Secure Cloud Computing

Sushil Jajodia • Krishna Kant
Pierangela Samarati • Anoop Singhal
Vipin Swarup • Cliff Wang
Editors

Secure Cloud Computing

 Springer

Editors
Sushil Jajodia
Center for Secure Information Systems
George Mason University
Fairfax, VA, USA

Krishna Kant
Center for Secure Information Systems
George Mason University
Fairfax, VA, USA

Pierangela Samarati
University of Milan
Crema, Italy

Anoop Singhal
Computer Security Division
National Institute of Standards
 and Technology (NIST)
Gaithersburg, MD, USA

Vipin Swarup
The MITRE Corporation
McLean, VA, USA

Cliff Wang
Computing and Information Science
 Division
Information Sciences Directorate
Triangle Park, NC, USA

Images can be viewed in color by visiting the book's web page on SpringerLink or downloading the eBook version.

ISBN 978-1-4939-4883-3   ISBN 978-1-4614-9278-8 (eBook)
DOI 10.1007/978-1-4614-9278-8
Springer New York Heidelberg Dordrecht London

Preface

Cloud computing continues to experience a rapid proliferation because of its potential advantages with respect to ease of deploying required computing capacity as needed and at a much lower cost than running an owned computing infrastructure. However, the lack of ownership brings in myriad security and privacy challenges that are quite difficult to resolve. The purpose of this book is to provide a state-of-the-art coverage of the techniques to address these issues at all levels of the stack ranging from hardware mechanisms to application level techniques. It is hoped that the book will be useful to researchers, practitioners, and students in further research on the subject and the implementation of the techniques in real-life systems.

The term cloud computing has been used for a variety of distributed computing environments including some traditional ones. For example, a computing infrastructure owned by the organization is often referred to as a "private cloud", which may or may not be any different from a traditional virtualized data center owned by the organization. The distinction may come if multiple entities or departments within the organization share the same infrastructure, but have their own privacy, information sensitivity, and security concerns. In contrast, a "public cloud" refers to a facility owned and operated by a separate entity and available for use by any organization or individual. Ownership and operation models in between these extremes are also possible, such as a cloud intended for use by enterprises that provides more restrictive use policies, tighter security, higher availability, etc. than public clouds. Such "community clouds" have domain specific characteristics, capabilities, and vulnerabilities different from private or public clouds.

User access to the cloud infrastructure could be provided at varying levels ranging from underlying physical infrastructure controlled directly by the user all the way up to built-in software exposed to the users. Traditionally, three specific levels have been identified: IaaS (Infrastructure as a Service), PaaS (Platform as a Service), and SaaS (Software as a Service). The challenges in providing the required security and privacy vary across the levels, with lower level access resulting in more difficult challenges in protecting the resources from misuse and attacks.

In recent years, there have been numerous incidents of exposure of confidential data either accidentally or as a result of hacker attacks. Although many of these incidents are not specific to cloud computing, the increasing adoption of cloud computing by the government and businesses has raised the specter of perhaps even more damaging information leaks in the future. For example, the Cloud Security Alliance (CSA) has identified "The Notorious Nine" cloud computing threats for 2013 that are likely to persist in the future as well (see https://cloudsecurityalliance. org/research/top-threats/). The most significant threats include: (a) exploitation of side-channel information by VMs to extract sensitive information about other VMs, including the cryptographic keys, (b) data loss due to accidents or physical hazards, (c) illegal access to credentials or penetration of critical entities such as hypervisor by hackers, (d) weak APIs and interfaces, (e) denial of service or other attacks using the cloud infrastructure, (f) and insider attacks (including the service or infrastructure providers). Significantly, a common theme identified in the list of threats is the vulnerabilities brought about by the solutions themselves. This is normally a result of increased complexity and hence vulnerabilities arising from software bugs and additional configuration data. For example, the keys and other parameters needed by cryptographic algorithms must themselves be managed and protected against attacks and accidental loss.

A key attribute of cloud computing is the involvement of multiple parties that provide or use the infrastructure or services. These parties could form a natural hierarchy with physical infrastructure providers at the bottom and the end users at the top. For example, a cloud computing service provider or a broker may use physical infrastructure provided by one or more lower level entities, and expose services or virtual infrastructures used by end users or application service providers. The sharing of increasingly sophisticated and larger computing infrastructures among multiple parties makes cloud computing security a very challenging undertaking. The main reasons include:

1. Lack of trust between various parties up and down the hierarchy (e.g., between the cloud service provider and the physical infrastructure provider if they are different, or between service provider and the user) and across a level (between service providers or users running on the same shared infrastructure). The trust model drives the level of information access granted among parties and protections implemented to avoid potential abuse. Some protections (e.g., encryption) may rule out certain operations within the cloud or make them very expensive.
2. Complex privacy and anonymity requirements for information exchanges between various parties. This drives mechanisms for obfuscating and restricting access to information content, a careful control of association between different pieces of information, and avoidance of attribution of information to specific parties. These requirements may dictate what data can be kept where and where the operations on the data take place.
3. Operational disruption, integrity violation, and information leaks caused by attacks that may originate not only from malicious outsiders but also from legitimate providers and users of the cloud. These aspects in turn drive the level of protection that needs to be built at various layers including physical infras- tructure, communication protocols, data storage and transmission, middleware, etc.

The chapters in this book address recent advances in addressing some of these security and privacy issues. Each chapter is intended to be self-contained, although the reader is expected to have working knowledge of the security and privacy field. It is hoped that the book will fill an important need in the rapidly emerging field of cloud computing security.

Images can be viewed in color by visiting the book's web page on SpringerLink or downloading the eBook version.

Fairfax, VA, USA	Sushil Jajodia
Fairfax, VA, USA	Krishna Kant
Crema, Italy	Pierangela Samarati
Gaithersburg, MD, USA	Anoop Singhal
McLean, VA, USA	Vipin Swarup
Triangle Park, NC, USA	Cliff Wang

Acknowledgements

We are extremely grateful to the numerous contributors to this book. In particular, it is a pleasure to acknowledge the authors for their contributions. Special thanks go to Courtney Clark, Associate Editor at Springer for her support of this project. We also wish to thank the Army Research Office for their financial support under the grant number W911NF-12-1-0595. Part of the work was performed while Sushil Jajodia was a Visiting Researcher at the US Army Research Laboratory.

Contents

Cryptographic Key Management Issues and Challenges in Cloud Services

Ramaswamy Chandramouli, Michaela Iorga, and Santosh Chokhani

Abstract To interact with various services in the cloud and to store the data generated/processed by those services, several security capabilities are required. Based on a core set of features in the three common cloud services – Infrastructure as a Service (IaaS), Platform as a Service (PaaS) and Software as a Service (SaaS), we identify a set of security capabilities needed to exercise those features and the cryptographic operations they entail. An analysis of the common state of practice of the cryptographic operations that provide those security capabilities reveals that the management of cryptographic keys takes on an additional complexity in cloud environments compared to enterprise IT environments due to: (a) difference in ownership (between cloud Consumers and cloud Providers) and (b) control of infrastructures on which both the Key Management System (KMS) and protected resources are located. This document identifies the cryptographic key management challenges in the context of architectural solutions that are commonly deployed to perform those cryptographic operations.

1 Introduction

Encryption and access control are the two primary means for ensuring data confidentiality in any IT environment. In situations where encryption is used as a data confidentiality assurance measure, the management of cryptographic keys is a critical and challenging security management function, especially in large enterprise

R. Chandramouli (✉) • M. Iorga
National Institute of Standards and Technology, 100 Bureau Drive, Mailstop 8930, Gaithersburg, MD 20899, USA
e-mail: mouli@nist.gov; Michaela.Iorga@nist.gov

S. Chokhani
CygnaCom Solutions, 7925 Jones Branch Drive, Suite 5400, McLean, VA 22102, USA
e-mail: SChokhani@cygnacom.com

S. Jajodia et al. (eds.), *Secure Cloud Computing*, DOI 10.1007/978-1-4614-9278-8_1, © Springer Science+Business Media New York 2014

data centers, due to sheer volume and data distribution (in different physical and logical storage media), and the consequent number of cryptographic keys. This function becomes more complex in the case of a cloud environment, where the physical and logical control of resources (both computing and networking) is split between cloud actors (e.g. Consumers, Providers and Brokers) (see Sect. 2.2 below and NIST SP 500-292 for more details).

The objectives of this chapter are to identify:

(a) The cryptographic key management issues that arise due to the distributed nature of IT resources, as well the distributed nature of their control, the latter split among multiple cloud actors. Furthermore, the pattern of distribution varies with the type of service offering – Infrastructure as a Service (IaaS), Platform as a Service (PaaS) and Software as a Service (SaaS), and
(b) The special challenges involved in deploying cryptographic key management functions that meet the security requirements of the cloud Consumers, depending upon the nature of the service and the type of data generated/processed/stored by the service features.

In this chapter, we address the following topics:

1. Section 1 provides an overview of cryptographic key management;
2. Section 2 provides a summary of the cloud computing concepts, including a reference architecture (cloud actors, cloud service types and deployment models) as identified in NIST standards; and
3. Section 3 builds on the previous sections to identify a core set of features for the three main cloud service types – IaaS, PaaS and SaaS: the security capabilities (SC) required to exercise those features, architectural solutions available to meet the security capabilities and the consequent key management challenges.

In order to ensure that cryptographic mechanisms provide the desired security, the following criteria should be met with regards to their three main components – Algorithms (and associated modes of operation), Protocols and Implementation:

1. The cryptographic algorithms and associated modes of operation deployed should have been scrutinized, evaluated, and approved using a review process that is open and includes a wide range of experts in the field. Examples of such approved algorithms and modes are found in National Institute of Standards and Technology's Federal Information Processing Standards (FIPS) and Special Publications (SPs), and in the Internet Engineering Task Force (IETF) Request for Comment (RFC) documents. The specific NIST documents pertaining to cryptographic algorithms and associated modes of operation are: FIPS 186-3 for Digital Signatures, FIPS 180-4 for Secure Hash, SP 800-38A for modes of operation and SP 800-56A & SP 800-56B for key establishment.
2. The cryptographic protocols used should have been scrutinized, evaluated, and approved using a review process that is open and includes a wide range of experts in the field. IETF protocol specifications for Secure Shell (SSH) and Transport Layer Security (TLS) are examples that meet these criteria.

3. The implementation of a cryptographic algorithm or protocol should undergo a widely recognized and reputable independent testing for verification of conformance to underlying specifications. NIST's Cryptographic Algorithm Validation Program (CAVP) and Cryptographic Module Validation Program (CMVP) are examples of such independent testing programs.

2 Cryptographic Key Management Overview

In this section, we review the two broad categories of cryptographic keys, list the most commonly used key types, identify the key states and chart the resulting transition diagram. We then proceed to describe the most important key management functions (also referred to as key lifecycle operations) and list the generic security requirements associated with these functions.

2.1 Key Types

Cryptographic keys fall into two broad categories:

1. **Secret key**: A key that is generally used to (1) perform encryption/decryption using symmetric cryptographic algorithms; and/or (2) to provide data integrity using message authentication codes (i.e., Hash based Message Authentication Code or HMAC) or an encryption mode of operation that also provide data integrity. A secret key is also called a symmetric key, since the same key is required for encryption and decryption or for integrity value generation and integrity verification.
2. **Public/Private Key Pair:** A pair of mathematically related keys used in asymmetric cryptography for authentication, digital signature or key establishment. As the name indicates, the private key is used by the owner of the key pair and kept secret and should be protected at all times, while the public key can be published and used be the relying party to complete the protocol or invert the operations performed with the private key.

From these broad categories one can determine the most commonly used key types in a cloud computing environment. This is not to say that a cloud implementation may not have additional types of keys.

1. **Public/Private Authentication Key Pair:** This key pair is used by one party (peer, client or server) to authenticate to the other party. Its typical use entails combining a random challenge with the signer-generated random number and signing the result for the benefit of the challenger who wishes to authenticate

the private-key holder. Examples of usage include client-authenticated Transport Layer Security (TLS), Virtual Private Network (VPN) authentication, and smart card-based logon. An authentication key pair is generally used in a network environment and is generally used for long-term use (e.g., up to 3 years)

2. **Public/Private Signature Key Pair:** This private key of the key pair is used by one party to digitally sign a message/data, and the corresponding public key is used to verify the signature. Examples of the usage of a signature key pair are signed Secure/Multipart Internet Mail Extensions (S/MIME) messages, signed electronic documents, and signed code. In some implementations, a key pair may be used for both authentication and signature functions. A signature key pair is generally used in a network environment and is generally used for long-term use (e.g., up to 3 years). It may also be used to generate and verify signatures on stored data.

3. **Public/Private Key Establishment Pair:** This key pair is used to securely establish a key between parties. Examples of the use of a key pair for key establishment are encrypting the symmetric key for S/MIME payload encryption/decryption and encrypting the random secret to be sent from a TLS client to a server. It is recommended that key establishment key pairs be distinct from authentication and signature key pairs. However, it is recognized that some devices such as web servers use the same key pair for key establishment and authentication. A key establishment key pair is traditionally used in a network environment, but some usage for stored data is also seen and can be envisioned. A key establishment key pair is generally used for a pre-defined period for encryption (e.g., up to 3 years), but is used for decryption for as long as the confidentiality of the data needs to be protected.

4. **Symmetric Encryption/Decryption Key:** A symmetric key is used to encrypt and decrypt data or messages. For data-in-transit, a symmetric encryption/decryption key may have a short life, typically for each message (e.g., S/MIME message) or for each session (for example a TLS session). For stored data, the symmetric life of the encryption/decryption key tends to be as long as the confidentiality of the data needs to be protected.

5. **Symmetric Message Authentication Code (MAC) Key:** A symmetric key is used to provide assurance for the integrity of data. There are three techniques used to provide this assurance: (1) use a symmetric encryption algorithm and a MAC mode of operation (e.g., CMAC using AES); (2) use a symmetric encryption algorithm and an authenticated encryption mode of operation (e.g., GCM or CCM using AES); and (3) use a hash-based MAC (HMAC). For data-in-transit, a symmetric MAC key has a short life, typically for a single message or for a single session (for example a TLS session). For stored data, the life of a symmetric MAC key tends to be for as long as the data needs to be protected. Note that when authenticated encryption mode is used, the same key is used for both the MAC and encryption/decryption, since both objectives are achieved by invoking a single mode of operation.

6. **Symmetric Key Wrapping Key:** A symmetric key is used to encrypt a symmetric key or an asymmetric private key. A Key Wrapping Key is also called a Key Encrypting Key.

2.2 Key States

A symmetric key or public/private key pair can undergo the following states. This is not to say that a key management implementation may not have additional states. Alternatively, a key management implementation may have a subset of these states.

- **Generation:** A symmetric key or public/private key pair is generated when required.
- **Activation:** A symmetric key or private key is activated when it is required to be used. A public key is activated when it is made available or on the date indicated in its associated metadata (e.g., notBefore date in an X.509 public key certificate).
- **Deactivation:** A symmetric key or private key is deactivated when it is no longer required for applying cryptographic protection to data. Deactivation of these keys may be followed by destruction or archival. A public key is not deactivated. It may expire (e.g., at the notAfter date in an X.509 public key certificate), or may be suspended (e.g., via certificate revocation list (CRL) [refer RFC 4949] in X.509 standard) or revoked (e.g., via CRL in X.509 standard).
- **Suspension:** A key may be suspended from use for a variety of reasons, such as an unknown status of the key or due to the key owner being temporarily away. In the case of the public key, suspension of the companion private key is communicated to the relying parties. This may be communicated as an "On hold" revocation reason code in a CRL and in an Online Certificate Status Protocol (OCSP) response
- **Expiration:** A key may expire due to the end of its crypto period [refer RFC 4949]. In the case of a public key, an expiration date is indicated in the associated metadata (e.g., notAfter date in X.509 certificates).
- **Destruction:** A key is destroyed when it is no longer needed.
- **Archival:** A key may be archived when it is no longer required for normal use, but may be needed after the key's cryptoperiod. An example for secret or private keys is the possible decryption of archived data. An example for public keys is the verification of archived signed documents.
- **Revocation:** A revocation is explicitly stated with respect to public keys; however, the revocation also applies to the corresponding private key. Revocation information is securely communicated to the relying parties, for example, as CRLs or OCSP responses, in the case of X.509 public key certificates. Secret keys are also "revoked", often by including them on lists, such as a compromised key list.

The following is the state diagram for the key states (Fig. 1).

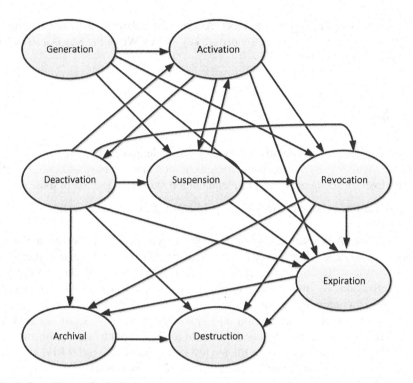

Fig. 1 State diagram for the key states

2.3 *Key Management Functions*

The following are the important key management functions:

- **Generate Key:** The generation of good-quality keys is critical to security. Keys for a cryptographic algorithm should be generated in cryptographic modules that have been approved for the generation of keys for that algorithm.
- **Generate Domain Parameters:** Discrete Logarithm-based algorithms require the generation of domain parameters prior to the generation of the keys; the keys are generated using those domain parameters. The domain parameters for an algorithm shall be generated in approved cryptographic modules that have been approved for their generation. Since domain parameters can be common to a broad community of users, key generation need not entail domain parameter generation. For example, defining Suite B P-256 curve defines all the domain parameters for the attendant ECDSA and ECDH algorithms.
- **Bind Key and Metadata:** A key may have associated data, such as the time period of use, usage constraints (such as authentication, encryption, and/or key establishment), domain parameters, and security services for which they are used, such as source authentication, integrity, and confidentiality protection. This function provides assurance that the key is associated with the correct metadata.

- **Bind a Key to an Individual:** The identifier of the individual or other entity that owns a key is considered as part of the key's metadata, but this association is sufficiently critical to be listed as a distinct function.
- **Activate Key:** This function transitions a key to the active state. It is often done in conjunction with key generation.
- **Deactivate Key:** This function is generally done when a key is no longer needed for applying cryptographic protection. For example, when a key has expired, or is replaced by another key.
- **Backup Key:** A key is backed by the owner, the key management infrastructure or a third party in order to reconstitute the key when it is accidentally destroyed or otherwise unavailable. When a private or secret key is backed up by the key management infrastructure or by a third party, the function is also referred to as "key escrow".
- **Recover Key:** This function is complementary to the key backup function and is invoked when the key is unavailable for some reason and is required by the authorized parties. Key backup and recovery generally applies to the symmetric and private keys.
- **Modify Metadata:** This function is invoked when metadata bound to a key needs to change. The renewal of a public key certificate is an example of this function where the validity period for the public key is changed.
- **Rekey:** This function is used to replace the existing key with a new key. Generally, the existing key (the key being replaced) plays a role in authentication and authorization for replacement.
- **Suspend a Key:** This function is used to temporarily cease the use of a key. It is akin to reversible revocation. This function may need to be invoked if the status of a key is undetermined or if the key owner wishes to temporarily suspend its use (e.g., for extended leave). For secret keys, this can also be accomplished via key deactivation. For public keys and the companion private key, this is generally done using suspension notification of the public key.
- **Restore a Key:** This function is used to restore a suspended key once its secure status is ascertained. For secret keys, this can also be accomplished via key activation. For public keys and the companion private keys, this is generally done using a revocation notification where the revoked public key entry is deleted implying the key is valid.
- **Revoke a Key:** This function is used to inform the relying parties to stop using a public key. There may be a variety of reasons for this, including the compromise of companion private key, and that the owner has stopped using the companion private key.
- **Archive a Key:** This function is used to store a key in long-term storage after it has been deactivated, expired, and/or compromised.
- **Destroy a Key:** This function is used to zeroize a key when it is no longer to be used.
- **Manage TA Store:** This function is used by the relying party to determine what trust anchors to trust for what purpose. A trust anchor is a public key and its associated metadata that the relying party explicitly trusts and uses to establish

trust in other public keys via transitive trust, such as a public-key certification path that is a series of public key certificates where the digital signature in one certificate can be used to verify the digital signature on the next certificate.

2.4 Key Management: Generic Security Requirements

The following are general key management security requirements:

1. Parties performing key management functions are properly authenticated and their authorizations to perform the key management functions for a given key are properly verified.
2. All key management commands and associated data are protected from spoofing, i.e., source authentication is performed prior to executing a command.
3. All key management commands and associated data are protected from undetected, unauthorized modifications, i.e., integrity protection is provided.
4. Secret and private keys are protected from unauthorized disclosure.
5. All keys and metadata are protected from spoofing, i.e., source authentication is performed prior to accessing keys and metadata.
6. All keys and metadata are protected from undetected, unauthorized modifications, i.e., integrity protection is provided.
7. When cryptography is used as a protection mechanism for any of the above, the security strength of the cryptographic mechanism used is at least as strong as the security strength required for the keys being managed,

There are significant challenges to implement these key management security requirements in cloud computing over unsecure public networks. In the next sections we review the cloud computing reference architecture and identify, for the three main cloud service types – IaaS, PaaS and SaaS, a core set of features, the security capabilities (SC) required to exercise those features, architectural solutions available to meet the security capabilities and the consequent key management challenges.

3 Cloud Computing Environment: Evolution and State of Practice

3.1 Three Generations of Internet

The evolution of the internet can be divided into three generations: in the 1970s the first generation was marked by expensive mainframe computers accessed from terminals; the second generation was born in the late 1980s and early 1990s, and was identified by the explosion of personal computers with Graphical User Interfaces (GUIs); the first decade of the twenty-first century brought the third generation, defined by mobile computing, the "internet of things" and cloud computing.

In 1997, Professor Ramnath Chellappa of Emory University, defined cloud computing for the first time while a faculty member at the University of South California, as an important new *"computing paradigm where the boundaries of computing will be determined by economic rationale rather than technical limits alone."* Even though the international IT literature and media have come forward since then with a large number of definitions, models and architectures for cloud computing, autonomic and utility computing were the foundations of what the community commonly referred to as "cloud computing". In the early 2000s, companies started rapidly adopting this concept upon the realization that cloud computing could benefit both the Providers as well as the Consumers of services. Businesses started delivering computing functionality via the Internet, enterprise-level applications, web-based retail services, document-sharing capabilities and fully-hosted IT platforms, to mention only a few cloud computing use cases of the 2000s. The latest widespread adoption of virtualization and of service-oriented architecture (SOA) promulgated cloud computing as a fundamental and increasingly important part of any delivery and critical-mission strategy, enabling existing and new products and services to be offered and consumed more efficiently, conveniently and securely. Not surprisingly, cloud computing became one of the hottest trends in the IT armory, with a unique and complementary set of properties, such as elasticity, resiliency, rapid provisioning, and multi-tenancy.

3.2   *Cloud Computing Definition (by NIST)*

Cloud computing is a model for enabling convenient, on-demand network access to a shared pool of configurable resources (e.g., networks, servers, storage, applications, and services) that can be rapidly provisioned and released with minimal management efforts or service provider interaction. Enterprises can use these resources to develop, host and run services and applications on demand in a flexible manner in any devices, anytime, and anywhere. According to the U.S. National Institute of Standards and Technology's (NIST) definition published in the NIST Special Publication SP 800-145, "cloud computing is a model for enabling ubiquitous, convenient, on-demand network access to a shared pool of configurable computing resources (e.g., networks, servers, storage, applications and services) that can be rapidly provisioned and released with minimal management effort or service provider interaction." This definition is widely accepted as a valuable contribution toward providing a clear understanding of cloud computing technologies and cloud services and it has been submitted as the U.S. contribution for an International standardization.[1]

The NIST definition also provides a unifying view of five essential characteristics that all cloud services exhibit: *on-demand self-service, broad network access,*

---

[1]http://www.nist.gov/itl/csd/cloud-102511.cfm

resource pooling, rapid elasticity, and *measured service.* Furthermore, NIST identifies a simple and unambiguous taxonomy of three "service models" available to cloud Consumers (Infrastructure-as-a-Service (IaaS), Platform-as-a Service (PaaS), Software-as-a-Service (SaaS)) and four "cloud deployment modes" (Public, Private, Community and Hybrid) that together categorize ways to deliver cloud services. Since the cloud service model is an important architectural factor when discussing key managements aspects in a cloud environment, we are reproducing below the definitions for the service models provided by NIST in SP 800-145, "The NIST definition of Cloud Computing":

1. Infrastructure as a Service (IaaS) – The capability provided to the Consumer is to provision processing, storage, networks, and other fundamental computing resources where the Consumer is able to deploy and run arbitrary software, which can include operating systems and applications. The Consumer does not manage or control the underlying cloud infrastructure, but has control over operating systems, storage, deployed applications, and possibly limited control of select networking components (e.g., host firewalls).
2. Platform as a Service (PaaS) – The capability provided to the Consumer is to deploy Consumer-created or acquired applications onto the cloud infrastructure that are created using programming languages and tools supported by the Provider. The Consumer does not manage or control the underlying cloud infrastructure, including network, servers, operating systems, or storage, but has control over the deployed applications and possibly the application-hosting environment configurations.
3. Software as a Service (SaaS) – The capability provided to the Consumer is to use the Provider's applications running on a cloud infrastructure. The applications are accessible from various client devices through a thin client interface, such as a web browser (e.g., web-based email). The Consumer does not manage or control the underlying cloud infrastructure, including network, servers, operating systems, storage, or even individual application capabilities, with the possible exception of limited user-specific application-configuration settings.

IaaS allows cloud Consumers to run any operating systems and applications of their choice on the hardware and resource abstraction layer (hypervisors) furnished by the cloud Provider. A Consumer's operating systems and applications can be migrated to the cloud Provider's hardware, potentially replacing a company's data center infrastructure.

PaaS allows Consumers to create their own cloud applications. Basically, the cloud Provider renders a virtualized environment and a set of tools to allow the creation of new web applications. The Cloud Provider also furnishes the hardware, operating systems and commonly used system software and applications, such as DBMS, Web Server, etc.

SaaS allows cloud Consumers to run online applications. Off-the-shelf applications are accessed over the Internet. The cloud Provider owns the applications, and the Consumers are authorized to use them in accordance with a Service Agreement signed between parties.

Cloud computing provides a convenient, on-demand way to access a shared pool of configurable resources (e.g., networks, servers, storage, applications, and services), which enables users to develop, host and run services and applications on demand in a flexible manner in any devices, anytime, and anywhere. Cloud services are those services that are expressed, delivered and consumed over a public network, a private network or in some combination (community or hybrid). These services are usually delivered in one of the following service categories identified by NIST: IaaS, PaaS and SaaS. Cloud Provider and Broker may also identify other Categories of services (such as Network-as-a-Service, Storage-as-a-Service, carrier-as-a-Service) that are practical components already embedded in the service models identified by NIST, and are not stand-alone service models that identify particular cloud architectures. Some cloud Providers might provide abstracted hardware and software resources that may be offered as a service. This allows customers and partners to develop and deploy new applications that can be configured and used remotely. Leveraging cloud services that provide opportunities to provision resources elastically enables enterprises to launch or change their business quickly and easily as needed.

3.3   Cloud Computing Reference Architecture (from NIST)

In the Special Publication SP 500-292, NIST has published the NIST Cloud Computing Reference Architecture[2] (RA). This architecture is a logical extension of the NIST cloud computing definition. It is a generic high-level conceptual model that is an effective tool for discussing the requirements, structures, and operations of cloud computing. The model is not tied to any specific vendor products, services or reference implementation, nor does it provide prescriptive solutions. The RA defines a set of cloud Actors and their activities and functions that can be used in the process of orchestrating a cloud Ecosystem. The Cloud Computing RA relates to a companion cloud computing taxonomy and contains a set of views and descriptions that are the basis for discussing the characteristics, uses and standards for cloud computing. The Actor-based model is intended to serve the expectations of the stakeholders by allowing them to understand the overall view of roles and responsibilities in order to assess and manage the risk by implementing adequate security controls.

The NIST Reference Architecture is intended to facilitate the understanding of the operational intricacies in cloud computing. It does not represent the system architecture of a specific cloud computing system; instead, it is a tool for describing, discussing, and developing a system-specific architecture using a common frame-work of reference.

---

[2]http://collaborate.nist.gov/twiki-cloud-computing/pub/CloudComputing/
ReferenceArchitectureTaxonomy/NIST_SP_500-292_-_090611.pdf

As shown in Fig. 2 this architecture outlines the five major cloud Actors; Consumer, Provider, Broker, Carrier and Auditor.

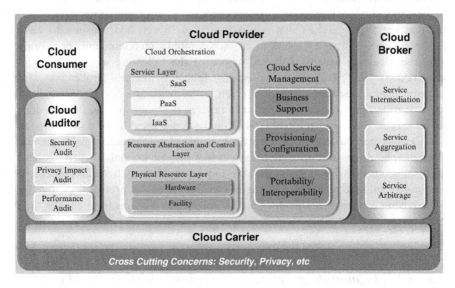

Fig. 2 NIST cloud computing security reference architecture approach (Courtesy of NIST, SP 500-292)

Each cloud Actor defined by the NIST RA is an entity (a person or an organization) that participates in a transaction or process and/or performs tasks in cloud computing. The definitions of the cloud Actors introduced by NIST in SP 500-292, NIST cloud Computing Reference Architecture, are reproduced below in Table 1.

Table 1 Cloud actor definitions (Courtesy of NIST, SP 500-292)

Actor	Definition
Cloud consumer	A person or organization that maintains a business relationship with, and uses service from, *Cloud Providers*
Cloud provider	A person, organization, or entity responsible for making a service available to interested parties
Cloud auditor	A party that can conduct an independent assessment of cloud services, information system operations, performance and security of the cloud implementation
Cloud broker	An entity that manages the use, performance and delivery of cloud services, and negotiates relationships between *Cloud Providers* and *Cloud Consumers*
Cloud carrier	An intermediary that provides connectivity and transport of cloud services from *Cloud Providers* to *Cloud Consumers*

In our latest work (draft documents and white papers), NIST identifies two types of cloud Providers:

1. Primary Provider and
2. Intermediary Provider,

and two types of cloud Brokers:

1. Business Broker and
2. Technical Broker.

Figure 3, below, graphically depicts these two types of Providers and the two types of Brokers. It is important to note that, in particular, cloud environments where an Intermediary Provider partners with a Primary Provider in offering cloud services, the key management functions that fall under the Provider's responsibilities might need to be divided among the two Providers, depending on the architectural details of the offered cloud service. From the cloud Consumer's perspective this segregation is not visible.

A Primary Provider offers services hosted on an infrastructure that it owns. It may make these services available to Consumers through a third party (such as a Broker or Intermediary Provider), but the defining characteristic of a Primary Provider is that it does not obtain the sources of its service offerings from other Providers.

An Intermediary Provider has the capability to interact with other cloud Providers without offering visibility or transparency into the Primary Provider(s). An Intermediary Provider uses services offered by a Primary Provider as invisible components of its own service, which it presents to the customer as an integrated offering. From a security perspective, all security services and components required of a Primary Provider are also required of an Intermediary Provider.

A Business Broker only provides business and relationship services, and does not have any contact with the cloud Consumer's data, operations, or artifacts (e.g., images, volumes, firewalls) in the cloud and, therefore, has no responsibilities in implementing any key management functions, regardless of the cloud architecture. Conversely, a Technical Broker *does* interact with a Consumer's assets; the Technical Broker aggregates services from multiple cloud Providers and adds a layer of technical functionality by addressing single-point-of-entry and interoperability issues.

There are two key defining features of a cloud Technical Broker that are distinct from an Intermediary Provider:

1. The ability to provide a single consistent interface (for business or technical purposes) to multiple differing Providers, and
2. The *transparent visibility* that the Broker allows into who is providing the services in the background – as opposed to Intermediary Providers that do not offer such transparency.

Since the Technical Broker allows for this transparent visibility, the Consumer is aware of which key management functions are implemented by each Actor. This case is different from the case in which an Intermediary Provider is involved, since

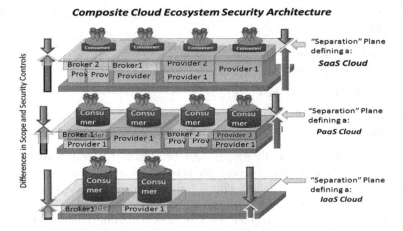

Fig. 3 Composite cloud ecosystem security architecture (Courtesy of NIST)

the Intermediary Provider is opaque, and the Consumer is unaware of how the key management functions are divided, when applicable, between the Intermediary Provider and the Primary Provider.

The NIST RA diagram in Fig. 2 also depicts the three service models discussed earlier: IaaS, PaaS and SaaS in the "inverted L" representations, highlighting the stackable approach of building cloud service. Additionally, the NIST RA diagram identifies, for each cloud Actor, their general activities in a cloud ecosystem. This Reference Architecture is intended to facilitate the understanding of the operational intricacies in cloud computing. It does not represent the system architecture of a specific cloud computing system; instead, it is a tool for describing, discussing, and developing a system-specific architecture using a common framework of reference that we plan to leverage in our later discussion of key management issues in a cloud environment.

Cloud computing provides enterprises with significant cost savings, both in terms of capital expenses (CAPEX) and operational expenses (OPEX), and allows them to leverage leading-edge technologies to meet their information processing needs. In a cloud environment, security and privacy are a cross-cutting concern for all cloud Actors, since both touch upon all layers of the cloud computing Reference Architecture and impact many parts of a cloud service. Therefore, the security management of the resources associated with cloud services is a critical aspect of cloud computing. In a cloud environment, there are security threats and security requirements that differ for different cloud deployment models, and the necessary mitigations against such threats and cloud Actor responsibilities for implementing security controls depend upon the service model chosen and the service categories elected. Many of the security threats can be mitigated with the application of traditional security processes and mechanisms, while others require cloud-specific solutions. Since each layer of the cloud computing Reference Architecture may have different security vulnerabilities and may be exposed to different threats, the architecture of a cloud-enabled service directly impacts its security posture and the system's key management aspects.

For each service model, Fig. 4 below uses a building-block approach to depict a graphical representation of the cloud Consumer's visibility and accessibility to the "Security and Integration" layer that hosts the key management in a cloud environment. As the figure shows, the cloud Consumer has high visibility into the "Security & Integration" layer and has control over the key management in a IaaS model, while the cloud Providers implement only the infrastructure-level security functions (which are always opaque to Consumers). The Consumer has limited visibility and limited key management control in a PaaS model, since the cloud Provider implements the security functions in all lower layers except the "Applications" layer. The cloud Consumer loses the visibility and the control in a SaaS model, and in general, all key management functions are opaque to the cloud Consumer, since the cloud Provider implements all security functions.

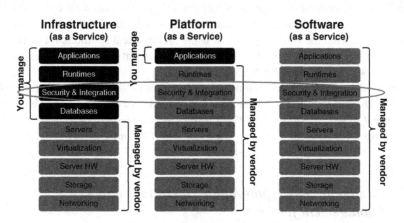

Fig. 4 Cloud service models and data protection (Courtesy of CIO Research Council [CRC])

In the following Section, we will discuss, for each service model, the Key Management challenges encountered by cloud Actors in different use cases.

4 Cryptographic Key Management Challenges in the Cloud

As stated in Sect. 2, the secure management of the resources associated with cloud services is a critical aspect of cloud computing. Cryptographic operations form one of the main tasks of secure management. Hence, while cloud services provide ubiquitous computing, elastic capabilities and self-configurable resources at lower costs, they also entail performing several cryptographic operations (from a cloud Consumer perspective) for the following:

- Secure Interaction of the Cloud Consumer with various services and
- Secure Storage of data generated/processed by those services.

The key management system (KMS) required to support cryptographic operations for the above functions can be complex, due to differences in ownership and control of underlying infrastructures on which the KMS and the protected resources are located. For example, though the ownership of data in cloud services rests with the cloud Consumer, the data is physically resident on storage resources controlled by the cloud Provider, and in many instances, the KMS required for managing the cryptographic keys needed to protect that data have to be run on the computing resources provided by the cloud Provider. This presents challenges to a cloud Consumer seeking to obtain the necessary security assurance from those cryptographic operations.

The driver for the set of cryptographic operations performed in the main cloud service models (IaaS, PaaS and SaaS) depends upon the features that constitute those services. Though there are slight variations in the feature set among different cloud Providers, it is possible to identify a core set of features. Based on these core set of features, we identify the security capabilities associated with the exercise of the features, and from the state of practices using architectural solutions for achieving those security capabilities, we derive the key management challenges for IaaS, PaaS and SaaS service types in Sects. 3.1, 3.2, and 3.3, respectively. *It must be noted upfront that in all architectural solutions where cryptographic keys are stored in the cloud, there is a limit to the degree of security assurance that the cloud Consumer can expect to get, due to the fact that the logical and physical organization of the storage resources are entirely under the control of the cloud Provider.*

4.1   Challenges in Cryptographic Operations and Key Management for IaaS

In the IaaS cloud type, the Consumer deploys its own computing resources in the form of virtual machines (VMs) or leases them from the cloud Provider. The leasing option involves checking out pre-built images offered by an IaaS cloud Provider. The VM images that are checked out must be authenticated to ensure that they are from authorized sources and have not been tampered with. After a VM is configured, it has to be launched in the cloud Provider's infrastructure to become a running VM instance. The operation of launching the VM and the subsequent lifecycle operations on the VM (such as Stop, Pause, Restart, Kill etc) are performed by the IaaS cloud Consumer through access to the management interface of the Hypervisor. Additionally, during operations or the use of cloud services, the IaaS cloud Consumer has to interact with running VM instances in a secure manner. These three operations – checking out a VM, performing lifecycle operations (including launching) on a VM instance and secure interaction with it – are performed by designated service-level administrators of the IaaS cloud Consumer. IaaS cloud service *security capabilities (SC)* that enable these operations are:

- **IaaS-SC1**: The ability to authenticate pre-defined VM Image Templates made available by a cloud Provider for building functional, customized VM instances that meet a cloud Consumer's needs,
- **IaaS-SC2**: The ability to authenticate the API calls sent by the cloud Consumer to the VM Management interface of the cloud Provider's Hypervisor environment, and
- **IaaS-SC3**: The ability to secure the communication while performing administrative operations on VM instances

For each of the three security capabilities identified above, possible *architectural solutions* (AS) are presented below that are based on known secure functions or protocols. The cryptographic key management challenges associated with these AS are also described and discussed.

IaaS-SC1 The ability to authenticate pre-defined VM Image Templates made available by a cloud Provider for building functional, customized VM instances that meet a cloud Consumer's needs (Server Authentication Mechanism).

Architectural Solution:
When leasing VMs from IaaS Providers, cloud Consumers are concerned that the VM image templates being checked out might not be authentic. To mitigate this concern, the templates can be digitally signed by the cloud Provider. The private key of a public/private key pair that is used to sign the VM image templates should be securely stored by the Provider and protected while in use (e.g., using FIPS 140-2 validated cryptographic module). The Provider needs to make the corresponding public key available to the Consumer in an authenticated manner (e.g., using an out-of-band means or using a public key certificate). Alternative means of assuring the integrity of the VM are: (a) the use of a cryptographic hash function (secure hash function), such as SHA-256 computed over the VM code, which Consumers should re-compute and verify against the value obtained using an out-of-band means; (b) the use of cryptographic message authentication code (MAC) mechanisms (i.e., HMAC or a block-cipher-based MAC) using a cryptographic algorithm and a secret shared by the Provider and the Consumers.

Key Management Challenges:
The authentication of the VM templates using one of the cryptographic techniques referred above (i.e., digital signature, cryptographic hash function, or message authentication code) entails the bootstrapping problem and hence, requires a comprehensive security analysis, rather than just an examination of the key management challenge. Appendix provides this analysis for the three possible cryptographic techniques for achieving IaaS-SC1 and a possible solution.

IaaS-SC2 The ability to authenticate the API calls sent by the cloud Consumer to the VM Management interface of the cloud Provider's Hypervisor environment.

Architectural Solution:
Although the responsibility for configuring the VMs lies with a cloud Consumer, an IaaS cloud Provider can implement functionality whereby the VM Management Interface of the Hypervisor only accepts and executes authenticated API calls. Cloud Consumers need to generate or possess a public/private key pair that will be used for signing the calls submitted to the VM Management interface. The public key needs to be bound to the Consumer's identity in a public key certificate signed by a trusted authority. The certificate is then made available to the VM Management Interface of the Hypervisor to verify the signature of the calls submitted by the Consumer to the VM instance. An alternative approach is to provide the capability for the cloud Consumer to set up a secure session with the VM Management interface using either SSH (refer IaaS-SC3) or TLS (refer IaaS-SC4).

Key Management Challenge:
Cloud Consumers need to secure the private key of the public/private key pair that is used to sign the VM Management commands on their system (both at rest and while in use).

IaaS-SC3 The ability to secure the communication while performing administrative operations on VM instances.

Architectural Solution:
The service-level administrators of the IaaS Consumer need root/administrator access to running VM instances deployed or leased by that Consumer. A typical mechanism deployed to secure this access is Secure Shell (SSH) that provides a framework for public/private (asymmetric) keys or password-based client authentication techniques. A public/private key technique requires the cloud Consumer to generate a public/private key pair and then associate the public key with the Consumer's account in the VM instance. The task of a VM recognizing the Consumer as the owner of the companion private key is accomplished by appending the public key to the authorized keys file in the VM instance that can support SSH login through protocols such as File Transfer Protocol (ftp), Secure Copy Protocol (scp), or console commands. Thus, SSH can be used to enable the VM instance to authenticate the Consumer using cryptographic means. Further details of the SSH protocol are described in Internet RFC 4253. This strong cryptographic authentication prevents anonymous connection attempts to the VM instance, as well as preventing authentication attacks (such as password guessing). Moreover, the SSH protocol permits asymmetric keys to be used to perform an authenticated ephemeral Diffie-Hellman (DH) key establishment. The symmetric session keys calculated during this process are used to encrypt the payload and to generate hash-based message authentication codes, thus providing both confidentiality and integrity security services. When SSH is used, not only is the administrator authenticated, but all the commands, responses, and payload are protected in both directions (Consumer $\longleftrightarrow$ VM) from eavesdropping and against undetected modifications, and are cryptographically authenticated.

Key Management Challenges:
Cloud Consumers need to secure the private key of the public/private key pair that is used to authenticate themselves, using the best enterprise security mechanisms. It is important to note that, the Diffie-Hellman keys and the derived session keys are ephemeral and generated or calculated on-the-fly. Thus, these keys do not require persistent storage, and hence, their key management is not an issue.

After the service-level administrator of the cloud Consumer authenticates pre-defined VM Images provided by the cloud Provider and checks them out (using capability IaaS-SC1), customizes them to its requirements, launches them securely in the hypervisor environment (using IaaS-SC2) of cloud Provider and performs configuration maintenance through secure interaction with the launched VM instances (using capability IaaS-SC3), the application-level administrator of the cloud Consumer installs and configures various servers (web servers, Database Management servers, etc.), application execution environments (i.e., Java VMs, Java run time modules, etc.) and application executables (and in some instances, source codes, as well) on those VM instances. Although the application-level administrators do not configure VM instances (such as allocation/resizing of virtual memory, CPU cores or virtual disks, etc.), they do have the need to setup secure sessions with VM instances prior to being authenticated. Hence, in most practical situations, the same service-level administrators of the cloud Consumer play the role of application-level administrators as well. The administrators use the same SSH technique and keys for secure application-level administration.

After applications are up and running on their leased VMs, the application users of an IaaS cloud Consumer would like to interact with these applications securely (through setting up secure sessions and strong authentication) and exercise the various application features – depending upon the set of assigned permissions or by assuming their assigned roles (which provide the permissions). Finally, there is the need for Data Storage services for all categories (service-level administrators, application-level administrators and application users) of IaaS Consumers. The data storage services required may span different types of data, such as: (a) Static Data – application source codes, Reference data used by applications, Archived data and Logs, and (b) Application data – those generated and used by applications. The application data in turn could be either Structured (e.g., Database data) or Unstructured (e.g., files from social feeds).

The challenges in the secure interaction of the application users (as opposed to application-level administrators) of IaaS cloud Consumers with IaaS cloud services (both main services, such as executing the applications on VM instances, as well as auxiliary services such as data storage) are:

- **IaaS-SC4**: The ability to secure the communication with application instances running on VM instances for application users during cloud-service usage,
- **IaaS-SC5**: The ability to securely store static application support data securely (data not directly processed by applications),

- **IaaS-SC6**: The ability to securely store application data in a structured form (e.g., relational form) securely using a Database Management System (DBMS),
- **IaaS-SC7**: The ability to securely store application data that is unstructured, and

IaaS-SC4 The ability to secure the communication with application instances running on VM instances for application users during cloud service usage.

Architectural Solution:
Application users (clients) generally interact with services by setting up a secure session (which can provide both confidentiality and integrity) with application (service) instances (e.g., Web server or DBMS server instances). The most common technology employed is the Transport Layer Security (TLS) protocol. TLS, just like SSH described earlier, can be used to enable the service instance and client to authenticate each other using a cryptographic means (as described in Internet RFC 5246), as well as to set up secure session keys for encrypting/decrypting and for generating message authentication codes.

Key Management Challenges:
The secure session requires the presence of an asymmetric key pair (private and public keys) for a service instance and an optional key pair on the client side, as well. The client-side private key can be managed by an enterprise key management system, and the server-side private key has to be managed by a key management system run by the IaaS cloud Provider.

IaaS-SC5 The ability to securely store static application support data securely.

Architectural Solution:
To support applications running on leased VM instances, IaaS cloud Consumers need secure storage services to store relatively static data such as application source codes, reference data used by applications, preferred VM Images and archived data and Logs. These types of data are different from data generated, processed and stored directly by the application. To store the former type of data, the cloud Providers offer a file-storage service.

Key Management Challenge:
The data that is not processed by or written to by applications can be encrypted at the cloud Consumer site before being uploaded to the cloud Providers file storage service. Hence, encryption keys (generally, symmetric keys) needed for encrypting the data at the cloud Consumer site and are under its administrative control and can thus be secured using enterprise key management solutions.

IaaS-SC6 *The ability to securely store application data in a structured form securely:* To store structured data generated by applications running on its VM instances, the IaaS cloud Consumer needs to subscribe to a Database service (generally a relational service offered by the Provider as an adjunct to its IaaS offering). The cloud Consumer subscribing to this service is generally provided with a DBMS instance with the ability to custom configure the instance to suit its business and security needs. The options available to provide confidentiality protection for data managed by the DBMS instance and the associated key management challenge are described below:

Architectural Solution-TDE: (Transparent/External Encryption):
Use the native encryption function that is provided as a feature within the DBMS engine or use a third party tool. This feature is called Transparent Data Encryption (TDE) and is a technique similar to storage-level encryption (the encryption engine operates at the I/O level and encrypts data just prior to being written to disk). The whole database is protected with a single Database Encryption Key (DEK) that is itself protected by more complex means, including the possibility of using a Hardware Security Module (HSM). Since TDE performs all cryptographic operation at the I/O level within the database system, there is no need to modify the application logic or the database schema.

Key Management Challenge:
Since the IaaS cloud Consumer has administrative control of the subscribed DBMS instance, it has control over the DEK as well. Since encryption is taking place at the I/O level, the DEK has to reside close to the storage resources designated for storage of the database data, and hence, the cloud Consumer has no other option other than storing the DEK in the same cloud where the DBMS instance is running. Although there are TDE implementations that offer column and table-level granularity for encryption, the most common usage is for storage-level encryption, and hence, the implementation cannot be configured to provide different set of encryption keys for different users based on their permission set (or assigned role).

Architectural Solution-ULE: (Database Level Encryption or User-Level Encryption)
Under this feature, users can choose to encrypt data at the column level, table level or even a set of data files corresponding to multiple tables or indexes.

Key Management Challenge:
This solution requires the use of a different encryption key for different database objects. An additional service is required (e.g., by a Security Server) that will map the set of session permissions of the user (based on the roles assumed) to the set of keys, and then make a call to a KMS to retrieve the required set of keys from key storage. For better security, the security server, the KMS and (persistent) key storage should be run in a cloud that is different than the DBMS instance or should be run on-premise by the cloud Consumer. The security server and KMS perform the role-to-key mapping and key retrieval functions, respectively, based on the authenticated credentials of the DBMS user. However, during a user's session (for key usage), the keys remain in a cache of the memory space created for the user session in the same cloud as the DBMS instance. The added challenge of retrieving the key from the KMS and providing it securely to the application running in the cloud Provider space also needs to be dealt with. One can argue that once the secure session with the DBMS application in the cloud is established, this security challenge is trivial. Alternatively, the cloud Consumer can run the security server and the KMS in the

same cloud as the DBMS application. This latter approach leaves the sensitive data vulnerable to access by the cloud Provider Administrators unless additional security measures are taken.

IaaS-SC7 *The ability to store unstructured application data securely:* This operation requires storage-level encryption similar to *Transparent/External encryption* (**Architectural Solution-1: (Transparent/External Encryption)**, and hence, the same key management challenges apply.

4.2 Challenges in Cryptographic Operations and Key Management for PaaS

The objective of a Platform as a Service (PaaS) offering is to provide a computational platform and the necessary set of application development tools to Consumers for developing or deploying applications. Although the underlying OS platform on which the development tools are hosted is known to the Consumer, the Consumer does not have control over its configuration functions and thus the resulting operating environment. Consumers interact with these tools (and associated data, such as development libraries) to develop custom applications. Consumers may also need a storage infrastructure to store both supporting data and application data for testing the application functionality. PaaS cloud service *security capabilities (SC)* that enable these operations are:

- **PaaS-SC1**: The ability to set up secure interaction with deployed applications and/or development tool instances,
- **PaaS-SC2**: The ability to securely store static data (data not directly processed by applications),
- **PaaS-SC3**: The ability to securely store application data in a structured form (e.g., relational form) using a Database Management System (DBMS), and
- **PaaS-SC4**: The ability to securely store application data that is unstructured.

The operations involved in exercising the above capabilities (PaaS-SC1 through PaaS-SC4) are identical to the operations involved in exercising capabilities IaaS-SC4 through IaaS-SC7, respectively and hence, the same cryptographic key management challenges apply.

4.3 Challenges in Cryptographic Operations and Key Management for SaaS

SaaS offerings provide access to applications hosted by the cloud Provider. An SaaS cloud Consumer would like to interact with these application instances securely (through setting up secure sessions and strong authentication) and exercise the various application features, depending upon the set of assigned permissions or by assuming their assigned roles (which provide the permissions). In addition, some SaaS Consumers would also like to store the data generated/processed by those applications in an encrypted form because of the following reasons: (a) to prevent exposure of their corporate data, due to loss of the media used by cloud Providers; and (b) surreptitious viewing of their data by an SaaS co-tenant or by a cloud Provider administrator. Though the former feature (secure interaction with application) is provided by the SaaS Providers, the second feature (storing data in an encrypted form) currently has to be provided entirely by the SaaS Consumer. The typical set of security capabilities (whether provided by an SaaS service or not) are:

- **SaaS-SC1**: The ability to set up secure interaction with an application, and
- **SaaS-SC2**: The ability to store application data (structured or unstructured) in an encrypted form.

The operations involved in exercising the SaaS-SC1 capability is identical to the operations involved in exercising the IaaS-SC4 capability, and hence, the same cryptographic key management challenges apply.

SaaS-SC2 The ability to store application data (structured or unstructured) in an encrypted form.

There are two operational scenarios here. If all fields in the database need to be encrypted, then the encryption capabilities have to reside with the cloud Provider because of the sheer scale of operation (see Architectural Solution – DVE below for description). On the other hand, if each cloud Consumer wants selective encryption of some subset of fields, and since that subset varies with each Customer, all encryption operations has to take place at the client (cloud Consumer) end (see Architectural Solution – GTE). The key management challenges for each of the two options are discussed below after a brief description of associated architectural solution.

Architectural Solution-DVE (Encryption of Entire Database):
For efficient encryption and storage of application data, SaaS cloud Providers divide the physical storage resources into logical storage chunks called disk volumes and assign different encryption keys over sets of disk volumes (e.g., assign an encryption key for two or three disk volumes).

Key Management Challenge:
Since all the encryption keys are under the control of the SaaS cloud Provider, this architectural solution does not provide assurance to the Consumer against the insider[3] threat unless additional measures are taken. Secondly, it is possible that data belonging to different Consumers reside on a single disk volume and is protected by a common encryption key, providing no cryptographic separation of the data belonging to different cloud Consumers. Furthermore, the sheer volume

---

[3]That is, cloud Provider Administrator.

of data stored in large SaaS cloud offerings requires a large number of keys, thus necessitating the need for the management of hundreds of symmetric encryption keys, possibly using multiple key management servers. If the key management function is carried out using an HSM, then it may require the creation and maintenance of multiple HSM partitions.

Architectural Solution-GTE (Selective Encryption of Database Fields):
For selective encryption of certain set of fields chosen by the Consumer (the selection of the set based on each Consumer's business requirements), an encryption gateway (generally running as an appliance) is usually employed inside the cloud Consumer's enterprise network. Architecturally, the gateway is located between the SaaS client application and SaaS cloud application (hosted by cloud SaaS Provider) and acts as a reverse proxy server that monitors all incoming and outgoing application traffic (e.g., HTTP, SMTP, SOAP and REST). The outgoing payload in this context will usually be the data that needs to be sent to the SaaS cloud application for storage. The gateway being configured with rules for encrypting different data items, encrypts or tokenizes the data in real time and forwards the modified data to the SaaS cloud application. Similarly, encrypted or tokenized data retrieved and returned by the SaaS cloud application is converted again, in real time, into clear text prior to being displayed by the SaaS client application. This encryption scheme thus requires no change either to the SaaS cloud Provider application or to the SaaS cloud Consumer's client application. Furthermore, all application functionality can be exercised normally since the encryption/decryption process performed by the encryption gateway is Format and Function-Preserving. Thus, the encryption gateway is the solution adopted under the following scenario:

- The SaaS cloud Consumer needs selective encryption of certain fields and hence all the processing (from the application functionality point of view) as well as encryption of those fields occurs at the Consumer side and the DBMS instance at the cloud is used just for storage (as opposed to computational processing) as far as those fields are concerned.
- The values in fields marked for encryption thus are in encrypted form at all times in the cloud (both during application processing in the cloud and storage in the cloud)
- Data in clear text is visible only to authorized clients using SaaS client application to interact with the SaaS cloud application through the encryption gateway

Key Management Challenge:
The encryption gateway may use a single key or different cryptographic keys for encrypting/decrypting different selected fields of the application. Irrespective of the number of cryptographic keys used, since the encryption gateway resides within the enterprise network perimeter, all cryptographic keys are fully under the control of the SaaS cloud Consumer and hence protected using in-house enterprise key management policies and practices.

Appendix A: Security Analysis of Cryptographic Techniques for Authenticating VM Templates in the Cloud

When leasing VMs from cloud Providers, cloud Consumers are concerned that the VM templates being checked out might not be authentic. To mitigate this concern, the following are some possible techniques:

1. A Digital Signature on the VM template,
2. The use of a Cryptographic Hash function,
3. The use of a Keyed Message Authentication Code, or
4. The use of cloud Provider Environment Discretionary Access Control.

Each of these techniques is described and analyzed below. Note that there are numerous variations for each technique and several other techniques, but these techniques were chosen to illustrate how to go about performing security analysis. Also note that, based on the cloud computing paradigm, it is assumed that the cloud Consumer will not download the VM template for authentication in the Consumer's Enterprise environment. Rather, the authentication will be performed in the Provider environment in which the VM is going to execute.

A.1 VM Template Authentication Using Digital Signature

As Fig. A.1, illustrates, the cloud Provider signs the VM template using the cloud Provider's private key once the VM template has been created. The signing function needs to be performed only once when the VM template is created.

Every time that a cloud Consumer checks out a VM template, he can verify the digital signature on the VM template using the public key of the cloud Provider. The cloud Consumer supplies the public key to the verification engine as illustrated in Fig. A.1.

This approach has the advantage that the cloud Provider is able to create and modify multiple VM templates, and all cloud Consumers can verify the source and integrity of the VM template via a digital signature verification. It also has the advantage of simplified key management. All that is required are the following: (a) the cloud Provider needs to create a single public/private signature key pair and protect the private key from unauthorized use and from unauthorized disclosure, (b) the cloud Provider needs to provide the public key in a trusted manner[1] to each cloud Consumer; and (c) the cloud Consumer needs to protect the public key from undetected, unauthorized modification.

The approach has some disadvantages as well. While on the surface, the approach seems highly secure, there are several security concerns with it:

---

[1]This can be easily accommodated using physical means during contract signing.

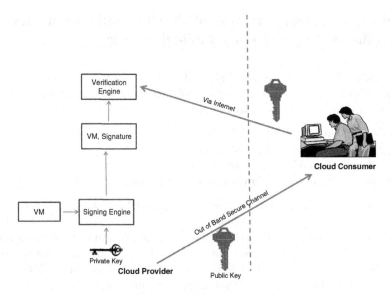

Fig. A.1 VM template authentication using digital signatures

1. First of all, how does the cloud Consumer communicate securely with the verification engine to provide the public key and to obtain the verification results. Let us assume that the cloud Consumer can establish a secure session using TLS or SSH.
2. Then the question becomes: how does the cloud Consumer trust the verification engine running in the cloud Provider. If the cloud Consumer cannot trust or authenticate the verification engine, it has no basis to trust the response from the verification engine regarding the VM template signature verification.
3. Furthermore, whatever means the cloud Consumer uses to establish trust in the verification engine, why not use the same means to trust the VM template and forego the extra step of having to first establish trust in the verification engine?

A.2   VM Template Authentication Using Cryptographic Hash Function

Another technique of assuring the integrity of the VM template is by using a cryptographic hash function, such as SHA-256, to compute a hash value on the VM template, and the Consumers obtaining the hash value using an out-of-band means as illustrated in Fig. A.2.

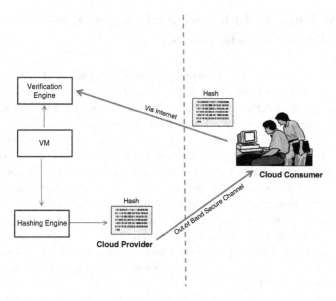

Fig. A.2 VM template authentication using cryptographic hash

The approach has the advantage of requiring no key management. However, the hash value of the VM template needs to be provided to the consumers using means that assure its integrity and source (e.g., physically). The cloud Consumer provides this hash value for comparison during VM template authentication.

The approach has several disadvantages. Some of the disadvantages are common to those for digital signatures:

1. This approach has the limitation that each time the VM template' is modified, a new hash value needs to be promulgated using a secure, out-of-band means.
2. The approach has the limitation that each VM template hash value needs to be promulgated using secure, out-of-band means. One can assume that the cloud will have multiple VM templates.
3. Just like the digital signature, this approach does not solve the problem of the cloud Consumer communicating securely with the verification engine to provide the hash value and obtaining the verification results. Let us assume that the cloud Consumer can establish a secure session using TLS or SSH.
4. Then the question becomes: how does the cloud Consumer trust the verification engine running in the cloud Provider. If the cloud Consumer cannot trust or authenticate the verification engine, it has no basis to trust the response from the verification engine regarding the VM template verification.
5. Furthermore, whatever means the cloud Consumer uses to establish trust in the verification engine, why not use the same means to trust the VM template and forego the extra step of having to first establish trust in the verification engine?

A.3 VM Template Authentication Using Message Authentication Code (MAC)

As illustrated in Fig. A.3, another approach is to use a MAC. A MAC is calculated using a cryptographic function, such as a keyed hash function or a mode of operation for a symmetric block cipher algorithm, that produces a message authentication code using a secret shared by the Provider and the Consumers.

The approach has the advantage of the cloud Provider being able to create and modify multiple VM templates and all cloud Consumers being able to verify the source and integrity of the VM template via MAC verification. It also has the advantage of simplified key management. All that is required are the following: (a) the cloud Provider needs to create a single secret key and protect it from unauthorized use and from unauthorized disclosure; (b) the cloud Provider needs to provide to each cloud Consumer with the secret key in a secure manner[2]; and (c) the cloud Consumer needs to protect the secret key from unauthorized disclosure.

The approach has several disadvantages. Some of the disadvantages are common to those for using digital signatures:

1. Unless the secret key is unique per Consumer, this approach is vulnerable to one Consumer modifying a VM template to compromise another Consumer. Having unique keys for each Consumer will increase a cloud Provider's key management challenge

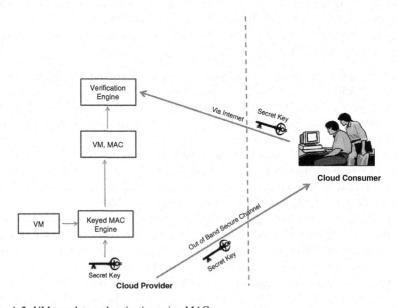

Fig. A.3 VM template authentication using MAC

---

[2]This can be easily accommodated using physical means during contract signing.

2. Just like the use of a digital signature, this approach does not solve the problem of the cloud Consumer communicating securely with the verification engine to provide the secret key and to obtain the verification results. Let us assume that the cloud Consumer can establish a secure session using TLS or SSH.
3. Then the question becomes: how does the cloud Consumer trust the verification engine running in the cloud Provider. If the cloud Consumer cannot trust or authenticate the verification engine, it has no basis to trust the response from the verification engine regarding the VM template authentication.
4. Furthermore, whatever means the cloud Consumer uses to establish trust in the verification engine, why not use the same means to trust the VM template and forego the extra step of having to first establish trust in the verification engine?

A.4   VM Template Authentication Based on Cloud Provider Discretionary Access Control

Under this approach Consumers obtain the VM template from a location that can be modified by the Provider only (i.e., the VM template is protected using discretionary access controls). Though this form of authentication is not a cryptographic technique, we have included this for completeness as a possible approach for VM template authentication.

A.5   Conclusion

In conclusion, one can see from our higher-level security analysis of the possible cryptographic techniques for authenticating VM templates, that none of them solve the twin problem of establishing trust in the VM template, as well as in the verification engine. Hence, our suggested solution for VM template authentication is:

1. The cloud Consumer should use SSL or SSH to establish a secure session with the VM template integrity verification engine.
2. The application instance housing the VM integrity verification engine needs to be configured to run as a secure appliance on a specially hardened VM. The verification engine should also include appropriate public keys, secret keys, and/or hash values, depending on the VM template authentication technique chosen by the cloud Provider. Note that this approach obviates the need for a secure, out-of-band channel between the cloud Provider and the cloud Consumer. This approach also allows the cloud Provider to change keys, algorithms, authentication method and/or a VM template without having a secure, out-of-band channel with the cloud Consumer. Note that a cloud Provider may use different cryptographic techniques (digital signatures, cryptographic hash, or MAC) to protect different VM templates.

3. The cloud Consumer should check out any VM template, and authenticate the VM template and launch the VM.

The advantage of having a verification engine as opposed to having a VM template under discretionary access control is the added flexibility for the cloud Provider to only secure the verification engine using discretionary access control, as opposed to a myriad of VM templates.

References

1. F. Liu, J. Tong, J. Mao, R. Bohn, J. Messina, L. Badger, and D. Leaf, NIST Cloud Computing Reference Architecture (NIST SP 500-292), National Institute of Standards and Technology, U.S. Department of Commerce (2011). http://www.nist.gov/customcf/get_pdf.cfm?pub_id=909505
2. P. Mell and T. Grance, The NIST definition of cloud computing (NIST SP 800-145), National Institute of Standards and Technology, U.S. Department of Commerce (2011) http://csrc.nist.gov/publications/nistpubs/800-145/SP800-145.pdf
3. L. Badger, D. Berstein, R. Bohn, F. de Valux, M. Hogan, J. Mao, J. Messina, K. Mills, A. Sokol, J. Tong, F. Whiteside, and D. Leaf, US government cloud computing technology roadmap volume 1: High-priority requirements to further USG agency cloud computing adoption (NIST SP 500-293, Vol. 1), National Institute of Standards and Technology, U.S. Department of Commerce (2011). http://www.nist.gov/itl/cloud/upload/SP_500_293_volumeI-2.pdf
4. L. Badger, R. Bohn, S. Chu, M. Hogan, F. Liu, V. Kaufmann, J. Mao, J. Messina, K. Mills, A. Sokol, J. Tong, F. Whiteside, and D. Leaf, US government cloud computing technology roadmap volume II: Useful information for cloud adopters (NIST SP 500-293, Vol. 2), National Institute of Standards and Technology, U.S. Department of Commerce (2011). http://www.nist.gov/itl/cloud/upload/SP_500_293_volumeII.pdf.
5. L. Badger, T. Grance, R. Patt-Corner, and J. Voas, Cloud Computing Synopsis and Recommendations (NIST SP 800-146), National Institute of Standards and Technology, U.S. Department of Commerce (2012). http://csrc.nist.gov/publications/nistpubs/800-146/sp800-146.pdf
6. W. Jansen and T. Grance, Guidelines on Security and Privacy in Public Cloud Computing (NIST SP 800-144). National Institute of Standards and Technology, U.S. Department of Commerce (2011). http://csrc.nist.gov/publications/nistpubs/800-144/SP800-144.pdf.
7. Secure Shell (SSH) Transport Layer Protocol, http://www.ietf.org/rfc/rfc4253.txt
8. The Transport Layer Security (TLS) Protocol Version 1.2, http://tools.ietf.org/html/rfc5246
9. Internet Security Glossary, Version 2, http://tools.ietf.org/rfc/rfc4949.txt
10. F.Bracci, A.Corradi and L.Foschini, Database Security Management for Healthcare SaaS in the Amazon AWS Cloud, IEEE Computer, 2012.
11. Understanding and Selecting a Database Encryption or Tokenization Solution, http://securosis.com
12. Best Practices in Securing Your Customer Data in Salesforce, Force.com, and Chatter, http://www.ciphercloud.com

Costs and Security in Clouds

Yao Chen and Radu Sion

Abstract Cloud computing has emerged as an important paradigm for deploying services and applications for both enterprises and end-users. In this chapter, we explore two important aspects of cloud computing – *costs* and *security*. We aim to answer two questions: (1) Is cloud computing a cost effective endeavor? (2) How much security can we afford in the cloud while maintaining the cost benefits of outsourcing?

To answer these questions, we start by looking at the economics of computing in general and clouds in particular. Specifically, we derive the end-to-end cost of a CPU cycle in various environments and show that its cost lies between 0.5 picocents in efficient clouds and nearly 27 picocents for small enterprises (1 picocent = $\$1 \times 10^{-14}$), values validated against current cloud pricing. We show that cloud computing makes sense only in scenarios when the clients distance can be offset by a minimal application computation footprint. We then explore the cost of common cryptography primitives as well as the viability of their deployment for cloud security purposes. It turns out that securing outsourced data and computation against untrusted clouds is often costlier than the associated savings, with outsourcing mechanisms up to several orders of magnitudes costlier than their non-outsourced locally run alternatives.

1 Introduction

As computing becomes embedded in the very fabric of our society, the exponential growth and advances in cheap, high-speed communication allow for unprecedented levels of global information exchange and interaction. As a result, new market forces

Y. Chen (✉) • R. Sion
Network Security and Applied Cryptography Lab, Stony Brook University,
Stony Brook, NY, USA
e-mail: yaochen@cs.stonybrook.edu; sion@cs.stonybrook.edu

S. Jajodia et al. (eds.), *Secure Cloud Computing*, DOI 10.1007/978-1-4614-9278-8_2,   31
© Springer Science+Business Media New York 2014

emerge that propel toward a fundamental, cost-efficient paradigm shift in the way computing is deployed and delivered: computing outsourcing.

Computing outsourcing provides great elasticity and scalability of resources. It minimizes client-side management overheads and benefit from a service provider's global expertise consolidation and bulk pricing, and helps users avoid the capital expense in acquiring computing resources. The past decades' traditional outsourcing paradigms have usually involved established service providers such as IBM that manage or host clients' machines in dedicated data centers. More recently, first storage and then computation outsourcing has been commoditized through the emergence of globally-sized enterprises such as Google, Yahoo, Amazon, and Sun which started offering increasingly complex storage and computation outsourcing "cloud" services. CPU cycles have become consumer merchandise.

So far, the end-to-end viability of cloud computing has mostly not been explored. Is a remotely hosted computing cycle in a cloud indeed cheaper than performing it locally *when considering the end-to-end bottom-line*? It seems the markets have spoken and the increasing number of service providers can be viewed as testimony that this indeed is the case. Yet by what margins? And what are the features of suitable applications for cloud deployment? As the migration from in-house data centers to the clouds is non-trivial and fraught with potentially large costs, asking these questions is essential.

In this chapter, to understand the viability of clouds, we provide a cost model for computing in different environments and derive the dollar cost of primitives such as CPU cycles, storage and network transfers. Using the model, we then evaluate cloud outsourcing end-to-end and derive a threshold principle defining when outsourcing indeed is economically viable, i.e., when computing-related savings outweigh the costs of networking. We then evaluate the footprints and types of applications most suited for cloud deployment.

Despite the associated buzz, clouds have been somewhat less successful in attracting medium to large size corporations. Such clients often fall under strict regulatory compliance requirements for manipulating information or simply are reluctant to place sensitive data and computation logic under the control of a remote, third-party provider, without practical assurances of privacy and confidentiality in which the provider is un-trusted. Significant challenges lie in the path of successful large-scale adoption.

To address this, existing secure outsourcing research addressed several issues including guaranteeing integrity, confidentiality and privacy of outsourced data to secure querying on outsourced encrypted database. Such assurances will likely require strong cryptography as part of elaborate intra- and client-cloud protocols. Yet, strong crypto is expensive. Thus, it is important to ask: how much cryptography can we afford in the cloud while maintaining the cost benefits of outsourcing?

Some believe the answer is simply *none*. For example, in an interview [56] Whitfield Diffie argued that "**current techniques would more than undo the economy [of] outsourcing and show little sign of becoming practical.**"

Here we set out to find out whether this holds and if so, by what margins. One way to look at this is in terms of CPU cycles. For each desired un-secured client CPU cycle, *how many additional cloud cycles can we spend on cryptography*, before its outsourcing becomes too expensive? We end up gaining the insight that today's secure data outsourcing primitives are often orders of magnitude more expensive than local execution, mainly due to the fact that we do not know how to process complex functions on encrypted data efficiently enough. And outsourcing simple operations – such as existing research in querying encrypted data, keyword searches, selections, projections, and simple aggregates – is simply not profitable. Thus, while traditional security mechanisms allow the elegant handling of inter-client and outside adversaries, today it is still too costly to secure against cloud insiders with cryptography.

2 Cost Models

To reach the granularity of compute cycles we explore the cost of running computing at different levels. We chose environments of increasing size: home, small enterprises, mid-size enterprises and large size data centers. The boundaries between these setups are often dynamic and the main reason we're using them is to help differentiate a set of key parameters.[1]

2.1 Levels

Home Users (H). We include this scenario as a baseline for a simple home setup containing several computers. This could correspond to individuals with spare time to maintain a small set of computers, or a very small home-based enterprise with no staffing overheads. It is important to consider this scenario as it represents a potentially large slice of the outsourcing market, especially through application such as mail, document, media and personal blog/web hosting. Also this niche is important as it features a set of peculiarities, including access to residential energy pricing, negligible cooling, rental and management costs (as we will not factor individuals' time in).

Small Enterprises (S). We consider here any scenario involving an infrastructure of up to 1,000 servers run in-house in a commercial enterprise. The cost structure will start to feature most of the usual suspects, including commercial energy and network pricing, cooling, space leases, staffing etc. Small enterprises however can not afford custom hardware, efficient power-distribution, and cooling or dedicated buildings among others. More importantly, in addition to power distribution

---

[1]We note it is not the subject of our work to explore in-depth data center infrastructures. A plethora of online sources discuss issues related to data centers, often focusing on power and overall efficiency (most notably James Hamilton's blog [27]).

inefficiencies, due to their nature, small enterprises cannot be run at high utilization as they would be usually under the incidence of business cycles and its associated peak loads.

Mid-size Enterprises (M). We consider here setups of up to 10,000 servers, run by a corporation, often in its own dedicated data center(s). Mid-size enterprises might have some clout and access to better service deals for network service as well as more efficient cooling and power distribution. They are not fully global, yet could feature several centers across one or two time zones, allowing increased independence from local load cycles as well as the ability to handle daily peaks better by shifting loads across timezones. All the above results ultimately in increased utilization (20–25 % est.) and overall efficiency.

Large Enterprises/Clouds (L). Clouds and large enterprises run over 10,000 servers, cross multiple time-zones, often literally at a global level, with large data centers distributed across all continents and often in tens to hundreds of countries. For example Google has built a 30-acre site in Dalles, Oregon, next to a hydroelectric dam providing cheap power. The site is composed of 34,000 sqft buildings [33]. Especially in cloud setups, high speed networks allow global-wide distribution and integration of load from thousands of individual points of load. This in turn flattens the 24-h overall load curve and allows for efficient peak handling and comparably high utilization factors (50–60 % est. [28]). Cloud providers run the most efficient infrastructures, and often are at the forefront of innovation. Moreover, clouds have access to bulk-pricing for network service from large ISPs, often one order of magnitude cheaper than mid-size enterprises.

2.2 Factors

We now consider the cost factors that come into play across all of the above levels. These can be divided into a set of inter-dependent vectors, including: hardware (servers, networking gear), building (floor space leasing), energy (running hardware and cooling), service (administration, staffing, software maintenance), and network service. Other breakdown layouts of these factors are possible.

Server Hardware. Hardware costs include servers, racks, power equipment, network equipment, cooling equipment etc. We will discuss network equipment later. Naturally, there are different choices for data centers to increase capacity. *Up-scaling* – the purchase of a smaller number of more expensive off-the-shelf multi-blade servers – is often considered in mid-size enterprises, and features lower software and infrastructure cost advantages. Scaling out – deploying massive numbers of low-cost, almost "expendable" custom-designed and often in-house built multi-CPU server boards – is a strategy available to large, cloud-size providers such as Google and Amazon. The advantages of this approach are low hardware costs, low inter-failure correlation and high overall efficiency factors. Sometimes these two approaches can be combined; e.g., servers embedded with 4–8 CPUs can be considered as scale-out architecture of scale-up nodes [25]. We note that these costs drop with time, likely even by the time this goes to print. For example, while many of the current documented mid-size deployments use single or multi-CPU System-X blade servers at around $1–2,000 each [32], large data centers deploy custom setups at about $3,000 for 4 CPUs, near-future developments could yield important changes.[2] We will be conservative and empirically assume home PC prices of around $750/CPU, small and mid-size enterprise costs of around $1,000/CPU (for 2 CPU blades) and cloud-level costs of no more than $500/CPU.

Energy. Energy in data centers does not only include power, computing and networking hardware but the entire support infrastructure, including cooling, physical security, and overall facilities. With the increasing density of today's rack structure, temperature rises more rapidly than in old server rooms [7]. For example, any additional 40 W/sqft can lead to a rise of 25 °F in 10 min. A simple rough way to infer power costs is by estimating the Power Usage Efficiency (PUE) of the data center. The PUE is a metric to evaluate the energy efficiency of a data center [24] (PUE = Total Power Usage/IT Equipment Power Usage). PUE ranges from 1.13 to 1.21 for big providers as claimed by Google, Facebook and 1.22 for efficient data center containers, to over 2 for typical data centers [44,51]. We will assume 1.2–1.5 PUE for large enterprises, 1.6–2 PUE for mid-size enterprises and 2–2.5 for small enterprises [44]. Costs of electricity are relatively uniform and documented [23].

Service. Evaluating the staffing requirements for data centers is an extremely complex endeavor as it involves a number of components such as software development and management, hardware repair, maintenance of cooling, building, network and power services.

Analytical approaches are challenged by the sparsity of available relevant supporting data sets. We deployed a set of commonly accepted rule of thumb values that have been empirically developed and validate well [29]: the server to administrator ratio varies from 2:1 up to experimental 2,500:1 values due to different degrees of automation and data management. In deployment, small to mid-size data centers feature a ratio of 100–140:1 whereas cloud level centers can go up to 1,000:1 [23, 28].

Network Hardware. To allow for analysis of network intensive protocols, we chose to separate network transport service costs from the other factors of impact in the bottom line for CPU cycle. Specifically, while the internal network infrastructure costs will be factored in the data center costs, network service will not. We will estimate separately the cost of transferring a bit reliably to/from the data center intermediated by outside ISPs' networks. Internal network infrastructure costs can be estimated by evaluating the number of required switches and routers. The design

---

[2]In one documented instance, e.g., Amazon is working with Rackable Systems to deliver an under $700 AMD-based 6 CPU board dubbed CEMS (Cooperative Expendable Micro-Slice Servers) V3.

of scalable large economy network topology with high inter-node bandwidth for data centers is an ever ongoing research problem [45]. We base our results on some of the latest state of the art research, deploying fat tree interconnect structures. Fat trees have been shown to offer significantly lower overall hardware costs with good overall connectivity factors. For example inter-connecting a 27,648 node cluster with Ethernet switching can be done for under $8.64 million [45], assuming $3,000 48-port GigE switches at the edge, aggregation and core layers.

Floor Space. Floor space costs vary wildly, by location and use. While office space can be had for up to tens of dollars/sqft/month in Manhattan, data center space can be had at much lower rates, being as low as $0.1/sqft/month [15,16,48]. While small to mid-size enterprises usually have data centers near their location (thus sometimes incurring office-level pricing), large companies such as Google and Microsoft tend to build data centers on owned land, in less populated place where the per sqft price can be brought down much lower, often amortized to zero over time.

We also note that floor surface is directly related to power consumption and cooling with designs supporting anywhere from 40 to 250 W/sqft [21]. Thus, the overall power requirements (driven by CPUs) impact directly the required floor space.

3 Cost Primitives

Armed with knowledge of the above factors, we now estimate the cost of basic computing primitives.

3.1 CPU Cycles

We start by evaluating the amortized dollar cost of a CPU cycle in Eq. (1). See notations in Table 1 and various setups' parameters in Table 2.

Table 1 Notations for Eq. (1)

Symbol	Definition
N_s, N_w	Number of servers, switches
α	administrator: server ratio
β	W/sqft
λ_s, λ_w	Server, switch price
λ_p, λ_f	Personnel, floor cost per second
λ_e	Electricity price/(W·s)
μ	CPU utilization
ν	CPU frequency
τ_s, τ_w	Servers, switches lifespan (5 years)
w_p, w_i	Server power at peak, idle

Table 2 Sample key parameters

Parameters	Home	Small	Medium	Large
CPU utilization	5–8 %	10–12 %	15–20 %	40–56 %
server:admin ratio	N.A.	100–140	140–200	800–1k
Space (sqft/month)	N.A.	$0.5	$0.5	$0.25
PUE	N.A.	2–2.5	1.6–2	1.2–1.5

Table 3 Current pricings of a CPU cycle from major cloud providers

Provider	Picocents
Amazon EC2	0.93–2.36
Google AppEngine	Up to 2.31
Microsoft Azure	Up to 1.96

$$CycleCost = \frac{Server + Energy + Service + Network + Floor}{Total\ Cycles}$$

$$= \frac{\lambda_s \cdot N_s / \tau_s + (w_p \cdot \mu + w_i \cdot (1-\mu)) \cdot PUE \cdot \lambda_e + \frac{N_s}{\alpha} \cdot \lambda_p + \lambda_w \cdot N_w / \tau_w + \lambda_f \cdot \frac{(w_p \cdot \mu + w_i \cdot (1-\mu)) \cdot PUE}{\beta}}{\mu \cdot v \cdot N_s}$$

$$(1)$$

The results are depicted in Fig. 1, costs ranging from 0.45 picocents/cycle in very large cloud settings all the way to (S), the costliest environment, where a cycle costs up to 27 picocents ($1\ US\ picocent = \$1 \times 10^{-14}$).

Fig. 1 CPU cycle costs

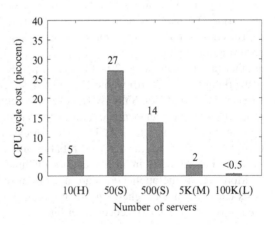

We validate our results by exploring the pricing of the main cloud providers (Table 3). The prices lie surprisingly close to each other and to our estimates, ranging from 0.93 to 2.36 picocents/cycle. The difference in cost is due to the fact that these points include not only CPUs but also intra-cloud networking, instance-specific disk storage and cloud providers' profit.

Table 4 Summarized network service costs [28, 49]

	H, S	M	L
Monthly	$44.90	$200	$95	$13
Bandwidth (d / u)	15/5 Mbps	per Mbps	per Mbps	
Dedicated	No	Yes	Yes	Yes
Picocent/bit	115/345	>7,000	3,665	500

Table 5 Per bit transfer costs

Settings	Cost (picocent)
(H, S) → Cloud	900
(M) → Cloud	4,500

3.2 Network Service

Published numbers place network service costs for large data centers at around $13/Mbps/month and for mid-size setups at $95/Mbps/month [28] for *guaranteed* bandwidth. Home user and small enterprise pricing usually benefits from economies of scale and numbers are readily available, e.g., Optimum Online provides 15/5 Mbps internet connection for small business starting at $44.9/month. We note however that the quoted bandwidth is not guaranteed and refers only to the hop connecting the client to the provider. However, if home users or small enterprises were to order *guaranteed* network service, the price is much higher (around $200/Mbps/month as quoted to us by network providers.). In this work, we mainly consider *non-guaranteed* network services for home users and small enterprises. We summarize these costs in Table 4.

The end-to-end cost of network transfer includes the cost on both communicating parties and the CPU overheads of transferring a bit from one application layer to another (a minimum about 20 CPU cycles per 32 bit data). Moreover, for reliable networking (e.g., TCP/IP) we need to also factor in the additional traffic and spent CPU cycles (e.g., SYN, SYN/ACK, ACK, for connection establishment, ACKs for sent data, window management, routing, re-transmissions, etc.). If we assume a 1 % TCP re-transmission rate, 1 ACK packet for every two data packets, it costs more than 900 picocents to transfer 1 bit reliably in the $S \to L$ scenario. We summarize the per bit transfer cost in other scenarios in Table 5.

Moreover, if the applications are not optimized to fully utilize payloads these costs could be much higher, e.g., if only a 32 bit value payload is sent, it would incur upwards of 10,000 picocents per bit.

3.3 Storage

Simply storing bits on disks has become truly cheap. Increased hardware reliability (with mean time between failures rated routinely above a million hours even for consumer markets) and economies of scale resulted in extreme drops in the costs of disks. Table 6 shows the costs of ownership and operation of a representative sample (by no means exhaustive) set of commonly available consumer-level disks (numbers were obtained in November 2009 from numerous online sources, including the disk vendors' sites, price search engines and independent online hardware discussion sites). Costs incorporate energy and amortized acquisition components. Energy is dominating at 60–70 % of the total cost. We note that actual observed MTBF are often up to about 3.4 times lower than advertised [53]. We considered this in computing the values in Table 6.

In terms of amortized acquisition costs, the Seagate Barracuda provides the best price/hardware/MTBF ratio at 7.67 picocents/bit/year. We observe that hardware constitutes only a small percentage of the overall costs, e.g., for the Maxtor, the amortized hardware acquisition being only 12.16 % of the overall ownership cost. And it holds across all considered (H,S,M,L) levels due to the fact that the existence of a critical mass of disk consumer level buyers results in economies of scale pricing available for everybody.

This leads to the insight that, if storage power and maintenance has been already factored in, then, for most scenarios direct storage hardware costs are very small and *can be mostly ignored when evaluating network and CPU intensive protocols*. Naturally this does not hold if the main costs include long-term data at rest with little or no computation and networking. But, as soon as data gets transferred or processed, direct storage costs become negligible.

4 To or Not To

The insights gained above in the costs of computation, network and storage enable us to explore the viability of the outsourcing endeavor.

We start by noting that it is easy to find scenarios for which it does *not* make sense to outsource to clouds from a strict cost-centric perspective. For example, the CPU cycle costs in Fig. 1 immediately show that it is not profitable to outsource personal workloads (H) to small (S) enterprises (we denote this $H \to S$) as it would naturally incur additional network bandwidth and CPU cycle costs are much higher for (S).

Yet, what about the other options, $\{H \to M, H \to L, S \to M, S \to L, M \to L\}$?

The answer in each of these cases is highly dependent on the type of applications outsourced. Basically, there are three main services the cloud provides: storage, networking and computation. The costs of these three primitives behave differently across computing environments of different scale, thus their outsourcing costs are different. Often the relation between these primitives in an application determines its outsourcing saving. In the following, we explore applications of different types in two outsourcing scenarios (single-client outsourcing and multi-client outsourcing).

Table 6 Magnetic disk storage costs

Disk	Cap. (GB)	Price (USD)	Adj. MTBF (milllion hours)	Amort. acq. (picocent/bit/year)	Power (W)	Power cost (picocent/bit/year)	Total cost (picocent/bit/year)	Aqc.%
Maxtor Diamond Max	500	53	0.35	32.89	10.85	237.62	270.50	12.16
Hitachi Deskstar 7k500	500	67	0.29	49.89	12.30	269.37	319.26	15.63
Hitachi Ultrastar A7K1000	1,024	153	0.35	46.36	11.50	122.97	169.33	27.38
WD Caviar GP Low Power	1,024	103	0.29	37.45	5.75	61.49	98.93	37.85
Seagate Barracuda 7200.10	750	63	0.35	26.06	10.95	159.87	185.93	14.02

4.1 Single-Client Model

One of the simplest computation outsourcing scenarios involves clients shifting their *own* CPU-intensive applications onto clouds, to save costs. Later *these same clients* (or delegates thereof) will access these cloud-hosted applications for their own use. An example of this are *large corporations considering migrating in-house data centers to clouds*.

Naturally, this is feasible when the savings outweigh the outsourcing overhead costs. In general, outsourcing a computation load from environment a to environment b is economically justified when

$$Savings = Cycles \times c_a - Cycles \times c_b - Trans_{a \to b} \geq 0$$

$$\Leftrightarrow Cycles \geq \frac{Trans_{a \to b}}{c_a - c_b} \qquad (2)$$

where *Cycles* is the number of CPU cycles needed per bit data, and c_x denotes the CPU cycle cost for environment $X \in \{H, S, M, L\}$. We call this the *first minimal CPU-intensive requirement criterion* (we will also call this the "first outsourcing criterion"):

> **First outsourcing criterion:**
>
> For an application accessed mainly by clients in environment a, outsourcing it from a to another environment b is economically justified iff. its computation load exceeds $\frac{Trans_{a \to b}}{c_a - c_b}$ compute cycles per transferred input bit.

To illustrate, consider a 32 bit item in the $S \to L$ case. We know from Sect. 3.2, that the cost of reliably transferring 32 bits can be anywhere 28,000 and 320,000 picocents depending on the nature of the connection and whether connection establishment costs are amortized across multiple sends. For consistency, we disregard for now any application-specific costs, such as the existence of results and their transfer costs. As a lower bound, we get

$$Cycles \geq \frac{Trans_{S \to L}}{c_S - c_L} \in (1{,}000, 12{,}000).$$

In other words, *if the task at hand requires anywhere less than 1,000 CPU cycles (in the most optimized possible case) per 32 bits of input data, it is not profitable to outsource from a home setting to a large cloud.*

Moreover, 1,000 turns out to also be a lower bound across all outsourcing options as can be seen in Fig. 2. For $H \to L$, we have anywhere between $Cycles > 6{,}400$

Fig. 2 Cost savings of outsourcing per 32 bit data from $S \to L, H \to L, M \to L$ with increasing application computation load. The lower bounds on the numbers of CPU cycles needed to justify cloud outsourcing are 1,000, 6,400, and 96,100 respectively

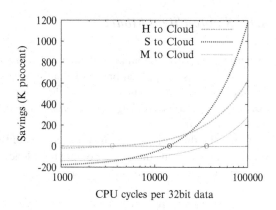

and $Cycles > 71,000$. For $M \to L$, due to the much higher network costs of (M), 32 bit transfers can cost anywhere between 144,000 and 1,615,000 picocents, which results in anywhere between $Cycles > 96,100$ and $Cycles > 1,070,000$.

Applications which are well suited in such CPU-intensive outsourcing include highly scientific computations [52], which usually consume large amounts of CPU. We note that recently Mathworks seems to have tapped this niche, by adding a parallel toolbox in Matlab which enables users to do parallel computing on the Amazon Elastic Compute Cloud [3].

We note that the above *minimal CPU-intensive requirement* criterion specifically refers to network costs that cannot be amortized over multiple transactions, hence the wording "per *transferred* input bit". Yet, often applications involve significant amounts of already cloud-hosted data inputs, and in such cases, the criterion simply refers to any data that is transferred to/from the cloud.

Simple Storage. Overall, the CPU-intensive requirement of the criterion suggests that purely storage-centric applications are not good candidates for unified-client outsourcing in the cloud. This indeed seems to hold for simple storage outsourcing in which a single data customer places data remotely for future access. For the $S \to L$ scenario, the amortized cost of storing a bit reliably either locally *or remotely* is under 9 picocents/month (including power). Network transfer however, is at least 900 picocents per accessed bit, a cost that is not amortized and two orders of magnitude higher than storing the data.

Thus, from a pure technological cost-centric point of view, it is simply not effective to store data remotely. Depending on the application network footprint, *outsourced storage costs (incl. network transfer cost) can be upwards of 2+ orders of magnitude higher than local storage*. It's worth noticing that cloud providers also allow users to mail a portable storage device and upload the data to the cloud over their local network [2]. Yet, as we discussed in Sect. 3.3, simple storage without data processing has become truly cheap even for end users. Using clouds as remote storage is not cost efficient.

Searchable Storage and Databases. Scenarios where outsourcing of data becomes viable include any data processing mechanisms that allow the amortization of networked data transfer over multiple queries to the data set.

Consider for example a searchable outsourced database of size n which allows queries of certain search selectivity s (search results are of size $n * s * S_r$, where S_r is the size of a single result) to be submitted. In this case, the intuition dictates that outsourcing is profitable for a CPU-intensive search process (e.g., for a large database size) and a high selectivity (very low s). For illustration, if searching involves a binary index ($O(\log n)$ CPU cycles), and a comparison takes $C_{compare} = 3$ cycles, we have

$$Savings = \log n \times C_{compare} \times (c_a - c_b)$$

$$Cost_{trans} = nsS_r Trans_{a \to b},$$

and, for cost viability, we want

$$\log n \times C_{compare} \times (c_a - c_b) \geq nsBTrans_{a \to b}$$

$$\Leftrightarrow s \leq \frac{\log n \times C_{compare} \times (c_a - c_b)}{nS_r Trans_{a \to b}}$$

In the $S \to L$ scenario, for a database of $n = 10^9$ keywords and $S_r = 32$ bits, this results in $s \leq 8.3 \times 10^{-11}$. And s will be even lower when database size grows.

4.2 Multi-Client Model

Yet, paradoxically, despite the above conclusion, storage outsourcing seems to be thriving. Just recently, Smugmug, a paid digital photo sharing website, announced $1M savings a year by outsourcing storage to Amazon S3 [1].

This can be explained as follows. The core storage costs coupled with the lack of an intense-enough CPU load, indeed do not justify outsourcing for a unified client scenario. Yet, web-based enterprises such as Smugmug, by their very nature provide services to third party clients and thus also require mechanisms to handle their clients' remote access, e.g., through often CPU-intensive web interfaces supported by web servers running on actual CPUs. This can increase the per-bit CPU footprint significantly. Moreover, network service pricing for mid-size enterprises can be up to one order of magnitude higher than for clouds, as can be seen in Table 4 – and in effect, clouds can afford to also operate as an efficient content distribution (CDN) service.

Overall, the case for cloud feasibility becomes more complicated in multi-client scenarios. The outsourcing criterion needs to be updated as a function also of the different network service deals of the two environments. Then, outsourcing is economically tenable when

$$Cycles \times c_a - Cycles \times c_b + (Trans_{c \to a} - Trans_{c \to b}) \geq 0 \qquad (3)$$

where c is the environment from which the majority of client accesses are coming to the outsourced application (Fig. 3). Then, the outsourcing criterion can be rewritten into a more complete ("second outsourcing criterion") form as follows:

Second outsourcing criterion:

For an application that resides in environment a, whose accesses come mainly from clients in environment c, outsourcing it from a to another environment b is economically justified iff.

its computation load exceeds $\frac{Trans_{c \to b} - Trans_{c \to a}}{c_a - c_b}$ compute cycles per transferred input bit – for $c_a \geq c_b$ and $Trans_{c \to a} \leq Trans_{c \to b}$, or,

its computation footprint is lower than $\frac{Trans_{c \to a} - Trans_{c \to b}}{c_b - c_a}$ compute cycles per transferred input bit – for $c_a \leq c_b$ and $Trans_{c \to a} \geq Trans_{c \to b}$

We can better understand Eq. (3) by detailing the following four cases:

(i) $c_a \geq c_b$ and $Trans_{c \to a} \geq Trans_{c \to b}$, in this case, savings are constantly positive, yielding no *CPU intensive requirement*;

(ii) $c_a \leq c_b$ and $Trans_{c \to a} \leq Trans_{c \to b}$, no savings can be achieved (constantly negative);

(iii) $c_a \geq c_b$ and $Trans_{c \to a} \leq Trans_{c \to b}$, then $Cycles \geq \frac{Trans_{c \to b} - Trans_{c \to a}}{c_a - c_b}$

(iv) $c_a \leq c_b$ and $Trans_{c \to a} \geq Trans_{c \to b}$, in this case, $Cycles \leq \frac{Trans_{c \to a} - Trans_{c \to b}}{c_b - c_a}$, this unusual case corresponds to an *upper bound* on the amount of computation an application can have before outsourcing becomes counter-productive;

We show in Fig. 3 the cost savings of $S, M \to L$ with different third party clients and applications at different CPU intensive levels. The CPU intensive requirements are much lower than in the single-client model. Note, given today's cost points, $M \to L$ is always profitable and falls into case (i). This may also explain the success of Smugmug outsourcing to Amazon S3. Moreover, if S requires guaranteed network service for the application (see numbers in Table 4), $S \to L$ also falls into case (i).

For completeness, the equation also covers cases when outsourcing occurs from larger to smaller scale environments, as in (iv). One illustrative instance of this is a large enterprise placing smaller data centers strategically closer to targeted clients. Although CPU cycles will cost more in these smaller data centers, this kind of outsourcing can effectively take advantage of its associated network proximity.

This illustrates another point of feasibility for clouds: content distribution for applications with numerous (often geographically dispersed) clients. This is not only profitable because of the better network service deals that clouds get from major ISPs, but also due to their on-demand scalability promise etc., which is outside of the scope of this chapter.

For multi-client applications such as content distribution or data processing, it is important to consider also intra-cloud communication as well as the actual

Fig. 3 Illustration of the cost savings of outsourcing per 32 bit of data from $a \in \{S, M\}$ to $b = L$ with $c \in \{S, M\}$ – with increasing computation load – according to Eq. (3) (corresponding to the second outsourcing criterion). For $a = S, c = S$, the CPU intensive requirement is 410 cycles per 32 bit

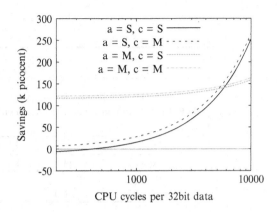

Table 7 Inter- and intra-cloud network transfer pricing (picocent)

	Amazon	Microsoft	Google
Data-in	1,164	1,164	1,164
Data-out	1,979	1,746	1,396
First 10 TB/month			
Next 40 TB/month	1,513	1,746	1,396
Next 100 TB/month	1,280	1,746	1,396
Next 150 TB/month	1,164	1,746	1,396
Intra-cloud/same region	0	0	0
Intra-cloud/inter-region	116	N/A	N/A

profit-including pricing of bit transfers in/out of clouds. For example, at the time of this writing, clouds charge 1,164 picocents per incoming bit, roughly double than what they are paying to ISPs. Table 7 illustrates these pricing points.

5 Cryptography

So far we know that a CPU cycle will set us back 0.45–27 picocents, transferring a bit costs at least 900 picocents, and storing it costs under 100 picocents/year. We now explore the costs of basic crypto and modular arithmetic. All values are in picocents. Note that CPU cycles needed in cryptographic operations often vary with optimization algorithms and types of hardware used (e.g., specialized secure CPUs and crypto accelerators with hardware RSA engines [4] are cheaper per cycle than general-purpose CPUs).

Symmetric Key Crypto. We first evaluate the per-bit costs of AES-128, AES-192, AES-256 and illustrate in Table 8. The evaluation is based on results from the ECRYPT Benchmarking of Cryptographic Systems (eBACS) [9].

Table 8 AES-128, AES-192, AES-256 costs (per byte) on 64-byte input

	AES-128	AES-192	AES-256
S	1.42E + 03	1.48E + 03	1.52E + 03
L	2.37E + 01	2.47E + 01	2.53E + 01

Table 9 Cost of RSA encryption/decryption on 59-byte messages (picocents)

	1,024 bit		2,048 bit	
	Encrypt	Decrypt	Encrypt	Decrypt
S	3.74E + 06	1.03E + 08	8.99E + 06	6.44E + 08
L	6.24E + 04	1.72E + 06	1.50E + 05	1.07E + 07

Table 10 DSA on 59-byte messages. The 1,024-bit DSA uses 148-byte secret key and 128-byte public key. The 2,048-bit DSA uses 276-byte secret key and 256-byte public key

	1,024 bit		2,048 bit	
	Sign	Verify	Sign	Verify
S	5.73E + 07	6.94E + 07	1.89E + 08	2.30E + 08
L	9.55E + 05	1.16E + 06	3.15E + 06	3.84E + 06

Table 11 Costs of ECDSA signatures on 59-byte messages (curve over a field of size 2^{163}, 2^{409}, 2^{571} respectively) (picocents)

	ECDSA-163		ECDSA-409	
	KG/SGN	Verify	KG/SGN	Verify
S	1.36E + 08	2.65E + 08	9.60E + 08	1.91E + 09
L	2.27E + 06	4.41E + 06	1.60E + 07	3.19E + 07
	ECDSA-571			
	KG/SGN		Verify	
S	2.09E + 09		4.18E + 09	
L	3.48E + 07		6.96E + 07	

RSA. Numerous algorithms aim to improve the speed of RSA, mainly by reducing the time to do modular multiplications. In Table 9, we illustrate the costs of RSA encryption/decryption using benchmark results from [9].

PK Signatures. We illustrate costs of DSA, and ECDSA signatures based on NIST elliptic curves [9] in Tables 10 and 11.

Cryptographic Hashes. We also show per byte cost of MD5 and SHA1 with varied input sizes in Table 12.

Table 12 Per-byte cost of MD5 and SHA1 (with 64- and 4,096-byte input)

	MD5		SHA1	
	4,096	64	4,096	64
S	1.52E + 02	3.75E + 02	2.14E + 02	6.44E + 02
L	2.53E + 00	6.25E + 00	3.56E + 00	1.07E + 01

6 Secure Outsourcing

Thus armed with an understanding of computation, storage, network and crypto costs, we now ask whether securing cloud computing against insiders is a viable endeavor.

We start by exploring what security means in this context. Naturally, the traditional usual suspects need to be handled in any outsourcing environment: (mutual) authentication, logic certification, inter-client isolation, network security as well as general physical security. Yet, all of these issues are addressed extensively in existing infrastructures and are not the subject of this work.

Similarly, for conciseness, within this scope, we will isolate the analysis from the additional costs of software patching, peak provisioning for reliability, network defenses etc.

6.1 Trust

We are concerned cloud clients being often reluctant to place sensitive data and logic onto remote servers without guarantees of compliance to their security policies [19, 35]. This is especially important in view of recent sub-poenas and other security incidents involving cloud-hosted data [13, 14, 42]. The viability of the cloud computing paradigm thus hinges directly on the issue of clients' trust and of major concern are cloud insiders. Yet how "trusted" are today's clouds from this perspective? We identify a set of scenarios.

Trusted clouds. In a *trusted* cloud, in the absence of unpredictable failures, clients are served correctly, in accordance to an agreed upon service contract and the cloud provider's policies. No insiders act maliciously.

Untrusted clouds. For *untrusted* clouds, we distinguish several cases depending on the types of illicit incentives existing for the cloud and the client policies with which these will directly conflict. We call a cloud *data-curious* if insiders thereof have incentives to violate confidentiality policies (mainly) for (sensitive) client data. Similarly, in an *access-curious* cloud, insiders will aim to infer client access patterns to data or reverse-engineer and understand outsourced computation logic. A *malicious* cloud will focus mainly on (data and computation) integrity policies and alter data or perform incorrect computation.

Reasonable cloud insiders are likely to factor in the potential illicit gains (the incentives to violate the policy), the penalty for getting caught, as well as the probability of detection. Thus for most practical scenarios, insiders will engage in such behavior only if they can get away undetected with high probability, e.g., when no (cryptographic?) safeguards are in place to enable the detection.

6.2 Secure Outsourcing

Yet, millions of users embrace free web apps in **an untrusted provider model**. This shows that today's (mostly personal) cloud clients are willing to trade their privacy for (free) service. This is not necessarily a bad thing, especially at this critical-mass building stage, yet raises questions of clouds' viability for commercial, regulatory-compliant deployment, involving sensitive data and logic. And, from a bottom-line cost-perspective, is it worth even trying? This is what we aim to understand here.

In the following **we will assess whether clouds are economically tenable if their users do not trust them and therefore must employ cryptography and other mechanisms to protect their data.** A number of experimental systems and research efforts address the problem of outsourcing *data* to *untrusted service providers*, including issues ranging from searching in remote encrypted data to guaranteeing integrity and confidentiality to querying of outsourced data. In favor of cloud computing, we will set our analysis in the most favorable $S \rightarrow L$ scenario, which yields most CPU cycle savings.

6.3 The Case for Basic Outsourcing

Before we tackle cloud security, let us look at the simplest computation outsourcing scenario (where clients outsource data to the cloud, expect the cloud to process it, and send the results back). In Chap. 1, we show that, to make (basic, unsecured) outsourcing cost effective, the cost savings (mainly from cheaper CPU cycles) need to outweigh the cloud's distance from clients. In $S \rightarrow L$, outsourced tasks should perform at least 1,000 CPU cycles per every 32 bit data, otherwise it is not worth outsourcing them.

6.4 Encrypted Data Storage with Integrity

With an understanding of the basic boundary condition defining the viability of outsourcing we now turn our attention to one of the most basic outsourcing scenarios in which a single data client places data remotely for simple storage purposes. In the $S \rightarrow L$ scenario, the amortized cost of storing a bit reliably either locally *or remotely* is under 9 picocents/month (including power). Network transfer however, is of at least 900 picocents per accessed bit, a cost that is not amortized and two orders of magnitude higher.

From a technological cost-centric point of view it is simply not effective to store data remotely: **outsourced storage costs can be upwards of** 2+ **orders of magnitude higher than local storage** for the $S \to L$ scenario *even in the absence of security assurances.*

Cost of Security. Yet, outsourced storage providers exist and thrive. This is likely due to factors outside of our scope, such as the convenience of being able to have access to the data from everywhere or collaborative application scenarios in which multiple data users share single data stores (multi-client settings). Notwithstanding the reason, since consumers have decided it is worth paying for outsourced storage, the next question we ask is, how much more would security cost in this context? We first survey some of the existing work.

Several existing systems encrypt data before storing it on potentially data-curious servers [10, 12, 43]. File systems such as I^3FS [34], GFS [22], and Checksummed NCryptfs [54] perform online real-time integrity verification.

It can be seen that two main assurances are of concern here: integrity and confidentiality. The cheapest integrity constructs deployed in most of the above revolve around the use of hash-based MACs. As discussed above, SHA-1 based keyed MAC constructs with 4,096-byte blocks would cost around 4 picocent/byte on the server and 200 picocents/byte on the client side, leading to a total cost of about 25 picocents/bit. This is at least four times lower than the cost of storing the bit for a year and at least one order of magnitude lower than the costs incurred by transferring the same bit (at 900+ picocents/bit). Thus, **for outsourced storage, integrity assurance overheads are negligible.**

For publicly verifiable constructs, crypto-hash chains can help amortize their costs over multiple blocks. In the extreme case, a single signature could authenticate an entire file system, at the expense of increased I/O overheads for verification. Usually, a chain only includes a set of blocks.

For an average of twenty 4,096 byte blocks[3] secured by a single hash-chain signed using 1,024-bit RSA, would yield an amortized cost approximately 1 M picocents per 4,096-byte block (30+ picocents/bit) for client read verification and 180+ picocents/bit for write/signatures. This is up to **8 times more expensive than the MAC based case.**

---

[3]Douceur et al. [20], show that file sizes can be modeled using a log-normal distribution. E.g, for $\mu^e = 8.46$, $\sigma^e = 2.4$ and 20,000 files, the median file size would be 4 KB, mean 80 KB, along with a small number of files with sizes exceeding 1 GB [5, 20].

6.5 Searches on Encrypted Data

Confidentiality alone can be achieved by encrypting the outsourced content before outsourcing to potentially access-curious servers. Once encrypted however, it cannot be easily processed by servers.

One of the first processing primitives that has been explored allows clients to search directly in remote encrypted data [6, 8, 17]. In these efforts, clients either linearly process the data using symmetric key encryption mechanisms, or, more often, outsource additional secure (meta)data mostly of size linear in the order of the original data set. This meta-data aids the server in searching through the encrypted data set while revealing as little as possible.

But is remote searching worth it vs. local storage? We concluded above that simply using a cloud as a remote file server is extremely non-profitable, up to several orders of magnitude. Could the searching application possibly make a difference? This would hold if either (i) the task of searching would be extremely CPU intensive allowing the cloud savings to kick in and offset the large losses due to network transfer, or (ii) the search is extremely selective and its results are a very small subset of the outsourced data set – thus amortizing the initial transfer cost over multiple searches.

We note that existing work does not support any complex search predicates outside of simple keyword matching search. Thus the only hope there is that the search-related CPU load (e.g., string comparison) will be enough cheaper in the cloud to offset the initial and result transfer costs.

Keyword searching can be done in asymptotically constant time, given enough storage or logarithmic if B-trees are used. While the client could maintain indexes and only deploy the cloud as a file server, we already discovered that this is not going to be profitable. Thus if we are to have any chance to benefit here, the index structures need to also be stored on the server.

In this case, the search cost includes the CPU cycle costs in reading the B-tree and performing binary searches within B-tree nodes. As an example, consider 32 bit search keys (e.g., as they can be read in one cycle from RAM), and a 1 TB database. One to three CPU cycles are needed to initiate the disk DMA per reading, and each comparison in the binary search requires another 1–3 cycles (for executing a comparison conditional jump operation). A B-tree with 16 KB nodes will have approximately a 1,000 fanout and a height of 4–5, so performing a search on this B-tree index requires about 100–300 CPU cycles. Thus in this simple remote search, $S \rightarrow L$ outsourcing would result in CPU-related savings of around 2,500–8,000 picocents per access. Transferring 32 bits from $S \rightarrow L$ costs upwards of 900 picocents. Outsourced searching becomes thus more expensive for any results upwards of 36 bytes per query.

6.6   Insights into Secure Query Processing

By now we start to suspect that similar insights hold also for outsourced query processing. This is because we now know that (i) the tasks to be outsourced should be CPU-intensive enough to offset the network overhead – in other words, outsourcing peanut counting will never be profitable, and (ii) existing confidentiality (e.g., homomorphisms) and integrity (e.g., hash trees, aggregated signatures, hash chains) mechanisms can "secure" only very simple basic arithmetic (addition, multiplication) or data retrieval (selection, projection) which would cost under a few of cycles per word if done in an unsecured manner. In other words, *we do not know yet how to secure anything more complex than peanut counting*. And outsourcing of peanut counting is counter productive in the first place. Ergo our suspicion.

We start by surveying existing mechanisms. Hacigumus et al. [26] propose a method to execute SQL queries over partly obfuscated outsourced data to protect data **confidentiality** against a data-curious server. The main functionality relies on (i) partly obfuscating the outsourced data by dividing it into a set of partitions, (ii) query rewriting of original queries into querying referencing partitions instead of individual tuples, and (iii) client-side pruning of (necessarily coarse grained) results. The information leaked to the server is balancing a trade-off between client-side and server-side processing, as a function of the data segment size. Hore et al. [30] explores optimal bucket sizes for certain range queries.

Ge et al. [55] discuss executing aggregation queries with confidentiality on an untrusted server. Unfortunately, due to the use of extremely expensive homomorphisms this scheme leads to large processing times for any reasonably security parameter settings (e.g., for 1,024 bit fields, 12+ days *per query* are required).

Other researchers have explored the issue of **correctness** in settings with potentially malicious servers. In a publisher-subscriber model, Devanbu et al. deployed Merkle trees to authenticate data published at a third party's site [18], and then explored a general model for authenticating data structures [39, 40]. In [46, 47] as well as in [37], mechanisms for efficient integrity and origin authentication for selection predicate query results are introduced. Different signature schemes (DSA, RSA, Merkle trees [41] and BGLS [11]) are explored as potential alternatives for data authentication primitives. In [36, 50] *verification objects* VO are deployed to authenticate data retrieval in "edge computing" In [31, 38] Merkle tree and cryptographic hashing constructs are deployed to authenticate range query results.

To summarize, existing secure outsourced query mechanisms deploy (i) partitioning-based schemes and symmetric key encryption for ("statistical" only) confidentiality, (ii) homomorphisms for oblivious aggregation (SUM, COUNT) queries (simply too slow to be practical), (iii) hash trees/chains and (iv) signature chaining and aggregation to ensure correctness of selection/range queries and projection operators. SUM, COUNT, and projection usually behave linearly in the database size. Selection and range queries may be performed in constant time, logarithmic time or linear time depending on the queried attribute (e.g., whether it is a primary key) and the type of index used.

For illustration purposes, w.l.o.g., consider a scenario most favorable to out-sourcing, i.e., assuming the operations behave linearly and are extremely selective, only incurring two 32-bit data transfers between the client and the cloud (one for the instruction and one for the result). Informally, to offset the network cost of $900 \times 32 \times 2 = 57{,}600$ picocents, only traversing a database of size at least 10^5 will generate enough CPU cycle cost savings. Thus it seems that with very selective queries (returning very little data) over large enough databases, outsourcing can break even.

Cost of Security. In the absence of security constructs, we were able to build a scenario for which outsourcing is viable. But what about a general scenario? What are the overheads of security there? It is important to understand whether the cost savings will be enough to offset them. While detailing individual secure query protocols is out of scope here, it is possible to reason generally and gain an insight into the associated order of magnitudes.

Existing integrity mechanisms deploy hash trees, hash chains and signatures to secure simple selection, projection or range queries. Security overheads would then include *at least* the (client-side) hash tree proof re-construction ($O(\log n)$ crypto-hashes) and subsequent signature verification of the tree's root. The hash tree proofs are often used to authenticate range boundaries. The returned element set is then authenticated often through either a hash chain (in the case of range joins, at least 30 picocents per byte) or aggregated signature constructs (e.g., roughly 60,000 picocents each, for selects or projections). This involves either modular arithmetic or crypto-hashing of the order of the result data set. For illustration purposes, we will again favor the case for outsourcing, and assume only crypto-hashing and a linear operation are applied.

Consider a database that has $n = 10^9$ tuples of 64 bits each. In that case (binary) hash tree nodes need to be at least 240 bits ($80 + 160$ bits $= 2$ pointers + hash value) long. If we assume 3 CPU cycles are needed per data item, the boundary condition results in selectivity $s \leq 0.00037$ before outsourcing starts to make economical sense. In a more typical scenario of $s = 0.001$ (queries are returning 0.1 % of the tuples), a per-query loss of over 0.3 US cents will be incurred.

The above holds only for the $S \to L$ scenario in which hash trees are deployed. In the case of signature aggregation [38, 47], the break-even selectivity would be even lower due to the higher computation overheads.

7   Conclusions

In this chapter, we mused on the dollar cost and security in cloud computing. We started by giving a cost model for computation, storage and networking in different environments. We saw that CPU cycles cost no less than 0.45 picocents, a bit cannot be transferred without paying at least 900 picocents, and stored a year without a pocket setback of at least 100 picocents. We validated the cost model with today's pricing points of clouds.

We determine two "outsourcing criteria", defining the boundary condition of cloud migration viability. The "first outsourcing criterion" considers unified client applications and postulates that, from a technological cost-centric perspective, outsourcing them *is profitable for computation intensive tasks*, specifically, *when its (mostly computation-related) cost savings are sufficient to offset client-cloud network distances*. This happens today for unified client applications requiring *no less than 1,000 CPU cycles per each 32 bits of client-cloud transferred input*.

In the case of applications with third-party clients, the feasibility equation changes dramatically. The "second outsourcing criterion" postulates that, for today's pricing points, for mid-size enterprises, it always makes sense to outsource to cloud. For small enterprises, to make outsourcing profitable, the CPU intensive requirement is much lower than in the single-client model (410 CPU cycles per 32 bit data) or even no CPU intensive requirement if they require guaranteed network service. This is mainly because of the dominating costs of networking, and the fact that in the single-client model, the comparison baseline would not include any networking costs (as the data would be accessed locally).

We also explored whether cryptography can be deployed to secure cloud computing against insiders. We estimated common cryptography costs (AES, MD5, SHA-1, RSA, DSA, and ECDSA) and finally explored outsourcing of data and computation to untrusted clouds. We showed that deploying the cloud as a simple remote encrypted file system is extremely unfeasible if considering only core technology costs. We also concluded that existing secure outsourced data query mechanisms are mostly cost-unfeasible because **today's cryptography simply lacks the expressive power to efficiently support outsourcing** to untrusted clouds. Hope is not lost however. We found borderline cases where outsourcing of simple range queries can break even when compared with local execution. These scenarios involve large amounts of outsourced data (e.g., 10^9 tuples) and extremely selective queries which return only an infinitesimal fraction of the original data (e.g., 0.00037 %).

References

1. Amazon s3: Show me the money. http://blogs.smugmug.com/don/2006/11/10/amazon-s3-show-me-the-money/.
2. Aws import/export. http://aws.amazon.com/importexport/.
3. Parallel computing with matlab on amazon elastic compute cloud (ec2). http://www.mathworks.com/programs/techkits/ec2-paper.html.
4. IBM 4764 PCI-X Cryptographic Coprocessor. Online at http://www-03.ibm.com/security/cryptocards/pcixcc/overview.shtml, 2007.
5. Nitin Agrawal, William J. Bolosky, John R. Douceur, and Jacob R. Lorch. A five-year study of file-system metadata. In *Proceedings of the 5th USENIX conference on File and Storage Technologies (FAST 07)*, Berkeley, CA, USA, 2007. USENIX Association.
6. Georgios Amanatidis, Alexandra Boldyreva, and Adam O'Neill. Provably-secure schemes for basic query support in outsourced databases. In Steve Barker and Gail-Joon Ahn, editors, *DBSec*, volume 4602 of *Lecture Notes in Computer Science*, pages 14–30. Springer, 2007.

7. AMD. Power and cooling in the data centers. Power and cooling in the data centers, Online at http://enterprise.amd.com/Downloads/34146A_PC_WP_en.pdf.
8. Mihir Bellare, Alexandra Boldyreva, and Adam O'Neill. Deterministic and efficiently searchable encryption. In Alfred Menezes, editor, *CRYPTO*, volume 4622 of *Lecture Notes in Computer Science*, pages 535–552. Springer, 2007.
9. Daniel J. Bernstein and Tanja Lange (editors). ebacs: Ecrypt benchmarking of cryptographic systems. Online at http://bench.cr.yp.to accessed 30 Jan. 2009.
10. M. Blaze. A Cryptographic File System for Unix. In *Proceedings of the first ACM Conference on Computer and Communications Security*, pages 9–16, Fairfax, VA, 1993. ACM.
11. D. Boneh, C. Gentry, B. Lynn, and H. Shacham. Aggregate and verifiably encrypted signatures from bilinear maps. In *EuroCrypt*, 2003.
12. G. Cattaneo, L. Catuogno, A. Del Sorbo, and P. Persiano. The Design and Implementation of a Transparent Cryptographic Filesystem for UNIX. In *Proceedings of the Annual USENIX Technical Conference, FREENIX Track*, pages 245–252, Boston, MA, June 2001.
13. CNN. Feds seek Google records in porn probe. Online at http://www.cnn.com, January 2006.
14. CNN. YouTube ordered to reveal its viewers. Online at http://www.cnn.com, July 2008.
15. Katherine Conrad. Data centers hot once again in the bay area. Online at http://findarticles.com/p/articles/mi_qn4176/is_20070401/ai_n18782997.
16. Qwest Communications Corp. Space furniture rental. Online at http://www.qwest.com/about/policy/docs/qcc/documents/WO-sfr-Amd52_111006.pdf.
17. Reza Curtmola, Juan Garay, Seny Kamara, and Rafail Ostrovsky. Searchable symmetric encryption: improved definitions and efficient constructions. In *CCS '06: Proceedings of the 13th ACM conference on Computer and communications security*, pages 79–88, New York, NY, USA, 2006. ACM.
18. Premkumar T. Devanbu, Michael Gertz, Chip Martel, and Stuart G. Stubblebine. Authentic third-party data publication. In *IFIP Workshop on Database Security*, pages 101–112, 2000.
19. Donna Bogatin. Google Apps data risks: Security vs. privacy. Online at http://blogs.zdnet.com/micro-markets/?p=1021, February 2007.
20. John R. Douceur and William J. Bolosky. A large-scale study of file-system contents. In *Proceedings of the ACM SIGMETRICS international conference on Measurement and modeling of computer systems*, pages 59–70. ACM New York, NY, USA, 1999.
21. Janice Fetzer. Internet data centers:end user & developer requirements. Online at http://www.utilityeda.com/Summer2006/Mares.pdf.
22. S. Ghemawat, H. Gobioff, and S. T. Leung. The Google File System. In *Proceedings of the 19th ACM Symposium on Operating Systems Principles (SOSP '03)*, pages 29–43, Bolton Landing, NY, October 2003. ACM SIGOPS.
23. Albert Greenberg, James Hamilton, David A. Maltz, and Parveen Patel. The cost of a cloud: Research problems in data center networks. In *SIGCOM Computer Communications Review*, 2009.
24. The Green Grid. Green grid metrics: Describing data center power efficiency. Online at http://www.thegreengrid.org/gg_content/Green_Grid_Metrics_WP.pdf.
25. The Clipper Group. Scale-up and scale-out architectures-ibm provides choice with the xseries. Technical report, 2005.
26. H. Hacigumus, B. Iyer, C. Li, and S. Mehrotra. Executing sql over encrypted data in the database-service-provider model. In *Proceedings of the ACM SIGMOD international conference on Management of data*, pages 216–227. ACM Press, 2002.
27. James Hamilton. Perspectives Blog. Online at http://mvdirona.com/jrh/work/.
28. James Hamilton. Internet-scale service efficiency. Large Scale Distributed Systems & Middleware (LADIS 2008),, 2008.
29. James Hamilton. On designing and deploying internet-scale services. Technical report, Windows Live Services Platform, Microsoft, 2008.
30. B. Hore, S. Mehrotra, and G. Tsudik. A privacy-preserving index for range queries. In *Proceedings of ACM SIGMOD*, 2004.

31. HweeHwa Pang and Arpit Jain and Krithi Ramamritham and Kian-Lee Tan. Verifying Completeness of Relational Query Results in Data Publishing. In *Proceedings of ACM SIGMOD*, 2005.
32. IBM. IBM blade servers. Online at http://www-03.ibm.com/systems/bladecenter/hardware/servers/.
33. Saul Hansell John Markoff. Hiding in plain sight, google seeks more power. Online at http://www.nytimes.com/2006/06/14/technology/14search.html.
34. A. Kashyap, S. Patil, G. Sivathanu, and E. Zadok. I3FS: An In-Kernel Integrity Checker and Intrusion Detection File System. In *Proceedings of the 18th USENIX Large Installation System Administration Conference (LISA 2004)*, pages 69–79, Atlanta, GA, November 2004. USENIX Association.
35. Larry Dignan. Will you trust Google with your data? Online at http://blogs.zdnet.com/BTL/?p=4544, February 2007.
36. M. Atallah and C. YounSun and A. Kundu. Efficient Data Authentication in an Environment of Untrusted Third-Party Distributors. In *24th International Conference on Data Engineering ICDE*, pages 696–704, 2008.
37. Maithili Narasimha and Gene Tsudik. DSAC: integrity for outsourced databases with signature aggregation and chaining. Technical report, 2005.
38. Maithili Narasimha and Gene Tsudik. Authentication of Outsourced Databases using Signature Aggregation and Chaining. In *Proceedings of DASFAA*, 2006.
39. C. Martel, G. Nuckolls, P. Devanbu, M. Gertz, A. Kwong, and S. Stubblebine. A general model for authenticated data structures, 2001.
40. Charles Martel, Glen Nuckolls, Premkumar Devanbu, Michael Gertz, April Kwong, and Stuart G. Stubblebine. A general model for authenticated data structures. *Algorithmica*, 39(1):21–41, 2004.
41. R. Merkle. Protocols for public key cryptosystems. In *IEEE Symposium on Research in Security and Privacy*, 1980.
42. Jeralyn Merritt. What google searches and data mining mean for you. Online at http://www.talkleft.com/story/2006/01/25/692/74066.
43. Microsoft Research. Encrypting File System for Windows 2000. Technical report, Microsoft Corporation, July 1999. www.microsoft.com/windows2000/techinfo/howitworks/security/encrypt.asp.
44. Rich Miller. Microsoft: Pue of 1.22 for data center containers. Online at http://www.datacenterknowledge.com/archives/2008/10/20/microsoft-pue-of-122-for-data-center-containers/.
45. Al-Fares Mohammad, Loukissas Alexander, and Vahdat Amin. A scalable, commodity data center network architecture. *SIGCOMM Comput. Commun. Rev.*, 38(4):63–74, 2008.
46. E. Mykletun, M. Narasimha, and G. Tsudik. Authentication and integrity in outsourced databases. In *Proceedings of Network and Distributed System Security (NDSS)*, 2004.
47. E. Mykletun, M. Narasimha, and G. Tsudik. Signature bouquets: Immutability for aggregated/condensed signatures. In *Computer Security - ESORICS 2004*, volume 3193 of *Lecture Notes in Computer Science*, pages 160–176. Springer, 2004.
48. Department of Administration. Records management fact sheet 13. Online at http://www.doa.state.wi.us/facts_view.asp?factid=68&locid=2.
49. Optimum. Optimum online plans. Online at http://www.buyoptimum.com.
50. HweeHwa Pang and Kian-Lee Tan. Authenticating query results in edge computing. In *ICDE '04: Proceedings of the 20th International Conference on Data Engineering*, page 560, Washington, DC, USA, 2004. IEEE Computer Society.
51. U.S. Environmental Protection Agency ENERGY STAR Program. Report to congress on server and data center energy efficiency public law 109–431, 2007.
52. J. J. Rehr, J. P. Gardner, M. Prange, L. Svec, and F. Vila. Scientific computing in the cloud, 2008.

53. Bianca Schroeder and Garth A. Gibson. Disk failures in the real world: what does an mttf of 1,000,000 hours mean to you? In *FAST '07: Proceedings of the 5th USENIX conference on File and Storage Technologies*, Berkeley, CA, USA, 2007.
54. G. Sivathanu, C. P. Wright, and E. Zadok. Enhancing File System Integrity Through Checksums. Technical Report FSL-04-04, Computer Science Department, Stony Brook University, May 2004. www.fsl.cs.sunysb.edu/docs/nc-checksum-tr/nc-checksum.pdf.
55. Tingjian Ge and Stan Zdonik. Answering aggregation queries in a secure system model. In *VLDB '07: Proceedings of the 33rd international conference on Very large data bases*, pages 519–530. VLDB Endowment, 2007.
56. Whitfield Diffie. How Secure Is Cloud Computing? Online at http://www.technologyreview.com/computing/23951/, November 2009.

Hardware-Enhanced Security for Cloud Computing

Jakub Szefer and Ruby B. Lee

Abstract Cloud computing has ushered in an era where cloud customers are able to rapidly access on-demand computing resources made available by third party cloud providers. The cloud providers who maintain these computing resources and lease them out to customers leverage economies of scale and sharing of resources to be able to provide these resources to customers at favorable prices. Cloud computing and this sharing of resources, however, introduces a number of security concerns. These concerns include other, potentially malicious, customers who are co-located on the same system as the customer; or even untrusted system software running on the remote systems where a customer's code and data execute or reside. To tackle these security concerns, we explore how secure hardware architectures can provide more protections to a customer's code and data in a cloud computing setting. In particular, we want to show that with hardware enhancements we can make computing in the cloud as secure as in your own dedicated facilities.

1 Introduction

Figure 1 shows the IaaS cloud computing model. Other cloud computing models, such as Platform-as-a-Service (PaaS) or Software-as-a-Service (SaaS), can be built on top of the IaaS model and could leverage the hardware security enhancements we present for the IaaS scenario. Before switching to using cloud computing, users may have run applications and an operating system (OS) on their own hardware. Now, these cloud customers use resources and remote servers of the cloud provider. Rather than have a physical machine, they now have a virtual machine (VM) that runs alongside other customers' VMs. The cloud provider runs a hypervisor, or a

J. Szefer (✉) • R.B. Lee
Department of Electrical Engineering, Princeton University,
Olden St., Princeton, NJ 08544, USA
e-mail: szefer@princeton.edu; rblee@princeton.edu

S. Jajodia et al. (eds.), *Secure Cloud Computing*, DOI 10.1007/978-1-4614-9278-8_3,
© Springer Science+Business Media New York 2014

virtual machine monitor, that virtualizes the system and orchestrates the sharing of the physical resources so that it can support many VMs on one physical system. This way, many customers' VMs can run on one server, consolidating resources and allowing the cloud provider to lease out the VMs to the customers at favorable prices. The cloud provider maintains many servers where customers' code and data are executed or stored. They also have management infrastructure including dedicated cloud management servers. This infrastructure is in place so that the customer's can easily provision and release computing resources. Customers often use the VMs to run some service (e.g., a web site) that is accessed by end users.

1.1 Security Concerns

While cloud computing provides many economic benefits, there are a number of new security concerns that need to be addressed. There are two main differences when using a virtual machine, versus executing or storing code and data on your own physical machine. First, there are the other customers' VMs that are running on the same system. These VMs should be properly isolated when running on top of a trusted hypervisor. Unfortunately, current hypervisors are susceptible to various vulnerabilities and bugs. A malicious cloud computing customer who is co-located on the same system as his or her competitor may attack the virtualization layer. Once the virtualization layer is compromised, its privilege level can be used to examine or obstruct other VMs. The second difference is the virtualization layer

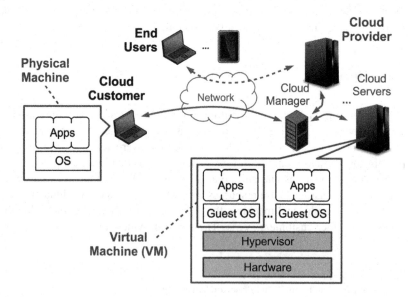

Fig. 1 The IaaS cloud computing model

itself, running underneath all the VMs. It is a privileged software layer which has access to all the resources of the system. It can affect confidentiality, integrity or availability of the different VMs. Normally, the hypervisor is trusted and is used to provide security for the rest of the system. If customers used virtualization on their own systems, they would know exactly the version and type of hypervisor used. In a cloud computing setting, however, customers have no control over the hypervisor. While the hypervisors are designed by reputable commercial vendors (e.g. VMWare [2]) or open-source projects (e.g. Xen [3]), they are still susceptible to bugs and vulnerabilities. Unlike in your own facilities, where you will not likely attack yourself, in a cloud computing setting one of the co-located VMs may belong to a different customer who may have incentive to compromise the hypervisor. Moreover, some cloud providers may be coerced to install a malicious hypervisor to spy on certain victim customers' VMs.

1.2 Approaches to Securing Cloud Computing

These security issues have been recognized by various researchers and many have worked on different approaches to securing cloud computing. Since the hypervisor is the key virtualization technology needed for cloud computing, most have focused on securing the hypervisor. Researchers have looked at minimizing the hypervisor code size [15, 17], as the number of bugs or vulnerabilities is often correlated to the code size. Others have explored re-writing the hypervisor to harden it against potential attacks [26]. Work has also been done on protecting different parts of the hypervisor, such as protecting the core hypervisor from the management OS [11]. A key duty of the hypervisor is to isolate the different VMs and research has been done on improving the isolation [8, 14]. Some researchers have also attempted to come ahead of the threats, and analyze or introspect the VMs to try to find attacks before they actually happen [9, 13, 16, 27]. While these approaches improve the security of the system, they still require a trusted hypervisor to be present for correct secure operation of the system. These are all software-based approaches, so far.

Hardware security approaches have also been explored. One example is the Trusted Platform Module (TPM) [22], which is a co-processor used for security-related functionality such as measurement and attestation of the software stack. The TPM can help measure the software at load time, but not actively protect it during runtime. More powerful co-processors [7] provide physical tamper prevention and a secure execution environment inside the co-processor. Such co-processors allow for secure execution of applications, but not entire VMs. Commercial processors have also included new extensions inside the main processor, mainly to support the extra software layer, i.e., the hypervisor. This, however, assumes a trusted all-powerful system software which runs in this new privileged mode. Academic projects have also looked at hardware-enhancements to improve security. A number of architectures have been proposed [5, 6, 10, 12, 18], many of these architectures focus on protecting software modules.

Rather than protecting software modules in an application, below we will describe how new hardware architecture can be used to enhance system security by protecting an entire virtual machine in a cloud computing setting – against the hypervisor as an adversary. Unlike software, hardware is mostly immutable. Any security features introduced in hardware chips are thus very difficult, if not impossible, to alter after the chip is manufactured. Also, hardware is logically the lowest layer in the system. For example, a security feature implemented in an OS running inside a VM can be bypassed by a malicious or compromised hypervisor (which is logically below the VM); there is not a layer below the hardware that can bypass security features implemented in hardware. Unlike other hardware approaches, we focus on protecting the entire VM, and consider the aggressive new threat model of a malicious or compromised hypervisor.

In particular, we describe our proposed concept of *hypervisor-secure virtualization* [19–21]. Architectures implementing hypervisor-secure virtualization include new hardware for protecting the confidentiality and integrity of a VM's memory, even from the (previously) all-powerful hypervisor. Hypervisor-secure virtualization architectures allow for a hypervisor to manage many VMs per system, share processor cores among different VMs, or even oversubscribe memory resources. These are all the features that can be done today, but the key difference is that thanks to the new hardware additions, the hypervisor can be untrusted. Using such architectures brings customers closer to the goal of being able to run their virtual machines remotely, and be as secure as if they were running the OS and applications locally on their own physical machine.

2   Hardware-Enhanced Security with HyperWall

We have realized hypervisor-secure virtualization in our HyperWall architecture [19–21]. The architecture uses resource isolation (focusing on the memory of the virtual machines), as opposed to cryptographic isolation, to implement hypervisor-secure virtualization. The architecture enhances today's multi-core server architectures by introducing new hardware additions. These additions enable selected portions of a virtual machine's memory to be isolated from the hypervisor, from DMA (direct memory access) by peripheral devices, and from other virtual machines. HyperWall's target usage scenario is the Infrastructure-as-a-Service (IaaS) cloud computing model, presented in the introduction, but the other cloud computing models can be built on top of it as well.

With HyperWall, cloud customers can run their virtual machines on the hosted infrastructure. Simultaneously, the infrastructure provider can host many other customers' virtual machines and run a hypervisor that the customer need not trust for the confidentiality and integrity of his or her code and data, because of our hardware enhancements. To enable the customer to protect a VM's code and data, the cloud customers are given the means to provide some specification of the confidentiality and integrity protection they want for the data and code that will run inside the VM.

Given the VM image and the requested protections, a HyperWall-enabled server can start and measure the VM and the protections. The attestation of the initialized VM and protections is communicated to the customer, and once they verify that the correct VM and protections indeed started, they can establish a secure channel with the VM. Any sensitive code or data can now be sent to the VM through the secure channel and executed remotely. When the VM is finished, the hardware properly cleans up the protected memory. The architecture and the various stages of the operation are discussed below, after the threat model.

2.1 Threat Model

The goal of HyperWall is to protect against confidentiality and integrity attacks by a malicious or compromised hypervisor. We want to retain an active hypervisor so that most of the features of today's cloud computing offerings can be supported (e.g., VM sharing processor cores or memory oversubscripiton). Thanks to the new, trusted hardware we can provide these protections. However, we do not consider attacks on availability, side-channels or physical attacks. In particular, a cloud provider needs a way to turn off VMs if customers stop paying or misbehave, so availability can not be guaranteed for customers. Side-channels are a separate research topic that has been explored [24, 25]. Hardware side-channel protections can be integrated with architectures such as HyperWall. We also expect a non-malicious infrastructure provider and secure facilities so that physical attack protection is not needed.

The protections focus on protecting entire VMs. The OS and applications inside a VM are assumed to be trusted by the customer. The customer is also assumed to know which memory regions inside the VM (in terms of guest physical pages) need protection, and the OS will not allocate sensitive code or data to the unprotected memory regions.

2.2 Memory Protection

With HyperWall, we opt for an isolation-based approach to memory protection where individual guest physical memory regions (e.g. consisting of multiple memory pages) are assigned to a virtual machine and the hardware enforces that only the owner virtual machine can access these pages. Memory isolation is not a new concept, but in today's commodity systems, the hypervisor software is relied on to provide and enforce the isolation. A powerful attack by the hypervisor is to give itself (directly, via a colluding VM, or via a device and direct memory access) the ability to snoop on some target VM's memory. To counter this, our hardware can enforce the memory isolation between the VMs and the hypervisor. Because hardware is logically below the hypervisor software, it can store protection specification data and contain security functionality which cannot be altered by the hypervisor.

Figure 2 shows the different memory regions in a HyperWall system. DRAM represents the machine memory. That memory is allocated to different VMs. In Fig. 2 we highlight different memory regions relevant to a protected VM.

First, there are the page table specifying address translation from guest physical pages (managed by the OS inside the VM) to the machine pages (managed by the hypervisor). This page table mapping is set by the hypervisor when it allocates memory for the VM. It is locked and protected by our new hardware when the VM is launched – thus preventing the hypervisor from updating the memory mapping without intervention by our new hardware. Memory update is discussed later in the chapter.

Second, there are the actual memory pages allocated to the VM and which have been loaded with the VM image (i.e., the code and data that makes up the OS and applications). These memory regions are defined by the page tables. The hardware uses the page tables to locate these pages and protect them according to the customer's specification.

Third, the customer's requested protections for the VM are a final part of memory which need to be protected. When the hypervisor loads the VM, it loads the VM images as well as these requested protections. The hardware needs to lock and protect these memory pages so that the hypervisor can not alter the requested protection data as the VM runs.

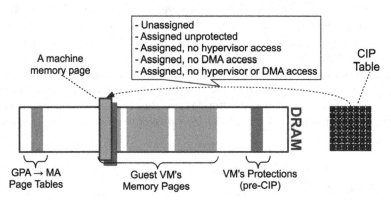

Fig. 2 The Confidentiality and Integrity Protection (CIP) table and the different protected memory regions

2.3 Confidentiality and Integrity Protection Table

A new feature introduced in HyperWall is the Confidentiality and Integrity Protection table (CIP table). The CIP table, shown on the right of Fig. 2, store the protection information for all machine memory pages, for all the VMs. An interesting aspect of the CIP table, is that it is actually stored in DRAM (as shown on the right side of Fig. 3).

We re-use existing DRAM to store the CIP protection data, which eliminates the need for special memory structures inside the processor or other parts of the system. That portion of DRAM is made hardware-only accessible, and is off limits to the hypervisor, the VMs, and the devices. During system boot up, our new hardware locks part of the DRAM so no software can access it. This is a very flexible approach as, for example, the memory can be updated – just install more DRAM – and when the system is rebooted the hardware will allocate a proportionally sized portion to be hardware-only accessible and to store the CIP table. Now hardware has an exclusive memory storage region where it can keep protection information.

A customer's specified protections come from the requested protection information (also called pre-CIP). Given a guest physical address (from the page tables), the pre-CIP data can be looked up to check the protections needed for the corresponding page. The guest physical to machine address translation from the page tables can be used to obtain the machine address where the guest physical page is mapped into. This information can be combined and is stored in the CIP table.

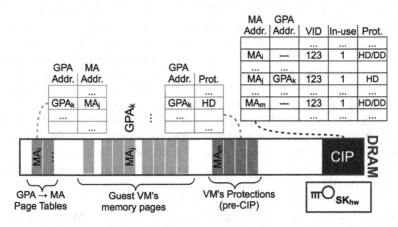

Fig. 3 Different tables and memory regions utilized by the HyperWall architecture: hypervisor-assigned page table is protected so the hardware knows the current memory mapping of the VM; the VM's memory itself is protected; the pre-CIP table is protected so the hypervisor cannot modify the requested protections. The CIP table stores the information about these three memory regions, and is stored in the hardware-only accessible memory. HD means Hypervisor Deny and DD means DMA Deny

Figure 3 shows more details of the different tables stored in the memory, along with sample guest physical addresses (GPA) and machine addresses (MA). The figure also shows a signing key, SK_{hw} that is unique to each processor supporting HyperWall architecture. Initialization and the use of the different memory regions, and the key, is discussed below.

2.4   Protecting Confidentiality and Integrity of VMs Under an Untrusted Hypervisor

There are three phases of the VM's execution during which memory needs to be protected by our new hardware to ensure the VM's confidentiality and integrity. First, the VM is initialized. Second, the VM runs. Finally, the VM is terminated.

VM Initialization

We have already discussed different memory regions relevant to a VM, shown in Fig. 2. These memory regions are loaded by the hypervisor before the VM is actually started. When the VM is launched, e.g., through the *vmlaunch* instruction, the new HyperWall hardware is triggered. The first duty of the hardware is to protect the memory regions by writing appropriate entries in the CIP table. The hardware assigns a VID (this VID is different from the VM identification assigned by the hypervisor, the hardware controls VIDs so the hypervisor cannot spoof them). The CIP table entries, as shown in Fig. 3 identify the owner VM of each machine memory page. For each page, the hardware first checks that the page is not in use (by using the machine address to index the CIP table and ensure that the page is free). If the page is free, the hardware assigns it to the VM. It writes the VID and marks the page as in-use. It also writes the protection information for this page, e.g., deny hypervisor accesses (HD) or deny DMA accesses from devices (DD). For the memory holding the page table and the requested protections, the memory is made inaccessible to the hypervisor and DMA.[1] For the memory pages of the VM, the hardware reads the page table entries and the requested protections information to see what protections were requested for the corresponding machine pages. If there is an error at any time, the VM launch is aborted.

Once all the memory pages are protected, and before the VM actually begins execution, the hardware calculates a cryptographic hash of the VM image and the requested protections. This is done because the (untrusted) hypervisor may have modified either of these before launching the VM. Once the memory pages are protected, the hypervisor cannot modify them and the contents of these pages can be measured. The measurements done by HyperWall are sent back to the customer. The measurements are cryptographically signed with the processor's signing key (shown as SK_{hw} in Fig. 3). The processor also has a digital certificate from the manufacturer. A customer, given reference measurements of the known good VM image and protections, signature of initialized VM's measurements, a hardware certificate and the hardware manufacturer's certificate can validate the received measurements. The measurement can be sent by the (untrusted) hypervisor and cloud infrastructure to the customer. We assume strong cryptography and that without access to the

---

[1] Note that the hardware checks that the page is not in use, so it is automatically not accessible to other VMs.

private portion of the cryptographic key, the signatures can not be forged. To ensure freshness and prevent replay attacks, the customer sends a nonce when requesting the VM, and that nonce is included in the measurements that are sent back to the customer.

VM Runtime

Once a VM is launched and running, the customer can start utilizing the protected environment offered by the HyperWall architecture. The first step is to establish a secure channel with the remote VM. Recall that the customer has already verified that his VM image and requested protections were started properly; or found out that they were not and stopped using that VM. Now the customer has the hardware certificate for the remote machine where their VM is running and the VID of their VM. We assume that the VM image originally contained no sensitive information, but only stock OS and common applications and libraries, e.g., OpenSSL library for cryptographic operations.

Establishing Secure Channel between Customer and VM   Figure 4 shows how a VM running on a HyperWall system can establish a secure channel with the customer. The key to the secure communication is the VM's protected memory. Once the VM is launched and the memory is protected, it can generate a public-private key pair (EK_{vm}, DK_{vm}). The hypervisor has no access to the protected memory, so it can not see these newly generated keys. Next, the VM can use HyperWall's new *sign_bytes* instruction to sign the EK_{vm} key. The signature also includes the VID and a nonce that the customer sends. It is made with the hardware's signing key. A hypervisor or another VM can not spoof the signature as they

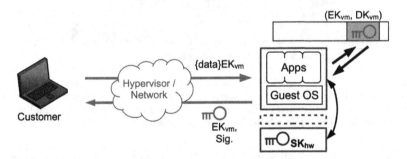

Fig. 4 Establishment of a secure communication channel with the VM

do not have access to the hardware signing key, SK_{hw}, and the VID is included automatically by hardware so other VMs cannot invoke the instruction and pretend to be a different VM. The key, EK_{vm}, and the signature are sent back to the customer. Once he or she verifies the signature, he or she can use the key to send sensitive code or data back to the VM (e.g., use it as part of a modified SSL protocol to establish a secure channel).

The code or data to be protected should be stored by the OS in the protected memory regions. Now, the code and data can execute, with the HyperWall hardware protecting the memory according to the customer's specification. Even a malicious or compromised hypervisor is not able to see into this memory.

Sharing Processor Cores Among VMs One of the features which makes cloud computing appealing is that many VMs can share the same system. Often, this requires scheduling more VMs than there are physical resources available, and switching between the VMs as they run. One key resource needed by VMs is the allocation of processor cores where the code actually executes. Scheduling many VMs on the same physical cores requires suspending them (when the hypervisor reads and saves processor state) and resuming them (when the hypervisor replaces saved state and triggers the VM to run again). It is critical to protect the VM when it is being suspended and resumed. The memory is already protected through the CIP table, even if the VM is suspended as the CIP table entries remain in the CIP until VM termination. The needed protections for suspending a VM are: protect the VM's virtual cores' state so that it is correctly resumed later, and protect the general-purpose registers which hold some of the code or data of the VM.

Figure 5 shows how a hypervisor could access contents of memory indirectly when it is reading the registers of a processor core. It could not only read the contents, but also modify them. To counter this, HyperWall encrypts general purpose registers[2] and generates a hash over the register state. When the VM is resumed, the hash is checked and the registers decrypted, if the hash verification succeeds.

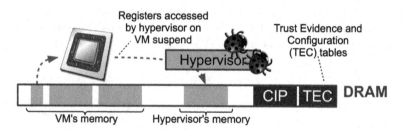

Fig. 5 Memory contents, copied to processor registers when the code executes, could be read or modified by the hypervisor as it suspends a VM and copies registers to its own memory. HyperWall protects register state on VM suspend and resume with the help of the Trust Evidence and Configuration (TEC) table, which hold one entry for each VM

The original HyperWall architecture [21] has been improved to prevent certain types of replay attacks during VM suspend and resume [19]. In our improved design, a new set of Trust Evidence and Configuration (TEC) table is introduced, which is also stored in the hardware-only accessible memory. These TEC table are used to keep some attestation and configuration related information about each VM. In particular, for each VM (as identified by its VID, which is the same VID as

---

[2]If the VM suspend reason is a hypercall then the registers are not encrypted as they are used to pass arguments to the hypercall.

used in the CIP table), the TEC table store a counter of the number of times the VM has been suspended. Each time the VM is suspended, and before hypervisor code gets to run and read the registers, the counter is incremented. This counter value is also used in a cryptographic keyed-hash generated by the hardware. When the hypervisor gets to execute, all the general purpose registers are encrypted, if it is not a hypercall, and a special new register holds the hash value of the general registers' contents concatenated back-to-back. These can be stored anywhere by the hypervisor.

When the VM is to be resumed, the hypervisor writes the register values and the hash value into processor registers. Before VM code starts to run, the hardware checks the values. If the hypervisor were to try to modify the register values or the hash, the hardware can detect it when it regenerates the hash and compares the values. Also, the hypervisor can not modify the suspend count stored in the TEC table, thus it cannot replay an old set of register values.

Memory Oversubscription In addition to being able to share processor cores, memory oversubscription is another key feature of many cloud computing deployments which our architecture supports. Memory ballooning [23] is a technique for dynamically changing the allocation of memory of a guest virtual machine, while the machine is running. Ballooning depends on the hypervisor's ability to dynamically change the guest physical to machine memory mapping of a VM as it runs.

Figure 6 shows conceptually the idea of memory ballooning. As an example, suppose a system has a total of 6 GB of memory, however, the administrator oversubscribes memory by allocating to each of two customers up to 4 GB of memory each for their VMs. In Fig. 6a we see that each VM initially has only 3 GB of memory allocated and a "balloon" taking up 1 GB of memory. At runtime, the hypervisor can cooperate with a "balloon driver" inside each VM, to change the memory allocation. If the first VM requires more memory, the hypervisor can take some memory pages away from the other VM (inflate its ballon) and give these pages to the first VM (deflate its balloon). This is shown in Fig. 6b. The reverse is shown in Fig. 6c. By adjusting the memory allocation as needed, many more VMs can run on the system than there are actual resources.

The key operation which allows memory ballooning is the ability of the hypervisor to change the memory allocation during a VM's runtime, i.e., change the page tables mapping guest physical addresses (GPA) to machine addresses (MA). The hypervisor can change the mapping and remove pages (i.e., inflate the balloon) or add new pages (i.e., deflate the balloon). The problem, however, is that a malicious hypervisor may try to read the contents of the memory pages it just removed from a VM, potentially leaking the VM's code or data. Alternatively, a hypervisor may try to add memory mappings such that two VMs would share some memory pages, thus again potentially leaking code or data. The HyperWall hardware tightly controls the type of memory update that could be performed by the hypervisor while still allowing the hypervisor to change the guest physical address (GPA) to machine address (MA) mapping.

Three security requirements needed to ensure a VM's confidentiality and integrity protection during memory update are:

- Scrubbing of memory pages: a machine memory page that is to be freed should be scrubbed before it becomes free and can be allocated to another VM (to prevent leaks leading to confidentiality breaches),
- No adding of in-use pages: a VM should not be allocated machine memory pages already in use by another VM (to prevent another VM from compromising the confidentiality or integrity of a victim VM's memory), and
- No swapping of pages within a VM: during the memory update, a VM's guest physical to machine memory page mappings should not be swapped (to prevent integrity breaches, and potential confidentiality breaches, where the hypervisor can swap memory contents).

To perform the memory update in HyperWall, the hypervisor specifies a new page table mapping. It then suspends a VM, and writes a pointer to the new page table mapping. On VM resume, the hardware can compare the page table pointer to recognize the changed value. This triggers the memory update. Now, hardware checks the new page tables and compares them to the contents of the CIP table.

The hardware can use the CIP table to recognize if a machine page is already in use. The VID in the CIP table entry is used to recognize the owner VM. If a hypervisor creates a new mapping, and assigns a new page to the VM, the hardware can check the VID in the CIP entry for this page – if the VID is not null, then the page is already in use and cannot be added. The update must abort. If there is no error, the hardware can read the requested protections data for the new page, and set the protections in the CIP table accordingly.

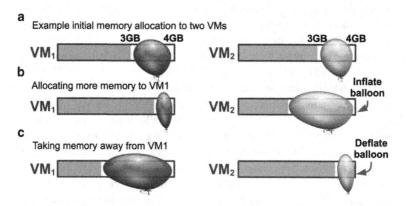

Fig. 6 Memory ballooning example

For pages that are to be deleted, we introduce a new "to-be deleted" bit in the page tables; the hypervisor marks pages to be deleted with this bit and the hardware can easily recognize which pages to delete. The hardware can compare the VIDs to make sure the page is indeed currently in use by the VM, then it can scrub the machine memory page and clear the CIP table entry to mark the page as free.

Memory swapping attempts can be recognized by comparing the guest physical page address (GPA) from the page tables, to the guest physical page address in the CIP table. If the page is present in the page tables (not a new added page) the hardware can read the CIP table entry to make sure that the machine page in the CIP table is for the guest physical page. If this reverse mapping does not match, then there is an attempt to swap pages and the update must be aborted.

VM Terminate

When the VM is terminated, its memory needs to be reclaimed. This can be done by the hypervisor by issuing the new *vmterminate* instruction with the VID being the identification of the VM that is to be terminated. The HyperWall state machine intercepts this instruction and begins VM termination. The HyperWall hardware traverses the page tables mapping to find all pages used by the VM. After each protected page is zeroed out by hardware, its entry in the CIP table is cleared so that this memory page can be freely accessed again. Once all the memory pages are removed from being protected, the memory holding the protection data needs to be unprotected. Then, the memory holding the page table mappings needs to be unprotected as well. Finally, all the entries for the VM in the TEC table are cleared. This clears and returns the memory as well as makes the VID number available for another VM to use. If a hypervisor fails to issue the *vmterminate* instruction or otherwise misbehaves, it remains locked out of the protected memory – this is a loss of availability of these memory pages, but no code or data is leaked.

3   HyperWall Architecture Summary

Figure 7 shows the hardware and software modifications required to implement the HyperWall architecture and to support the operations described above. Also, Table 1 lists the new or modified instructions used by HyperWall. The new instructions (A), e.g. *vmterminate*, were introduced along with new registers (B), e.g. the VM_suspend_hash register. A cryptographic engine (C) is needed for performing encryption, decryption, hashing and signing (using the SK_{hw} key). A hardware random number generator (D) is added to support the new *trng* instruction used in secure channel establishment. The bulk of the HyperWall logic is in a state machine (E) which is responsible for updating the CIP and TEC tables when a VM is created, updated or terminated. In particular, the state machine ensures the protections are maintained when the memory mapping for a guest VM is updated. This is done by the hardware mediating updates to the guest physical address to machine address page table mappings. The TLB logic (F) is expanded to consult the CIP table before inserting an address translation into the TLBs. To improve performance, the access checks are done when the address translation is performed during the handling of a TLB miss. If there is no violation, the address is cached in the TLB

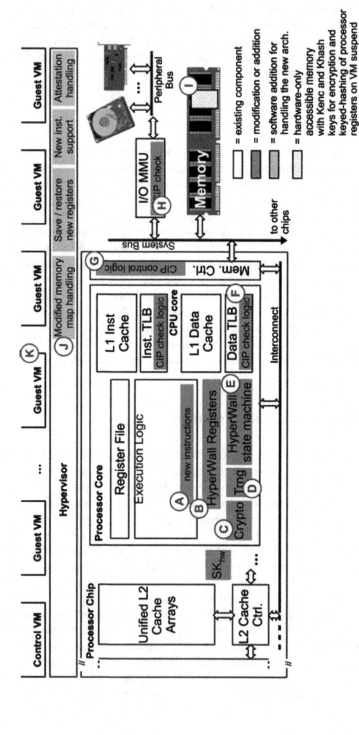

Fig. 7 Summary of the hardware, and related software, modifications in the processor needed to support the HyperWall architecture

Table 1 Summary of new or modified instructions in HyperWall architecture

Instruction (Inputs)	Description
generate_trust_evidence (VMID)	Request current trust evidence of VM with VID to be copied into processor registers
sign_bytes (Addr, Size)	Use hardware's private key to sign specified data
trng ()	Access true random number generator to retrieve 64 bits of randomness
vmterminate (VID)	For a VID, signal hardware to scrub the VM's memory and terminate the VM
vmlaunch ()	Existing instruction, modified to trigger our HyperWall mechanisms on VM launch

and the CIP table check can be avoided in the future, for a TLB hit. To prevent stale mappings, however, the TLBs need to be flushed whenever the CIP table are updated. The memory controller (G) is updated with configuration registers and CIP control logic to walk the CIP table on a hypervisor or DMA access. Similarly to the address translation in the main processor, the I/O MMU (H) needs to have extra logic to consult the CIP table. We re-use a portion of DRAM (I), the hardware-only accessible memory, to store the CIP and TEC tables.

While HyperWall is a hardware architecture, the software needs to be modified to interact with the new modified hardware. The hypervisor (J), as the entity in charge of the platform, needs to interact with our new hardware architecture. It needs to save and restore the new registers when VMs are interrupted and resumed (as it does already with other state today). It needs to use a modified procedure for updating the memory mapping during VM runtime (i.e., specify a new page table mapping, rather than modify individual entries in the old page table mapping). During a VM's runtime, it needs to issue our new *generate_trust_evidence* instruction to read the trust evidence data and return it to the customer when requested. When terminating the VM, it needs to issue our new *vmterminate* instruction.

The guest VM (K) needs small modifications to use the *trng* instruction for obtaining randomness (rather than from other means, such as from interrupts, that could be controlled by the hypervisor). It also needs to use the *sign_bytes* instruction to get information, e.g. an attestation report, signed by the hardware before sending it to the customer. The OS should properly load code and data so that sensitive code or data are never placed in the unprotected guest physical memory regions.

4 Trust Evidence

An interesting new feature introduced in HyperWall is the trust evidence it collects and can provide to the customer. We already discussed how at VM launch, the HyperWall hardware measures the VM image and the requested protections. This information is digitally signed and can be sent back to the customer for verification. More interestingly, however, HyperWall also performs measurements at VM runtime. In particular, we introduced new counters, akin to performance counters, which keep track of attempts to violate memory protections. For each VM, there is a set of trust evidence counters ($VCNT$ and $VMAD$, described below), stored in the Trust Evidence and Configuration table (TEC table).

As the VM runs, the hardware protects its memory from hypervisor and/or DMA accesses (Direct Memory Access from/to I/O devices). From Fig. 8, we can see that the hypervisor or DMA could attempt to access the VM's memory. The hardware intercepts and blocks such accesses (if the memory is specified to be protected in the CIP table). Moreover, when such a malicious (or erroneous) access is detected, the hardware counters associated with the VM are incremented. There is the $VCNT$ counter which keeps track of the number of attempted violations. There is also the $VMAD$ register, which keeps track of the last memory address where an attempted memory access violation occurred.

These measurements are digitally signed by the hardware, again using the SK_{hw} key and can be sent back to the customer, upon the customer's request. The customer can then use this information to examine the state of the system. While the hardware protects the VMs, if there is a large number of attempted violations, the customer may choose to stop utilizing that VM, as something suspicious is happening on the remote system.

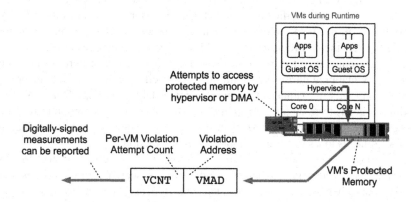

Fig. 8 New trust evidence mechanisms keep track of attempts to violate memory protections. These attestation measurements are digitally signed by the hardware and can be reported to the customer for checking

5   Further Research Directions

HyperWall provides a significant step towards making computing in the cloud as secure as in your own dedicated facilities. But many research challenges remain. In particular, can computing in the cloud be made even more secure than on your own machine?

There are many other interesting and relevant threat models, where research in hardware-enahanced security architectures could yield significant improvements in system security. Figure 9 shows a few of these different threat models. On the left in Fig. 9a we show a conventional trust chain, where each level of the software stack must be trusted by the level above. This is the case today, where the hardware is assumed trusted, the hypervisor is assumed trusted, and the OS is also trusted, in order to run trusted software applications securely. Architectures built on this threat model require trust in all the different software components, in addition to the hardware. TPM [22] or ARM's TrustZone [1] assume this threat model.

Moving to the right, Fig. 9b shows a threat model where the hypervisor is trusted, but the OS is untrusted. A cloud provider can run a trusted hypervisor as the virtualization layer, and try to provide protection for its customers' applications. But the cloud provider may not want to have to trust today's bloated, commodity OSes which are vulnerable to bugs. Bastion [4, 5] architecture is one example of a hardware-software security architecture which assumes this threat model. Bastion's strategy is to combine software flexibility (it uses a trusted hypervisor to protect and manage the TSMs) with hardware immutability and performance (to protect the hypervisor). For example, Bastion's hardware offers mechanisms for the secure launch of the hypervisor, as well as for protecting the hypervisor during runtime. Bastion's trusted hypervisor in turn protects the Trusted Software Modules (TSMs); it can securely launch TSMs during runtime, perform secure memory management, provide secure inter-module control flow, and provide secure storage, in addition to providing runtime memory integrity and confidentiality protection against physical attacks. One of the key features of Bastion is its tailored attestation. Unlike HyperWall's trust evidence which gives information about an entire VM, Bastion's attestation can provide information about individual TSMs. Future work

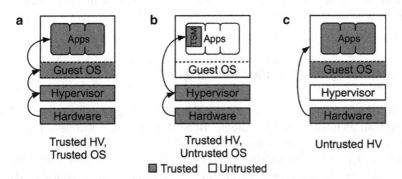

Fig. 9 Figure showing different threat models, dark-gray components are trusted; HV is the hypervisor, OS is the operating system, TSM is a Trusted Software Module

could look at how to partition the applications into the TSMs (something that is currently done manually and in an ad-hoc manner today), as just one example.

Another threat model relevant to cloud computing is shown in Fig. 9c. Here the guest OS is assumed trusted (by the customer of the virtual machine in which it runs), but the hypervisor may be untrusted or compromisable. This is a likely situation for a customer who has fully tested his own trusted applications and trusted OS, but is hoping to run this in a virtual machine to benefit from the lower cost and flexibility of cloud computing, where he has no control of the hypervisor. We described HyperWall as one example of an architecture which fits this threat model. Future work could explore how to do even more layer-skipping of untrusted software layers – yet still have a secure trust chain, by using new hardware security mechanisms. Prior to cloud computing, hardware security architectures explored protection of applications by hardware, but did not consider cases that involve a hypervisor [6, 10, 12, 18]. Also, ideas of Bastion's tailored attestation could be combined with HyperWall's trust evidence to provide even better attestation mechanisms.

In addition to providing secure cloud servers, future research should also address security in the client devices that use cloud computing resources. Mobile devices like smartphones and tablets are the portals into cloud computing, and can access all kinds of important and sensitive information though the cloud. Hence, security in client devices is an important research direction, and very relevant to secure cloud computing.

As important as designing new hardware-enhanced security architectures is the security testing and verification of these new architectures and new hardware-software mechanisms. Security testing with known attacks is invaluable, but it can only show the presence of certain security vulnerabilities – not the absence of all exploitable vulnerabilities. Security verification tries to show that security properties hold, or will not be violated. While it may be able to leverage some tools from functional verification, security verification has additional requirements. Hence, research towards a systematic methodology and tools that enable security verification at design time can go a long way to providing better security in tomorrow's computing systems.

6 Summary and Further Readings

We have defined *hypervisor-secure virtualization* architectures and described our HyperWall architecture as an example. HyperWall uses new hardware features to protect the confidentiality and integrity of a VM's memory from an untrusted or malicious hypervisor. With HyperWall, a hypervisor, while untrusted with respect to the confidentiality and integrity of the VMs' memory, is still able to run and perform management duties, such as sharing processor cores among VMs or performing runtime memory reallocation. Having an untrusted hypervisor is an aggressive new threat model, not previously tackled by other architectures, which almost always assume a trusted hypervisor. Our new CIP (Confidentiality and Integrity Protection) table and new hardware mechanisms ensure that the memory of the VMs is protected and the untrusted hypervisor cannot maliciously alter these protections. Hence we can allow an untrusted, commodity hypervisor to run, thus providing rich runtime functionality for the VMs. We also introduced the concept of the hardware-only accessible DRAM memory, which is used to store the CIP table and the TEC (Trust Evidence and Configuration) table for the VMs.

Interested readers are encouraged to read the original paper describing hypervisor-secure virtualization [20]. Details of the HyperWall architecture are available in a conference paper [21]. Improvements and updates, as well as full details of the architecture, are available in [19]. Other hardware-enhanced approaches to security are also discussed in [4–7, 10, 12, 18, 22, 24, 25].

Acknowledgements This work was supported in part by NSF grants CNS-1218817, CCF-0917134 and EEC-0540832.

References

1. ARM, TrustZone. http://www.arm.com/products/processors/technologies/trustzone.php, accessed April 2013.
2. VMWare. http://www.vmware.com/, accessed April 2013.
3. Xen. http://www.xen.org, accessed May 2013.
4. David Champagne. *Scalable Security Architecture for Trusted Software*. PhD thesis, Princeton University, 2010.
5. David Champagne and Ruby B. Lee. Scalable architectural support for trusted software. In *Proceedings of the 16th International Symposium on High Performance Computer Architecture*, HPCA, pages 1–12, 2010.
6. Jeffrey S. Dwoskin and Ruby B. Lee. Hardware-rooted trust for secure key management and transient trust. In *Proceedings of the 14th ACM Conference on Computer and Communications Security*, CCS '07, pages 389–400, 2007.
7. Joan G. Dyer, Mark Lindemann, Ronald Perez, Reiner Sailer, Leendert van Doorn, Sean W. Smith, and Steve Weingart. Building the IBM 4758 Secure Coprocessor. *Computer*, 34:57–66, 2001.
8. Tal Garfinkel, Ben Pfaff, Jim Chow, Mendel Rosenblum, and Dan Boneh. Terra: A virtual machine-based platform for trusted computing. *SIGOPS Oper. Syst. Rev.*, 37(5):193–206, 2003.
9. Tal Garfinkel and Mendel Rosenblum. A virtual machine introspection based architecture for intrusion detection. In *Proceedings Network and Distributed Systems Security Symposium*, pages 191–206, 2003.
10. Ruby B. Lee, Peter Kwan, John Patrick McGregor, Jeffrey Dwoskin, and Zhenghong Wang. Architecture for protecting critical secrets in microprocessors. In *Proceedings of the International Symposium on Computer Architecture*, ISCA, pages 2–13, 2005.
11. Chunxiao Li, Anand Raghunathan, and Niraj K. Jha. Secure virtual machine execution under an untrusted management OS. In *Proceedings Conference on Cloud Computing (CLOUD)*, pages 172–179, 2010.
12. David Lie, John C. Mitchell, Chandramohan A. Thekkath, and Mark Horowitz. Specifying and verifying hardware for tamper-resistant software. In *Proceedings of Symposium on Security and Privacy*, S&P, pages 166–177, 2003.
13. Ryan Riley, Xuxian Jiang, and Dongyan Xu. Guest-transparent prevention of kernel rootkits with vmm-based memory shadowing. In Richard Lippmann, Engin Kirda, and Ari Trachtenberg, editors, *Recent Advances in Intrusion Detection*, volume 5230 of *Lecture Notes in Computer Science*, pages 1–20. Springer Berlin Heidelberg, 2008.

14. Reiner Sailer, Enriquillo Valdez, Trent Jaeger, Ronald Perez, Leendert Van Doorn, John Linwood Griffin, Stefan Berger, Reiner Sailer, Enriquillo Valdez, Trent Jaeger, Ronald Perez, Leendert Doorn, John Linwood, and Griffin Stefan Berger. sHype: Secure Hypervisor Approach to Trusted Virtualized Systems. Technical Report RC23511, IBM Research, 2005.
15. Arvind Seshadri, Mark Luk, Ning Qu, and Adrian Perrig. SecVisor: A tiny hypervisor to provide lifetime kernel code integrity for commodity OSes. *SIGOPS Oper. Syst. Rev.*, 41(6):335–350, 2007.
16. Monirul I. Sharif, Wenke Lee, Weidong Cui, and Andrea Lanzi. Secure in-vm monitoring using hardware virtualization. In *Proceedings of the 16th ACM Conference on Computer and Communications Security*, CCS '09, pages 477–487, 2009.
17. Udo Steinberg and Bernhard Kauer. NOVA: A microhypervisor-based secure virtualization architecture. In *European Conference on Computer Systems*, pages 209–222, 2010.
18. G. Edward Suh, Dwaine Clarke, Blaise Gassend, Marten van Dijk, and Srinivas Devadas. AEGIS: Architecture for tamper-evident and tamper-resistant processing. In *Proceedings of the 17th annual International Conference on Supercomputing*, ICS '03, pages 160–171, 2003.
19. Jakub Szefer. *Architectures for Secure Cloud Computing Servers*. PhD thesis, Princeton University, 2013.
20. Jakub Szefer and Ruby B. Lee. A Case for Hardware Protection of Guest VMs from Compromised Hypervisors in Cloud Computing. In *Proceedings of the Second International Workshop on Security and Privacy in Cloud Computing*, SPCC, pages 248–252, 2011.
21. Jakub Szefer and Ruby B. Lee. Architectural Support for Hypervisor-Secure Virtualization. In *Proceedings of International Conference on Architectural Support for Programming Languages and Operating Systems*, ASPLOS, pages 437–450, March 2012.
22. Trusted Computing Group Trusted Platform Module main specification version 1.2, revision 94. http://www.trustedcomputinggroup.org/resources/tpm_main_specification, accessed April 2013.
23. Carl A. Waldspurger. Memory resource management in VMware ESX server. In *5th Symposium on Operating Systems Design and Implementation (OSDI)*, pages 181–194, 2002.
24. Zhenghong Wang and Ruby B. Lee. New cache designs for thwarting software cache-based side channel attacks. In *Proceedings of the 34th annual International Symposium on Computer Architecture*, ISCA '07, pages 494–505, 2007.
25. Zhenghong Wang and Ruby B. Lee. A novel cache architecture with enhanced performance and security. In *Proceedings of the 41st annual IEEE/ACM International Symposium on Microarchitecture*, MICRO 41, pages 83–93, 2008.
26. Zhi Wang and Xuxian Jiang. HyperSafe: A Lightweight Approach to Provide Lifetime Hypervisor Control-Flow Integrity. In *Proceedings of the 2010 IEEE Symposium on Security and Privacy*, S&P, pages 380–395, May 2010.
27. Zhi Wang, Xuxian Jiang, Weidong Cui, and Peng Ning. Countering kernel rootkits with lightweight hook protection. In *Proceedings of the 16th ACM Conference on Computer and Communications Security*, CCS, pages 545–554, 2009.

Cloud Computing Security: What Changes with Software-Defined Networking?

Maurício Tsugawa, Andréa Matsunaga, and José A.B. Fortes

Abstract Broadly construed, Software-Defined Networking (SDN) refers to the use of a standards-based open architecture and its supporting open source and open interfaces technologies to enable the deployment, management, and operation of networks. While traditional network management relies on vendor-specific hardware, protocols, and software, SDN systems are architected to have well-defined control and data planes offering flexible management interfaces. The enhanced control enabled by SDN opens opportunities for better cloud security engineering. At the same time, new vulnerabilities are potentially exposed as new technologies are introduced. This chapter discusses how SDN impacts cloud security, and potential risks that need to be addressed when SDN is deployed within and across clouds.

1 Introduction

The Open Networking Foundation (ONF), a non-profit consortium that promotes Software-Defined Networking (SDN), defines SDN as an architecture that enables direct programmability of networks [23]. According to [17], SDN is an approach that enables applications to converse with and manipulate the control software of network devices and resources. Even though the SDN functionality is present in "closed" form (as opposed to using an open architecture) in today's network infrastructure, the programmability of traditional network hardware is highly tied to particular implementations by different vendors, making it difficult to realize an end-to-end SDN. Much flexibility, compared to proprietary vendor-specific interfaces (i.e., software packages, scripts, and APIs), is needed to unleash the full potential

M. Tsugawa (✉) • A. Matsunaga • J.A.B. Fortes
Advanced Computing and Information Systems Laboratory, Department of Electrical and Computer Engineering, University of Florida, Gainesville, FL 32611-6200, USA
e-mail: tsugawa@ufl.edu; ammatsun@ufl.edu; fortes@ufl.edu

S. Jajodia et al. (eds.), *Secure Cloud Computing*, DOI 10.1007/978-1-4614-9278-8_4,
© Springer Science+Business Media New York 2014

of SDN. This flexibility can be accomplished by separating the control plane of network hardware (e.g., switches) from the data plane as depicted in Fig. 1. As illustrated by the OpenFlow approach [15, 21], the basic idea is to let a control entity (software), which is physically separated from the data plane, to define how data flows (i.e., how network messages/packets are forwarded and routed), instead of instructing and configuring multiple independent controllers (integrated and running in each individual network hardware – e.g., switch, router, firewall, and intrusion detection system) as in traditional networks.

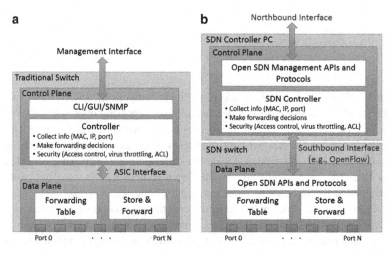

Fig. 1 Control and data plane separation in SDN (**b**) when compared to a traditional all-in-one switch (**a**) – control is performed external to the store-and-forward hardware as opposed to an integrated solution in traditional switches. Both control and data planes export programming APIs (northbound and southbound, respectively), which are being standardized

In this chapter, SDN refers to the emerging network architecture that allows flexible and vendor-independent management and operation of networks. The needed standards and open specifications are being developed by organizations and consortiums (e.g., Internet Engineering Task Force [10], and ONF [23]) with participation of industry and research communities. The most popular specification, adopted by many SDN developers, is OpenFlow [15, 21].

The enhanced control offered by SDN aligns well with cloud computing networking needs. Due to the scale and dynamic nature of resources (physical and virtual) and users, cloud infrastructure and applications require efficient mechanisms to rapidly change how networks operate according to how users and applications come and go. Without SDN, cloud operators rely on a combination of vendor-provided and in-house software to control cloud networking. Cloud security, related to networking, is accomplished by (1) trusting the complex network configuration generated manually by network administrators or management software; and (2) isolating network management traffic from regular data, so only cloud administrators can interact with network hardware. As SDN shifts network management from network configuration to network "programming", an important question arises: from a security stand point, how do SDN-based clouds compare to traditional (i.e., pre-SDN) clouds? Can SDN address security vulnerabilities of traditional architecture? Do new SDN technologies expose vulnerabilities not present in the traditional architecture? What are the mechanisms that need to be developed or reused to secure SDN-enabled clouds?

In order to answer the above questions, this chapter discusses different aspects of cloud security and how SDN impacts them when used in lieu of traditional networking architectures.

2   Introduction to SDN: What Is Changing?

Today's networking infrastructure is very complex, with a variety of vendor-dependent mechanisms to address different problems, and inflexible (i.e., difficult to accommodate innovations without fully upgrading hardware and software). This fact is best illustrated by the difficulty to widely adopt the Internet Protocol version 6 (IPv6). IPv6 was developed in late 1990s, and it was meant to replace IP version 4 (IPv4) to deal with the address space exhaustion problem. However, as of 2013, IPv6 traffic share is only around 1 % [5]. OpenFlow was initially proposed as an academic research project, led by Nick McKeown (Stanford University) with the goal of enabling scientists to run network experiments in real world campus networks. As depicted in Fig. 1, the idea is to achieve vendor-independent flexibility by clearly separating the control plane (software system that makes decisions about where traffic is sent) and the data plane (hardware that can forward traffic at line rate to the destination selected by the control plane). OpenFlow was developed to be an open interface so that the communication between the control and data planes (Southbound Interface in Fig. 1) could be standardized. With standard interfaces, vendors would be able to implement switches that support OpenFlow without exposing details of the internal data plane. By enabling programmability of the network, many software engineering techniques can be applied, and the hope is that exposing the right abstraction on upper layers (Northbound Interface in Fig. 1), it will be possible to achieve simplicity. Interestingly, the term Software-Defined Networking was coined by Kate Greene, a science and technology journalist, while working on an article describing the research of Nick McKeown's team on OpenFlow [6]. Understandably, OpenFlow is closely related to SDN, and plays an important role defining the Southbound Interface. An OpenFlow-enabled switch implements a flow table, illustrated in Fig. 2, and OpenFlow protocol to access the flow table. Each entry in flow table specifies rules to match a packet (based on MAC address, IP address, TCP/UDP port, VLAN, and switch port) and the action to be taken upon a match (forward the packet to particular switch port(s), drop the packet, forward to the controller, and/or send to normal processing pipeline).

This functionality opens a wide range of opportunities to the controller: it is possible to implement a broadcasting hub, learning switch, multicast, and firewall all with line rate performance.

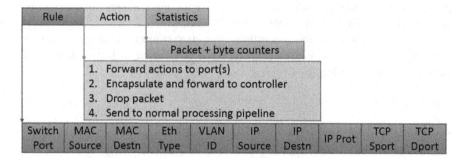

Fig. 2 OpenFlow version 1.0 flow table entry [14]. An OpenFlow-enabled switch can take actions based on L2, L3, and transport layer headers flowing through the data plane

This clean and flexible architecture offered by SDN is extremely appealing for managing networks in a cloud environment. For example, VLAN technology [12], used in many cloud systems to keep multiple tenants isolated from each other, requires reconfiguration of network hardware every time a VM is instantiated or shutdown. Manual configuration by network administrators logging in to every affected switch is impractical in a very dynamic cloud environment. Automation requires understanding well command-line/web interfaces exposed by vendors and writing programs/scripts to parse such interfaces, which are different for each vendor and can change after a firmware upgrade. An open and standardized Northbound interface illustrated in Fig. 3 will significantly simplify the integration of network functions in cloud middleware: (1) the cloud middleware consults its database to check which VMs (VM1, VM2, and VM3) belong to a particular tenant (Tenant_A), and where those VMs are running (physical host and/or SDN switch that each VM is connected); (2) the cloud middleware invokes a SDN Northbound API to create a VLAN (VLAN_A) and connect the tenant's VM on the new VLAN; (3) the SDN controller computes the necessary Southbound instructions and contacts the affected SDN switches. Moreover, using SDN mechanisms it would be possible to implement VLAN-like functionality without the 4096 ID limit of IEEE 802.1Q standard: for example, isolation can be enabled by allowing communication only among media access control (MAC) addresses of a particular tenant (this would entail the SDN controller to compute rules based on MAC addresses to be placed on switches).

SDN has attracted interest from both industry and academia, leading to the release of many controllers, and OpenFlow-enabled hardware/software. Many believe that SDN is applicable not only for campus networks (as initially designed), but everywhere. While studies and deployments of SDN across wide-area networks (WAN) exist [9, 11, 28], there is currently low interest in applying the technology

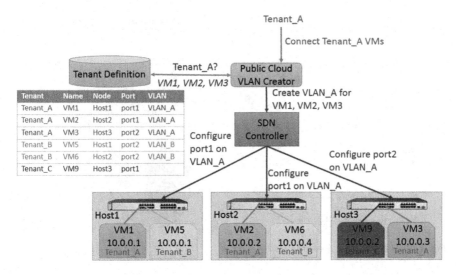

Fig. 3 Example of how cloud middleware uses SDN interfaces to control the network. The figure illustrates that VLAN management can be achieved by simply invoking a Northbound API exposed by a SDN controller. Southbound instructions to achieve the desired functionality are computed and transmitted by the SDN controller

in the Internet core. As further discussed in the next sections, security aspects (especially user authentication and access control) are not yet defined for SDN, and in the Internet core where multiple providers/administrative domains are traditionally organized as "independent" autonomous systems (AS), the open access and logically centralized view of the network will require further development to deal with multiple potentially conflicting interests. As illustrated in Fig. 4, SDN deployments concentrate on the edge of the Internet within a single administrative domain. The majority of deployments are within a private LAN, with SDN replacing the traditional network management/operation and offering agile reconfiguration mechanisms to deal with and implement policies for the Bring Your Own Device (BYOD) movement. In larger deployments (in a datacenter, campus or enterprise networks), different network services such as firewalls (higher performance as rules are distributed among switches and processed at line rate, instead of concentrating on a single appliance with potential packet processing speed limitations) and quality-of-service differentiation (offer different network paths favoring bandwidth or latency) are cleanly implemented. WAN deployments require dedicated links across sites and are typically under a single administrative domain. A typical application in this scenario is to best utilize the network infrastructure and provide resiliency given the deterministic knowledge offered by the SDN logical central controller.

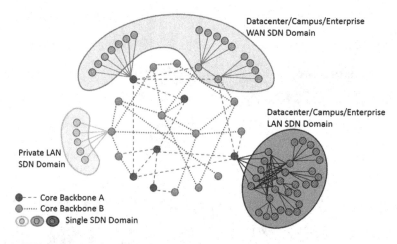

Fig. 4 SDN deployment domains

3   Cloud Security with SDN: Opportunities and Vulnerabilities

SDN and OpenFlow development has mainly focused on improving network functionality (e.g., by adding network programmability). An increase in functions or features represents a larger surface area where exploitable weakness can exist (less security), and also a system that is more difficult to use since users will need to understand and learn a larger set of functions (less useable) – this fact is well illustrated in the Security/Functionality/Ease-of-use triad as in Fig. 5 [34]. From a networking perspective, the most secure system is the one that is not connected – i.e., zero functionality and completely unusable. Too much security will make the system very difficult to use, and too much functionality will make it difficult to track all potential vulnerabilities (this is well exemplified by the high number of vulnerabilities in computer operating systems). Readers should consider two points going through the next subsections discussing cloud security with SDN: (1) every aspect, including the ones intuitively unrelated, affects security; and (2) given the trade-off, a compromise needs to be found for an acceptable level of security.

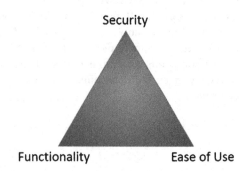

Fig. 5   Security/
Functionality/ Ease-of-use
triad

3.1   Network Management Complexity and Change in Personnel

Without SDN, network administrators are forced to use non-standardized APIs and develop in-house software and scripts to configure the network. Writing such program is an error-prone activity, which reflects the complexity of today's networks. SDN will not reduce the complexity of networks – i.e., the large number of devices to manage, and the large number of protocols to support will remain unchanged or keep growing – and SDN programming is expected to be equally error-prone. However, with the adoption of standardized interfaces (such as OpenFlow, which one can view as "network" instruction set), network "programs" should become more readable to a larger number of developers/administrators, which will help the debugging process and trustworthiness of network management codes. This is particularly important when change in personnel takes place. Typically, a network administrator that inherits a network decides to develop management tools and scripts from scratch. The main reasons are: (1) the inherited configuration is not well documented, and (2) previous administrators may have left back doors that would compromise security.

It is expected that new abstractions will be created (through the Northbound interfaces) so that users will not need to deal with the complex low-level Southbound interfaces. Many researchers advocate that applying software engineering and creating the correct abstractions will lead to a simpler system, enabling easier debugging [8] and use of formal verification techniques [32].

3.2   Autonomous Systems Versus Logically Centralized Management

SDN advocates a logically centralized management of networks (i.e., global network view), in which a controller (or a collaborating set of controllers) operates and defines the flow of data. With Autonomous Systems (AS), an administrator of a particular domain can focus in protecting its own site, with little interaction with a limited number of neighboring AS. The global network view approach of SDN raises obvious scalability concerns, but researchers believe that scalability is not going to be a problem since while the data plane operates at line rate (Gbps), the control plane exchanges messages at a much lower rate. The global view, however, requires a well-defined model for collaboration and federation – how network resources are programmed, what can be programmed, and who can program. In a scenario where multiple users/cloud tenants share the network infrastructure, the boundaries of what each user of network programs can do need to be well defined. Creating a hierarchical structure where the SDN domain can delegate limited functionality to its tenants is a possible evolution when dealing with the logical central control. This issue is closely related to intercloud security as discussed in [2].

3.3 Restricted Management Access Versus Open Management Access

Management networks are traditionally isolated, often times physically, from regular network traffic. Even if access to configuration of network devices is done through insecure mechanisms, the infrastructure would be protected from attackers since only network administrators have access to the management network. SDN can be deployed in a similar way so that only network administrators have access to programming interfaces. Security in this case depends on how well network administrators can operate the infrastructure, and it is independent whether or not SDN is used. However, the SDN vision is to allow applications and end users interact directly with the network, the same way they interact with compute and storage resources. Thus, mechanisms to control access to programming interfaces and coordinate the use of network resources become necessary. Currently, the majority of deployments consider the SDN to be isolated from the data network. Much research and development are still needed, but some features can be seen in network operating systems (e.g., NOX [7, 20]) and network "hypervisors" (e.g., FlowVisor [29, 30]).

3.4 Isolation Among Users/Tenants

Cloud providers make use of several techniques to achieve maximum isolation among users (or tenants), including firewall configurations and use of VLANs. For example, in the advanced networking model of CloudStack [1] (an open-source Infrastructure-as-a-Service cloud middleware), each user is assigned an independent VLAN. VLAN technology [12] allows multiple isolated broadcast domains to co-exist in a LAN, and a specific VLAN header (tag) is processed by switches. SDN can make the complex management of VLANs more controllable (i.e., through the use of standard interfaces), or alternatively, achieve tenant isolation using SDN programming. SDN controllers can implement firewall rules since they control how packets/frames flow through the data plane. The level of isolation will depend on how well SDN programs are written.

From a performance perspective, cloud resource sharing is susceptible to denial-of-service attacks by exhaustion. An attacker can potentially deny CPU or disk I/O to other users by putting an extremely high load on shared resources. Similarly, an attacker can try to congest the network sending unnecessary messages, or attack the machine running the SDN controller. There are two arguments that support SDN to better handle such attacks: (1) it is possible to quickly detect such patterns and isolate the traffic so regular users are unharmed; and (2) modern switches can handle line rates (1 Gbps or 10 Gbps) per port, and SDN can group flows or traffic per port.

3.5 Response to Attacks

SDN has two main advantages over traditional networks in regards to detection and response to attacks: (1) the (logically) centralized management model of SDN allows administrators to quickly isolate or block attack traffic patterns without the need to access and reconfigure several heterogeneous hardware (switches, routers, firewalls, and intrusion detection systems); (2) detection of attacks can be made a distributed task among switches (SDN controllers can define rules on switches to generate events when flows considered malicious are detected), rather than depending on expensive intrusion detection systems. SDN can also be used to control how traffic is directed to network monitoring devices (e.g., intrusion detection systems) as proposed in [31]. Quick response is particularly important in highly dynamic cloud environments. Traditional intrusion detection systems (IDS) mainly focus on detecting suspicious activities and are limited to simple actions such as disabling a switch port or notifying (sending email) to a system administrator. SDN opens the possibility of taking complex actions such as changing the path of suspicious activities in order to isolate them from known trusted communication. Research will focus on how to recast existing IDS mechanisms and algorithms in SDN contexts, and development of new algorithms to take full advantage of multiple points of action. For example, as each switch can be used to detect and act on attacks, [16] has shown the improvement of different traffic anomaly detection algorithms (Threshold Random Walk with Credit Based rate limiting, Maximum Entropy, network traffic anomaly detection based on packet bytes, and rate limiting) using Openflow and NOX by placing detectors closer to the edge of the network (home or small business networks instead of the ISP) while maintaining the line rate performance.

3.6 Network Statistics Monitoring

While mechanisms to access network statistics data from switches and routers are available (e.g., using Simple Network Management Protocol – SNMP [4]), such data are rarely made available to end users. SDN switches are designed to match flows (based on MAC, IP, switch port, VLAN, etc.) and process the flows according to rules defined by a controller. The hardware used to match flows has built-in performance counters, which are also exposed through programming interfaces. These counters can be used to define matching rules based on either statistics or fine-grain monitored network data. By leveraging this feature, service level agreements (SLA) between cloud providers and users can be made easier to manage. With a reliable source of statistics data, cloud providers and users can both verify when and how a network-related SLA has been violated.

3.7 Data Confidentiality

Confidentiality is very challenging to achieve at the network level. First, the network always knows the source and destination of packets (otherwise it would not know how to route messages), and second, if encryption is implemented at the network level, users would need to trust the network devices. True end-to-end data confidentiality can be only accomplished if secrets (i.e., encryption keys) are only known to the source and destination parties. SDN is unlikely to offer confidentiality or encrypted communication since there are many validated application level protocols that ensure data confidentiality. Applications could (and should) continue to rely on traditional methods when processing sensitive data.

3.8 VM Migration

The use of VM migration intra- and inter-clouds has been actively investigated due to its potential to offer better cloud resource management. Complex network reconfigurations (in traditional networks), or programs (in SDN) are needed when a VM moves from one server to another – i.e., to keep the same VLAN configuration, access, and firewall policies unchanged. The complexity increases depending on the migration distance, i.e., in increasing order: within a rack (same switch), across racks, across server rooms, across buildings, and across WAN. Realizing a SDN-based WAN requires further research, as already exemplified by the RouteFlow [18] SDN switch-based architecture. As SDN evolves and gets deployed, more network programs and interfaces supporting VM migration will be made available. SDN mechanisms could be used to isolate the traffic related to VM migrations, potentially leading to improved security. However, attackers may also take advantage of SDN mechanisms to reroute and gain access to VM migration traffic, thus, the VM migration process itself will still need to use appropriate and secure application-layer protocols.

3.9 Reliability

With traditional network switches, failure in any component would affect only a partial part of the entire network. In particular, failure of a management server, which is used to communicate with switches and routers when configuration changes are needed, minimally affects the operation of the network since it will only prevent new configurations to be propagated. In a cloud, it could prevent accepting new users (if a VLAN needs to be created), but running systems will continue to work. Failure of a SDN controller can potentially have catastrophic consequences – in the worst case, the network can completely shutdown.

3.10 Opportunities for Attackers

SDN exposes new interfaces to control and operate the network, which can be potential source of security risks. If communication between control plane and data plane is not properly secured (e.g., physically isolated communication channels, or use of secure channels and protocols), security of the entire network can be easily compromised. Moreover, as discussed above, a compromised controller can affect the security of the entire network, so SDN controllers and their access control policies need to be carefully designed and implemented. As low level network functions and services are exposed to more users, attacks that are difficult or impractical for regular users may become possible once SDN is available (e.g., while in traditional networks interception of packets to perform man-in-the-middle attacks would require privileged access to network devices, with SDN it can be potentially achieved through interactions with the controller). SDN controllers run on traditional computers that are known to have exploits. Securing properly these points of entry will be essential for maintaining the security currently dependent on network configurations.

4 SDN/OpenFlow Security Research

SDN research has been centered on the development and unveiling of a new networking paradigm, the definition of flexible management/programming interfaces, and the implementation of prototypes and simulators to attract the interest of network hardware vendors. The success of these activities is well illustrated in presentations and tutorials from Open Networking Summit events [24], and while security aspects of SDN have not yet received full attention, an increasing body of research work is becoming available. A snapshot of this work, at the time of writing of this chapter, is discussed below.

Researchers from SRI International and Texas A&M University maintain the OpenFlowSec website [22], where solutions to SDN security challenges are made available through reference implementations, papers, presentations and demonstrations. The group has developed tools that can help experts to study different aspects of OpenFlow security. FORT-NOX [26] extends the NOX OpenFlow controller platform [7] implementing a security kernel that mediates OpenFlow rule insertion requests by applications. The FORT-NOX security policy enforcement kernel implements a rule-conflict detection engine that, in conjunction with a role-based authorization mechanism, decides whether OpenFlow rule insertions or deletions should be accepted or not. FRESCO is a security application development framework for OpenFlow-based SDN. The FRESCO scripting language makes it possible to write security applications with fewer lines of source code compared to writing OpenFlow applications from scratch, enabling developers to focus on security aspects of OpenFlow applications.

Tools to develop OpenFlow or OpenFlow-based security applications, closely related to OpenFlowSec, have also been studied by different researchers. FlowVisor [29] uses network slicing to create multiple logical networks, and evaluates OpenFlow rule conflicts between the logical networks. The Resonance architecture [19] recognizes the need for fine-grained security policies that can be changed dynamically in response to network monitoring, and implements a security system that tracks different states of each host to apply security policies accordingly. Researchers in [27] propose the development of network programming language abstractions to help guarantee the consistency of rules in SDNs.

Research on how to recast existing security mechanisms using the SDN paradigm has also been conducted. The work in [33] is the most relevant to this article as it touches two services offered by Amazon Elastic Compute Cloud (EC2): elastic IP and security groups. An elastic IP is a static IPv4 address leased by Amazon to a particular cloud user that can be programmatically mapped to an instance (a VM). Security groups are groups of EC2 instances (an instance can belong to one or more security groups) to which users can assign firewall rules. Authors show in [33] how these two services can be implemented using OpenFlow mechanisms, and also how they can be integrated into existing open source cloud middleware.

Authors in [35] propose the use of OpenFlow mechanisms to improve the security of guest WiFi services, more specifically the separation of authentication, access, and accounting. A prototype of OpenWiFi is implemented using off-the-shelf WiFi access points (APs) with modified firmware in order to make them OpenFlow-enabled APs. The OpenFlow ability to collect flow statistics is highlighted in this work for improved accounting.

An interesting approach to uncover and mitigate cyberthreats is the use of "Big Data Security" [25]. The key idea is to treat the entire network traffic of an organization as Big Data (i.e., a very large and complex data set from which traditional analysis tools are unable to efficiently extract useful information), and use Big Data mechanisms to implement security solutions. Piper [25] introduces security intelligence and analytics (SIA), by Solera Networks, as a potential solution. SIA captures every packet and flow that traverses a network, and can potentially detect threats that would be impossible using traditional solutions. It is expected that SDN can further improve the performance and functionality of Big Data security solutions such as SIA.

5 Needed SDN Research and Development for Cloud Security

As SDN moves from configuration of network devices to the notion of programming the network, and the idea of a "network" instruction set can be conceptualized. OpenFlow specification mainly focuses on this layer, defining what and how the control plane interacts with the data plane. Similar to computer architecture where stand-alone applications directly access the hardware without operating system control, it is possible to directly use the network instructions to implement stand-alone SDN controllers – which are the majority of OpenFlow controllers currently available, and sufficient for small deployments (Fig. 6). Even with this simple setup many SDN aspects can be studied: how the controller should be protected against external attacks, how to properly isolate the control messages from the data plane, what is the right set of "network instructions" to be exposed, how many switches a single controller can handle, how to implement a distributed controller, among others.

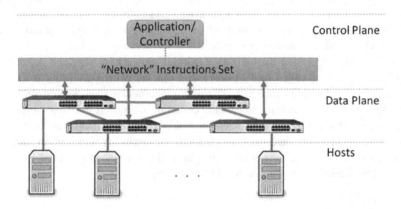

Fig. 6 Stand-alone SDN controller

In a cloud environment, it is likely that multiple controllers will be needed to accommodate the different, and often conflicting, needs among providers, system administrators, and end users. A network operating system (NOS) that can coordinate multiple applications and resolve potential conflicts (e.g., as proposed in [26]) is then needed (Fig. 7). Security studies should then focus on the NOS layer: what is the appropriate set of interfaces exported by a NOS, does a function expose vulnerabilities, how well each application is isolated from each other. Lessons learned from years of computer operating systems development should be leveraged.

Further, network hypervisors that are able to coordinate the action of multiple network operating systems (e.g., FlowVisor [29]) would enable maximum flexibility in network programming. Similar to computer systems, every layer needs security considerations (Fig. 8).

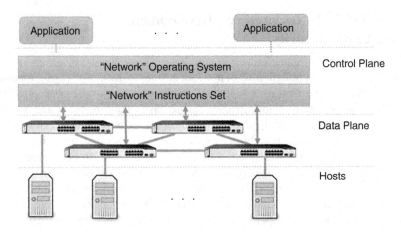

Fig. 7 Network operating system

SDN is a step forward to realize the vision of fully virtualized datacenters, campus-based networking test beds and networked sandboxes offering missing network virtualization services to clouds. As an emerging technology, much research and development are needed to understand its security implications. Making an analogy with machine virtualization, virtual networking services, as needed by cloud providers, users, and middleware, can be developed using a layered architecture as illustrated in Fig. 8. The data plane/network instruction set needs to be able to securely accept and execute commands/instructions from the control plane. Substantial effort has been spent in making open specifications for the data and control planes interface, with much focus on flexibility and less on security. Many argue that this interface needs to be physically isolated and secured, and only accessed by trusted controller, network OS, or hypervisor.

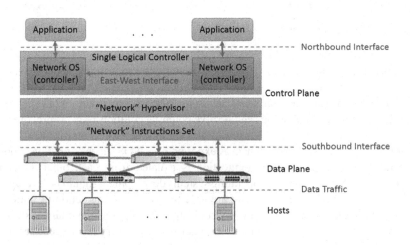

Fig. 8 Network virtualization using SDN

In the control plane, sophisticated authentication and access control are needed. In deployed clouds there already exists a user base, with well defined mapping between resources and users. For example, in an IaaS cloud, the mapping between a given user and running VMs is clear. Network hypervisors will need to restrict the actions of a controller to a particular set of VMs. This task becomes much more complex when multiple clouds are involved [3, 13], and solutions to cloud federation/collaboration should be leveraged.

6   Conclusions

This chapter discusses software-defined networking and its impact on cloud computing security. As SDN changes network management from device configuration to network programming, it exposes a large amount of interfaces with potential security vulnerabilities. If SDN is just used as a better technology to operate networks and interfaces are physically restricted to system and network administrators, substantial changes to cloud network management security are not expected. Assuming that SDN programming is properly done, security of network management will remain the same with similar vulnerabilities and threats. Many deployments will follow the administrators-only network management model, at least in the initial phases of SDN deployment. As SDN matures, mechanisms to securely expose SDN programmability to a wider range of users will be needed, and increasingly complex security considerations will be incorporated into SDN design. The security topics discussed in this paper, while not exhaustive, are the ones that the authors feel in need of immediate attention.

Configuration and operation of networks is a complex and error-prone activity with or without SDN. Unintended security vulnerabilities will continue to exist and even increase in certain scenarios since SDN promotes a larger community to be involved in interacting with the network control plane. At the same time, the flexibility in manipulating low level network components offered by SDN will enable the development of new ways of improving security not possible before. Security highly depends on how network programs are implemented. Similar to computer programs, high quality secure programs and badly implemented and insecure programs will co-exist.

A layered approach similar to computer systems can be used to coordinate the sharing of network programming responsibilities among multiple users, administrators, and middleware. The programming interfaces in the data plane can be considered a "network" instruction set, with network hypervisors coordinating multiple network operating systems, which in turn offer services to multiple applications. Each layer will need to be appropriately secured.

Still, access to network services will need to be well controlled and coordinated, so that applications do not interfere with each other. Therefore, a complex control of users is needed, and federation and interoperation challenges similar to the ones faced by clouds emerge. SDN should be included in the intercloud discussion, as it can take advantage of the sophisticated authentication and authorization mechanisms, and in turn, offer a flexible networking environment for improved and secure cloud experiences.

Acknowledgements This work is supported in part by National Science Foundation (NSF) grants No. 0910812, 1139707, 1240171 and the AT&T Foundation. Any opinions, findings and conclusions or recommendations expressed in this material are those of the authors and do not necessarily reflect the views of the NSF, and AT&T Foundation.

References

1. Apache CloudStack Project. http://www.cloudstack.org. Cited 14 June 2013.
2. Bernstein D and Vij D (2010) Intercloud Security Considerations. In *2010 IEEE Second International Conference on Cloud Computing Technology and Science (CloudCom)*. 537–44. IEEE, Indianapolis, USA. doi:10.1109/CloudCom.2010.82.
3. Bernstein D, Ludvigson E, Sankar K, Diamond S, and Morrow M (2009) Blueprint for the Intercloud - Protocols and Formats for Cloud Computing Interoperability. In *Fourth International Conference on Internet and Web Applications and Services 2009 (ICIW '09)*. 328–36. Venice/Mestre. doi:10.1109/iciw.2009.55.
4. Case JD, Fedor M, Schoffstall ML, and Davin J (1990) *A Simple Network Management Protocol (SNMP)*. IETF RFC 1157, 1–36.
5. Google - IPv6 statistics. http://www.google.com/intl/en/ipv6/statistics.html. Cited 14 June 2013.
6. Greene K (2009) *TR10: Software-Defined Networking*. Technology Review (MIT). http://www2.technologyreview.com/article/412194/tr10-software-defined-networking/. Accessed 14 June 2013.
7. Gude N, Koponen T, Pettit J, Pfaff B, Casado M, McKeown N et al. (2008) NOX: towards an operating system for networks. *ACM SIGCOMM Computer Communication Review* **38**, 105–10. doi:10.1145/1384609.1384625.
8. Handigol N, Heller B, Jeyakumar V, Maziéres D, and McKeown N (2012) Where is the debugger for my software-defined network? In *Proceedings of the first workshop on Hot topics in software defined networks*. Vol. pp. 55–60, ACM, Helsinki.
9. Hölzle U (2012) *OpenFlow@Google*. Open Networking Summit 2012. http://www.youtube.com/watch?v=VLHJUfgxEO4. Accessed 14 June 2013.
10. Internet Engineering Task Force. http://www.ietf.org. Cited 14 June 2013.
11. Internet2 (2012) *Internet2 Innovation Platform FAQ*. Internet2. http://www.internet2.edu/pubs/Internet2-Innovation-Platform-FAQ.pdf. Accessed 14 June 2013.
12. Interworking Task Group of IEEE 802.1 (2011) IEEE Standard for Local and metropolitan area networks–Media Access Control (MAC) Bridges and Virtual Bridged Local Area Networks. *IEEE Std 802.1Q-2011 (Revision of IEEE Std 802.1Q-2005)* 1–1364. doi:10.1109/ieeestd.2011.6009146.
13. Keahey K, Tsugawa M, Matsunaga A, and Fortes JAB (2009) Sky Computing. In *IEEE Internet Computing*. Vol. 13, pp. 43–51.
14. McKeown N (2008) *Why can't I innovate in my wiring closet?* The Stanford Clean Slate Program. http://www.openflow.org/documents/OpenFlow.ppt. Accessed 14 June 2013.
15. McKeown N, Anderson T, Balakrishnan H, Parulkar G, Peterson L, Rexford J et al. (2008) OpenFlow: enabling innovation in campus networks. *ACM SIGCOMM Computer Communication Review* **38**, 69–74. doi:10.1145/1355734.1355746.

16. Mehdi SA, Khalid J, and Khayam SA (2011) Revisiting traffic anomaly detection using software defined networking. In *Proceedings of the 14th international conference on Recent Advances in Intrusion Detection (RAID'11)*. 161–80. Springer-Verlag, Menlo Park, CA. doi:10.1007/978-3-642-23644-0_9.

17. Nadeau T and Pan P (2011) Software Driven Networks Problem Statement. *IETF Internet-Draft (work-in-progress)* draft-nadeau-sdnproblem-statement-01.

18. Nascimento MR, Rothenberg CE, Salvador MR, Corrêa CNA, Lucena SCd, and Magalhães MF (2011) Virtual routers as a service: the RouteFlow approach leveraging software-defined networks. In *Proceedings of the 6th International Conference on Future Internet Technologies*. 34–7. ACM, New York, NY, Seoul, Republic of Korea. doi:10.1145/2002396.2002405.

19. Nayak AK, Reimers A, Feamster N, and Clark R (2009) Resonance: dynamic access control for enterprise networks. In *Proceedings of the 1st ACM workshop on Research on enterprise networking*. 11–8. ACM, doi:10.1145/1592681.1592684.

20. NOX OpenFlow Controller. http://www.noxrepo.org. Cited 14 June 2013.

21. OpenFlow. http://www.openflow.org. Cited 14 June 2013.

22. OpenFlowSec. http://www.openflowsec.org. Cited 14 June 2013.

23. Open Networking Foundation. http://www.opennetworking.org. Cited 14 June 2013.

24. Open Networking Summit. http://www.opennetsummit.org. Cited 14 June 2013.

25. Piper S (2013) In *Big Data Security for Dummies*. John Wiley & Sons, Inc.

26. Porras P, Shin S, Yegneswaran V, Fong M, Tyson M, and Gu G (2012) A security enforcement kernel for OpenFlow networks. In *Proceedings of the first workshop on Hot topics in software defined networks*. 121–6. ACM, New York, NY, Helsinki, Finland. doi:10.1145/2342441.2342466.

27. Reitblatt M, Foster N, Rexford J, and Walker D (2011) Consistent updates for software-defined networks: Change you can believe in! In *Proceedings of the 10th ACM Workshop on Hot Topics in Networks*. ACM, Cambridge. doi:10.1145/2070562.2070569.

28. Rothenberg CE, Nascimento MR, Salvador MR, Corrêa CNA, Lucena SCd, and Raszuk R (2012) Revisiting routing control platforms with the eyes and muscles of software-defined networking. In *Proceedings of the first workshop on Hot topics in software defined networks*. 13–8. ACM, Helsinki, Finland. doi:10.1145/2342441.2342445.

29. Sherwood R, Gibb G, Yap K-K, Appenzeller G, Casado M, McKeown N et al. (2009) *FlowVisor: A Network Virtualization Layer*. OpenFlow Switch Consortium, Tech. Rep. OPENFLOW-TR-2009-1.

30. Sherwood R, Gibb G, Yap K-K, Appenzeller G, Casado M, McKeown N et al. (2010) Can the Production Network Be the Testbed? In *9th USENIX Symposium on Operating Systems Design and Implementation (OSDI)*. 365–78. USENIX Association, Vancouver, BC, Canada.

31. Shin S and Gu G (2012) CloudWatcher: Network security monitoring using OpenFlow in dynamic cloud networks (or: How to provide security monitoring as a service in clouds?). In *2012 20th IEEE International Conference on Network Protocols (ICNP)*. 1–6. Austin, TX. doi:10.1109/icnp.2012.6459946.

32. Skowyra R, Lapets A, Bestavros A, and Kfoury A (2013) Verifiably-Safe Software-Defined Networks for CPS. In *Proceedings of the 2nd ACM International Conference on High Confidence Networked Systems (HiCoNS 2013), Philedelphia, PA, USA*. ACM, Philadelphia.

33. Stabler G, Rosen A, Goasguen S, and Wang K-C (2012) Elastic IP and security groups implementation using OpenFlow. In *Proceedings of the 6th international workshop on Virtualization Technologies in Distributed Computing Date*. ACM, Delft, The Netherlands. doi:10.1145/2287056.2287069.

34. Waite A (2010) *InfoSec Triads: Security/Functionality/Ease-of-use*. http://blog.infosanity.co.uk/2010/06/12/infosec-triads-securityfunctionalityease-of-use/. Accessed 14 June 2013.

35. Yap K-K, Yiakoumis Y, Kobayashi M, Katti S, Parulkar G, and McKeown N (2011) *Separating authentication, access and accounting: A case study with OpenWiFi*. Technical report, OpenFlow 2011-1.

Proof of Isolation for Cloud Storage

Zhan Wang, Kun Sun, Sushil Jajodia, and Jiwu Jing

Abstract Cloud services help users reduce operational costs by sharing the hardware resources across multiple tenants. However, due to the shared physical resources, malicious users can build covert channels to leak sensitive information (e.g., encryption keys) between co-resident tenants. Cloud service providers have proposed to mitigate these concerns by offering physically isolated resources; however, cloud users have no ways to verify the actual configuration and level of the resource isolation. To increase the observability of disk storage isolation, we introduce two Proof of Isolation (PoI) schemes that enable cloud users to verify separated disk storage and dedicated disk storage, respectively. Our experimental results show that our PoI schemes are practical in both private and public cloud environments.

1 Introduction

As the cloud service becomes more popular to help users reduce operational costs and simplify technical management, it gains greater adoption across enterprises, government agencies, and individuals. Gartner's report [27] indicates that global spending on public cloud services is expected to grow 18.6 % in 2012 to $110.3 billion, and the total market is expected to grow to $210 billion in 2016. Cloud providers deliver their services in a scalable way by sharing the infrastructures,

Z. Wang (✉) • J. Jing
State Key Laboratory of Information Security, Institute of Information Security, Chinese Academy of Sciences, 87A Minzhuang Road, Beijing 100093, China
e-mail: zwang@lois.cn; jing@lois.cn

K. Sun • S. Jajodia
Center for Secure Information Systems, George Mason University, Fairfax, VA 22030-4422, USA
e-mail: ksun3@gmu.edu; jajodia@gmu.edu

S. Jajodia et al. (eds.), *Secure Cloud Computing*, DOI 10.1007/978-1-4614-9278-8_5, © Springer Science+Business Media New York 2014

platforms, and applications across multiple tenants. Meanwhile, the vulnerability of shared technology is among the top nine critical threats to cloud security according to a Cloud Security Alliance (CSA) report [17]. Sensitive information could be compromised through the covert channels built upon the shared CPU cache [49], memory bus [47], and hard disks [34, 43] in the cloud. For instance, a malicious virtual machine (VM) is capable of retrieving the encryption keys from a victim VM hosted on the same physical machine [53].

To ease the security concerns on co-resident data, cloud service providers (CSPs) are motivated to offer physically isolated resources to certain users who have high security requirements. Nowadays a correct deployment of isolation configuration solely relies on the Service Level Agreements (SLAs) signed between a CSP and its users. If the CSP violates the commitments in the SLAs either accidentally or intentionally, the users may not detect those violations until actual economic loss has occurred. Therefore, it is critical to investigate technical approaches that enable the users to verify the commitments in the SLAs.

Two factors enormously increase the difficulties on verifying the SLAs in the cloud. First, the CSP has no motivation to provide sufficient supports for its users to verify its SLA commitments. Therefore, the users may have to perform the SLA verification independently against untrusted and/or uncooperative CSPs. Second, the cloud users merely have a logical view of their resources in the cloud due to the abstraction layer or the business model of cloud computing [31]. Researchers have proposed a number of techniques on verifying SLA commitments such as fault tolerance [11], geographical replication [8, 46], confidentiality [22], integrity [5], and VM isolation [52]. However, the research on verifying the disk storage isolation remains an open problem in the cloud.

In this chapter, we introduce two Proof of Isolation (PoI) schemes for cloud users to verify the actual implementation of storage isolation without any cooperation from CSPs. We first formalize two storage isolation requirements, *separation* and *dedication*. Separation requires that the data owned by two users with conflict of interests should be physically isolated on different storage devices (e.g., hard disks). Note that access control policies (e.g., Chinese Wall Security Policy [13]) cannot guarantee a complete isolation due to the covert channels on disk storages. Dedication requires that a physical storage device can only be used to save the data for one user, who does not want to share the underlying storage device with any other users.

We propose two PoI schemes for *separation* verification and *dedication* verification. The basic idea of the separation verification scheme [43] is to measure the time for simultaneously accessing the conflicting files. When the conflicting files are stored on the same hard drive, the reading time is longer than that when they are on different hard drives, mainly due to the contentions of I/O resources. We propose *TerraCheck* [44], a dedication verification scheme, to help cloud users verify if the unallocated disk space on a hard disk has been occupied by undesired users. It places shadow data on the unallocated disk space and verifies the dedication by detecting the changes to the shadow information.

The rest of this chapter is organized as follows. Section 2 discusses the threat model. We formalize the isolation requirements on cloud disk storage in Sect. 3. Sections 4 and 5 present the two proof of isolation schemes on separation and dedication, respectively. Section 6 discusses the related work on remote verification in the cloud. Section 7 concludes this chapter.

2 Threat Model

Covert channels against the shared disk can be effectively prevented by storing the two conflict-of-interest files on two separated or dedicated hard disks. Both separation and dedication requirements on cloud storage can be enforced by the commitment terms in SLAs. However, a misbehaved cloud provider may fail to meet such requirements due to economic considerations or accidental configuration errors. For instance, even if two conflicting files are required to be put onto two hard disks, the cloud provider may instead store them on the same hard disk.

We consider the misbehaved cloud service providers as *honest-but-greedy*. *Honest* means that the CSPs are not motivated to corrupt user's data or violate the data privacy with respect to the business reputation. However, the CSPs may be *greedy* for either storing conflicting data on the same storage disk or allocating the storage not in use by the dedicated user to other users. Consequently, the security and privacy of the existing user's data may be threatened by the co-resident users through exploiting covert channels to retrieve encryption keys [53], obtain other sensitive information [34], or violate the access control policy [43].

3 Cloud Storage and Storage Isolation Requirements

A cloud infrastructure includes two basic types of storage: direct attached storage and network based remote storage. As shown in Fig. 1, the direct attached storage is the storage media attached to each virtual machine, and the remote storage devices can be accessed by users through Internet (dashed arrow) or by the VMs through the internal network (solid arrow) within the cloud datacenter.

For both types of storage, the resources of cloud storage service can be viewed as a large set of physical storage devices S. The number of storage devices is $|S|$, and $\mathscr{P}(S)$ is the power set of S. Suppose one user u stores n files $D_u = \{d_u^1, d_u^2, \ldots, d_u^n\}$ to $|S|$ devices, where $n > 0$. Storage placement for user u can be characterized by a function $f : D_u \to \mathscr{P}(S)$ that maps the set of files D_u into the set of physical storage devices S. Note one file may be mapped to more than one storage devices.

Separation: To remove the covert channels, the conflict-of-interest datasets should by physically separated on different storage devices, and we call this requirement as

Separation. Suppose user u has a conflicting file set $C_{u,v}$ with user v, where $C_{u,v} = \{(d_u^i, d_v^j) \mid d_u^i \text{ has conflicts with } d_v^j, d_u^i \in D_u, d_v^j \in D_v\}$, separation requires that

$$\forall d_u^i \in D_u, \forall d_v^j \in D_v, (d_u^i, d_v^j) \in C_{u,v} \Rightarrow f(d_u^i) \bigcap f(d_v^j) = \varnothing. \qquad (1)$$

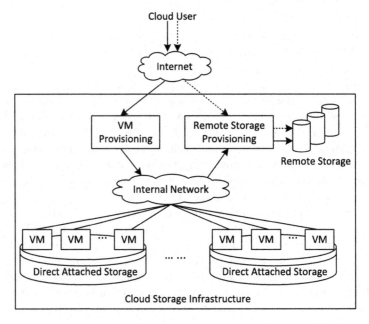

Fig. 1 Architecture of a cloud storage infrastructure

Dedication: Cloud service provides support dedicated storage [3] where one tenant will never share the underlying physical storage devices with any other tenants. Given a user u's storage placement $f(D_u)$, the set of disks used by u is $S_u = \bigcup_{i=1}^{n} f(d_u^i)$. For all the users in the user set U, dedication requirement by user u can be satisfied if

$$\forall v \in U, v \neq u, S_u \bigcap S_v = \varnothing. \qquad (2)$$

4 Separation Verification

Storage separation verification helps the cloud users to verify if the conflict-of-interest files are placed separately by the CSP and cannot be accessed from the same hard disk.

The basic idea is to measure the time when accessing the conflicting files at the same time. If the two files are stored on the same hard drive, the reading time is longer than that when they are on different hard drives due to the contentions of the I/O resources. However, several factors, such as sequential read or random read, affect the file access time and may impact the accuracy of the separation verification. We study such factors for both direct attached storage access and remote cloud storage access, and then introduce effective countermeasures to mitigate the influence of these factors.

4.1 Hard Disk I/O Contention

We take advantage of the contention of I/O resources to detect the file co-residency and verify the storage separation. Three features of hard disk, namely *disk head contention*, *I/O request blocking*, and *disk cache miss*, have obvious impacts on the response time for accessing two co-resident files.

Disk Head Contention. Disk access speed is determined by both transfer rate and access time. The transfer rate is the rate at which data flows between the drive and the host, and it is a relative constant for a given hard disk in a computer. The access time consists of two parts. The *seek time* measures the time for the disk arm to move the disk heads to the cylinder containing the desired sector, and the *rotational latency* is the time to rotate the platter and position the desired sector under the disk head [36]. Therefore, when we simultaneously read two files stored on the same hard disk, disk head has to move between at least two storage areas on the disk platter. It causes a large amount of disk movements and results in longer access time. However, if the two files are stored on different hard disks, no disk head contention exists.

I/O Request Blocking. I/O scheduler maintains a request queue that lists all the I/O requests from different processes and dispatches the shared I/O resource for each request in an optimal order. From the earliest Elevator I/O scheduler to the recent Complete Fair Scheduler (CFS) which is configured as the default I/O scheduler in current Linux Kernel [10], they provide a better prevention against the starvation and improve the overall I/O throughput. The I/O scheduler assigns incoming I/O requests to specific queues based on the process originating the I/O requests and then serves a configurable number of requests (by default, 4 in CFS) for each queue before continuing onto the next. However, if two I/O requests on two different files are issued to the same hard drive around the same time, when one process seizes the disk I/O, the other has to wait. If the two files are stored on different disks, it has less impact since I/O requests will be served by two devices at the same time.

Disk Cache Miss. Modern hard disk drives provide caching and prefetching mechanism with their on-chip CPU and memory unit. When an operating system issues a request to read a block from the hard drive, if the data of that block is found in the disk cache memory, the read request can be served without any disk mechanical movement. This makes hard disk drives have faster response time overall, especially for sequential access time. To improve the overall throughput of hard disk, a common strategy is not to start any prefetch if there are I/O requests waiting to be served. Furthermore, another common strategy is to preempt or terminate any ongoing prefetch as soon as a new I/O request arrives [30]. Therefore, when we read two files on the same disk at the same time, the access time won't be significantly reduced by disk cache prefetch. In contrast, if two files are stored on different disks, when we read the two files at the same time, disk cache prefetch may help reduce the access time.

4.2   Verification of Direct Attached Storage

In the cloud, each VM has certain amount of attached storage for loading OS images or serving as regular purpose storage. Accessing this form of cloud storage is similar to accessing the local file system since the customers can decide the file systems and can fully control the associated operating system. Since all the I/O requests should go through the hypervisor or VM monitor, the I/O scheduling deployed by the hypervisor may affect the disk access time. However, the functionality of hypervisor I/O scheduling aims to guarantee that all the VM can fairly access I/O resources. Therefore, it will not affect our verification process significantly. When we design a verification scheme for direct attached storage, we must consider two major factors, *query mode* and *OS page cache*, that affect the accuracy of the verification.

Query Mode. The query mode includes the query size, query pattern and query range. We need to find the query modes that generate more disk head contentions and thus enlarge the access time of co-resident files. Bowers et al. [11] identified that the seek time dominates the reading time for smaller blocks, such as 256 KB. Actual file access time, however, is highly dependent on the pattern of disk head movement. For instance, only one seek is required to read sequential file blocks on one hard disk. In contrast, random block accesses incur a highly varying seek time. Therefore, random read helps to enlarge the access time of co-resident files. Additionally, the size of the file determines the minimum range that the disk head has to move around. When the disk head needs to move within a larger space on the disk platter, it takes more seek time. Therefore, randomly fetching small blocks from a large area on disk would cause the greatest disk contention.

OS Page Cache. Modern operation system borrows the available physical memory for the disk caching in order to reduce the low-speed disk accesses (e.g., *kmem_cache* facility in Linux kernel [10]). Read-ahead is another important feature of memory cache management. The default read-ahead size in Linux is 32 pages (4 KB per page), which can be scaled up and down by the read-ahead algorithm. If the operating system detects that current disk accessing is sequentially reading, the size of read-ahead will be increased automatically. When the operating system detects that the current disk access is random, it will decrease the size of read-ahead.

A simple way to remove the impact of OS memory cache is disabling the memory cache in the operating system. This operation works well in local environment. Sometimes, this operation is impossible to be executed, for example, in a cloud provider controlled environment where storage server is invisible to the customers. Alternatively, randomly reading proper size of blocks from the disk may minimize such impact.

Therefore, we find that the optical query pattern will enlarge the disk contention, and meanwhile minimize the impact of OS page cache. In section "Local Isolation Checking", we will identify the practical query pattern for storage verification.

4.3   Verification of Network Based Cloud Storage

In the cloud, large amount of storage are fabric network based, such as Amazon S3 [3]. Besides the factors in local disk access, we need to consider more factors that may introduce uncertainties when measuring the access time from a cloud storage. In this case, the following factors should be considered.

Network Variability. When the cloud storage is network based, the network variability should be mitigated for accurately measuring the file access time. Bowers et al. [11] has done excellent work to evaluate the network delay. We can further reduce the network latency and variability during the verification by using the computing resources located in the same datacenter.

Multi-tenant Contention. Due to the unique feature of multi-tenant in the cloud, I/O request contention from co-located tenants always exists; however, cloud providers have done considerable work to minimize the service latency. Thus, such contention is relatively small even when a large number of simultaneous disk I/O access are requested from different storage devices. Another way to mitigate such variability is to launch the verification at different time of a day.

Cloud Storage Layout. Different cloud storage providers may have various implementations of the storage layouts, which are important for selecting the appropriate parameters for file co-residency verification. Three aspects of cloud storage layout should be considered.

Disk Model Diversity. Most cloud storage infrastructures are established upon the commodity hardware with less I/O throughput rather than high-end enterprise facilities. The disk features such as seek time and cache algorithms vary from different disk models. We assume that hard drives within one datacenter have similar specification.

Data Partition. Cloud storage typically splits a big file into small chunks and each chunk is entirely stored on one hard disk. There is little public information about the exact chunk size adopted by each public cloud storage provider. Microsoft Azure announced that the chunk and the replica unit is 100 MB in their Azure storage architecture article [15]; Google File System [28] adopts 64 MB as its chunk size. We believe that the chunk size is on the order of tens of megabytes in public cloud storage.

Data Replication. In a cloud environment, all the data are stored with redundancy for the purposes of both fault tolerance and load balance. Each query may be answered by any replica that resides on the healthy and less busy storage device. Amazon S3 introduces two data redundant storage options. The standard storage can sustain the concurrent loss of data in two facilities, and the Reduced Redundancy Storage (RRS) can only sustain the loss of data in a single facility [2]. The scheduler

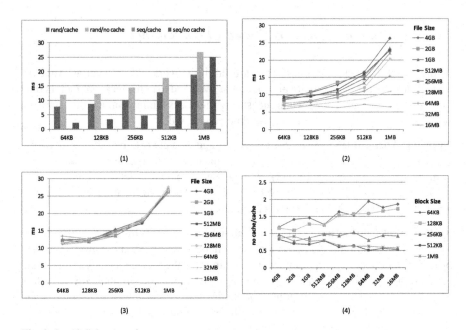

Fig. 2 Local disk contention

of cloud storage provider determines a replica to serve certain query. Our scheme verifies that the conflict-of-interest files are accessed from different storage devices at any time even if some of their replicas are physically stored on the same storage device.

4.4 Experiments

We conduct experiments on both direct attached cloud storage and network based cloud storage and test our mechanism of separation storage verification.

Local Isolation Checking

Localisolation checking aims to verify if two conflicts files are stored separately in the attach based cloud storage. We set up a virtualization environment to simulate the attach based cloud storage. The host machine has an Intel Core i5 CPU 3.10 GHz and 4 GB RAM. Two Seagate ST3500418AS hard disks attached with the local computer have the same capacity (500 GB), disk cache[1] size (16 MB), average seek time (less than 8.5 ms), latency (4.16 ms) and rotation speed (7,200 rpm). To reduce the disk activities triggered by the operating system (OS), we turn off all possible background processes in Ubuntu 12.04 (64-bit) operating system and keep the CPU utilization lower than 1 % such that the disk contentions from other processes can be minimized. Xen [7] virtualization platform is installed on the host machine. The management domain Dom0 is located at the first hard disk *sda*. Each guest VM can be launched on any hard disks-*sda* and *sdb*.

Disk Contention Benchmark. The isolation verification on single file is conducted on a guest VM that is installed on *sda*. One logical volume on *sdb* is attached to the guest VM. The activities of both Dom0 and guest VM OS have minimal impacts on the disk access. We generate random files with sizes from 16 MB to 4 GB on the disk.

Four factors will affect the block reading time from different parts of a single file. They are the block size for each read, the reading pattern (sequential/random), file size, and OS page cache (enable/disable). We test the impacts of all above factors and determine the query mode for verifying the isolation of two conflict files. Generally, the seek time dominates the reading time for small blocks. The blocks with the size smaller than 64 KB tend to have the same reading time regardless the disk manufacturers [11]. To have more accurate controls on the disk head movement and create sufficient disk contention, we read small blocks with sizes from 64 KB to 1 MB.

For the sequential reading, we select 50 sequential blocks from one 1 GB file that is stored on one disk. For random reading, we randomly select 50 blocks from an individual file with the sizes from 16 MB to 4 GB, respectively. Each test is repeated 200 times with different files in order to mitigate the file layout variability on the hard disk. Between each test, we clean both OS page cache and disk cache. The experimental results are shown in Fig. 2.

Figure 2 (1) shows that random reading creates more considerable disk contention than sequential reading regardless of the status of OS page cache, especially when the block size is relatively small. There are two reasons. First, disk head has to move further for random read than the movements for sequential read. Second, random read cannot take full advantage of the read-ahead mechanism provided by the OS page cache. The results also show that enabled OS page cache dramatically reduces the reading time for smaller blocks. When the block size is small, the

---

[1]In this paper, we call the memory on the disk drive as disk cache. The physical memory used as disk buffer is referred as page cache.

sequential reading has significant advantage since the seek time dominates the access time. When the block size increases to 1 MB, the data transfer time is dominant in both random and sequential pattern. Therefore, reading random small blocks enlarges disk contention.

Figure 2 (2) and (3) represent the random reading time of different block sizes from different files with OS page cache enabled and disabled, respectively. When OS page cache is enabled, the random reading time is affected by the file sizes. When the file is small, the page cache greatly benefits the random reading. We also observe that reading the same number of blocks from a larger file takes longer since the disk head has to move across a larger range on the disk platter surface. We compare the impact of OS page cache on different sizes of blocks as shown in Fig. 2(4). When the block size is 256 KB, the status of OS page cache has minimal affect on the average reading time. Therefore, we choose randomly reading 256 KB as the query pattern for verifying the isolation of two files so that the impact of the OS page cache is minimal; meanwhile the disk contention is considerable.

In-House Cloud Experiments. We exploit the above observations to check if two conflicting files are stored on the same hard disk. The separation verification on conflicting file pairs is conducted on different pairs of guest VMs. The virtualization platform has done lots of work to fairly assign CPU time to each VM so that the CPU contention between VMs is negligible. We create three pairs of guest VMs as follows:

- *Pair I.* Each VM is attached by the disk volume from different disks.
- *Pair II.* Both VMs are attached by the disk volume from the same disk. The distances of two volume on the disk is 10 GB.
- *Pair III.* Both VMs are attached by the disk volume from the same disk. The distances of two volume on the disk is 20 GB.

As we show in the analysis in Sect. 4.3, the common practice of data partition is less than 100 MB. We generate random files on each VM with sizes of 16, 32, 64, and 128 MB. We compare the average random reading time from different pairs of VMs. We read 50 blocks (256 KB each) from each file with different sizes. The results are shown in Fig. 3. For small files, such as 16 MB, the difference between reading from one disk and two disks is small. The reason is that the small co-resident files cannot cause enough disk movements to increase the reading time. However, when the file size is no less than 32 MB, the time difference becomes larger than 40 %. When the disk space attached to a pair of VMs is larger, the access time is slightly increased since the disk head has to move in a larger area on the disk platter. However, such difference is small since the disk seek time is in the range of 2–10 ms.

Public Cloud Experiments. We launch a *t1.micro* EC2 instance in Amazon cloud with a 160 GB hard disk. We compare the 256 KB block reading time. As shown in Fig. 4, reading two files from one disk takes double longer than reading one file from an individual disk. Therefore, our mechanism is practical in public clouds.

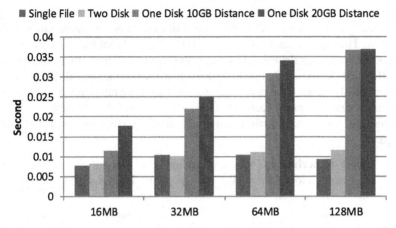

Fig. 3 Eucalyptus experiment

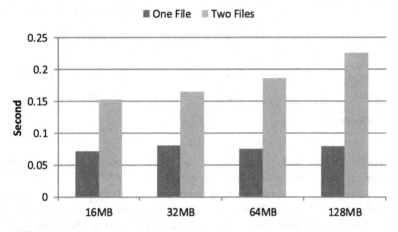

Fig. 4 EC2 experiment

Remote Separation Checking

Remote separation checking aims to verify whether or not two conflicts files are stored separately in the network based cloud storage. We conduct the experiments on both in-house cloud and public cloud. We store the conflicting files on the network based storage services, *Walrus* on Eucalyptus [25] and *S3* on Amazon cloud [3]. Both are widely used network based cloud storage nowadays. We discuss the exploitation of our verification mechanism in public cloud.

In-House Cloud Experiments. We deploy the open source cloud platform Eucalyptus 3.1 and its object based storage service *Walrus* on our host machine to evaluate the isolation verification of remote conflicting files. The interface of Eucalyptus is completely compatible with Amazon cloud [3]. Two hard disks serve the Walrus service. We upload different sizes of files on each hard disk. We randomly read 256 KB blocks from file pairs stored either on the same disk or separately. The experimental results are shown in Fig. 5. From Fig. 5(1), we observe that reading from a single disk takes more than two times longer than reading from two different disks. We randomly read 100 pairs of files on the same disk and another 100 pairs of file on different disk. Each pair of files have randomly different sizes. The average reading time of each 256 KB files are shown in Fig. 5(2). With 0.02 s as the threshold, we can successfully distinguish the isolated storage and co-resident storage.

Public Cloud Experiments. We also evaluate our storage isolation checking method in Amazon cloud, one of the most popular cloud platforms. Amazon S3

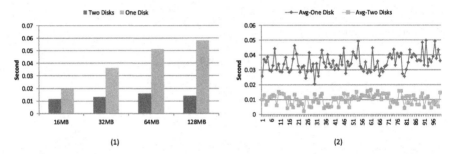

Fig. 5 Eucalyptus experiment

organizes the data by buckets and objects. Each bucket can contain unlimited number of objects. The object is like the file in common PC. In S3, all the buckets share a unique name space. However, Amazon rarely discloses the implementation details such as data partition and replication. We get the following clues majorly from the officially published S3 best practice [20], S3 patent [1], and our observations.

- *Network Variability*: According to Amazon's website [3], making GET requests against Amazon S3 from within Amazon EC2 instances can minimize network variability.
- *Bucket Separation*: Multiple buckets that start with different alphanumeric characters will ensure a degree of partitioning from the start [20]. It implicates that objects logically in the buckets with different initial letters must not reside on the same disk.
- *Object Layout*: [20] also mentions that performing GETs in any sorted order can increase the throughput. The smaller the objects, the more significant impact on the overall throughput. For files with small size, sequential reading may benefit from the disk cache and prefetch. We infer that a number of sequentially uploaded small files should be stored on the same disk.
- *Data Replication*: For simplicity, we adopt RRS for all the experimental data. With RRS, all the objects have two replicas in Amazon Cloud.

Based on the limited Amazon S3 storage implementation details, we read the pairs of files in three modes:

- *Two Buckets with Different Initials*: Reading two files from two buckets with the same initial letter in the same region.
- *Two Buckets with Same Initial*: Reading two files from two buckets with different initial letters in the same region.
- *One Bucket*: Reading two files from one bucket.

We launch two EC2 *m1.medium* instances with the same configuration in US east region to execute the three reading modes. We create S3 buckets with different initial letters located in the same region with the EC2 instances. For each bucket, we upload 100 different 1 MB files with the RRS option. Most of these 100 small files should be stored on the same storage device according to the analysis above. We issue the GET requests from two EC2 instances at the same time. We evaluate the correlation coefficient of reading time recorded by two VMs. The result is shown in Fig. 6. We conduct the experiment at different time of a day and repeated during 2 weeks. We can observe that the reading time from the same bucket or from two buckets with the same initial name has an order larger correlation coefficient than reading from buckets with different initial letters. Therefore, our storage separation verification method can be extended to distinguish accessing the same hard disk from accessing different hard disks in real cloud environment.

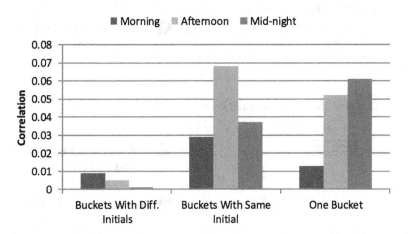

Fig. 6 Co-residency checking in cloud

5   Dedication Verification

We propose *TerraCheck* [44] to help cloud users verify if their dedicated storage devices have been misused to store other users' data. *TerraCheck* detects the malicious occupation of the dedicated device by monitoring the change of the shadow data that are residual bits intentionally left on the disk and are invisible by the file system. When the cloud providers share the dedicated disk with other users, such misuses can be detected since the shadow data will be overwritten and become irretrievable. We describe the theoretical framework of *TerraCheck* and show experimentally that it works well in practice.

5.1 System Model

We assume the usage of the dedicated storage is well-planned by one user. For example, the user allocates a determined amount of dedicated disk space to each

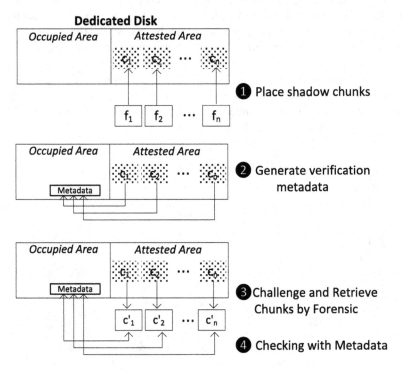

Fig. 7 Overview of *TerraCheck*

VM. This is a common practice [31] for resource management in the cloud. When the user launches a small number of VMs, only part of the dedicated storage is allocated. The rest of the dedicated storage should be protected from being exploited by other users due to both security and performance reasons. We refer to this part of the disk space as *attested area*. The disk space being used by the dedicated user is called *occupied area*. Additionally, the attested area may scale up and down based on the occupation of the dedicated disk. *TerraCheck* requires a small amount of trusted disk space for storing verification metadata on the *occupied area*. We assume the *occupied area* is trusted, since an *honest-but-greedy* cloud provider is trustworthy for managing user data.

Suppose a user C pays and possesses a dedicated disk with the capacity of s in the cloud. The dedicated disk is divided into two areas as shown in Fig. 7. The *occupied area* with the capacity of s_a disk space has been allocated by C for storing the data. The *attested area* with the capacity of s_u disk space remains unallocated where $s_u = s - s_a$. When C needs more disk space and increases the size of occupied area, the size of attested area will shrink accordingly. The goal of *TerraCheck* is to verify if the attested area has been misused by other users or the cloud provider.

TerraCheck consists of four major procedures, as shown in Fig. 7. First, it places shadow chunks in the attested area of the target disk. The shadow chunks are deleted files which cannot be accessed from the file system. Shadow chunks can be recovered by disk forensics technique as long as they have not been overwritten. Second, it generates metadata, such as the hash value of the shadow chunks, for monitoring the alternation of shadow chunks. The metadata is stored on the occupied area. Third, *TerraCheck* challenges the shadow chunks by using disk forensic techniques to recover them. Lastly, it compares the forensics results with the verification metadata. If any shadow chunk has been altered and cannot be recovered, a violation of dedication requirement is detected.

Verification Requirements

A solution for verifying the dedicated storage should satisfy the following technical requirements.

- *Trustworthy.* The verification mechanism should provide the users high confidence in the result of the verification. When the cloud provider has to pay higher storage overhead to defeat our verification mechanism, we can ensure our checking capability from the economic consideration.
- *Efficiency.* The verification procedure should be fast, without obviously interrupting the disk activities against the allocated part of the disk. Moreover, The metadata used for verification should be small; otherwise, it is unacceptable to use the same amount or more disk space to store the original shadow data on the local disk.
- *Scalability.* When the dedicated user occupies or releases more disk space, for example, for running more VMs or shutting down existing VMs, the disk area to be attested varies. When the customer needs to scale the disk space up or down, the affected shadow chunks should be as few as possible.

System Operations

TerraCheck consists of five basic operations. *ChunkGen* generates the shadow chunks and places them on the *attested area*. *MetaGen* generates the verification metadata and stores them on the *occupied area*. *ChalGen* generates the information

Table 1 Summary of operation parameters

Variable	Meaning
C	The cloud user who possesses the dedicated device and executes dedication verification
n	The number of shadow chunks placed on attested disk area
l_k	Length of each shadow chunk
t_h	Header tag of each chunk
t_f	Footer tag of each chunk
K	The set of shadow chunks
s_u	Size of unallocated disk space
id_{k_i}	ID of shadow chunk i
F	The set of files for generating shadow chunks
img_{AA}	Disk image of attested area
$meta_{DB}$	File for storing verification metadata
b_i	Starting disk address of chunk i on attested area
e_i	Ending disk address of chunk i on attested area
id_{AR_x}	ID of attested region x
$meta_{FILTER}$	File for storing Bloom filter

of challenged chunks. *Retrieve* executes the forensics of challenged chunks and calculates their hash values. *Verify* operation compares the result of *Retrieve* with the verification metadata recorded in *MetaGen* and performs dedication verification. Table 1 summarizes all the variables used in the rest of this chapter.

- **ChunkGen$(n, l_k, t_h, t_f) \rightarrow K = \{k_1, k_2, \ldots, k_n\}$:** TerraCheck fills *attested area* with a set of chunks $K = \{k_1, k_2, \ldots, k_n\}$ and $n * l_k = s_u$. Each chunk k_i has a header tag t_h and a footer tag t_f to represent the start and the end of a chunk, respectively. The total length of the header and the footer $l_{t_h} + l_{t_f}$ is less than l_k. This algorithm takes the number of chunks, the length of each chunk, the header t_h, the footer t_f as inputs and generates n temporary files $F = \{f_1, f_2, \ldots, f_n\}$ first. Each file f_i in F starts with t_h, ends with t_f and the rest of it is filled by random bits. Each file f_i has the same length as l_k. All the files in F are stored on attested area and then deleted from the file system. The bits left on attested area associated with each file f_i are the set of chunks $K = \{k_1, k_2, \ldots, k_n\}$. Each chunk contains three parts – the header, the footer, and a random body.
- **MetaGen$(n, t_h, t_f, img_{AA}, h) \rightarrow \{meta_{DB}, \bot\}$:** It takes the number of chunks, the header, footer tag information, the disk image of *attested area* and a hash function as inputs, returns the verification metadata or abortion. $h : \{0, 1\}^* \rightarrow \{0, 1\}^m$ denotes a fixed hash function that outputs m bits hash value. The MetaGen algorithm retrieves the chunks from img_{AA} by matching the t_h and t_f and calculates the hash value of each chunk. The results of verification metadata $meta_{DB}$ are stored on occupied area. $meta_{DB} = \{(id_{k_i}, b_i, e_i, h(k_i)) | i \in \{1, 2 \ldots n\}, k_i \in K\}$ lists the ID of a chunk and the boundary of each chunk on the disk, such as the start block number b_i and the end block number e_i of chunk k_i, and the hash value of each chunk $h(k_i)$. Each chunk can be retrieved from the raw disk based on the start

and end block number without the help of the file system. Let $|meta_{DB}|$ be the number of items in $meta_{DB}$. If $|meta_{DB}| \neq n$, it indicates that some chunks cannot be recovered from the disk image of attested area or there is a mismatched header (or footer) among the chunks. In this case, MetaGen fails and outputs abortion symbol $\perp$.

- **ChalGen**$(meta_{DB}, id_{k_i}) \to chal$: This algorithm generates a challenge $chal$ based on $meta_{DB}$ and the ID of the queried chunk. $chal = (id_{k_i}, b_i, e_i, h(k_i)) \in meta_{DB}$ is the chunk to be examined.
- **Retrieve**$(chal, h) \to result$: It takes the challenge and the hash function as inputs and calculates the hash value after retrieving the chunk based on the information specified in $chal$. It returns the hash value of the chunk in $chal$.
- **Verify**$(result, chal) \to \{$**"success"**, **"failure"**$\}$: The Verify algorithm takes $result$ and $chal$ as inputs and compares the hash value in $result$ with that in $chal$. If the two hash values match, it outputs "success" and otherwise outputs "failure".

5.2 Basic Scheme

Our goal is to make sure that the attested area hasn't been allocated to other users. The basic *TerraCheck* scheme consists of four phases.

- **Initial.** In the initial phase, the attested area is filled with all zeros. This operation prevents the existing content on the disk from affecting our placement results.
- **Placement.** We place the shadow chunks on the attested area by using the *ChunckGen* and *MetaGen* algorithms. If $MetaGen \to \perp$, a failure occurs, *TerraCheck* should be restarted from the initial phase. Otherwise, *MetaGen* generates valid verification metadata $meta_{DB}$.
- **Verification.** It is a procedure to patrol on the dedicated storage device and collect the evidence for the undesired occupation by calling *Challenge*, *Retrieve* and *Verify* algorithms until each shadow chunk placed in the attested area has been checked. The *Verification* phase would be stopped once *Verify* algorithm returns a "failure" for any chunk. The dedication property is preserved if all the chunks passed the examination.
- **Update.** It will be executed when the size of attested area is subject to changes. It is difficult to predict the set of affected chunks since the allocation of disk space depends on the disk scheduling. Therefore, both the shadow chunks and their associated verification metadata become useless and subject to deletion. The initial phase and placement phase should be restarted with the new attested area.

The basic *TerraCheck* scheme can successfully check the dedication requirement with high accuracy. However, it has two major limitations:

- *Computational Cost.* The verification phase has to read through the whole *attested area* and calculate the hash value for each shadow chunk.

- **Update Operation.** When the size of *attested area* has been changed, *TerraCheck* should be restarted from the initial phase against the new *attested area*.

5.3   Advanced Scheme

To mitigate the limitations of the basic *TerraCheck* scheme, we propose a probabilistic based *TerraCheck* scheme. To reduce the computational cost, we randomly sample the chunks during the *Verification* procedure. Moreover, to provide a more efficient update operation, we introduce multiple regions called *attested region* within the attested area. The attested region is the smallest unit for C to scale up the size of the occupied area. For example, C plans to attach a certain size of disk space to a newly launched VM. When the size of the occupied area is shrunk due to the termination of a VM, a new attested region will be created. Each attested region contains multiple shadow chunks. The shadow chunk is the smallest unit for challenge and verification. In addition, we use Bloom filter to reduce the storage for saving the verification metadata.

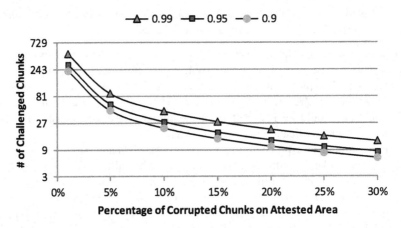

Fig. 8 Probabilistic framework of advanced *TerraCheck*

Attested Region

We introduce attested region for conveniently scaling up and down the size of attested area. The attested area is divided into multiple attested regions. The size of attested region depends on how a user uses the dedicated disk. For example, if it uses the disk as the attached secondary storage for running VMs, and each VM is attached by a fixed amount of disk space, such amount is an optimal size for each attested region. When an attested region should be deleted, the related verification metadata are deleted and excluded from the *TerraCheck* procedure.

Probabilistic Verification

Chunk sampling can greatly reduce the computational cost, while still achieving a high detection probability. Suppose a user probes p chunks during the *Challenge* phase and t chunks have been tampered and become unrecoverable. If the total number of chunks is n, the probability that at least one of the probed chunks matches at least one of the tampered chunks is $\rho = 1 - \frac{n-t}{n} \cdot \frac{n-t-1}{n-1}, \ldots, \cdot \frac{n-p+1-t}{n-p+1}$. Since $\frac{n-t-i}{n-i} \geq \frac{n-t-i-1}{n-i-1}$, it follows that $\rho \geq 1 - (\frac{n-t}{n})^p$.

When t is a fraction of the chunks, the user can detect misbehaviors by asking for a constant amount of chunks, independently on the total number of file blocks. As shown in Fig. 8, if $t = 1\%$ of n, then *TerraCheck* asks for 459 chunks, 300 chunks and 230 chunks in order to achieve the probability of at least 99, 95 and 90 %, respectively. When the number of corrupted chunks goes up to 10 % of the total chunks, the violation can be detected with 95 % probability, by only challenging 29 chunks. As the number of corrupted chunks increases, the number of chunks required to be checked is decreased. The sampling is overwhelmingly better than scanning all chunks in the basic *TerraCheck* scheme. Therefore, we can challenge a fixed number of chunks to achieve certain accuracy. The size of each chunk will determine the computation cost. When the size of each chunk is small, the overhead for retrieving all challenged chunks from dedicated disk is low.

Advanced Operations

Our advanced *TerraCheck* scheme consists of the same phases as the basic *TerraCheck*. We need to refine both the *MetaGen* and *ChalGen* algorithms in the advanced scheme. Also, the update phase should be modified.

MetaGen($n, t_h, t_f, img_{AA}, h) \rightarrow \{meta_{DB}, \perp\}$. The results of verification metadata $meta_{DB} = \{(id_{AR_x}, id_{k_i}, b_i, e_i, h(k_i)) | i \in \{1, 2 \ldots n\}, k_i \in K\}$. It lists the ID of the located attested region, the ID of a chunk and the boundary of each chunk on the disk, such as the start block number b_i and the end block number e_i of chunk k_i, and the hash value of each chunk $h(k_i)$. Each chunk can be retrieved from the raw disk based on the start and end block number and the ID of the attested region without the help of the file system.

ChalGen $(meta_{DB}) \xrightarrow{r} chal$. It randomly generates a challenge $chal$ based on $meta_{DB}$. $chal = (id_{AR_r}, id_{k_r}, b_r, e_r, h(k_r)) \in meta_{DB}$ is the chunk to be examined.

Update. Since the attested area is further divided into attested regions, when a user needs to extend or shrink the disk space for occupied area, only limited number of attested regions are deleted or added so that the *TerraCheck* against the rest of chunks remains valid. When the occupied area scales up, the metadata related to the erased attested region will be deleted. The rest of metadata is still available for *TerraCheck*.

Reducing Metadata Storage

In the basic *TerraCheck* scheme, the size of $meta_{DB}$ for storing the verification metadata is linear to the number of shadow chunks. The number of chunks could be very large if the user wants to achieve a lower computational cost, as we discussed in the probabilistic verification. Therefore, we use Bloom filter to reduce the amount of storage for verification metadata in *TerraCheck*.

Bloom filter [9] is a space-efficient data structure for representing a set in order to support membership queries. Bloom filter is suitable to the place where one might like to keep or send a list for verification, but a complete list requires too much space. We use Bloom filter to represent a set $S = \{x_1, x_2, \ldots, x_n\}$ of n elements as an array of m counters, initially all set to 0. It uses k independent hash functions $h_1, h_2, \ldots, h_k$ with range $[1, m]$. For mathematical convenience, we make the natural assumption that these hash functions map each item in the universe to a random number over the range $\{1, \ldots, m\}$. For each element $x \in S$, the bits $h_i(x)$ are set to 1 for $1 \leq i \leq k$. A location can be set as 1 multiple times. To check if an item y is a member of S, we check whether all $h_i(y)$ are 1. If not, then clearly y is not a member of S. If all $h_i(y)$ are 1, we assume that y is in S.

Bloom filter may yield a false positive, where it suggests that an element x is in S even though it is not. The probability of a false positive for an element not in the set, or the false positive rate, can be estimated, given our assumption that hash functions are perfectly random. After all the elements of S are hashed into the Bloom filter, the probability that a specific bit is still 0 is $PR_{zero} = 1 - \frac{1}{m}^{kn} \approx e^{-\frac{kn}{m}}$. The probability of a false positive is $(1 - PR_{zero})^k$. A Bloom filter with an optimal value for the number of hash functions can improve storage efficiency.

We modify our *TerraCheck* model for utilizing Bloom filter to reduce the storage cost of the verification metadata.

- **BF-MetaGen**$(t_h, t_f, img_{AA}, h) \rightarrow \{meta_{FILTER}, \perp\}$ The algorithm takes the header and footer tag information, the disk image of *attested* area and a hash function as inputs, returns the verification metadata or an abortion. $meta_{FILTER}$ is a Bloom filter which involves the hash value of each shadow chunk.
- **BF-Verify**$(result, meta_{FILTER}) \rightarrow \{\text{"success"}, \text{"failure"}\}$: It takes *result* and $meta_{FILTER}$ as inputs and checks if the hash value in *result* is valid and associates with any chunks. If the hash value can be found from $meta_{FILTER}$, the algorithm outputs "success" and otherwise "failure".

5.4   Experiments

We implement and evaluate both basic *TerraCheck* scheme and advanced *TerraCheck* scheme. All experiments are conducted on a Dell PowerEdge460 server with Intel Core i5 CPU running at 3.10 GHz, and with 4,096 MB of RAM. The system runs Ubuntu 12.04 (LST) that is configured with Xen Hypervisor. The dedicated storage device is a WestDigital SATA 7,200 rpm hard disk with 1 TB capacity and 64 MB cache. For evaluation purpose, we used SHA-1 as the hash function h. The random values used for challenging the chunks in the advanced *TerraCheck* are generated using the function proposed by Shoup [21]. All data represent the mean of 20 trials.

We implement a large attested area in basic *TerraCheck* and implement an attested region in advanced *TerraCheck* as a logical volume. The occupied area may involve multiple logical volumes. LVM (Logical Volume Management) technology is exploited to automate the update operation when the size of the occupied disk space varies. We rely on the retrievability of the shadow chunks on each logical volume to check the dedication property. We utilize Scalpel [29], an open source file recovery utility with an emphasis on speed and memory efficiency, to retrieve the shadow chunks based on their header tag and footer tag. To perform file recovery, Scalpel makes two sequential passes over each disk image. The first pass reads the entire disk image and searches for the headers, footers and a database of the locations of these headers. The second pass retrieves the files from the disk image based on the location information of the header and footer. Scalpel is file system-independent and will carve files from FATx, NTFS, ext2 and ext3, or raw partitions.

We evaluate the computation overhead and storage cost during each phase of *TerraCheck*.

Initial Phase. During the initial phase, the attested area is filled with all zeros. The time for this phase is determined by, and linear to the size of attested area s_u. It takes about 10 s for cleaning 1 GB of the attested area. Both basic *TerraCheck* and advanced *TerraCheck* have the same performance at this phase.

Placement Phase. There are two steps for placing the chunks. The first step is to generate and store the chunks to the attested area. The cost of this operation is determined by the chunk size and the size of the attested area. On our testbed, it takes 12 s to store 100 MB of shadow chunks. The second step is to generate the metadata. It takes 8.198 s for Scalpel to scan 1 GB of the attested area in the first pass and store the location information.

Verification Phase. The basic *TerraCheck* examines all the chunks based on the verification metadata recorded in $meta_{DB}$. Therefore, the time for generating the challenge can be ignored. The advanced *TerraCheck* randomly challenges the chunks. The generation of random number takes less than 0.1 ms. The challenged chunks are retrieved from the *attested area* based on the start and end location recorded as the verification metadata. Therefore, the performance is determined by the disk access time. Table 2 shows the disk access time in our experiment.

Table 2 Time for retrieving chunks

Chunk size	512 KB	1 MB	2 MB	4 MB	8 MB	16 MB
Retrieve time	13 ms	15 ms	20 ms	29 ms	48 ms	86 ms

After retrieving the challenged chunks, *TerraCheck* compares the hash value of the retrieved chunk with the verification information. In basic *TerraCheck*, all the chunks residing on the attested area should be checked, which uses the time for calculating the hash value of all the chunks. The advanced *TerraCheck* scheme randomly challenges the chunks to achieve the detection of undesired disk occupation. We simulate the behaviors that a proportion of attested area is altered. For instance, if a random 1 % of an attested area with 10,000 chunks are altered, such a situation could be detected with a 90 % probability by challenging 217 chunks on average, which is close to the theoretical result.

Update Phase. For the basic *TerraCheck* scheme, the performance of the update is same as the overhead of executing the initial and placement phases. The performance of the advanced *TerraCheck* scheme depends on the change of the size of the attested area. When the occupied area is extended, the advanced *TerraCheck* scheme only needs to update the $meta_{DB}$ by deleting the items of affected chunks. When the occupied area is shrunk, more attested regions should be created on the attested area. The generation of each attested region takes about 400 ms regardless the size of the attested region.

Reducing Metadata Storage. *apgbmf* [4] is originally used to manage Bloom filter for restricting password generation in APG password generation software [37]. We use *apgbmf* version 2.2.3 as a standalone bloom filter management tool.

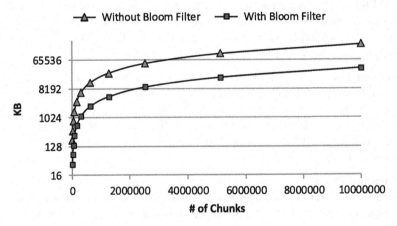

Fig. 9 Comparison of the storage cost with/without Bloom filter (%1 fault positive rate allowed)

We consider each hash value of the shadow chunk as an item of password dictionary in the context of *apgbmf*. We create a Bloom filter for such hash value dictionary. During the verification phase of *TerraCheck*, if a recovered chunk is unaltered, its hash value will pass the Bloom filter, i.e., the hash value is one of the hash values which associates with an original shadow chunk with a high probability. When we allow a 1 % fault positive rate, the storage cost with Bloom filter is reduced 5.5 times as shown in Fig. 9. When the number of chunks is more than 10 million, the metadata only requires 36 MB as compared to 200 MB without using Bloom filter.

6   Related Work

Enforcement and *verification* are two research directions for securing and protecting the data stored in the cloud. Virtualization technology [6, 14, 26, 33, 42, 51] and cryptographic approaches [38, 39, 50] have been exploited to enforce the authorized access to the data and secure the search and computation against the encrypted data [18, 40]. However, enforcement based methods usually require a large amount of operations and supports from data owners. To reduce such burden, more researches on remote verification of security properties have been emerging to increase visibility on the correct operations of cloud.

Reliability.   Data redundancy is the key to preventing data loss and achieving fault tolerance in cloud storages. Bowers et al. [11] proposed RAFT which allows users verify that a file is stored with sufficient redundancy by measuring the response time for accessing "well-collected" file blocks. Wang et al. [45] proposed a layout-free scheme to verify the redundancy level deployed by the cloud provider within one datacenter. Some other works [8, 16, 46] proposed mechanisms to verify that the cloud storage provider replicates the data in multiple geo-locations by measuring the network latency.

Integrity.   Ateniese et al. [5] proposed PDP (Provable Data Possession) to verify the integrity of the data stored in the cloud. PDP lowers the computational overhead by sampling and applying HVT (Homomorphic Verifiable Tags) to the data. Some other works improved PDP scheme by supporting the integrity verification of dynamic data [24, 41] and multiple replication data [19], and by protecting the privacy [35] of the verified data. PoR (Proof of Retrievability) [23] proves that the data stored in the cloud is intact and retrievable. PoR enables verification of an entire data collection without first retrieving it from the cloud. Later, Bowers et al. [12] and Juels and Oprea [32] integrated PoR scheme into an auditing framework HAIL (High-Availability and Integrity Layer) to detect and recovery from data corruption.

Confidentiality.   To strongly protect against unauthorized access or disclosure of the data stored in the cloud, some cloud providers promise to encrypt user data at rest. In order to provide the transparency to tenants, Dijk et al. [22] proposed *Hourglass* scheme to ensure the implementation of the encryption by the cloud provider. *Hourglass* proves the correct handling of cloud-managed data encryption by imposing a resource requirement (e.g., time, storage or computation) on the process of translating files from the plain-text to the cipher-text.

Isolation. Recent researches [34,47,48] have indicated that side channels in shared hardware may enable attackers to exfiltrate sensitive data (e.g., encryption keys [53]) across virtual machines (VMs). In view of such risks, cloud providers may promise physically isolated resources to select tenants, but a challenge remains: tenants still need to be able to verify physical isolation of their VMs, storage and network. Zhang et al. [52] detects the co-resident VMs by monitoring the activities in the CPU cache. Our work focuses on verifying the isolation of disk storage [43,44].

7   Conclusion and Future Work

In this chapter, we present the requirements of storage isolation in the cloud from the perspective of cloud users. Next, we introduce two Proof of Isolation (PoI) schemes to allow cloud users technically verify the implementation of storage isolation without any cooperation from cloud providers. PoI schemes provide cloud users more observability of the cloud-managed isolation. In the future, we will extend our isolation schemes to work on more diverse storage media, such as SSD (Solid State Drive) and RAID, and study their performance.

Acknowledgements This material is based upon work supported by the National Science Foundation under grant CT-20013A, by US Army Research Office under MURI grant W911NF-09-1-0525 and DURIP grant W911NF-11-1-0340, and by the Office of Naval Research under grant N0014-11-1-0471.

References

1. A. K. Fischman, A. H. Vermeulen: Keymap service architecture for a distributed storage system (2010)
2. Amazon Simple Storage Service (S3): URL http://aws.amazon.com/s3/
3. Amazon Web Services: URL aws.amazon.com
4. apgbfm, http://linux.die.net/man/1/apgbfm: URL http://linux.die.net/man/1/apgbfm
5. Ateniese, G., Burns, R., Curtmola, R., Herring, J., Kissner, L., Peterson, Z., Song, D.: Provable data possession at untrusted stores. In: Proceedings of the 14th ACM conference on Computer and communications security, CCS '07, pp. 598–609. ACM, New York, NY, USA (2007). DOI 10.1145/1315245.1315318. URL http://doi.acm.org/10.1145/1315245.1315318
6. Azab, A.M., Ning, P., Wang, Z., Jiang, X., Zhang, X., Skalsky, N.C.: Hypersentry: enabling stealthy in-context measurement of hypervisor integrity. In: Proceedings of the 17th ACM conference on Computer and communications security, CCS '10, pp. 38–49. ACM, New York, NY, USA (2010). DOI 10.1145/1866307.1866313. URL http://doi.acm.org/10.1145/1866307.1866313
7. Barham, P., Dragovic, B., Fraser, K., Hand, S., Harris, T.L., Ho, A., Neugebauer, R., Pratt, I., Warfield, A.: Xen and the art of virtualization. In: SOSP, pp. 164–177 (2003)

8. Benson, K., Dowsley, R., Shacham, H.: Do you know where your cloud files are? In: CCSW, pp. 73–82 (2011)
9. Bloom, B.H.: Space/time trade-offs in hash coding with allowable errors. Commun. ACM **13**(7), 422–426 (1970)
10. Bovet, D.P., Cesati, M.: Understanding the Linux Kernel - from I/O ports to process management: covers version 2.6 (3. ed.). O'Reilly (2005)
11. Bowers, K.D., van Dijk, M., Juels, A., Oprea, A., Rivest, R.L.: How to tell if your cloud files are vulnerable to drive crashes. In: ACM Conference on Computer and Communications Security, pp. 501–514 (2011)
12. Bowers, K.D., Juels, A., Oprea, A.: Hail: a high-availability and integrity layer for cloud storage. In: Proceedings of the 16th ACM conference on Computer and communications security, CCS '09, pp. 187–198. ACM, New York, NY, USA (2009). DOI 10.1145/1653662. 1653686. URL http://doi.acm.org/10.1145/1653662.1653686
13. Brewer, D.F.C., Nash, M.J.: The chinese wall security policy. In: IEEE Symposium on Security and Privacy, pp. 206–214 (1989)
14. Butt, S., Lagar-Cavilla, H.A., Srivastava, A., Ganapathy, V.: Self-service cloud computing. In: ACM Conference on Computer and Communications Security, pp. 253–264 (2012)
15. Calder, B., Wang, J., Ogus, A., Nilakantan, N., Skjolsvold, A., McKelvie, S., Xu, Y., Srivastav, S., Wu, J., Simitci, H., Haridas, J., Uddaraju, C., Khatri, H., Edwards, A., Bedekar, V., Mainali, S., Abbasi, R., Agarwal, A., ul Haq, M.F., ul Haq, M.I., Bhardwaj, D., Dayanand, S., Adusumilli, A., McNett, M., Sankaran, S., Manivannan, K., Rigas, L.: Windows azure storage: a highly available cloud storage service with strong consistency. In: SOSP, pp. 143–157 (2011)
16. Chen, B., Curtmola, R.: Towards self-repairing replication-based storage systems using untrusted clouds. In: Proceedings of the third ACM conference on Data and application security and privacy, CODASPY '13, pp. 377–388. ACM, New York, NY, USA (2013). DOI 10.1145/2435349.2435402. URL http://doi.acm.org/10.1145/2435349.2435402
17. Cloud Security Alliance: The notorious nine: Cloud computing top threats in 2013 (2013)
18. Curtmola, R., Garay, J., Kamara, S., Ostrovsky, R.: Searchable symmetric encryption: improved definitions and efficient constructions. In: Proceedings of the 13th ACM conference on Computer and communications security, CCS '06, pp. 79–88. ACM, New York, NY, USA (2006). DOI 10.1145/1180405.1180417. URL http://doi.acm.org/10.1145/1180405.1180417
19. Curtmola, R., Khan, O., Burns, R., Ateniese, G.: Mr-pdp: Multiple-replica provable data possession. In: Proceedings of the 2008 The 28th International Conference on Distributed Computing Systems, ICDCS '08, pp. 411–420. IEEE Computer Society, Washington, DC, USA (2008). DOI 10.1109/ICDCS.2008.68. URL http://dx.doi.org/10.1109/ICDCS.2008.68
20. Dan@AWS: Best Practices for Using Amazon S3 (2009). URL http://aws.amazon.com/articles/1904
21. Dent, A.W.: The cramer-shoup encryption scheme is plaintext aware in the standard model. In: EUROCRYPT, pp. 289–307 (2006)
22. Dijk, M.V., Juels, A., Oprea, A., Rivest, R.L., Stefanov, E., Triandopoulos, N.: Hourglass schemes: How to prove that cloud files are encrypted. In: ACM Conference on Computer and Communications Security (2012)
23. Dodis, Y., Vadhan, S.P., Wichs, D.: Proofs of retrievability via hardness amplification. In: Theory of Cryptography Conference, pp. 109–127 (2009)
24. Erway, C., Küpçü, A., Papamanthou, C., Tamassia, R.: Dynamic provable data possession. In: Proceedings of the 16th ACM conference on Computer and communications security, CCS '09, pp. 213–222. ACM, New York, NY, USA (2009). DOI 10.1145/1653662.1653688. URL http://doi.acm.org/10.1145/1653662.1653688
25. Eucalyptus, http://www.eucalyptus.com: URL www.eucalyptus.com
26. Garfinkel, T., Pfaff, B., Chow, J., Rosenblum, M., Boneh, D.: Terra: a virtual machine-based platform for trusted computing. SIGOPS Oper. Syst. Rev. **37**(5), 193–206 (2003). DOI 10. 1145/1165389.945464. URL http://doi.acm.org/10.1145/1165389.945464
27. Gartiner, Inc.: Forecast overview: Public cloud services, worldwide, 2011–2016, 4q12 update (2013)

28. Ghemawat, S., Gobioff, H., Leung, S.T.: The google file system. In: SOSP, pp. 29–43 (2003)
29. III, G.G.R., Roussev, V.: Scalpel: A frugal, high performance file carver. In: DFRWS (2005)
30. Jacob, B., Ng, S., Wang, D.: Memory Systems: Cache, DRAM, Disk. Morgan Kaufmann Publishers Inc. (2007)
31. Jhawar, R., Piuri, V.: Fault tolerance management in iaas clouds. In: Proc. of the 1st IEEE-AESS Conference in Europe about Space and Satellite Telecommunications (ESTEL 2012), ESTEL 2012. Rome, Italy (2012)
32. Juels, A., Oprea, A.: New approaches to security and availability for cloud data. Commun. ACM **56**(2), 64–73 (2013). DOI 10.1145/2408776.2408793. URL http://doi.acm.org/10.1145/2408776.2408793
33. Keller, E., Szefer, J., Rexford, J., Lee, R.B.: Nohype: virtualized cloud infrastructure without the virtualization. In: Proceedings of the 37th annual international symposium on Computer architecture, ISCA '10, pp. 350–361. ACM, New York, NY, USA (2010). DOI 10.1145/1815961.1816010. URL http://doi.acm.org/10.1145/1815961.1816010
34. Ristenpart, T., Tromer, E., Shacham, H., Savage, S.: Hey, you, get off of my cloud: exploring information leakage in third-party compute clouds. In: ACM Conference on Computer and Communications Security, pp. 199–212 (2009)
35. Shah, M.A., Swaminathan, R., Baker, M.: Privacy-preserving audit and extraction of digital contents. IACR Cryptology ePrint Archive **2008**, 186 (2008)
36. Silberschatz, A., Galvin, P.B., Gagne, G.: Operating system concepts (7. ed.). Wiley (2005)
37. Spafford, E.: Opus: Preventing weak password choices
38. di Vimercati, S.D.C., Foresti, S., Jajodia, S., Paraboschi, S., Samarati, P.: Over-encryption: management of access control evolution on outsourced data. In: Proceedings of the 33rd international conference on Very large data bases, VLDB '07, pp. 123–134. VLDB Endowment (2007). URL http://dl.acm.org/citation.cfm?id=1325851.1325869
39. di Vimercati, S.D.C., Foresti, S., Jajodia, S., Paraboschi, S., Samarati, P.: Support for write privileges on outsourced data. In: SEC, pp. 199–210 (2012)
40. Wang, C., Ren, K., Wang, J., Urs, K.M.R.: Harnessing the cloud for securely solving large-scale systems of linear equations. In: ICDCS, pp. 549–558 (2011)
41. Wang, Q., Ren, K., Yu, S., Lou, W.: Dependable and secure sensor data storage with dynamic integrity assurance. TOSN **8**(1), 9 (2011)
42. Wang, Z., Jiang, X.: Hypersafe: A lightweight approach to provide lifetime hypervisor control-flow integrity. In: Proceedings of the 2010 IEEE Symposium on Security and Privacy, SP '10, pp. 380–395. IEEE Computer Society, Washington, DC, USA (2010). DOI 10.1109/SP.2010.30. URL http://dx.doi.org/10.1109/SP.2010.30
43. Wang, Z., Sun, K., Jajodia, S., Jing, J.: Disk storage isolation and verification in cloud. In: Globecom 2012. Anaheim, CA, USA (2012)
44. Wang, Z., Sun, K., Jajodia, S., Jing, J.: Terracheck: Verification of dedicated cloud storage. In: 27th Annual IFIP WG 11.3 Working Conference on Data and Applications Security and Privacy (DBSec '13). Newark, NJ, USA (2013)
45. Wang, Z., Sun, K., Jajodia, S., Jing, J.: Verification of data redundancy in cloud storage. In: Proceedings of the 2013 International Workshop on Security in Cloud Computing (To Appear)
46. Watson, G.J., Safavi-Naini, R., Alimomeni, M., Locasto, M.E., Narayan, S.: Lost: location based storage. In: Proceedings of the 2012 ACM Workshop on Cloud computing security workshop, CCSW '12, pp. 59–70. ACM, New York, NY, USA (2012). DOI 10.1145/2381913.2381926. URL http://doi.acm.org/10.1145/2381913.2381926
47. Wu, Z., Xu, Z., Wang, H.: Whispers in the hyper-space: High-speed covert channel attacks in the cloud. In: the 21st USENIX Security Symposium (Security'12) (2012)
48. Xiao, J., Xu, Z., Huang, H., Wang, H.: A covert channel construction in a virtualized environment. In: ACM Conference on Computer and Communications Security, pp. 1040–1042 (2012)
49. Xu, Y., Bailey, M., Jahanian, F., Joshi, K.R., Hiltunen, M.A., Schlichting, R.D.: An exploration of l2 cache covert channels in virtualized environments. In: CCSW, pp. 29–40 (2011)

50. Yu, S., Wang, C., Ren, K., Lou, W.: Achieving secure, scalable, and fine-grained data access control in cloud computing. In: INFOCOM, pp. 534–542 (2010)
51. Zhang, F., Chen, J., Chen, H., Zang, B.: Cloudvisor: retrofitting protection of virtual machines in multi-tenant cloud with nested virtualization. In: Proceedings of the Twenty-Third ACM Symposium on Operating Systems Principles, SOSP '11, pp. 203–216. ACM, New York, NY, USA (2011). DOI 10.1145/2043556.2043576. URL http://doi.acm.org/10.1145/2043556. 2043576
52. Zhang, Y., Juels, A., Oprea, A., Reiter, M.K.: Homealone: Co-residency detection in the cloud via side-channel analysis. In: IEEE Symposium on Security and Privacy, pp. 313–328 (2011)
53. Zhang, Y., Juels, A., Reiter, M.K., Ristenpart, T.: Cross-vm side channels and their use to extract private keys. In: Proceedings of the 2012 ACM conference on Computer and communications security, CCS '12, pp. 305–316. ACM, New York, NY, USA (2012). DOI 10.1145/2382196.2382230. URL http://doi.acm.org/10.1145/2382196.2382230

Selective and Fine-Grained Access to Data in the Cloud

Sabrina De Capitani di Vimercati, Sara Foresti, and Pierangela Samarati

Abstract This chapter surveys some of the research results related to the protection and efficient access to data stored and managed by external cloud servers. We first provide an overview of the security and privacy problems and challenges that need to be considered, and then illustrate emerging approaches for protecting data externally stored, and for enforcing fine-grained (queries) and selective (access control) accesses on them. Finally, we show how the combined application of the solutions discussed may introduce privacy problems that should be carefully considered.

1 Introduction

Emerging paradigms like data outsourcing and cloud computing have attracted the attention of the research and industrial communities thanks to their advantages in terms of reduced costs for IT resources, increased storage, flexibility in resource management, and higher scalability. These advantages however do not come for free. In fact, these emerging paradigms also introduce a number of privacy and security risks that may represent a serious obstacle for their wide development and for their acceptance by users and companies. Security and privacy may relate to different aspects, including resources, data and network isolation, attacks to the cloud servers, compliance with laws and regulations, reliability of applications and services, protection of the confidentiality and integrity of data, and data availability (e.g., [11,19,38,39,44]). In this chapter, we will provide an overview of the problems and solutions related to the proper protection of the confidentiality of the data and to the efficient access to them. These problems become quite complex in a

S. De Capitani di Vimercati • S. Foresti • P. Samarati (✉)
Università degli Studi di Milano – Dipartimento di Informatica
Via Bramante 65, 26013 Crema, Italy
e-mail: pierangela.samarati@unimi.it

S. Jajodia et al. (eds.), *Secure Cloud Computing*, DOI 10.1007/978-1-4614-9278-8_6,
© Springer Science+Business Media New York 2014

cloud scenario since users release and store their data on external servers that are outside their control. Also, the advances in the Information and Communication Technologies (ICTs), including the possibility of combining and analyzing more information from several data sources, intensify the data protection problem.

The protection of potentially sensitive data stored and managed by external cloud servers poses interesting challenges. In fact, cloud servers can be characterized by different levels of trust, ranging from *honest-but-curious* servers, meaning that they are trusted for the management of the data but cannot know (access) the data they store, to servers that may intentionally behave improperly in the storing and processing of the data. Data are therefore encrypted by the data owner before their storage in the cloud. Since cloud servers cannot decrypt data, there is the problem of defining techniques (e.g., indexes) for enforcing fine-grained retrieval of the data without compromising their privacy. However, techniques that support effective and efficient accesses to the outsourced data are not enough. In fact, if the server (or a generic observer) monitors the accesses by users, it may be able to draw inferences on which data have been accessed. Also, the presence of multiple users who rely on external storage for making their data available to others, introduces the problem of enforcing selective (read and write) access to the outsourced data.

In this chapter, after a brief overview of the different security and privacy problems that can arise in a cloud computing scenario, we survey and discuss research results related to the protection of the privacy of outsourced data, and on the fine-grained and selective retrieval of data. We also show that the combination of techniques addressing a specific problem can cause privacy breaches. The remainder of the chapter is organized as follows. Section 2 provides an overview of the main security and privacy risks in a cloud scenario. Section 3 illustrates some approaches and open issues related to the protection of data confidentiality, indexing for query support, and selective access. Section 4 describes how the combination of indexes for query support and fragments for data confidentiality can cause leakage of confidential information. Section 5 describes how the combination of indexes and selective encryption may allow unauthorized users to infer (or reduce their uncertainty on) information that they are not authorized to access. Finally, Sect. 6 provides our conclusions.

2   Security and Privacy in the Cloud

The security and privacy problems that arise when data are stored at external servers have been the subject of many studies (e.g., [22, 31, 37]). Depending on the considered aspect, the security and privacy problems can be related to: (i) the privacy of users; (ii) the privacy and integrity of data storage; (iii) the privacy and integrity of queries; and (iv) the secure and private data computations involving multiple providers. Figure 1 illustrates the reference cloud scenario where users interact with external cloud servers for accessing data and services, and different

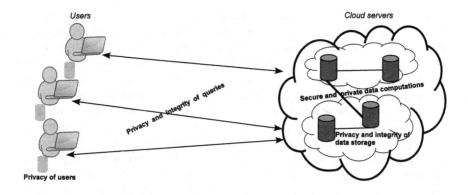

Fig. 1 Reference cloud scenario

cloud servers collaborate for offering a service or responding to a query. In the remainder of this section, we provide a description of each of the four categories of security and privacy problems mentioned above.

Privacy of users. Cloud services allow users to access applications and data on demand every-time they need. To successfully complete the required access, users may be asked to provide some information while however wishing to protect their identities for privacy reasons. For instance, a user can be interested in querying a cloud server for collecting information about a given illness without revealing her identity to avoid possible correlations between the illness and herself or a person close to her. The techniques developed for supporting anonymous communication between parties and attribute-based access control can be helpful in protecting the privacy of the users. In fact, anonymous communication techniques allow users to communicate on the Internet without revealing their identities [9], meaning that an observer cannot trace who is communicating with whom, or who is interacting with which server or searching for which data. Attribute-based access control solutions allow users to access resources or data without reveling their identities [13]. The idea is that, instead of declaring their identities, users prove that they satisfy the conditions needed for the access. To this purpose, a user can disclose a *credential* (a set thereof) certifying the information necessary for the access. The server verifies whether the credential is valid and whether the information it certifies satisfies the policy regulating access to the resource. The research community has also devoted considerable attention to the use of *anonymous credentials* [16] for access control (e.g., [4]). An anonymous credential allows a user to make statements about attribute values, maintaining the values private. For instance, anonymous credentials permit to selectively release a subset of the properties in a credential or to prove that they satisfy some conditions, without revealing any information about their values. Anonymous credentials can be at the basis of a new generation of access control policy languages that can be particularly suited to open and dynamic scenarios like the cloud.

Recently, some proposals have started to address the problem of regulating the release of users' personal information according to privacy preferences expressed by the users themselves. These proposals have introduced models relying on user preferences that permit to associate a higher or lower sensitivity with the combined release of a set of properties/credentials (e.g., [5–7,40,53]). For instance, a user may consider the joint release of her name and credit card number more sensitive than the release of each information singularly taken. Although these solutions represent a first step towards the definition of a comprehensive approach for the protection of users' privacy, there are still several open issues: the development of user-friendly approaches for expressing privacy preferences; the ability of defining privacy preferences that depend on the context; and the integration of these approaches with server-side solutions supporting fine-grained policy disclosure, which permit the server to obfuscate the portions of its policies considered sensitive, while providing the user with enough information for releasing the information necessary to possibly gain access (e.g., [8]).

Privacy and integrity of data storage. When data are outsourced to an external server that is outside the control of the data owner, the protection of the confidentiality and of the integrity of the data, as well as the efficient access to them become clearly of paramount importance. In this context, the research community has been very active and produced advancements in several areas: solutions for *protecting data confidentiality* (e.g., encryption and fragmentation [1, 21, 37]); *indexes* for supporting queries (e.g., [17, 37]), solutions for supporting *selective access* to outsourced data (e.g., [24]), solutions for ensuring *data integrity* (e.g., signatures [14, 35, 43]). These approaches typically consider a scenario where a *data owner* outsources her data to an *external server* that can be trusted to properly manage the data, making them available to requesting *users*, but it is not trusted to read the content of the data it stores (i.e., *honest-but-curious* server). The outsourced data can be of any type, including files and relational tables. In the remainder of this chapter, for simplicity and without loss of generality, we will assume that the outsourced data are organized in a single relation r, stored in a (distributed) relational database. Relation r is defined over relational schema $R(a_1, \ldots, a_n)$, with attribute a_i defined over domain D_i, $i = 1, \ldots, n$. The presentation of solutions and issues related to the protection of the privacy of outsourced data will be the subject of the following sections.

Privacy and integrity of queries. Accessing information from external cloud servers and performing queries over outsourced data introduce several privacy and integrity issues. Existing data management architectures typically assume that the data obtained from distributed parties have not been tampered with, and are available only to authorized parties. Such assumptions do not apply anymore in cloud scenarios, where multi-tenant infrastructures orchestrate different services. Assurances on the fact that the privacy of the queries is preserved and that computations on data are processed in the expected way (integrity and verifiability) are becoming more and more important. In fact, there is an increasing need for novel techniques that support not only data privacy, but also the privacy of the accesses that users make on such data. This problem has been traditionally addressed by Private Information Retrieval (PIR) proposals (e.g., [18]), which provide protocols for querying a database that prevent the external server from inferring which data are being accessed. PIR solutions however have high computational complexity, and alternative approaches have been proposed. These novel approaches rely on the Oblivious RAM structure (e.g., [33, 47, 48]) or on the definition of specific tree-based data structures combined with a dynamic allocation of the data (e.g., [29, 30]). The goal is to support the access to a collection of encrypted data while preserving access and pattern confidentiality, meaning that an observer can infer neither what data are accessed nor whether two accesses aim to the same data. Besides protecting access and pattern confidentiality, it is also necessary to design mechanisms for protecting the integrity and authenticity of the computations, that is, to guarantee the correctness, completeness, and freshness of query results. Most of the techniques that can be adopted for verifying the integrity of query results operate on a single relation and are based on the idea of complementing the data with additional data structures (e.g., Merkle trees) or of introducing in the data collection fake tuples that can be efficiently checked to detect incorrect or incomplete results (e.g., [41, 46, 50–52]). Interesting aspects that need further analysis are related to the design of efficient techniques able to verify the completeness and correctness of the results of complex queries (e.g., join operations among multiple relations, possibly stored and managed by different cloud servers with different levels of trust).

Secure and private data computations. More and more emerging scenarios require different cloud servers to cooperate to the aim of sharing information and/or performing distributed computations. This sharing process can be clearly selective, meaning that different servers may have different access privileges. Recently, a significant amount of research has addressed the problem of processing distributed queries under protection requirements (e.g., [2, 15, 26]). Some proposals are based on the concept of access pattern, a profile associated with each relation/view [15]. For each attribute of the relation/view, the access pattern includes a value that may be either i for input or o for output. When accessing a relation, the values for all i attributes must be supplied to obtain the corresponding values of o attributes. Sovereign joins [2] are an alternative solution for securely processing joins. This solution is based on a secure coprocessor, which is involved in query execution, and exploits cryptography. Other approaches propose an authorization model to regulate the view that each server can have on the data, ensuring that query computation exposes to each server only the data that the server can view [26]. The idea is that a relation (base or resulting from the evaluation of a query) can be released to a server whenever the information it carries (either directly or indirectly when the relation has been obtained as the result of a query) is visible from the receiving party. The proposed authorization model operates at the schema level and supports the definition of generic view patterns, thus nicely meeting both expressiveness and simplicity requirements.

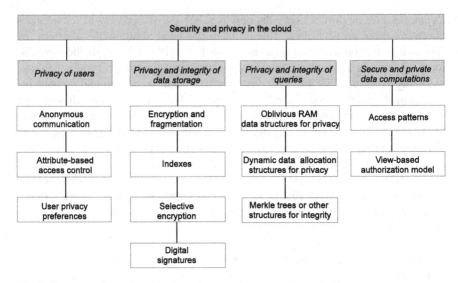

Fig. 2 Summary of security and privacy issues and corresponding solutions

Figure 2 summarizes the main categories of security and privacy issues discussed above (gray boxes) along with some of the corresponding solutions (white boxes). Note that this classification does not aim to be complete but only to provide a quick overview of the solutions mentioned.

3 Privacy of Data Storage

The problem of protecting outsourced data while enjoying effective and efficient data management and retrieval operations has attracted the attention of many researches, and several investigations have been carried out. The problem is quite complex and involves several aspects, including basic techniques for protecting data at rest (Sect. 3.1), techniques for efficiently accessing encrypted data without compromising their confidentiality (Sect. 3.2), and data-centric techniques for supporting selective access to the outsourced data without relying on the data owner and/or on the honest-but-curious server storing the data (Sect. 3.3). We now describe more in details these aspects.

3.1 Encryption and Fragmentation

The problem of protecting the confidentiality of outsourced data has been one of the first issues investigated in the data outsourcing and cloud scenarios. In fact, the risk that unauthorized parties (or even the external server itself) can access sensitive

a

PATIENTS

	SSN	Name	YoB	Job	Disease
t_1	123456789	Alice	1980	Clerk	Asthma
t_2	234567891	Bob	1980	Doctor	Asthma
t_3	345678912	Carol	1970	Nurse	Asthma
t_4	456789123	David	1970	Lawyer	Bronchitis
t_5	567891234	Eva	1970	Doctor	Bronchitis
t_6	678912345	Frank	1960	Doctor	Gastritis
t_7	789123456	Gary	1960	Teacher	Gastritis
t_8	891234567	Hilary	1960	Nurse	Diabetes

b

$c_0 = \{\texttt{SSN}\}$
$c_1 = \{\texttt{Name, Disease}\}$
$c_2 = \{\texttt{Name, Job}\}$
$c_3 = \{\texttt{Job, Disease}\}$

Fig. 3 An example of plaintext relation (**a**) and of a set of confidentiality constraints over it (**b**)

information is one of the main factors for which users (and not only) are often reluctant to adopt the cloud for storing their data. The solutions proposed to protect data confidentiality are based on *encryption* and *fragmentation*, which can be used either singularly or in combination.

Encryption consists in wrapping a protective layer of encryption around data before storing them at an external server (e.g., [17, 34, 37, 44]). Since the encryption key is known only to the data owner and to authorized users, this technique protects the data against both external (malicious) parties, and the server itself. While effective, this approach is based on the conservative assumption that all the outsourced data are equally sensitive and must therefore be protected. However, as first observed in [1, 20, 21], often data are not sensitive per se but what is sensitive is their association with other data. As an example, the list of the names of hospitalized patients and the list of diseases cured in a hospital are not sensitive. On the contrary, the association of patients' names with the illness they suffer from is highly sensitive and should therefore be kept confidential. Data confidentiality can then be achieved by properly protecting sensitive associations. Given a relation r over relation schema $R(a_1,\ldots,a_n)$, both sensitive attribute values and sensitive associations among them can be modeled through *confidentiality constraints* [1]. A confidentiality constraint c over R is a subset of the attributes in R (i.e., $c \subseteq R$), modeling a sensitive association on the values of the attributes in c. Constraint c states that, for each tuple t in r: (i) value $t[a]$ is considered sensitive per se, if c is a singleton constraint (i.e., $c = \{a\}$); (ii) the joint visibility of the values of the attributes in c is considered sensitive, if c is an association constraint (i.e., $c = \{a_i,\ldots,a_j\}$). For instance, Fig. 3b illustrates a set of confidentiality constraints over relation PATIENTS in Fig. 3a. Singleton constraint c_0 states that the list of Social Security Numbers is considered sensitive per se. The remaining association constraints state that the association of: patients' name with the disease they suffer from (c_1), patients' names with their job (c_2), and patients' job with their disease (c_3) are considered sensitive, respectively.

Given a relation r and a set C of confidentiality constraints over it, the goal is to combine fragmentation and encryption techniques to guarantee that sensitive values and sensitive associations are properly obfuscated. Intuitively, singleton

constraints are enforced by encrypting the attribute values before outsourcing or by
not outsourcing the attribute values at all. Association constraints are enforced by
partitioning the attributes in R in different subsets (*fragments*), or by not releasing
(in clear form) at least one of the attributes in the constraint. A fragmentation
correctly enforces the confidentiality constraints if no fragment stored at the external
server represents all the attributes in a constraint in clear form, and fragments cannot
be joined by unauthorized users.

The approaches that rely on fragmentation and encryption for enforcing confidentiality constraints differ in how they guarantee that fragments cannot be joined,
and in how they protect attribute values considered sensitive per se. Based on these
differences, existing techniques can be classified as follows.

- *Non-communicating pair of servers* [1]. The data owner partitions relation R in
  two fragments, F_1 and F_2, stored at two non-communicating servers. Those
  attributes that cannot be stored at any of the two servers without violating
  confidentiality constraints are encoded and the result is stored at the two servers
  (e.g., the attribute values are encrypted via one-time-pad, and the result of
  encryption is stored at one server, while the key is stored at the other one).
  Only users who can access both the versions of an encoded attribute can
  reconstruct its plaintext values. Figure 4 illustrates an example of fragmentation
  for relation PATIENTS in Fig. 3a that satisfies the confidentiality constraints in
  Fig. 3b. It is composed of fragments $F_1 = \{\underline{\texttt{tid}}, \texttt{Name}, \texttt{YoB}, \texttt{SSN}^k, \texttt{Disease}^k\}$
  and $F_2 = \{\underline{\texttt{tid}}, \texttt{Job}, \texttt{SSN}^k, \texttt{Disease}^k\}$. Attribute $\texttt{tid}$ is a tuple identifier
  introduced in the two fragments to permit authorized users to correctly join F_1
  and F_2 to reconstruct the original content of relation PATIENTS. Attributes $\texttt{SSN}^k$
  and $\texttt{Disease}^k$ represent the encoded version of attributes $\texttt{SSN}$ and $\texttt{Disease}$,
  respectively.
- *Multiple fragments* [21]. The data owner partitions relation R in an arbitrary
  set of fragments, $\{F_1, \ldots, F_m\}$, possibly stored at the same server. Fragments
  are disjoint, meaning that no attribute is represented in clear form in more than
  one fragment. All the attributes in R that are not represented in clear form in
  a fragment are however represented in encrypted form in the fragment (i.e.,
  each fragment is complete). Figure 4 illustrates an example of fragmentation
  for relation PATIENTS in Fig. 3a that satisfies the confidentiality constraints in
  Fig. 3b. It is composed of three fragments: $F_1 = \{\underline{\texttt{salt}}, \texttt{enc}, \texttt{Name}, \texttt{YoB}\}$,
  $F_2 = \{\underline{\texttt{salt}}, \texttt{enc}, \texttt{Job}\}$, and $F_3 = \{\texttt{salt}, \texttt{enc}, \texttt{Disease}\}$. Attribute
  $\texttt{salt}$ is a randomly chosen value, different for each tuple in each fragment.
  Attribute $\texttt{enc}$ is the result of the encryption of the attributes in the original
  relation that are not represented in clear form in the fragment, concatenated with
  $\texttt{salt}$. For readability, in all our examples tuples in fragments are in the same
  order as in the original relation, even if the order in which tuples are stored in
  fragments is independent from the order in which they appear in the original
  relation. Note that the possibility of using an arbitrary number of fragments has
  the advantage that all attributes that are not involved in singleton constraints can
  be represented in clear form in a fragment (in the worst case, we can have a
  fragment for each attribute), as it is visible from the example above.

F_1

tid	Name	YoB	SSN^k	Disease^k
1	Alice	1980	jdkis	hyaf4k
2	Bob	1980	u9hs9	j97;qx
3	Carol	1970	j9und	9jp'md
4	David	1970	p0vp8	p;nd92
5	Eva	1970	8nn[	0-mw-n
6	Frank	1960	j9jMK	wqp9[i
7	Gary	1960	87l'D	L0MB2G
8	Hilary	1960	8pm}n	@h8hwu

F_2

tid	Job	SSN^k	Disease^k
1	Clerk	uwq8hd	jsd7ql
2	Doctor	j-0.dl;	0],nid
3	Nurse	8ojqdkf	j-0/?n
4	Lawyer	j0i12nd	5lkdpq
5	Doctor	mj[9;'s	j0982e
6	Doctor	aQ14l[	jnd%d
7	Teacher	8qsdQW	OP['
8	NURSE	0890UD	UP0D@

Non-communicating pair of servers (two can keep a secret) [1]

F_1

salt	enc	Name	YoB
s_{11}	Bd6!l3	Alice	1980
s_{12}	Oij3X.	Bob	1980
s_{13}	9kEf6?	Carol	1970
s_{14}	ker5/2	David	1970
s_{15}	C:mE91	Eva	1970
s_{16}	4lDwqz	Frank	1960
s_{17}	me3,op	Gary	1960
s_{18}	zWf4g>	Hilary	1960

F_2

salt	enc	Job
s_{21}	8de6TO	Clerk
s_{22}	X'mlE3	Doctor
s_{23}	wq.vy0	Nurse
s_{24}	nh=I3a	Lawyer
s_{25}	hh%kj)	Doctor
s_{26}	;vf5eS	Doctor
s_{27}	e4+YUp	Teacher
s_{28}	pgt6eC	Nurse

F_3

salt	enc	Disease
s_{31}	ew3)V!	Asthma
s_{32}	LkEd69	Asthma
s_{33}	w8vd66	Asthma
s_{34}	1"qPdd	Bronchitis
s_{35}	(mn2eW	Bronchitis
s_{36}	wD}x1X	Gastritis
s_{37}	0opEl	Gastritis
s_{38}	Sw@Fez	Diabetes

Multiple fragments [21]

F_o

tid	SSN	Job	Disease
1	123456789	Clerk	Asthma
2	234567891	Doctor	Asthma
3	345678912	Nurse	Asthma
4	456789123	Lawyer	Bronchitis
5	567891234	Doctor	Bronchitis
6	678912345	Doctor	Gastritis
7	789123456	Teacher	Gastritis
8	891234567	Nurse	Diabetes

F_s

tid	Name	YoB
1	Alice	1980
2	Bob	1980
3	Carol	1970
4	David	1970
5	Eva	1970
6	Frank	1960
7	Gary	1960
8	Hilary	1960

Departing from encryption (keep a few) [20]

Fig. 4 An example of fragmentation of relation PATIENTS in Fig. 3a according to the non-communication pair of servers, multiple fragments, and departing from encryption scenarios

- *Departing from encryption* [20]. The data owner partitions relation R in two fragments, F_o and F_s, and locally stores one of them (F_o), while the other is outsourced to an external server (F_s). Since only authorized users can access F_o, neither the server nor unauthorized users can join F_o and F_s to possibly reconstruct sensitive associations. Note that fragment F_o can both include attributes considered sensitive per se and sensitive associations. This solution completely departs from encryption, but it requires the data owner to locally store a portion of her data and to cooperate with the external server in query evaluation. Figure 4 illustrates an example of fragmentation for relation PATIENTS in Fig. 3a that satisfies the confidentiality constraints in Fig. 3b. It is composed of fragment $F_o = \{\underline{tid}, SSN, Job, Disease\}$ stored at the data owner side, and fragment $F_s = \{\underline{tid}, Name, YoB\}$ stored at the external server side.

PATIENTS^k

tid	enc	I_n	I_y	I_j	I_d
1	T8/lO?	π	α	δ	η
2	1wfTg<	π	α	ε	θ
3	vFe!d2	ρ	β	δ	ω
4	f3iJ:y	ρ	β	ζ	κ
5	;x0d9D	σ	β	ε	λ
6	kO6i)G	σ	γ	ε	μ
7	u2eW[b	τ	γ	ζ	ν
8	vY7'.1	τ	γ	δ	ξ

Fig. 5 An example of encrypted and indexed version of relation PATIENTS in Fig. 3a

Encryption, fragmentation, and their combinations are powerful mechanisms for protecting data confidentiality. However, there are still several open issues that need to be further investigated. In fact, fragmentation and encryption break associations among attribute values that could be considered of interest for final recipients, thus compromising the utility of released data. Alternative solutions that protect data while preserving a certain utility are therefore needed [25]. Also, confidentiality constraints are defined over relation schemas, while they could be extended to operate at the instance level (i.e., at the attribute values level). We also observe that encryption and fragmentation work under the assumption that the data collection never changes. Techniques supporting updates to the outsourced data collection without compromising confidentiality still need to be designed.

3.2 Indexes

The adoption of encryption for protecting data confidentiality makes query execution difficult. In fact, confidentiality demands that data decryption must be possible only at the user side. Solutions have been then developed to enable cloud servers to execute queries directly on encrypted data. These solutions complement the outsourced relation with a set of *indexes*, which are metadata information built on the plaintext values of the attributes [44]. Formally, a relation r, defined over schema $R(a_1, \ldots, a_n)$, is represented at the server side through an encrypted relation r^k over schema $R^k(\underline{tid}, enc, I_{i_1}, \ldots, I_{i_j})$. Attribute tid is a numerical attribute added to the original relation and acting as a primary key. Attribute enc represents the encrypted tuple. Attribute I_{i_l}, $l = 1, \ldots, j$, is the index defined over attribute a_{i_l} in R. Each tuple t in r is represented by an encrypted tuple t^k in r^k where $t^k[enc] = E_k(t)$, with E a symmetric encryption function with key k, and $t^k[I_{i_l}] = \iota(t[a_{i_l}])$, with ι an index function defined over D_{i_l}. Note that R^k has an index only for those attributes in R on which conditions need to be evaluated. Figure 5 illustrates an example of encrypted and indexed version of relation PATIENTS in Fig. 3a, with indexes over attributes Name (I_n), YoB (I_y), Job (I_j), and Disease (I_d).

Different indexing techniques have been proposed in the literature to support different kinds of conditions. Most of these indexing techniques can be classified in the following three classes, depending on how the corresponding index function ι maps the original values to the corresponding index values.

- *Direct index.* Index function ι maps each plaintext value to a different index value and vice versa. An example of direct index is represented by *encryption-based indexes* (e.g., [22]). For each tuple $t \in r$, the value of index I, defined over attribute a, is computed as $\iota(t[a]) = E_k(t[a])$. For instance, index I_y in relation PATIENTS^k in Fig. 5 represents an example of direct index over attribute YOB of relation PATIENTS in Fig. 3a.

- *Bucket-based index.* Index function ι maps different plaintext values to the same index value, generating collisions. Each plaintext value is however mapped to only one index value. An example of bucket-based index is represented by *partition-based indexes*, which partition the domain D of attribute a into non-overlapping subsets of contiguous values, and associate a label with each partition (e.g., [37]). For each tuple $t \in r$, the value of index I, defined over attribute a, corresponds to the label of the unique partition to which value $t[a]$ belongs. For instance, index I_n in relation PATIENTS^k in Fig. 5 represents an example of partition-based index over attribute Name of relation PATIENTS in Fig. 3a. The domain of attribute Name has been partitioned in four intervals depending on the initial of the name, with labels: π for names with initial in the range [A,B], ρ for names with initial in the range [C,D], σ for names with initial in the range [E,F], and τ for names with initial in the range [G,H]. Another example of bucket-based index is represented by the *hash-based indexes* (e.g., [17]). For each tuple $t \in r$, the value of index I, defined over attribute a, is computed as $\iota(t[a]) = h(t[a])$, where h is a secure hash function that generates collisions. For instance, index I_j in relation PATIENTS^k in Fig. 5 represents an example of hash-based index over attribute Job of relation PATIENTS in Fig. 3a. The hash function adopted generates collisions and, in particular, is defined as follows: $h(\text{Clerk}) = h(\text{Nurse}) = \delta$, $h(\text{Doctor}) = \varepsilon$, and $h(\text{Lawyer}) = h(\text{Teacher}) = \zeta$.

- *Flattened index.* Index function ι maps each plaintext value to a set of index values to guarantee that all index values have the same number of occurrences (flattening). Each index value represents one plaintext value only. The index can be obtained by applying an encryption function to the plaintext values of the attribute and a post processing that flattens the distribution of the index values (e.g., [45]). For instance, index I_d in relation PATIENTS^k in Fig. 5 represents an example of flattened index over attribute Disease of relation PATIENTS in Fig. 3a, where each index value has exactly one occurrence.

These indexing techniques support the partial evaluation at the server-side of SQL queries. Given a query q, it is translated into a query q_s executed at the server side on the encrypted relation, and a query q_c executed at the client side on the decrypted result of q_s. Query q_c includes all conditions that cannot be evaluated by the server and aims at eventually discarding all *spurious tuples* returned by q_s, that is, all tuples that do not satisfy the original query submitted by the user.

The translation of query q into query q_s and q_c depends both on the kind of indexes defined for the attributes involved in the query and on the kind of query. As an example, consider query $q = $ "SELECT Att FROM R WHERE $Cond$", where $Att \subseteq R$ and $Cond$ is a set of equality conditions of the form $a = v$, with $a \in R$ and v a constant value in the domain D of a. Each equality condition $a = v$ is translated into an equivalent condition I IN $\iota(v)$, with I the index defined over a and ι the corresponding index function. Query q is then translated into query $q_s = $ "SELECT enc FROM R^k WHERE $Cond^k$", where $Cond^k$ includes, for each equality condition $a = v$, the equivalent condition I IN $\iota(v)$. The client will decrypt the result of q_s computed by the server, and will execute query q_c that eliminates spurious tuples, evaluates conditions that cannot be performed at the server side, and projects only the attributes in Att to obtain the result of q. For instance, query $q = $ SELECT Name FROM PATIENTS WHERE Job = 'Nurse' AND Disease = 'Asthma' is translated into query $q_s = $ SELECT enc FROM PATIENTS^k WHERE $I_j = \delta$ AND $I_d \in \{\eta, \theta, \omega\}$, which returns the first and third tuples in Fig. 5. The client then filters spurious tuples from the result of q_s by evaluating query $q_c = $ SELECT Name FROM $D_k(Res^k)$ WHERE Job = 'Nurse', where Res^k is the encrypted result returned by the server and D the symmetric decryption function with key k. Query q_c returns the value of attribute Name of tuple t_1 in Fig. 3a, which corresponds to the result of the original query q formulated by the user.

Indexing techniques specifically aimed at supporting the efficient evaluation of range conditions are based on order preserving encryption schemas (e.g., [3, 45]). Indexes that support aggregate functions and the basic arithmetic operators (i.e., $+, -, \times$) rely on homomorphic encryption techniques (e.g., [32, 36]). Additional indexing techniques, which cannot be classified as mentioned above, are based, for example, on the definition of data structures (e.g., $B+$-tree) coupled with the encrypted relation and stored at the server [22].

The definition of indexes over outsourced relations must balance precision in query evaluation and privacy of the data [17]. In fact, more precise indexes provide more efficient query execution, at the price of a greater exposure to possible privacy violations. Also, the number of indexes complementing an outsourced relation should be carefully tuned, since each additional index may cause a rapid growth to the risk of privacy violations.

3.3 Selective Encryption

In many real-world systems, different users may have different privileges on the outsourced data. Traditional access control architectures are based on the presence of a trusted component, called *reference monitor*, that is in charge of enforcing the access control policy defined by the data owner. In a cloud scenario, however, neither the data owner (for efficiency reasons) nor the cloud server storing the data (for privacy reasons) can enforce the access control policy. An interesting solution addressing this issue consists in adopting *selective encryption* [24], meaning that

	t_1	t_2	t_3	t_4	t_5	t_6	t_7	t_8
A	1	0	0	1	0	1	1	0
B	0	1	0	1	1	1	1	0
C	0	0	0	1	0	1	1	1
D	0	1	1	1	1	1	0	0
E	0	1	0	0	1	1	1	0

Fig. 6 An example of access matrix regulating access to relation PATIENTS in Fig. 3a

different keys are used for encrypting different data. The encryption keys are then (directly or indirectly) released only to the users authorized to access the corresponding data. The idea of using different keys for enforcing access control is not new and has been first introduced in other contexts. For instance, in [42] the authors propose to store encrypted XML documents on (potentially insecure and vulnerable) Web servers. The decisions about access rights to different portions of an XML document can be made by the document creator and are immediately applied to the XML document by using different encryption keys for different portions of the same XML document. To enforce access restrictions, users then obtain only the keys associated with the portions of XML documents for which they have an access right. Other proposals put forward the idea of using hierarchical-based access control in the context of distributed environments and broadcast pay tv content (e.g., [12, 49]). In the remainder of this section, we describe the main characteristics of the selective encryption approach in [24], specifically designed for the cloud scenario.

Given a set U of users and a relation r, the authorization policy regulating access to tuples in r is represented by an access matrix M, with a row for each user $u \in U$ and a column for each tuple $t \in r$. Cell $M[u,t]$ is equal to 1 (0, respectively), if user u can (cannot, respectively) access tuple t. For each tuple t, $acl(t)$ denotes the set of users who can access it (i.e., its access control list). For instance, Fig. 6 illustrates an example of access matrix regulating access to the tuples of relation PATIENTS in Fig. 3a by a set $U = \{A, B, C, D, E\}$ of users.

The authorization policy defined by the data owner is translated into an *equivalent encryption policy*. The encryption policy regulates keys used to encrypt tuples as well as key distribution to users and must be equivalent to the access control policy defined by the data owner, that is, each user can decrypt all and only the tuples she is authorized to access.

The translation of an authorization policy into an equivalent encryption policy is driven by two requirements: (i) each user must manage at most one key, and (ii) each tuple must be encrypted at most once (i.e., no replication). To satisfy these two desiderata, the approach in [24] adopts a *key derivation technique* based on public tokens, which permit to compute the value of an encryption key starting from the knowledge of another key and a piece of publicly available information [10]. Each key k_i is associated with a public label l_i and, given keys k_i and k_j, token $token_{i,j}$ is computed as $k_j \oplus h(k_i, l_j)$, with $\oplus$ the bitwise xor operator, and h a deterministic cryptographic function. Token $token_{i,j}$ permits to derive key k_j from k_i and public label l_j. Key derivation techniques are based on the definition of a *key derivation*

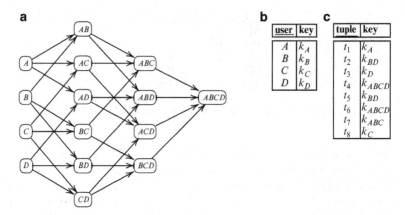

Fig. 7 An example of encryption policy equivalent to the access control policy in Fig. 6, considering the subset $\{A,B,C,D\}$ of users

graph, specifying which keys can be derived from other keys. A key derivation graph is a directed acyclic graph whose vertices represent keys, and whose edges represent tokens. The existence of a path from key k_i to key k_j in the key derivation graph denotes the fact that k_j can be (directly or indirectly, via a chain of tokens) derived from k_i. A key derivation graph correctly enforces an authorization policy M if each user $u_i \in U$ can derive, starting from the key she knows, the keys used to encrypt all and only the tuples $t_j \in r$ that she can access (i.e., with $M[u_i,t_j]=1$). To define such a graph, the idea is to exploit the set containment relationship $\subseteq$ over U. A key derivation graph induced by $\subseteq$ over U has a vertex for each subset of users in U and a path from vertex v_i to vertex v_j if v_i represents a subset of the users represented by v_j. The correct enforcement of the policy is guaranteed if each user knows the key of the vertex representing herself in the graph, and each tuple is encrypted with the key of the vertex representing its acl. For instance, consider the portion of the access matrix in Fig. 6 defined for the subset $\{A,B,C,D\}$ of users. The encryption policy in Fig. 7 is equivalent to the access control policy represented by the first four rows in Fig. 6. For readability, each vertex in the graph of Fig. 7 is labeled with the set of users it represents. As an example, user A can decrypt tuples t_1, t_4, t_6, and t_7 since she can derive, starting from vertex labeled A, the keys with which these tuples are encrypted.

Although effective for enforcing the authorization policy, the solution above defines more keys and tokens than necessary. Since the number of tokens in the system influences the access time, the proposal in [24] reduces the number of tokens by removing from the key derivation graph the vertices and edges that are not necessary to enforce M. The problem of minimizing the number of edges in a key derivation graph is however NP-hard. In [24] the authors propose an heuristic approach, which has been proved to obtain good results, based on two observations: (i) the vertices needed for correctly enforcing an authorization policy are those representing singleton sets of users and the acls of tuples in r; (ii) when two or more vertices have more than two common direct ancestors, the insertion of a vertex representing the set of users corresponding to these ancestors reduces the total number of tokens. Figure 8a illustrates an example of key derivation graph obtained adopting the approach in [24] over the access matrix in Fig. 6. As it is visible from the figure, the graph includes a vertex for each user and for each acl of a tuple in the system. It also includes an additional vertex (i.e., *ABC*), introduced to limit the number of tokens in the system. Clearly, the encryption policy in Fig. 8 is more convenient than the one in Fig. 7, as it reduces both the number of keys and the number of tokens in the system, while managing an additional user.

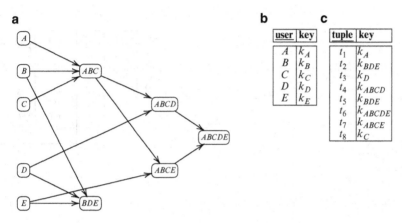

Fig. 8 An example of encryption policy equivalent to the access control policy in Fig. 6

Since the keys used to encrypt tuples depend on their access control lists, whenever the authorization policy changes, the tuples involved in the policy update may need to be re-encrypted to guarantee the equivalence of the encryption policy. For instance, assume that user E is revoked the privilege to read tuple t_6. Such a tuple should be first decrypted using key k_{ABCDE}, and then encrypted using key k_{ABCD}. However, re-encryption requires the direct involvement of the data owner and can be computationally expensive. The number of re-encryption operations are therefore minimized by adopting two layers of encryption that allow the server to manage policy update operations [24]. The *Base Encryption Layer* (BEL) is applied by the data owner before transmitting the relation to the server and consists in encrypting the tuples according to the authorization policy existing at initialization time. The *Surface Encryption Layer* (SEL) is performed by the server over the tuples already encrypted by the data owner. It enforces the dynamic changes over the policy. The basic idea consists in over-encrypting the tuples so that a user can access a tuple only if she knows or can derive the key used for encrypting the tuples at both levels.

The solution in [24] enforces read privileges only and has been complemented with another technique that allows the management of write operations [23]. This work associates each tuple with a *write tag*. The write tag is a random value chosen by the data owner independently from the tuple content, and is encrypted with a key known only to users who can modify the tuple and to the external server. The server will then enforce a write operation on a tuple only if the requesting user proves to know the write tag of the tuple. The proposal in [23] extends the key derivation graph with a key for the server and the keys necessary for protecting write tags. For instance, consider the read privileges in Fig. 6 over relation PATIENTS in Fig. 3a, and assume that: tuples t_1, t_4, and t_7 can be modified by user A only; tuples t_2 and t_6 can be modified by B, D, and E; tuples t_3 and t_5 can be modified by D; and tuple t_8 can be modified by C. Figure 9 illustrates the encryption policy in Fig. 8, extended to properly enforce write privileges. In the figure, we denote the external server as S.

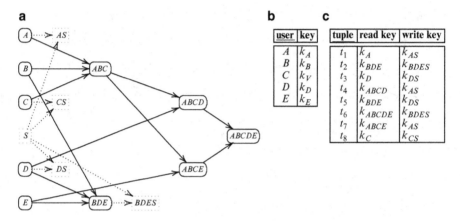

Fig. 9 Encryption policy in Fig. 8, extended to enforce write authorizations

Open issues that still need to be addressed are related to the expressive power of the supported access control policy, especially considering the ever-increasing bring-your-own-device (BYOD) trend. In fact, it would be interesting to develop solutions that will allow the specification of fine-grained restrictions, based on the users' context and on the specific device adopted for accessing data.

4 Indexes and Fragmentation

The fragmentation works illustrated in Sect. 3.1 permit to delegate to the server the evaluation of any condition over attributes appearing plaintext in a fragment. However, the client still needs to evaluate those queries that operate on encrypted attributes, or that involve attributes that are not represented in plaintext in the same fragment. For instance, consider the fragmentation in Fig. 4 obtained in the multiple fragments scenario of relation PATIENTS in Fig. 3a. Query q = SELECT Name FROM PATIENTS WHERE YoB = 1980 AND Disease = 'Asthma' cannot be evaluated by the server, since attributes YoB and Disease do not appear in the clear in the same fragment and the server can neither decrypt attribute enc nor join F_1 and F_3. Hence, one of the two conditions in q must be evaluated by the client. To mitigate the client's overhead in query evaluation, fragments can be complemented with indexes over encrypted attributes. Figure 10 illustrates three versions of fragment F_1 in Fig. 4, complemented with index I_d over attribute Disease, which has been computed using each of the three kinds of indexes illustrated in Sect. 3.2. The presence of indexes in a fragment could however cause unintended leakage of sensitive information [28]. The exposure to leakage varies depending on the knowledge that a curious observer (e.g., the external server) can exploit and the kind of indexes. In particular, the following two kinds of knowledge can be exploited for breaching data confidentiality.

a F_1

salt	enc	Name	YoB	I_d
s_{11}	Bd6!l3	Alice	1980	α
s_{12}	Oij3X.	Bob	1980	α
s_{13}	9kEf6?	Carol	1970	α
s_{14}	ker5/2	David	1970	β
s_{15}	C:mE91	Eva	1970	β
s_{16}	4lDwqz	Frank	1960	γ
s_{17}	me3,op	Gary	1960	γ
s_{18}	zWf4g>	Hilary	1960	δ

b F_1

salt	enc	Name	YoB	I_d
s_{11}	Bd6!l3	Alice	1980	ε
s_{12}	Oij3X.	Bob	1980	ε
s_{13}	9kEf6?	Carol	1970	ε
s_{14}	ker5/2	David	1970	η
s_{15}	C:mE91	Eva	1970	η
s_{16}	4lDwqz	Frank	1960	θ
s_{17}	me3,op	Gary	1960	θ
s_{18}	zWf4g>	Hilary	1960	ε

c F_1

salt	enc	Name	YoB	I_d
s_{11}	Bd6!l3	Alice	1980	κ
s_{12}	Oij3X.	Bob	1980	λ
s_{13}	9kEf6?	Carol	1970	μ
s_{14}	ker5/2	David	1970	ν
s_{15}	C:mE91	Eva	1970	ξ
s_{16}	4lDwqz	Frank	1960	π
s_{17}	me3,op	Gary	1960	ρ
s_{18}	zWf4g>	Hilary	1960	σ

Fig. 10 Fragment F_1 in Fig. 4 complemented with a direct index (**a**), a bucket-based index (**b**), and a flattened index (**c**) over attribute Disease

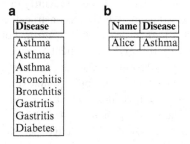

a

Disease
Asthma
Asthma
Asthma
Bronchitis
Bronchitis
Gastritis
Gastritis
Diabetes

b

Name	Disease
Alice	Asthma

Fig. 11 An example of vertical (**a**) and horizontal (**b**) knowledge by an observer

- *Vertical knowledge* is the knowledge of the projection of attribute a over relation r, and is due to the presence of attribute a in the clear in one fragment and indexed in other fragments. Vertical knowledge does not require any additional external information for an observer since, apart from the case where the attribute appears in a singleton constraint, it refers to information immediately present in other accessible fragments. For instance, fragment F_3 in Fig. 4 makes visible the plaintext values (and their number of occurrences) of attribute Disease (see Fig. 11a).
- *Horizontal knowledge* is the knowledge of the presence of a tuple t (or a set thereof) in r, and is due to external knowledge by an observer. For instance, an observer may know that Alice suffers from Asthma (see Fig. 11b).

Let us now examine the exposure risk of indexed fragments under the assumptions of horizontal and vertical knowledge and of the presence of indexes belonging to the three categories discussed in Sect. 3.2 [28].

- *Direct index.* Index function ι preserves the frequency distribution of plaintext values, which can be exploited to reconstruct the value-index association by an observer with vertical and/or horizontal knowledge. Vertical knowledge permits to precisely reconstruct the value-index association for values characterized by a unique number of occurrences (outliers). For instance, consider the indexed fragment in Fig. 10a and the vertical knowledge in Fig. 11a. It is immediate to see that $\iota(\text{Asthma}) = \alpha$ and $\iota(\text{Diabetes}) = \delta$ since these are the only plaintext and index values with 3 occurrences and 1 occurrence, respectively. Hence, an observer can infer that Alice, Bob, and Carol have Asthma and Hilary has Diabetes. Horizontal knowledge permits to precisely reconstruct the value-index association for the plaintext value $v = t[a]$ known by the observer, exposing all the tuples in r with value v for attribute a. For instance, in the example above, knowing that Alice suffers from Asthma permits an observer to infer that $\iota(\text{Asthma}) = \alpha$ and then that also Bob and Carol suffer from the same illness.
- *Bucket-based index.* Index function ι does not preserve the frequency distribution of plaintext values. However, the index value corresponding to plaintext value v will have a frequency equal to or higher than (in case of collisions) the frequency of v. Values with a high number of occurrences (outliers) are then still exposed. Vertical knowledge permits to identify the index values associated with frequent plaintext values, and then to reconstruct the value-index association for such values with a known probability of error. For instance, consider the indexed fragment in Fig. 10b and the vertical knowledge in Fig. 11a. Clearly, $\iota(\text{Asthma}) = \varepsilon$ since this is the only index value with at least 3 occurrences. Also, $\iota(\text{Diabetes}) = \varepsilon$ since Diabetes is the only plaintext value with 1 occurrence. An observer can then infer that three patients among Alice, Bob, Carol, and Hilary has Asthma (each with probability 0.75) and one has Diabetes (each with probability 0.25). Horizontal knowledge permits to identify the index value representing the known plaintext value $v = t[a]$. This index value may however correspond also to other plaintext values, limiting the observer's ability to precisely reconstruct value-index associations. For instance, in the example above, knowing that Alice suffers from Asthma permits an observer to infer that $\iota(\text{Asthma}) = \varepsilon$. However, nothing can be said about Bob, Carol, and Hilary since ε could also represent other plaintext values (different from Asthma). By combining horizontal with vertical knowledge, however, she can infer that two among Bob, Carol, and Hilary suffer from Asthma (each with probability 0.66) and one suffers from Diabetes (each with probability 0.33).
- *Flattened index.* Index function ι flattens the frequency distribution of index values. Vertical knowledge does not help in establishing correspondences between plaintext values and index values. Horizontal knowledge permits to identify one of the index values representing the known plaintext value $v = t[a]$, exposing only the tuples associated with this index value (in contrast to the possibly larger

$$F_1$$

salt	enc	Name	YoB	I_d
s_{11}	Bd6!l3	Alice	1980	α
s_{12}	Oij3X.	Bob	1980	α
s_{13}	9kEf6?	Carol	1970	δ
s_{14}	ker5/2	David	1970	β
s_{15}	C:mE91	Eva	1970	β
s_{16}	4lDwqz	Frank	1960	γ
s_{17}	me3,op	Gary	1960	γ
s_{18}	zWf4g>	Hilary	1960	δ

Fig. 12 Fragment F_1 in Fig. 4 complemented with a flattened index with collisions over attribute Disease

set of tuples with value v for a). For instance, consider the indexed fragment in Fig. 10c and the horizontal knowledge in Fig. 11b. An observer can only learn that $\iota(\text{Asthma}) = \kappa$. However, no other association is exposed, because κ has only one occurrence in F_1 (although Asthma has frequency 3 in F_3).

An index function ι that flattens the frequency distribution of index values and that generates collisions provides protection against both horizontal and vertical knowledge. In fact, as illustrated above, inference attacks caused by vertical knowledge can be counteracted by flattening the frequency distribution of index values. Inference attacks caused by horizontal knowledge are mitigated by index functions that map different plaintext values to the same index value, generating collisions. For instance, Fig. 12 illustrates fragment F_1 in Fig. 4 complemented with a flattened index with collisions over attribute Disease. This indexed fragment is protected against both vertical and horizontal knowledge in Fig. 11. Indeed, vertical knowledge cannot be exploited for frequency-based attacks (all the index values have two occurrences). Horizontal knowledge permits to infer that $\iota(\text{Asthma}) = \alpha$ but, since ι generates collisions, the observer cannot say anything about the disease from which Bob suffers. Although the proposal in [28] is focused on the adoption of one index, the discussion can easily be extended to the case where fragments are complemented with multiple indexes. In fact, flattening and collisions provide adequate protection in different scenarios (e.g., multiple indexes in one fragment, a same attribute indexed in different fragments, two attributes appearing one in plaintext and the other indexed in one fragment and reversed in another fragment).

Although effective to protect data at rest, a flattened index function with collisions has the disadvantage of reducing the performance in query evaluation. In fact, flattening requires to retrieve different index values when searching for one plaintext value, and collisions require a post-processing at the client side to remove spurious tuples in the query result computed by the server. As an example, consider fragment F_1 in Fig. 12, condition Disease = 'Asthma' translates into condition I_d IN $\{\alpha, \delta\}$. The evaluation of this condition would however return a tuple with value Diabetes for attribute Disease (i.e., tuple t_8), since Asthma and Diabetes are both mapped to value δ. Also, flattened indexes with collisions remain still vulnerable to dynamic observations (i.e., to adversaries who can observe users' queries). In

a

t	acl(t)
t_1	A
t_2	BDE
t_3	D
t_4	ABCD
t_5	BDE
t_6	ABCDE
t_7	ABCE
t_8	C

b

PATIENTS

	SSN	Name	YoB	Job	Disease
t_1	123456789	Alice	1980	Clerk	Asthma
t_2					
t_3					
t_4	456789123	David	1970	Lawyer	Bronchitis
t_5					
t_6	678912345	Frank	1960	Doctor	Gastritis
t_7	789123456	Gary	1960	Teacher	Gastritis
t_8					

c

PATIENTS^k

tid	enc	I_n	I_y	I_j	I_d
1	T8/lO?	π	α	δ	η
2	1wfTg<	π	α	ε	θ
3	vFe!d2	ρ	β	δ	ω
4	f3iJ:y	ρ	β	ζ	κ
5	;x0d9D	σ	β	ε	λ
6	kO6i)G	σ	γ	ε	μ
7	u2eW[b	τ	γ	ζ	ν
8	vY7'.1	τ	γ	δ	ξ

Fig. 13 Knowledge of user A over relation PATIENTS (**b**) and PATIENTS^k (**c**)

fact, by observing a long enough sequence of queries, an observer can easily infer the index values to which each plaintext value has been mapped, since they always appear together in query conditions. With reference to the example above, every query including condition Disease = 'Asthma' is translated into a query including condition I_d IN $\{\alpha, \delta\}$. An observer can then easily infer that α and δ represent the same plaintext value (Asthma, in our example). The protection against dynamic observations represents an open issue that still needs to be addressed, along with the problem of defining an efficient index function that provides both flattening and collisions.

5 Indexes and Selective Encryption

Selective encryption approaches illustrated in Sect. 3.3 enforce access control restrictions over outsourced data by guaranteeing that each user can decrypt all and only the tuples she is authorized to access. However, when data are made selectively available, the combination of selective encryption with indexes used for enabling efficient query execution on encrypted data may open the door to inferences. In fact, users may have visibility of indexes even of tuples they are not allowed to access. Such visibility, together with their ability to view data for which they are authorized, can allow them to possibly infer plaintext values of tuples they should not be able to read. In the following, for clarity in the exposition but without loss of generality, we will refer the discussion to one attribute a only.

The knowledge that a user u can exploit for inferences can be summarized as follows: (i) index function ι used to define index I over attribute a (necessary to translate user' queries into queries that operate at the server side); (ii) plaintext tuples that the user can access (i.e., t such that $u \in acl(t)$); (iii) all the encrypted tuples in r^k. For instance, consider relation PATIENTS in Fig. 3a and the authorization policy in Fig. 6 (which is also summarized in Fig. 13a for the reader's convenience), Fig. 13b,c illustrate the knowledge of user A over the plaintext and encrypted relation. Gray cells denote values that A is not authorized to read.

The information that a user with this knowledge can infer depends on the kind of index adopted (see Sect. 3.2), as illustrated in the following [27].

a

t	acl(t)
t_1	A
t_2	BDE
t_3	D
t_4	ABCD
t_5	BDE
t_6	ABCDE
t_7	ABCE
t_8	C

b PATIENTS

	SSN	Name	YoB	Job	Disease
t_1	123456789	Alice	1980	Clerk	Asthma
t_2			1980		Asthma
t_3			1970		Asthma
t_4	456789123	David	1970	Lawyer	Bronchitis
t_5			1970		Bronchitis
t_6	678912345	Frank	1960	Doctor	Gastritis
t_7	789123456	Gary	1960	Teacher	Gastritis
t_8			1960		

c PATIENTS^k

tid	enc	I_n	I_y	I_j	I_d
1	T8/lO?	π	α	δ	η
2	1wfTg<	π	α	ε	θ
3	vFe!d2	ρ	β	δ	ω
4	f3iJ:y	ρ	β	ζ	κ
5	;x0d9D	σ	β	ε	λ
6	kO6i)G	σ	γ	ε	μ
7	u2eW[b	τ	γ	ζ	ν
8	vY7'.1	τ	γ	δ	ξ

Fig. 14 Knowledge inferred by user A over relation PATIENTS

- *Direct index.* Index function ι is a bijective function that maps each plaintext value to one index value (and vice versa). It then exposes all the tuples with the same plaintext value for attribute a of a tuple that the user is authorized to access. For instance, index I_y over attribute YoB in Fig. 13c has been computed using a direct index function. Since user A can access tuple t_1, she knows that $\iota(1980) = \alpha$. She can then infer that $t_2[\text{YoB}] = 1980$, even if she is not authorized to access tuple t_2. In a similar way, A can also infer that $\iota(1970) = \beta$ and that $\iota(1960) = \gamma$ (i.e., she knows the plaintext value of attribute YoB of each tuple in PATIENTS). The user also knows index function ι. Hence, she can compute the index value $\iota(v)$ associated with each value v in the domain of attribute a, and possibly reconstruct the value that attribute a assumes in each tuple t of the outsourced relation, independently from her access privileges over t.

- *Bucket-based index.* Index function ι is a surjective function that maps multiple plaintext values to one index value. The inference risks described for direct indexes are mitigated by collisions. In fact, multiple occurrences of a same index value may correspond to different plaintext values. The user's knowledge of index function ι could however reduce the uncertainty over the value assumed by attribute a in a tuple t that she is not authorized to access. For instance, index I_j over attribute Job in Fig. 13c has been computed using a bucket-based index function. Since user A can access tuple t_1, she knows that $\iota(\text{Clerk}) = \delta$. However, she does not know with certainty whether $t_3[\text{Job}] = \text{Clerk}$ and $t_8[\text{Job}] = \text{Clerk}$ since function ι may generate collisions and map different plaintext values to index value δ.

- *Flattened index.* Index function ι is an injective function that maps a plaintext value to multiple index values, guaranteeing a flat distribution of the number of occurrences of index values. Like direct indexes, flattened indexes expose all the tuples with the same plaintext value for attribute a of a tuple that the user is authorized to access. In fact, when decrypting a tuple t that she can access, the user knows one of the index values representing value $v = t[a]$. By computing $\iota(v)$, she exactly knows which tuples in r^k have value v for attribute a. For instance, index I_d over attribute Disease in Fig. 13c has been computed using a flattened index function. Since user A can access tuple t_1, she knows that $\iota(\text{Asthma}) = \eta$ and, since she can compute $\iota(v)$ for any v in the domain of attribute Disease, she can compute the set of index values representing Asthma, that is, $\{\eta, \theta, \omega\}$. She can then infer that $t_2[\text{Disease}] = t_3[\text{Disease}] = \text{Asthma}$.

a   PATIENTS^k

tid	enc	I_y
1	T8/lO?	α_A
2	1wfTg<	$\alpha_B, \alpha_D, \alpha_E$
3	vFe!d2	β_D
4	f3iJ:y	$\beta_A, \beta_B, \beta_C, \beta_D$
5	;x0d9D	$\beta_B, \beta_D, \beta_E$
6	kO6i)G	$\gamma_A, \gamma_B, \gamma_C, \gamma_D, \gamma_E$
7	u2eW[b	$\gamma_A, \gamma_B, \gamma_C, \gamma_E$
8	vY7'.1	γ_C

b   PATIENTS^k

tid	enc	I_y
1	T8/lO?	α_A
2	1wfTg<	$\alpha_B, \alpha_D, \alpha_E$
3	vFe!d2	β_D
4	f3iJ:y	$\beta_A, \beta_B, \beta_C, \beta'_D$
5	;x0d9D	$\beta'_B, \beta''_D, \beta_E$
6	kO6i)G	$\gamma_A, \gamma_B, \gamma_C, \gamma_D, \gamma_E$
7	u2eW[b	$\gamma'_A, \gamma'_B, \gamma'_C, \gamma'_E$
8	vY7'.1	γ''_C

Fig. 15 An example of encrypted and indexed version of relation PATIENTS with index I_y over YOB computed using a user-dependent function (**a**) and a salted user-dependent function (**b**)

Inferences by user A over relation PATIENTS are summarized in Fig. 14, where light-gray cells represent values, reported in italic, that A is not authorized to access but that she can infer from her knowledge.

From the observations above, we note that inference is mainly caused by the presence of the same index value associated with tuples characterized by different authorizations. In [27] the authors proposed a solution, which is focused on direct indexes since they represent the worst case scenario, based on the principle that different occurrences of the same index value must be mapped to different index values when they should be visible to different subsets of users. The index value to which $t[a]$ should be mapped therefore depends, not only on value $v = t[a]$, but also on $acl(t)$. To this purpose, each user u has its own index function ι_u, which depends on a private piece of information that she shares with the data owner. Given a tuple t, the data owner computes a different index value $\iota_u(\,t[a])$ for each $u \in acl(t)$. Each user will then use her index function ι_u to formulate queries to be evaluated by the external server over indexes. For instance, Fig. 15a illustrates relation PATIENTS^k, where the index over attribute YOB has been computed adopting a user-dependent function. In the figure, for simplicity, we indicate with a sub-script the user whose index function generated the value (i.e., v_u is a value generated by ι_u). Note that $v_{u_i} \neq v_{u_j}$.

Since all the index values associated with a specific plaintext value of attribute a are visible to all the users in the system, the adoption of user-dependent index functions is not sufficient to block all the inferences. In fact, tuples sharing the same value for attribute a that are characterized by different but overlapping acls, called *conflicting tuples*, are exposed to inferences by users who can access at least one of these tuples. For instance, with reference to relation PATIENTS^k in Fig. 15a, user A cannot exploit her knowledge of tuple t_1 to infer the value of $t_2[\text{YOB}]$. However, by observing that β_D appears in tuples t_4 together with β_A, A can infer that β_D represents value 1970 and hence that $t_3[\text{YOB}] = t_4[\text{YOB}] = t_5[\text{YOB}] = 1970$. To block this inference channel, conflicting tuples must be associated with disjoint sets of index values. To impose diversity of indexes, the value computed by index function ι_u is differentiated by applying different randomly generated salts to conflicting tuples. For instance, Fig. 15a illustrates relation PATIENTS^k, where the index over attribute YoB has been computed adopting a salted user-dependent function. In the figure, we denote salted versions of value v as v' and v''.

While effective, the solution illustrated above presents similar privacy risks to the one described in Sect. 4. More precisely, this indexing technique remains vulnerable to dynamic observations, since monitoring a sufficient number of queries would permit an observer to reconstruct which (salted) index values represent the same plaintext value. Furthermore, collusion between authorized users and the external server may put data confidentiality at risk. The protection against these threats still remains an open issue.

6 Conclusions

Cloud computing offers a variety of new opportunities to users and companies, and many efforts have been therefore dedicated to the design of cloud-based services, applications, and infrastructures. While appealing, cloud computing however introduces new security and privacy issues. In this chapter, we analyzed the data protection issues, and described approaches for the protection of data confidentiality, and for the efficient and selective access to data. We also illustrated open problems arising from the combined application of such solutions and highlighted possible directions to address them.

Acknowledgements The chapter is based on joint work with Sushil Jajodia and Stefano Paraboschi. This work was supported in part by the Italian Ministry of Research within PRIN 2010–2011 project "GenData 2020" (2010RTFWBH), and by Google under the Google Research Award program.

References

1. Aggarwal, G., Bawa, M., Ganesan, P., Garcia-Molina, H., Kenthapadi, K., Motwani, R., Srivastava, U., Thomas, D., Xu, Y.: Two can keep a secret: A distributed architecture for secure database services. In: Proc. of CIDR 2005. Asilomar, CA, USA (January 2005)
2. Agrawal, R., Asonov, D., Kantarcioglu, M., Li, Y.: Sovereign joins. In: Proc. of ICDE 2006. Atlanta, GA, USA (April 2006)
3. Agrawal, R., Kierman, J., Srikant, R., Xu, Y.: Order preserving encryption for numeric data. In: Proc. of SIGMOD 2004. Paris, France (June 2004)
4. Ardagna, C.A., Camenisch, J., Kohlweiss, M., Leenes, R., Neven, G., Priem, B., Samarati, P., Sommer, D., Verdicchio, M.: Exploiting cryptography for privacy-enhanced access control: A result of the PRIME project. JCS 18(1), 123–160 (2010)
5. Ardagna, C.A., De Capitani di Vimercati, S., Foresti, S., Paraboschi, S., Samarati, P.: Minimizing disclosure of private information in credential-based interactions: A graph-based approach. In: Proc. of PASSAT 2010. Minneapolis, MN, USA (August 2010)

6. Ardagna, C.A., De Capitani di Vimercati, S., Foresti, S., Paraboschi, S., Samarati, P.: Supporting privacy preferences in credential-based interactions. In: Proc. of WPES 2010. Chicago, IL, USA (October 2010)

7. Ardagna, C.A., De Capitani di Vimercati, S., Foresti, S., Paraboschi, S., Samarati, P.: Minimising disclosure of client information in credential-based interactions. IJIPSI 1(2/3), 205–233 (2012)

8. Ardagna, C.A., De Capitani di Vimercati, S., Paraboschi, S., Pedrini, E., Samarati, P., Verdicchio, M.: Expressive and deployable access control in open Web service applications. IEEE TSC 4(2), 96–109 (April-June 2011)

9. Ardagna, C.A., Jajodia, S., Samarati, P., Stavrou, A.: Providing users' anonymity in mobile hybrid networks. ACM TOIT (2013)

10. Atallah, M., Blanton, M., Fazio, N., Frikken, K.: Dynamic and efficient key management for access hierarchies. ACM TISSEC 12(3), 18:1–18:43 (January 2009)

11. Bertoni, G., Breveglieri, L., Koren, I., Maistri, P., Piuri, V.: On the propagation of faults and their detection in a hardware implementation of the advanced encryption standard. In: Proc. of ASAP 2002. San Jose, CA, USA (July 2002)

12. Blanton, M., Frikken, K.: Efficient multi-dimensional key management in broadcast services. In: Proc. of ESORICS 2010. Athens, Grece (September 2010)

13. Bonatti, P., Samarati, P.: A uniform framework for regulating service access and information release on the Web. JCS 10(3), 241–272 (2002)

14. Boneh, D., Gentry, C., Lynn, B., Shacham, H.: Aggregate and verifiably encrypted signatures from bilinear maps. In: Proc. of EUROCRYPT 2003. Warsaw, Poland (May 2003)

15. Calì, A., Martinenghi, D.: Querying data under access limitations. In: Proc. of ICDE 2008. Cancun, Mexico (April 2008)

16. Camenisch, J., Lysyanskaya, A.: An efficient system for non-transferable anonymous credentials with optional anonymity revocation. In: Proc. of EUROCRYPT 2001. Innsbruck, Austria (May 2001)

17. Ceselli, A., Damiani, E., De Capitani di Vimercati, S., Jajodia, S., Paraboschi, S., Samarati, P.: Modeling and assessing inference exposure in encrypted databases. ACM TISSEC 8(1), 119–152 (February 2005)

18. Chor, B., Kushilevitz, E., Goldreich, O., Sudan, M.: Private information retrieval. Journal of ACM 45(6), 965–981 (April 1998)

19. Cimato, S., Gamassi, M., Piuri, V., Sassi, R., Scotti, F.: Privacy-aware biometrics: Design and implementation of a multimodal verification system. In: Proc. of ACSAC 2008. Anaheim, CA, USA (December 2008)

20. Ciriani, V., De Capitani di Vimercati, S., Foresti, S., Jajodia, S., Paraboschi, S., Samarati, P.: Keep a few: Outsourcing data while maintaining confidentiality. In: Proc. of ESORICS 2009. Saint Malo, France (September 2009)

21. Ciriani, V., De Capitani di Vimercati, S., Foresti, S., Jajodia, S., Paraboschi, S., Samarati, P.: Combining fragmentation and encryption to protect privacy in data storage. ACM TISSEC 13(3), 22:1–22:33 (July 2010)

22. Damiani, E., De Capitani di Vimercati, S., Jajodia, S., Paraboschi, S., Samarati, P.: Balancing confidentiality and efficiency in untrusted relational DBMSs. In: Proc. of CCS 2003. Washington, DC, USA (October 2003)

23. De Capitani di Vimercati, S., Foresti, S., Jajodia, S., Livraga, G. Paraboschi, S., Samarati, P.: Enforcing Dynamic Write Privileges in Data Outsourcing. COSE 39(A), 47–63 (November 2013)

24. De Capitani di Vimercati, S., Foresti, S., Jajodia, S., Paraboschi, S., Samarati, P.: Encryption policies for regulating access to outsourced data. ACM TODS 35(2), 12:1–12:46 (April 2010)

25. De Capitani di Vimercati, S., Foresti, S., Jajodia, S., Paraboschi, S., Samarati, P.: Fragments and loose associations: Respecting privacy in data publishing. PVLDB 3(1), 1370–1381 (September 2010)

26. De Capitani di Vimercati, S., Foresti, S., Jajodia, S., Paraboschi, S., Samarati, P.: Authorization enforcement in distributed query evaluation. JCS 19(4), 751–794 (2011)

27. De Capitani di Vimercati, S., Foresti, S., Jajodia, S., Paraboschi, S., Samarati, P.: Private data indexes for selective access to outsourced data. In: Proc. of WPES 2011. Chicago, IL, USA (October 2011)

28. De Capitani di Vimercati, S., Foresti, S., Jajodia, S., Paraboschi, S., Samarati, P.: On information leakage by indexes over data fragments. In: Proc. of PrivDB 2013. Brisbane, Australia (April 2013)

29. De Capitani di Vimercati, S., Foresti, S., Paraboschi, S., Pelosi, G., Samarati, P.: Efficient and private access to outsourced data. In: Proc. of ICDCS 2011. Minneapolis, MN, USA (June 2011)

30. De Capitani di Vimercati, S., Foresti, S., Paraboschi, S., Pelosi, G., Samarati, P.: Supporting concurrency in private data outsourcing. In: Proc. of ESORICS 2011. Leuven, Belgium (September 2011)

31. De Capitani di Vimercati, S., Foresti, S., Samarati, P.: Protecting data in outsourcing scenarios. In: Das, S., Kant, K., Zhang, N. (eds.) Handbook on Securing Cyber-Physical Critical Infrastructure. Morgan Kaufmann (2012)

32. Gentry, C.: Fully homomorphic encryption using ideal lattices. In: Proc. of STOC 2009. Bethesda, MA, USA (May 2009)

33. Goodrich, M., Mitzenmacher, M., Ohrimenko, O., Tamassia, R.: Privacy-preserving group data access via stateless Oblivious RAM simulation. In: Proc. of SODA 2012. Kyoto, Japan (January 2012)

34. Hacigümüs, H., Iyer, B., Mehrotra, S.: Providing database as a service. In: Proc. of ICDE 2002. San Jose, CA, USA (February 2002)

35. Hacigümüs, H., Iyer, B., Mehrotra, S.: Ensuring integrity of encrypted databases in database as a service model. In: Proc. of DBSec 2003. Estes Park, CO, USA (August 2003)

36. Hacigümüs, H., Iyer, B., Mehrotra, S.: Efficient execution of aggregation queries over encrypted relational databases. In: Proc. of DASFAA 2004. Jeju Island, Korea (March 2004)

37. Hacigümüs, H., Iyer, B., Mehrotra, S., Li, C.: Executing SQL over encrypted data in the database-service-provider model. In: Proc. of SIGMOD 2002. Madison, WI, USA (June 2002)

38. Jhawar, R., Piuri, V.: Fault tolerance management in IaaS clouds. In: Proc. of ESTEL 2012. Rome, Italy (October 2012)

39. Jhawar, R., Piuri, V., Samarati, P.: Supporting security requirements for resource management in cloud computing. In: Proc. of CSE 2012. Paphos, Cyprus (December 2012)

40. Kärger, P., Olmedilla, D., Balke, W.T.: Exploiting preferences for minimal credential disclosure in policy-driven trust negotiations. In: Proc. of SDM 2008. Auckland, New Zealand (August 2008)

41. Li, F., Hadjieleftheriou, M., Kollios, G., Reyzin, L.: Dynamic authenticated index structures for outsourced databases. In: Proc. of SIGMOD 2006. Chicago, IL, USA (June 2006)

42. Miklau, G., Suciu, D.: Controlling access to published data using cryptography. In: Proc. of VLDB 2003. Berlin, Germany (September 2003)

43. Mykletun, E., Narasimha, M., Tsudik, G.: Authentication and integrity in outsourced databases. ACM TOS 2(2), 107–138 (May 2006)

44. Samarati, P., De Capitani di Vimercati, S.: Data protection in outsourcing scenarios: Issues and directions. In: Proc. of ASIACCS 2010. Beijing, China (April 2010)

45. Wang, H., Lakshmanan, L.: Efficient secure query evaluation over encrypted XML databases. In: Proc. of VLDB 2006. Seoul, Korea (September 2006)

46. Wang, H., Yin, J., Perng, C., Yu, P.: Dual encryption for query integrity assurance. In: Proc. of CIKM 2008. Napa Valley, CA, USA (October 2008)

47. Williams, P., Sion, R.: Single round access privacy on outsourced storage. In: Proc. of CCS 2012. Raleigh, NC, USA (October 2012)

48. Williams, P., Sion, R., Carbunar, B.: Building castles out of mud: Practical access pattern privacy and correctness on untrusted storage. In: Proc. of CCS 2008. Alexandria, VA, USA (October 2008)

49. Wong, C., Gouda, M., Lam, S.: Secure group communications using key graphs. IEEE/ACM TON 8(1), 16–30 (February 2000)

50. Xie, M., Wang, H., Yin, J., Meng, X.: Integrity auditing of outsourced data. In: Proc. of VLDB 2007. Vienna, Austria (September 2007)
51. Xie, M., Wang, H., Yin, J., Meng, X.: Providing freshness guarantees for outsourced databases. In: Proc. of EDBT 2008. Nantes, France (March 2008)
52. Yang, Y., Papadias, D., Papadopoulos, S., Kalnis, P.: Authenticated join processing in outsourced databases. In: Proc. of SIGMOD 2009. Providence, RI, USA (June-July 2009)
53. Yao, D., Frikken, K., Atallah, M., Tamassia, R.: Private information: To reveal or not to reveal. ACM TISSEC 12(1), 1–27 (October 2008)

Enabling Collaborative Data Authorization Between Enterprise Clouds

Meixing Le, Krishna Kant, and Sushil Jajodia

Abstract We consider a collaborative enterprise computing environment where a group of enterprises or parties maintain their own relational databases to which they allow restricted access to other parties. The access is regulated by means of a set of authorization rules that may be defined using relational calculus, including joins over relations from multiple parties. In this chapter, we provide an overview of the issues that arise in such an environment and some solutions. In particular, since individual parties are likely to formulate the rules in a somewhat piecemeal manner, the rules may be mutually inconsistent or inadequate to answer the desired queries. We address the issues of detecting inconsistencies and methods for fixing them. We also discuss the question of enforceability (or adequacy) of the rules. When rules, as given, are not enforceable, we can either augment the access rights or employ trusted third parties to perform unenforceable operations. We also address the issue of handling dynamic changes to rules. Finally, we consider the problem of generating efficient query plans in this environment.

1 Introduction

Enterprises increasingly need to collaborate to provide rich business services to clients and with minimal manual intervention. This requires the enterprises involved in the service path to share data in an orderly manner. For instance, an automated determination of patient coverage and costs requires that a hospital and insurance company be able to make certain queries against each others' databases. Similarly, to arrange for automated shipping of merchandise and to enable automated status checking, the e-commerce vendor and shipping company should be able to exchange relevant information, perhaps in form of database queries. To achieve collaborative

M. Le (✉) • K. Kant • S. Jajodia
Center for Secure Information Systems, George Mason University, Fairfax, VA, USA
e-mail: mlep@gmu.edu; kkant@gmu.edu; jajodia@gmu.edu

S. Jajodia et al. (eds.), *Secure Cloud Computing*, DOI 10.1007/978-1-4614-9278-8_7,
© Springer Science+Business Media New York 2014

computation, data owners need to provide access to their data to other parties based on the needs of the allowable queries. It is also important not to release more information than necessary. For example, an insurance company may wish to access patient data at hospital for the individuals that it insures. However, it would be highly undesirable for the hospital to release information about patients that are not the clients of the said insurance company. In relational terms, this means that the access granted to the insurance company is over the join of its client table and hospital's patient table projected over the desired columns. With multiple parties involved, each with their own data sharing and protection requirements, the picture could get rather complicated, thereby leading to the problems such as conflicts between rules or insufficient access to answer the desired queries. These are the issues of primary concern in this chapter. In the rest of the chapter, we introduce the cooperative data access model and problems in Sect. 2. We discuss the mechanisms to solve the various problems in Sect. 3. In Sect. 4, we discuss use of trusted third parties for collaboration and handling of authorization rule changes. At last, we conclude our discussion and list interesting future directions for research in Sect. 5.

2   Cooperative Data Access Model

Without loss of generality, we assume each collaborative party or enterprise maintains its own data in its private cloud. Such a party may have its own data center running the private cloud or possibly running the cloud on infrastructures rented from a provider. We assume here that all data is stored in relational form and structured in a standard form such as BCNF. The latter property allows for lossless joins over keys. It may be possible to extend the analysis to more general data models, but that aspect is beyond the scope of this chapter.

As the enterprises need to collaborate with one another to fulfill the desired business requirements, they will negotiate among themselves suitable access rights. For instance, an insurance company may request access to some hospital data, perhaps in exchange for providing some of its data to the hospital. We define the data access privileges using a set of authorization rules. Since we are dealing with the relational model, the authorization rules are made over the original tables belonging to enterprises or over the lossless joins ($\bowtie$) over two or more relational tables. The join operations, coupled with appropriate projection and selection operations define the access restrictions. In order to enable working with only the schemas, in this chapter, we do not consider the selection operation. We use the join operation over the relations because it can implicitly constrain the tuples being released to the authorized party and it meets the requirement of cooperative data access. For example, if the hospital thinks the insurance company should be able to obtain the patient information but only these patients who have plans with this insurance company, then the authorization given to the insurance company is defined only on the join result of hospital and insurance tables.

We assume that the authorization rules themselves are not considered sensitive and are visible to all parties. In cases where this is not desirable, all the rules could be managed by a trusted third party but this only affects where the algorithms considered in this chapter can run. In either case, we assume that all rules are available in a central place for manipulations. The purpose of cooperative data access is for parties to run queries against one-another's databases. Thus, we first need to check if the information requested by the querier (or client) is authorized, and if so build a query execution plan to retrieve the desired data. The query execution plan must follow the given authorization rules at every step. Figure 1 shows a possible architecture for this environment. As a client initiates a query, it is first handled by the query planner which checks authorizations and generates a safe query plan.

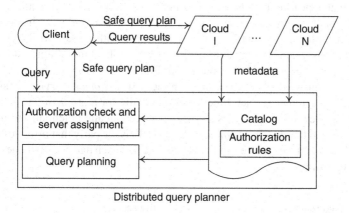

Fig. 1 Centralized authorization rule control

For simplicity, we assume simple select-project-join queries (e.g., no cyclic join schemas or queries). In general, the join operation cannot be done on any two arbitrary attributes, and the possible joins between different relations are usually limited. We assume that the join schema is given – i.e., all the possible join attributes between relations are known. Each join in the schema is assumed to be lossless so that a join attribute is always a key attribute of some relations. We also assume that the collaborating parties are non-malicious and strictly follow the given rules. Finally, we assume that there is only one authorization rule over each distinct join operation.

2.1 Notations and Definitions

We first introduce our authorization model. An **authorization rule** r_t is a triple $[A_t, J_t, P_t]$, where J_t is called the join path of the rule, A_t is the authorized attribute set, and P_t is the party authorized to access the data.

Definition 1. A **join path** is the result of a series of join operations over a set of relations $R_1, R_2 \ldots R_n$ with the specified equi-join predicates $(A_{l1}, A_{r1}), (A_{l2}, A_{r2}) \ldots (A_{ln}, A_{rn})$ among them, where (A_{li}, A_{ri}) are the join attributes from the two relations. We use JR_t to indicate the set of relations in a join path J_t. The **length** of a join path is the cardinality of JR_t.

We can consider a join path as the result of join operations with all the attributes intact. Then A_t can be interpreted as set of attributes projected on the join path accessible to party P_t. Table 1 shows an example set of rules given to the cooperative parties. The first column is the rule number, the second column gives the attribute set of the rules, the third column is the join path, and the last column shows the authorized parties of the rule. Only one rule can be given to a party on a given join path. We assume that each authorization rule includes all of the key attributes of the relations that appear in the join path. In other words, a rule has all the join attributes on its join path. We believe that this is a reasonable assumption as in most cases when the information is released, it is released along with the key attributes.

Table 1 corresponds to our running example throughout this chapter. It concerns an e-commerce scenario with four parties (or Enterprises): (a) *E-commerce*, denoted as E, is a company that sells products online, (b) *Customer_Service*, denoted C, that provides customer service functions (potentially for more than one company), (c) *Shipping*, denoted S, provides shipping services (again, potentially to multiple companies), and finally (d) *Warehouse*, denoted W, is the party that provides storage services. To keep the example simple, we assume that each party has but one relation described as follows:

Table 1 Authorization rules for e-commerce cooperative data access

Rule no.	Authorized attribute set	Join path	Party
1	{pid, location}	W	P_W
2	{oid, pid}	E	P_W
3	{oid, pid, location}	$E \bowtie_{pid} W$	P_W
4	{oid, pid, total}	E	P_E
5	{oid, pid, total, issue}	$E \bowtie_{oid} C$	P_E
6	{oid, pid, total, issue, address}	$S \bowtie_{oid} E \bowtie_{oid} C$	P_E
7	{oid, pid, location, total, address}	$S \bowtie_{oid} E \bowtie_{pid} W$	P_E
8	{oid, pid, issue, assistant, total, address, delivery}	$S \bowtie_{oid} E \bowtie_{oid} C \bowtie_{pid} W$	P_E
9	{oid, address, delivery}	S	P_S
10	{oid, pid, total}	E	P_S
11	{oid, pid, total, address, delivery}	$E \bowtie_{oid} S$	P_S
12	{oid, pid, total, location}	$E \bowtie_{pid} W$	P_S
13	{oid, location, pid, total, address, delivery}	$S \bowtie_{oid} E \bowtie_{pid} W$	P_S
14	{oid, pid}	E	P_C
15	{oid, issue, assistant}	C	P_C
16	{oid, pid, issue, assistant}	$E \bowtie_{oid} C$	P_C
17	{oid, pid, issue, assistant, total, address, location}	$S \bowtie_{oid} C \bowtie_{oid} E \bowtie_{pid} W$	P_C

1. E-commerce (<u>order_id</u>, product_id, total) as E
2. Customer_Service (<u>order_id</u>, issue, assistant) as C
3. Shipping (<u>order_id</u>, address, delivery_type) as S
4. Warehouse (<u>product_id</u>, location) as W

In the following, we use *oid* to denote *order_id* for short, *pid* stands for *product_id*, and *delivery* stands for *delivery_type*. The possible join schema is also given in Fig. 2. Relations *E*, *C*, *S* can join over their common attribute *oid*; relation *E* can join with *W* over the attribute *pid*. The relations are in BCNF, and the only FD (Functional Dependency) in each relation is the underlined key attribute determines the non-key attributes.

Fig. 2 The given join schema for the example

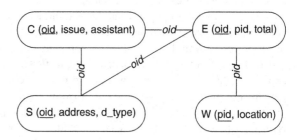

When a query is given, it should be answered by one of the parties that have the authorization. Since our authorization model is based on attributes, any attribute appearing in the Selection predicate in an SQL query is treated as a Projection attribute. In other words, the authorization of a PSJ query is transformed into an equivalent Projection-Join query authorization. Thus, a query q can be represented by a pair $[A_q, J_q]$, where A_q is the set of attributes appearing in the Selection and Projection predicates, and the query join path J_q is the FROM clause of an SQL query. For instance, there is an SQL query:

"Select *oid,total,address* From *E* Join *S* On *E.oid* = *S.oid* Where *delivery* = 'ground'"

The query can be represented as the pair $[A_q, J_q]$, where A_q is the set $\{oid, total, address, delivery\}$; J_q is the join path $E \bowtie_{oid} S$. In fact, each join path defines a new relation/view, and we say two join paths J_i and J_j are **equivalent**, noted as $J_i \cong J_j$, if any tuple in J_i appears in J_j and vice versa. As information release is explicitly defined by the rules, an authorized query must have a matching rule to allow the access.

Definition 2. A query q is **authorized** if there exists a rule r_t such that $J_t \cong J_q$ and $A_q \subseteq A_t$.

The rule and the authorized query must have the equivalent join paths. Otherwise, the relation/view defined by the rule will have fewer or more tuples than the query asks for. Here we don't consider the situation where the projections on two different join paths get the same result (e.g., by joining on foreign keys) since data coming from different parties usually does not have foreign key constraints. For instance, the example query Q_1 is authorized by r_{11}, but it cannot be authorized by r_{13}. Although all the required attributes are authorized by r_{13}, their join paths are not equivalent.

2.2 Issues in Collaborative Data Access

The data authorization rules are supposed to satisfy the requirements laid down by each enterprise, but without a careful analysis of interactions between them, we may find that the rules are either mutually inconsistent or inadequate to allow desired queries. For example, a hospital may choose to release data to an insurance company without realizing what additional information the insurance company can get from other parties such as a credit card company. If the data that the insurance receives from hospital and credit card company is joinable, it can perform the join and thereby effectively have access to data that is not authorized for it by any explicitly stated rule. In other words, we now have an authorization rule that was perhaps not intended to be granted. For example, the insurance company can now deduce credit score of the patients at the hospital in question. We say such a rule is inconsistent relative to the set of intended authorizations. Rule inconsistency is obviously undesirable since it amounts to information leakage without explicit knowledge of the parties involved.

Another problem is inadequacy of the given rules, which may cause a query to be authorized but not implementable. The simplest way to illustrate this problem is by considering the following situation: a rule specifies access to $R \bowtie S$ (where R and S are relations owned by two different parties); however, no party has access to both R and S individually and thus no party is able to do the join operation! In such case, a query requesting the data on the join result of R and S is authorized by the rule, but the query cannot be answered. We say that a rule can be enforced among the cooperative parties if there exists a series of operations among the cooperative parties that is allowed by the rule permissions and the final result is exactly the information conveyed by the rule.

One way to enforce a rule is to introduce a trusted third party that is given enough accesses in order to compute and supply the missing information. In the above example, if there is a trusted third party trusted by owners of R and S, they can supply it with relations R and S so that the third party can generate the missing $R \bowtie S$. We shall discuss different third party models to enforce the rules and answer queries. A third party may either act as an opaque service provider that does not retain any data, or provide richer functionality such as caching of data or query results. Multiple third parties may be needed to provide data isolation, handle trust issues, or to simply improve performance. In any case, it may be desirable to minimize third party involvement due to risk of data exposure (in transit or due to hacking), data transfer costs/delays, or the money charged by third parties.

If a query is authorized and the corresponding rule(s) can be enforced, we still need a safe query execution plan to answer the query. In spite of vast literature on query planning, the problem here requires a new approach because of the access restrictions and involvement of multiple parties.

2.3 Related Work

The problem of controlled data release among collaborating parties has been studied in [14]. The basic model in this paper is identical to ours and provides the motivation for our work. Its main contribution is an algorithm to check if a query with a given query plan tree can be safely executed. However, it does not address the problem of rule enforceability. Without a trusted third party, the unenforceable rules are inaccurate configurations and need to be revised, and we address that in our work. In another work [13], the same authors evaluate whether the information release the query entails is allowed by all the authorization rules given to a particular user, which considers the possible combinations of rules and assumes that the rules are defined in an implicit way. In our work, we assume authorizations are explicitly given, and data release is prohibited if there is no explicit authorization. While they focus on the problem of query authorization, we emphasize the executability of the authorized queries.

Processing distributed queries under protection requirements has been studied in [6, 18]. In these works, data access is constrained by a limited access pattern called binding pattern, and the goal is to identify the classes of queries that a given set of access patterns can support. These works with access patterns only considers two subjects, the owner of the data and a single user accessing it, whereas the authorization model considered in this work involves independent parties who may cooperate in the execution of a query. There are also classical works on distributed query processing [5, 17]. Most of these techniques aim to improve performance of query processing in the distributed environments, and minimize the data transmission among the different sites. In our scenario, authorization rules made by the data owners put constraints on data access privilege. When processing the queries, we should not only optimize for performance but also make sure no security constraint is violated.

Answering queries using views [16] is close to our work also since each rule can be thought as a view over basic relations. Answering queries using views can be used for query optimization [15], maintaining physical data independence and data integration [8]. Different methods can be applied, materialized views can be treated as new options and put into the conventional query plan enumeration to find better query plan, queries can also be rewritten using given views with query rewriting techniques, and sometimes conjunctive queries are used to evaluate the query equivalence and information containment. However, these works do not consider the collaboration relationships among different parties, which make our problem different from them.

In the area of outsourced database services, some works [1, 7] discuss how to secure the data in such environments, and there are also services like Sovereign joins [2]. Such a service receives encrypted relations from the participating data providers, and sends the encrypted results to the recipients. These methods are useful to enforce our authorization rules. For instance, we can use Sovereign joins [2] as a join service in our trusted third party model. The given authorization rules is also similar to the firewall rules, which indicates what types of queries can go through. As firewall rules are need to be enforceable and accurate [4, 12], we have the same requirements in our situation.

This chapter is mostly based on our previous works [9–11, 20]. Authorization rule consistency problem is address in [9], and [10] discusses the authorization rule enforcement checking problem. The mechanism to generate safe query plans is discussed in [20], and [11] deals with the problem of using trusted third parties in a minimal way.

3 Enabling Cooperative Data Access

In this section, we discuss the mechanisms to solve various problems in cooperative data access environment. These problems include achieving authorization rule consistency, checking rule enforcement and generating safe query plans for authorized queries.

3.1 Rule Consistency

Rules can be specified in two styles. An *implicit specification* means any valid compositions of the given rules are also considered as valid rules. In contrast, an *explicit specification* lists out all the allowed accesses and any access not included in the list is not allowed. In general, if a party obtains two joinable relations, say R and S according to two different explicit rules, it is free to join them to obtain $R \bowtie S$. With implicit specification, such a composition is, by definition, allowed and the parties involved must accept the risks of additional information leakage. However, with explicit specification, the composition is clearly not intended and we need to resolve the inconsistency. This can be done in two basic ways: (a) addition of the derived authorization such as $R \bowtie S$ to the rules, or (b) additional restrictions to disallow access to the composition.

In this work, we focus only on (a) and rely on the enterprises to expand their rules suitably so that access to compositions is explicitly included in the rules. This is a reasonable approach since it is not possible to prevent private computation by a party without restricting the component information itself. Approach (a) effectively implies that we generate a closure of the given set of rules. Formally, if rules r_i, r_j of party P can be joined losslessly according to the given join schema, and the resulting information $[A_i \bigcup A_j, J_i \bowtie J_j]$ is also authorized by another rule r_k of party P, then we say the two rules are **"upwards closed"**. For a set of rules, if any two rules that can be joined losslessly are "upwards closed", we say the set of rules is **consistent**, and the rules form a **consistent closure**. In the following, we shall consider how to systematically and efficiently generate the consistent closure of given set of rules.

Although approach (a) is straightforward, there are many instances where approach (b) is highly desirable. This happens when the association of two pieces of information is more sensitive than the individual pieces of information. For example, a hospital may not want the insurance company to be able to correlate medical diagnosis of its patients with their insurance claim histories, even though it does want to convey diagnosis information to the insurance company. The only way to restrict composition ability is to deny unrestricted access to one of the two basic relations involved in the composition. For example, if it is problematic to allow party P_t to have access to $R \bowtie S$, we must ensure that P_t can access either R or S but not both. In particular, P_t may be given unrestricted access to R, but for any queries involving S, it needs to go through a third party that controls the amount of data transferred. Thus, P_t cannot reliably construct the full $R \bowtie S$. (As usual, it is necessary to assume that P_t cannot accumulate up to date version of the entire S over time via a series of small queries. Without such an assumption, giving any access to tuples of a relation would amount to allowing access to the entire relation.)

Returning to approach (a), it is expected that the original authorization rules specified by the participating enterprises will usually be inconsistent and we need to identify the missing compositions that would remove the inconsistency. In the following we consider the consistency problem from the perspective of an individual party, but the same procedure needs to be repeated for every party.

We start by introducing the notion of key attribute hierarchy, which is useful for iterative construction of the closure. Consider two relations R and S with key attributes $R.K$ and $S.K$ respectively. If these relations can join losslessly, then the joining attribute must be the key attribute in at least one of them [3]. That is, either the join is performed on $R.K$, $S.K$, or $R.K$ is the same attribute as $S.K$. In either case, one key attribute from a basic relation is also the key attribute of the join result of the two relations. If the join is performed over the attribute $S.K$ ($R.K \neq S.K$), then the attribute $R.K$ can functionally determine the relation S. In such case, we say $R.K$ is at a higher level than $S.K$, denoted $R.K \rightarrow S.K$. If $R.K = S.K$, there is no hierarchy, and such key attribute of R and S is also the key attribute of the join result. For a given valid join path, the key attribute of the join path is always a key attribute from a basic relation. We call the key attribute of the join path in an authorization rule as **key** of the rule. Also, the join attributes in the join paths are always key attributes of some basic relations and these join attributes form the hierarchal relationship. For instance, in the given example rules, the key attribute oid is at the top level and $oid \rightarrow pid \rightarrow sid$.

Now for each key attribute of the basic relation, we create a group for the rules, called *join group* that takes this attribute as its key attribute. Since the rules within this group share the same key attribute, any two of them can join over their key attributes. More formally, a **join group** is a group of authorization rules associated with a key (join) attribute, where all the attributes in these rules functionally depend on this attribute. If a join group is **consistent**, then it is called a **consistent join group**.

Since some rules can be the result of private computation over other rules with respect to join paths, the rules themselves have relationships. Given a rule r_t with join path J_t, we call a join path as a **sub-join path** of J_t if it is a join path that contains a proper subset of relations of JR_t. We say a rule defined on a sub-join path of J_t is a **relevant rule** to r_t. A rule r_t can be generated only by combining the information from its relevant rules, since any other combination will contain extra information from relations not in J_t. Thus we can organize the rules into a **relevance graph** where each node is a rule marked by its join path and the nodes are connected by the relevance relationship. For instance, Fig. 3 shows a relevance graph. Here J_5 is a sub-path of J_6, and r_5 is a relevant rule to r_6, the rules are connected in the graph.

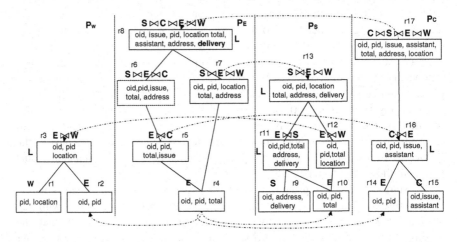

Fig. 3 Graph structure built for the example

It is now possible to outline the closure algorithm, although for brevity we refer the reader to [9] for details. The algorithm first divides rules into join groups and generates consistent join groups. Next, based on the join attribute hierarchy, each join attribute is considered for deriving further rules, and any such rules are added to the rule closure. When this procedure terminates, we have the entire consistent closure.

3.2 Rule Enforcement

In Sect. 2.1, we introduced the concept of query authorization. However, "authorized" is only a necessary condition for a query to be answered but not sufficient. To perform the required join operations to answer the query, we need to find appropriate parties that have the sufficient privileges to do these joins. Therefore, at least one legitimate query execution plan is required to answer a given query. A **query execution plan** or "query plan" for short, includes several ordered steps of operations over authorized and obtainable information and provides the composed results to a party. A query plan generates relational results, which can also be represented with the triple $[A_{pl}, J_{pl}, P_{pl}]$. All the operations executed and the final results produced by a valid query plan should be authorized by some given authorization rules. A query plan pl answers a query q, if the final generated relational result of the plan satisfies $J_{pl} \cong J_q \cong J_t$, $A_q = A_{pl} \subseteq A_t$ and $P_{pl} = P_t$. An authorization rule defines the maximal set of attributes that a query on the specified join path can retrieve. Thus, each rule can also be treated as a query. We call the query plan to enforce a rule as an **enforcement plan** or "plan" for short in the following.

Definition 3. A rule r_t can be *totally enforced*, if there exists a plan pl such that $J_t \cong J_{pl}$, $A_t = A_{pl}$, $P_t = P_{pl}$. r_t is *partially enforceable*, if it is not totally enforceable and there is a plan pl that $J_t \cong J_{pl}$, $A_t \supset A_{pl}$, $P_t = P_{pl}$. Otherwise, r_t is not enforceable. A join path J_t is enforceable if there is a plan pl that $J_t \cong J_{pl}$.

If a rule can be correctly enforced, there should be at least one valid enforcement plan for it. To enforce a rule with a long join path, we need to access the information from its underlying relations. Hence, whether a long join path can be enforced depends on the enforceability of the shorter join paths relevant to it. An rule enforcement plan with a long join path also uses the results of enforcement plans with shorter join paths. To that end, the enforcement plan building process requires a systematic walk through the rules with increasing join path length. At the beginning, the rules involving the basic relations (i.e., access rights of an enterprise to its own data) are trivially known to be totally enforceable. In the next step, we consider enforcement of rules with join path length of 2, and so on. In considering enforcement of a rule involving join of data from two distinct parties, we may need transmission of attributes from an owner party to another one that has access to it but does not own it. We call a plan as **joinable plan** if it contains all the key attributes of the basic relations in its join path. In some cases, a rule does not have a total enforcement plan. However, there are plans whose results implement subsets of the rule attribute set. We say that an attribute set is a **maximal enforceable attribute set** for a rule, if it is the result of a valid plan, and there is no other plan of the same rule that can implement a superset of these attributes. If a rule is totally enforceable, its maximal enforceable attribute set is the rule attribute set. Each rule has only one maximal enforceable attribute set.

It is obvious that not all the rules are enforceable. Whether an enforcement plan exists depends on whether pieces of enforceable information on shorter join paths are available and whether they can be joined losslessly at some place. In a cooperative environment, the enforceable information on remote cooperative parties may also be helpful to construct an enforcement plan. We do need a mechanism to check rule enforcement so as to tell which rules can be enforced and what are their maximal enforceable attribute sets. We address the rule enforcement checking problem in two steps. First, we examine the enforceability of each authorization rule in a constructive bottom-up manner, and build a relevance graph that captures the relationships and the enforceability among the rules. Second, we deal with the unenforceable information in the examined rules.

Unenforceable rules can be handled in two ways. The first choice is that we keep only the found enforceable rules with their maximal enforceable attribute sets, and rules that are not enforceable as well as the unenforceable attributes are removed from the rule definitions. In other words, the algorithm finds all the information that can be safely retrieved according to the given set of rules, and all inaccurate and unenforceable definitions are removed. This solution can be thought as a conservative one since it prohibits some authorized information to be released because of the enforceability. The second choice is to modify the rules as needed. For this, we take the view that all the information regulated by the rules is authorized, and authorized information should be retrievable. Whenever any information in the defined rules cannot be enforced, we change the rule configurations by granting more privileges so as to make this information enforceable. Since there are different ways to modify the rules, we prefer to find the way that has minimum impact on the existing rules. That is, we try to find the minimum amount of additional information to release. We have developed algorithms of both flavors and the details can be found in [10].

3.3 Query Planning

Once the enforceability of a query – or rather a rule satisfying the query – is known, we need a mechanism to generate the detailed query plan. A query plan is generated top-down by considering operations over sub-plans until the sub-plans refer to basic relations. The possible operations on plans are projection, join and data transmission. For instance, there is an enforcement plan for r_3 in Table 1, and such a plan contains a join over two sub-plans on the data authorized by r_1 and r_2 respectively. P_W owns the information authorized by r_1, and the sub-plan for it is an access plan reading the table W. The sub plan for r_2 includes an access plan reading table S at P_S, and another operation transmitting the data from P_S to P_w. The example plan authorized by r_3 has the $J_{pl} = E \bowtie_{pid} W$, and $A_{pl} = \{oid, pid, location\}$. We say a rule r_t **authorizes** ($\succeq$) a plan pl, if $J_{pl} \cong J_t$, $P_{pl} = P_t$, and $A_{pl} \subseteq A_t$.

Definition 4. An operation in a query plan is **consistent** with the given rules R, if for the operation, there exist rules that authorize access to the input tuples of the operation and to the resulting output tuples.

For the three types of operations in our scenario, we give the corresponding conditions for consistent operation.

1. For a projection (π) to be consistent with the rules, there must be a rule r_p authorizes ($\succeq$) the input information.

2. Join ($\bowtie$) involves two input subplans pl_{i1} and pl_{i2} to generate the resulting plan $pl_o = pl_{i1} \bowtie pl_{i2}$. For a join operation to be consistent with R, all the three plans need to be authorized by rules. Since join is performed at a single party, and rules are upwards closed, if the input plans are authorized by rules, the join operation is consistent.

3. Data transmission ($\rightarrow$) is an operation that involves two parties. The input is a plan pl_i on a party P_i, and the output is a plan pl_o for a party P_o, where $pl_o = pl_i \rightarrow P_o$. As each join path defines a different relation, the receiving party must have a rule that is defined on the equivalent join path as the information being sent. Otherwise, the transmission is not safe. Therefore, a data transmission operation to be consistent with R, if $\exists r_i, r_o \in R, J_i \cong J_o, P_i \neq P_o$ and $r_i \succeq pl_i, r_o \succeq pl_o$. If P_i is sending information with attributes not in A_o, P_i should do a projection operation $\pi_{A_o}(pl_i)$ first.

In the example, r_8 authorizes P_E to get information on ($S \bowtie E \bowtie C \bowtie W$). If P_S sends the information of r_{11} to P_E, it will not be allowed. Although the attribute set of r_{11} is contained by r_8, there is no rule for P_E to get data on the join path of ($E \bowtie S$), and the data transmission is disallowed.

Definition 5. A query execution plan pl is **consistent** with the given rules R, if for each step of operation in the plan is consistent with the given rule set R.

Let us now consider the basic query planning problem: given a set of authorization rules R and an incoming query q against enforceable information, generate a consistent query plan pl that is optimal and satisfies all the rules.

Due to the difficulties in enumerating all possible ways of answering a query, we consider a greedy algorithm based on the relevance graph [20]. To generate a consistent query plan, we need to make sure all the join operations in a join path can be safely implemented. In other words, we need to find a way of enforcing the query join path and retrieve all the attributes for the query. To find an efficient consistent query plan, we always choose the optimal join path enforcement plan first, and then apply the greedy mechanism to obtain required relevant rules. The problem of covering all the required attributes is similar to the classical weighted set covering problem, and hence the greedy algorithm also follows a similar approach.

The optimal enforcement plan for a join path on a specified party can be precomputed by extending the rule enforcement checking algorithm using a dynamic programming approach. Such a plan only enforces the join operations in query and usually results in missing attributes. To retrieve missing attributes, we traverse the graph structure again to decompose the target rule into a set of relevant rules that can provide these attributes. We record the required operations among these rules, and then recursively find ways to enforce these relevant rules to generate a query plan. With the greedy heuristic, we always try to decompose a rule into a minimal number of relevant rules. As we recursively look for the plans to enforce the relevant rules, we try to use the intermediate results as much as possible to improve the performance. The details of the algorithm and proofs of correctness can be found in [20].

The time complexity of the proposed greedy algorithm is $O(N^3)$, where N is the total number of rules. In addition, we evaluated the generated query plans of the algorithm. Since the optimal plan cannot be found in general, we cannot compare the resulting query plans with the optimal ones. Thus, we use simple case studies, where manually finding the optimal plans becomes possible, and we compare the results on these cases. The results show that the greedy query planning algorithm is effective in finding a good query plan for an authorized query. In most of the cases, it generated the optimal plans, and it gave close to optimal plans in the remaining cases.

4   Other Authorization Issues

We discuss several other issues in this section. The first problem is using a trusted third party in a minimal way to enforce rules that are not enforceable among existing collaborating parties. The second problem is maintaining the rule consistency property in the case of rule changes.

4.1   Rule Enforcement with Trusted Third Parties

As discussed earlier, the enforcement checking may reveal that no party is capable of performing certain operations. One way to handle such a case is by introducing trusted third parties that provided required data accesses in order to enforce unenforceable rules. However, third parties may be expensive to use and the data given to them could be at greater risk of exposure than the data maintained by original parties. Therefore, we focus on the problem of using third parties minimally in order to deliver the information regulated by the given authorization rules. We model the cost of using third party by communication and computing costs. It is not surprising that finding the minimal cost with third party to implement a given rule is NP-hard, and thus a greedy algorithm becomes essential.

We assume that a trusted third party (TP) is not among the existing cooperative parties and can receive information from any cooperative party. We assume that the TP always performs required operations honestly, and does not leak information to any other party. The simplest third party model is one of memoryless service provider. That is, each time we want to enforce a rule, we need to send all relevant information to the third party. The third party does its job, returns the results and then completely cleans up its storage space (i.e., no retention of data between successive requests). With the existence of a third party, we can always enforce a rule by sending relevant information from cooperative parties to TP.

Since each rule defines a relational table, we can quantify the amount of information represented by a rule. This can be exploited in minimizing the amount of information used by third parties. All the selected rules must be relevant to the target rule r_t that is to be enforced. If a relevant rule of r_t is not relevant to any other relevant rules of r_t with longer join paths on the same party, we call it a *Candidate Rule*. We only choose from candidate rules to decide the data that needs to be sent to the *TP*. Sending minimal information to the third party can minimize not only communication cost but also computation costs. However, estimating computation costs precisely can be challenging.

Suppose that we have a set of cooperative parties $\{P_1, P_2 \ldots P_m\}$ together with a set of rules $R = \{r_1, r_2 \ldots r_n\}$ and a *target rule* r_t to be enforced at the third party *TP*. The amount of the information is quantified by sum of the number of attributes picked from each rule multiplied by the number of tuples in that selected rule. Thus, we want to minimize the communication cost $Cost = \sum_{i=0}^{k} \pi(r_i) * card(r_i)$, where r_i is a selected rule, k is the number of selected rules, and $\pi(r_i)$ is the number of attributes selected to be sent, and $card(r_i)$ is the number of tuples in r_i. More specifically, the communication cost can be defined as follows:

$$cost(C) = \sum_{i=1}^{k} w(S_i)\pi(S_i), \pi(S_i) = \begin{cases} |S_j \cap (U \setminus \bigcup_{j=1}^{i-1} S_j)|, & \text{if}(key(S_i) \notin \bigcup_{j=1}^{i-1} S_j) \\ |S_j \cap (U \setminus \bigcup_{j=1}^{i-1} S_j)| + 1, & \text{if}(key(S_i) \in \bigcup_{j=1}^{i-1} S_j) \end{cases}$$

(1)

In Eq. (1), the function $key(S_i)$ gives the key attribute of candidate rule r_i. In general, this can depend on the number of attributes selected by the rule r_i. To illustrate, suppose that we have a rule $\{oid, total, pid, location\}, (E, W) \rightarrow$ Party E. Even though *oid* is the key of the entire rule, if we only need *location* in this rule, *pid* can be the key of the selected rule. In such a case, if *oid* is covered by previous selected rules but *pid* is not, then using *pid* as the key can reduce the overall cost. However, due to the complexity of these situations, we assume function $key(S_i)$ always gives the key of r_i, which is *oid*. We can think $w(S_i)$ is the per attribute cost for the rule r_i which is mostly determined by $card(r_i)$. In fact, the number of tuples in a relation/join path depends on the length of the join paths and the join selectivity among the different relations. Join selectivity [17] is the ratio of tuples that agree on the join attributes between different relations, and it can be well estimated using the historical and statistical data of these relations in many cases.

The "computing cost" is defined as the cost of CPU usage and disk I/O. These costs are incurred as the third party fetches data from storage devices, performs join operations, and writes out the join results. (The I/O cost of receiving the incoming data from cooperative parties and relaying results to them is counted as part of communication cost and not included in the computation cost.) The computing cost is difficult to estimate because of the different access methods for relations (e.g., index scan or sequential scan), and different join methods (e.g., nested loop, sort-merge, hash-join, etc.) Moreover, the order of joins and the size of the input data and join results also influence the computing cost. We assume the sizes (in terms of number of tuples) of the basic relations and results of joins are known. We denote the cost of a resulting relation on join path J_i as $w(J_i)$, which can be estimated as discussed above. We also assume all the joins are done with nested loop method, and given n rules, the third party always does $n-1$ sequential join operations. We assume the relations have indices on the join attributes. For a nested loop join with two input relations, the cost can be estimated as: $Access(Outer) + (Card(Outer) * Access(Inner))$, where $Access(R)$ is the cost of access the relation R, and $Card(R)$ is the number of tuples in R. Obviously, we always prefer using the smaller input relation as the outer relation. In addition, as we need to perform $n-1$ joins, we keep the intermediate join results of the previous joins. The result of a join can be estimated as $Access(Result) = Access(Out * Inner * SelectivityFactor)$, where $SelectivityFactor$ is the estimate of what fraction of input tuples will be in the result. Therefore, the total cost of $n-1$ join operations is:

$$CompCost = Access(R_1) + \sum_{i=1}^{n-1} (Card(JR_i) * Card(R_{i+1}) * Attr(R_{i+1}) * SF_{JR_i,R_{i+1}})$$

In the above equation, R_1 is the selected rule with least cost $w(J_i)$, and $Access(R) = Card(R) * Attr(R)$, where $Attr(R)$ is the number of attributes of R. JR_i is the join results of the rules from R_1 to R_i, and $SF_{JR_i,R_{i+1}}$ is the selectivity factor for each join operations. To minimize $CompCost$, it is preferred to have fewer operations, and for each operation, one with smaller cardinality should be used as the *Outer* relation. Given a set of selected relevant rules generated by the previous algorithms, we calculate the computing cost using the above model. Our experiments indicate that the communication cost and computing cost are generally closely related in practice (even though counterexamples are easy to construct). For the detailed algorithms and the comparisons with brute force algorithms, please refer to [11].

4.2 Handling Rule Changes

Until now, we have assumed the rules to be static. In practice, the rules may change with varying frequencies. One potential reason is simply a change in business policies, which is expected to occur only occasionally. The other case is where the interaction might involve multiple phases or stages with different (or somewhat different) rules in each phase. Other intermediate situations are also possible – such as when access rights are couple with some kind of reputation system. In the following we briefly consider the issues that may arise due to changes in access rules.

In general, a change of authorization rule that meets the new requirement and also has minimal impact on the remaining authorization rules is the optimal solution. In the algorithm considered here, we simply minimize the number of rules that need to be modified; however, in general, several other considerations may apply. For instance, some authorization rules may be more important than the others, and this aspect may need to be considered in minimizing the change. Similarly, some parties may collaborate more intimately or be more trustworthy than the others, and the changes should consider this gradation as well.

As rules are being changed, usually we need to modify a set of rules to maintain the rule consistency property. There are basically two types of rule changes. The first type of rule change is granting or revoking non-key attributes (non-join attributes) to an existing rule. In such scenarios, we can take advantage of the relevance graph to maintain the rule consistency. In case of rule grant, we search upwards in the relevance graph starting from the rule being modified, and this can be done with a depth first search. If the rule being inspected does not have the newly granted attributes, then the algorithm adds these attributes to the rule. If the rule being inspected already has these attributes, the search along this path will stop and another path will be picked. Consequently, the added attributes will be propagated to all the related rules that are at a higher level from the rule being changed. In the case of revocation, we search the relevance graph downwards, and the process is similar.

There is another type of rule change, where a rule with a new join path is granted to a party or an existing rule is completely revoked. We first discuss the new rule grant. In such a case, we need to check if this rule can join with existing rules to generate legitimate new rules. The mechanism is similar to the previous approach for generating the consistent closure. As the newly added rule has a new join path, we first obtain the key attribute of it, and then the rule is put into its corresponding join group. Within this group, as a new rule is added, the algorithm recomputes the consistent join group. This can be done efficiently since these rules all can join over their key attributes. The new rule is inserted into the graph of the join group. The algorithm will not check all its relevant rules in the graph since their composition will not create new join paths. All the other rules are checked and the new rule can join with each of them to form another new rule and be put into the consistent join group. In the next step, each of the added rules is iterated to see what are the other rules that can be generated based on it. By iterating the key attributes and the consistent join groups associated with them, the algorithm adds all the generated rules into the rule set so as to complete it as a consistent closure.

If an existing rule is completely revoked, we need to make sure that such a join path can no longer be generated from the remaining relevant rules. Therefore, each possible ways to enforce the join path need to be obtained and the possible pairs should be taken out. To achieve that, we use an algorithm taking advantage of the relevance graph as well. In the graph, only the *direct relevant rules* of the revoked rule denoted as r_v are examined. The direct relevant rules of r_v are the relevant ones in the graph that directly connect with r_v with one edge. For each of the directly connected rule r_d, the algorithm computes its matching rule r_m if it exists. Given the join schema and relevance graph, r_m can be efficiently determined, and (r_d, r_m) forms a pair which means a join over them can enforce the join path of rule r_v.

For each found pair of rules, the algorithm needs to remove one rule from it so as to make the join path no longer enforceable. If a rule in the pair is not locally enforceable, we prefer to remove it since it does not cause cascade revocations. In contrast, if a rule in the pair is locally enforceable, by removing this rule, we need to make sure all the rules that can compose this one are taken out. Thus, a cascade of revocations will occur. As this is a recursive process, we want to revoke minimal number of rules so that the impact is minimal. Hence, when iterating each pair of rules, the algorithm also records the number of appearances of the rules. The rule with most appearances is preferred to be removed since removing one such rule can break several pairs. In the worst case, half of the existing rules need to be removed from the rule set. The detailed algorithms for this are available in [9].

5 Conclusions and Future Work

In this chapter, we considered scenarios that require different parties and enterprises to cooperate with one another to perform computations to satisfy business requirements. Each of these enterprises owns and manages its data independently using a private cloud, and these parties need to selectively share some information with one another. We considered an authorization model where authorization rules are used to constrain the access privileges based on the results of join operations over relational data.

In such an environment, we identified the problems of rule consistency and rule enforcement. For a query requesting enforceable information, consistent query plans are required so as to answer the query. We introduced the notion of consistent query plan and a mechanism to generate such plans. For the authorization rules that cannot be enforced among the cooperative parties, we proposed to use a trusted third party to perform the required join operations. We defined cost models to minimize the interactions between cooperative parties and third parties. Finally, we discussed how to maintain the rule consistency when some rules are modified.

We assumed that the collaborating parties first make the rules via negotiations, and then check whether a query is authorized and the safe ways to answer the query. It is possible to consider reversing the process. That is, we may want to figure out the complete set of queries that should be answered to meet business requirements, and after that we design authorization rules for cooperative parties so that only these wanted queries can be answered. However, due to the local computation, we may authorize extra information when granting privileges for this set of queries. Thereby, the problem becomes to find the best way of making rules so that minimal amount of extra information will be released together with the rules. To achieve that, we may also need a limited number of third parties are given, and there is a problem of finding the optimal solution under such a scenario.

We studied the rule consistency problem with infrequent rule changes. In a military or workflow scenario, the permissions as well as the data may change on a per mission basis so that an authorization rule given to a party applies only for a short period of time. Since the relevant data also changes frequently in this case, it will become useless after some time. In such environments, the authorization rule can be granted dynamically based on the demands. For instance, for each step in a query, we can grant permissions to authorize the operation on the fly. Once such a step is executed, the authorizations are revoked. This is similar to the workflow scenario. By granting privileges for a short time period, the extra information that is obtainable via local computation can be limited. The challenging problem becomes finding a way to schedule the queries as well as the time points to grant the authorizations so that minimal amount of extra information is released.

In our current model, access privileges are specified at the attribute level. Once a party can access an attribute, it can get all the tuples projected on that attribute. Since certain tuples can be more sensitive than others, restrictions on the tuple level are also necessary to prevent undesired data release. Thus if would interesting to consider simplified forms of selection operations that can be handled by the same framework. In addition, it is also interesting to consider the write permissions. Our current models assume that only the data owners may change their data and other parties just read the data from these owners. In some situations, it is desirable that a collaborating party can also modify the data owned by others. In addition to the synchronization problems, there is also the challenging problem of organizing the privileges and correctly granting and revoking write privileges to certain parties.

Our current model does not assume any malicious insiders and all the parties are expected to strictly follow the given authorization rules. In practice, a party may not behave honestly during the collaboration. For instance, a party may obtain some authorized information from a data owner, and then leak it to some unauthorized parties. As another example, a party that receives data from the data owner and sends it to another party according to the generated query plan may change some of the data. Thus, it is required to have a mechanism that can verify the integrity of the received data. One possibility is to use the existing mechanisms such as hash values, Merkle trees, and signatures to ensure the data integrity [22,23]. Considering the properties in the collaboration environment, it may be possible to check the data integrity through collaboration. In cooperative data access, there may exist more than one legitimate data transmission path beginning from the data owner to the authorized party. Therefore, parties can exchange the information they have. By doing that, if the number of misbehaving parties is limited, it is possible to detect them. It is also possible to define rules in such a way that each query be answered in at least k ways (for some k), and misbehaviors can be detected if only fewer than $k/2$ ways behave irregularly. Furthermore, existing mechanisms such as reputation systems [19] and trust management [21] can be considered to ensure the data integrity in the cooperative data access environments.

Our third party model has been rather simplistic. It is possible to consider more sophisticated models where the third party can store data and even the intermediate results for more efficient enforcement. Because of the limited availability of storage, and the varying potential of reuse of stored data, one needs to design caching policies carefully. The optimal cache policy of the third party can be different from the file cache and process cache because the relational data is structured and we can cache the data on a per tuple or column basis. Since the business data of the cooperative parties may be changing dynamically, caching also introduces the tricky problem of maintaining synchronization between original data and its copies.

To build a private cloud, different parties may rent the cloud infrastructure from the same service provider. It is also possible for an enterprise to build a hybrid cloud where the data owner manages the sensitive data locally, but the data for sharing is put in a public cloud. These emerging trends create new challenges and opportunities for secure cooperative data access. If cooperative parties use the same cloud provider, then the cloud provider could be used as a partially trusted third party to help enforce the security policies. In addition, it may be possible to perform privacy preserving join operations in such an environment. The expected mechanism can be a hybrid of using a trusted third party and the secure multiparty computation. Also, the cost model should also be revised under such situations.

References

1. G. Aggarwal, M. Bawa, P. Ganesan, and etc. Two can keep A secret: A distributed architecture for secure database services. In CIDR 2005, pages 186–199.
2. R. Agrawal, D. Asonov, M. Kantarcioglu, and Y. Li. Sovereign joins. In , ICDE 2006, 3–8 April 2006, Atlanta, GA, USA, page 26, 2006.
3. A. V. Aho, C. Beeri, and J. D. Ullman. The theory of joins in relational databases. ACM Transactions on Database Systems, 4(3):297–314, 1979.
4. E. Al-Shaer, A. El-Atawy, and T. Samak. Automated pseudo-live testing of firewall configuration enforcement. IEEE Journal on Selected Areas in Communications, 27(3):302–314, 2009.
5. P. A. Bernstein, N. Goodman, E. Wong, C. L. Reeve, and J. B. Rothnie, Jr. Query processing in a system for distributed databases (SDD-1). ACM Transactions on Database Systems, 6(4):602–625, Dec. 1981.
6. A. Cali and D. Martinenghi. Querying data under access limitations. In ICDE 2008, April 7–12, 2008, Cancun, Mexico, pages 50–59, 2008.
7. S. De Capitani di Vimercati, S.Foresti, S.Jajodia, S.Paraboschi, and P.Samarati. Keep a few: Outsourcing data while maintaining confidentiality. In ESORICS 2009, pages 440–455.
8. R. Pottinger and A. Y. Halevy. Minicon: A scalable algorithm for answering queries using views. VLDB Journal, 10(2–3):182–198, 2001.
9. M. Le, K. Kant, and S. Jajodia. Access rule consistency in cooperative data access environment. In 8th IEEE International Conference on Collaborative Computing: Networking, Applications and Worksharing, 2012.
10. M. Le, K. Kant, and S. Jajodia. Rule configuration checking in secure cooperative data access. In 5th Symposium on Configuration Analytics and Automation (SafeConfig), 2012.
11. M. Le, K. Kant, and S. Jajodia. Rule enforcement with third parties in secure cooperative data access. In 27th IFIP WG 11.3 Working Conference on Data and Applications Security and Privacy (DBSec), 2013.
12. A. Wool. A quantitative study of firewall configuration errors. IEEE Computer, 37(6):62–67, 2004.
13. S. De Capitani di Vimercati, S. Foresti, S. Jajodia, S. Paraboschi, and P. Samarati. Assessing query privileges via safe and efficient permission composition. In CCS 2008, Virginia, USA, October 27–31, 2008.
14. S. De Capitani di Vimercati, S. Foresti, S. Jajodia, S. Paraboschi, and P. Samarati. Controlled information sharing in collaborative distributed query processing. In ICDCS 2008, Beijing, China, June 2008.
15. J. Goldstein and P. Larson. Optimizing queries using materialized views: A practical, scalable solution. In SIGMOD 2001, pages 331–342.
16. A. Y. Halevy. Answering queries using views: A survey. VLDB Journal,10(4):270–294,2001.
17. D. Kossmann. The state of the art in distributed query processing. ACM Comput. Survey, 32(4):422–469, 2000.

18. C. Li. Computing complete answers to queries in the presence of limited access patterns. VLDB Journal, 12(3):211–227, 2003.
19. K. Hoffman, D. Zage, and C. Nita-Rotaru, A survey of attack and defense techniques for reputation systems, ACM Computing Surveys (CSUR), vol. 42, no. 1, p. 1, 2009.
20. M. Le, K. Kant, and S. Jajodia. Consistent query plan generation in secure cooperative data access. Under submission. http://mason.gmu.edu/~mlep/submission.pdf
21. R. K. Ko, P. Jagadpramana, M. Mowbray, S. Pearson, M. Kirchberg, Q. Liang, and B. S. Lee, Trustcloud: A framework for accountability and trust in cloud computing, in Services (SERVICES), 2011 IEEE World Congress on, 2011, pp. 584–588.
22. J. Buchmann, E. Dahmen, E. Klintsevich, K. Okeya, and C. Vuillaume, Merkle signa- tures with virtually unlimited signature capacity, in Applied Cryptography and Net- work Security, 2007, pp. 31–45.
23. C. Wang, Q. Wang, K. Ren, and W. Lou, Privacy-preserving public auditing for data storage security in cloud computing, in INFOCOM, 2010 Proceedings IEEE, 2010, pp. 1–9.

Making Query Execution Over Encrypted Data Practical

Ken Smith, M. David Allen, Hongying Lan, and Andrew Sillers

Abstract The benefits of data outsourcing continue to grow, however owners of sensitive data cannot take full advantage due to its risk profile. Encrypted query processing promises to change this situation and allow data owners to securely outsource their sensitive data: data is encrypted, installed in a database on a remote (e.g., cloud) server, and standard queries are processed against the remote encrypted data. Correct query answers are returned without ever exposing plaintexts or decryption keys at the server. This chapter addresses three key challenges to realizing, as a practical option, the promise of encrypted query processing: handling query operations which cannot execute in ciphertext, implementing a working system, and achieving acceptable query performance.

1 Background: Clouds and Outsourcing

The trend to outsource data to third party clouds continues to grow, however for owners of sensitive data, clouds hold both great promise and vexing problems.

1.1 Outsourcing Data Management: The Promise

Renting a computing infrastructure frequently makes much better sense than owning and running one. Outsourcing the management of computing assets allows an organization to focus personnel, training, and hiring on their core business. It also offers unprecedented agility, such as near instant expansion and contraction of the organization's IT footprint as software development cycles and seasonal business

K. Smith (✉) • M.D. Allen • H. Lan • A. Sillers
The MITRE Corporation, McLean, VA, USA
e-mail: kps@mitre.org; dmallen@mitre.org; hlan@mitre.org; asillers@mitre.org

S. Jajodia et al. (eds.), *Secure Cloud Computing*, DOI 10.1007/978-1-4614-9278-8_8,   171

demands require, and takes advantage of the cost efficiencies of a volume provider of computing services, which have been compared to the efficiencies of household gas, water, and electric utilities. Especially in the era of big data, the cost of servers, disks, space, power, and cooling can far exceed the budget. Once purchased, computing assets must be actively patched, repaired, and upgraded; such costs can be avoided by renting.

In addition, outsourcing providers now offer a continually growing array of services that its customers could not afford to develop themselves. For example, Amazon Web Services offers rentable services such as inexpensive data archival, on-demand map reduce clusters, and subnets with private IP addresses [18].

This combination of rentable computing infrastructure and novel computing services makes widely available modes of computation which were previously impossible, or out of reach due to cost. Consider a medical experiment which generates and analyzes huge genetic datasets. The research funding to rent storage and computing on an as needed basis is far less than that required to purchase these and to pay professional staff to manage them. Using an outsourced infrastructure, novel studies can be proposed which might not otherwise be feasible under research funding.

1.2 Outsourcing Data Management: The Problem

Owners of *sensitive* datasets however, can be caught between the promise of outsourcing and the problem of losing control of part of the computing stack (Fig. 1). For an infrastructure as a service (IaaS) cloud, these stack layers include: hardware, virtualization, fabric, and customer-installed software applications (e.g., DBMS, web server, GUI); customers only control the final layer. Even with full confidence in cloud-supplied layers (e.g., the customer does not expect hypervisors to ever be compromised), cloud security engineering requires careful teamwork between

Fig. 1 Cloud security: the
challenge of letting go

the outsourcing vendor and the customer. The security features of vendor-supplied layers and customer-supplied layers must mesh without a flaw when they are used to implement a solution together. In this case, the utility analogy breaks down, because consumers rarely interact with their household and gas utilities beyond simply paying bills and turning service on and off.

Owners of sensitive datasets must also worry about the other participants in a cloud ecosystem. Unlike a self-managed infrastructure, the cloud ecosystem includes *cloud neighbors*, who typically belong to unknown organizations. In several published attacks, the attacker becomes a cloud neighbor of their target to stage the attack. For example, [22] illustrates a *side-channel* attack on a physically collocated virtual machine (i.e., one sharing the same physical host as the attacker's virtual machine), enabling the attacker to steal a cryptographic key in the target virtual machine by examining shared hardware resources.

The cloud ecosystem also includes vendor-supplied *cloud administrators*, who are typically assumed to be "honest but curious" [11]. However, this is not always the case. Recently, German citizens hiding their money in Swiss bank accounts to evade high national taxation rates were identified because the German government bribed the bank's database administrator [17]. Owners of sensitive government data cringe at the thought that a foreign government could influence a cloud administrator to do something like this.

In addition, in the advanced persistent threat (APT) attacker model [21], cited for the exfiltration of significant amounts of intellectual property, any person's online identity can be compromised (e.g., via a phishing attack) allowing the APT attacker to masquerade with the full privileges of the compromised identity. Therefore, any member of a cloud ecosystem could potentially become an attacker.

Due to such problems, owners of sensitive data are currently conflicted with respect obtaining the agility, services, division of labor, and efficiencies clouds can offer.

2 Using Data Encryption

A potentially game-changing strategy is the use of encryption to protect sensitive data in clouds. Encrypted data is mathematically transformed so only the possessor of a decryption key can reconstitute the original *plaintext* data without A prohibitively expensive computational effort. Thus, if sensitive cloud data is encrypted, an exfiltration attack does not truly succeed unless the attacker can additionally obtain the decryption key, or successfully attack the cryptosystem. This is true *regardless* of the stack layer the attack originates from, or the cloud denizen who executes it.

2.1 Pre-transmission Dataset Encryption

A simple strategy having these benefits is to encrypt each dataset prior to its transmission to the cloud, and to only decrypt it upon retrieval from the cloud. The downside of this strategy is that cloud applications cannot operate over these encrypted datasets, they must be downloaded before use. Consider the query "What is the location of helicopter 21?". In a normal cloud database deployment, the database would look up helicopter 21, and return a very small result relative to the size of the entire data set. For monolithic encrypted files and datasets, there is no way for the server to look up helicopter 21. Instead of returning a small answer, the entire database would need to be retrieved. With "big data" era terabyte and larger datasets, downloading the entire dataset before use is simply impractical.

2.2 Data-at-Rest Encryption

Data at rest encryption protects sensitive data in a storage system, can be used with cloud-based data, and allows computation over that data. Data is encrypted when stored on any cloud storage device, and decrypted when requested by an application. Data at rest encryption is used for many types of sensitive data, including personal health data covered by HIPAA, and sensitive but unclassified military information. Data at rest encryption is especially useful against physical attacks, such as a stolen laptop or disk drive, and mature products exist in which the user need not be an expert cryptographer or make large performance sacrifices. For example, Oracle's Transparent Database Encryption product (TDE) [14] now provides at rest encryption for Oracle DBMS's, exploiting new hardware encrypt/decrypt instructions [10].

Unfortunately, data at rest encryption does not protect *data in use*. It requires a decryption key to be available in the cloud so data can be decrypted and used by applications. As mentioned earlier, many attacks are aimed exactly at obtaining the decryption key. Furthermore, the moment a query hits a cloud application (e.g., a TDE encrypted database), data is decrypted and brought into cloud memory as plaintext. Thus, attackers do not actually need to obtain the key to defeat data at rest encryption, they simply need to exfiltrate plaintexts from cloud memory. Note that performing *data in use* encryption has not been added to standard security requirements simply because useful commercial solutions do not exist at this time.

2.3 Homomorphic Encryption and Computing Over Ciphertexts

Homomorphic cryptosystems promise the best of both worlds:

1. The ability to expose neither plaintext data nor decryption keys in clouds.

2. The ability for applications to nonetheless compute over encrypted data while it resides in the remote cloud.

Cryptosystems are valued primarily for their ability to secure information. As a side-effect, however, operations on their corresponding ciphertexts in some cryptosystems correspond to useful operations on plaintexts, which is called a *homomorphism* [5].

For example, in the Paillier [15] cryptosystem, the modular multiplication of two ciphertexts corresponds to the addition of their plaintexts. Thus, for two plaintext numbers m_1 and m_2, given only $E(m_1)$ and $E(m_2)$ (the encryptions of m_1 and m_2 respectively), and the public encryption key, it is possible to compute $E(m_1 + m_2)$ without access to the corresponding plaintexts. Other pairs of ciphertext and plaintext operations, although not strictly homomorphic provide identical utility. For example, in any deterministic cryptosystem, equality tests on ciphertexts correspond to equality tests on plaintexts. Thus, through the use of such cryptosystem properties, it is possible to perform useful operations on data *without ever decrypting it*.

Paillier is *additively* homomorphic because its homomorphism implements addition over plaintexts. Other cryptosystems (e.g., RSA) are *multiplicatively* homomorphic. The question naturally arises as to whether any cryptosystem is *fully homomorphic*, enabling *any* computable operation over plaintexts to be performed using ciphertext datasets.

Since being posed in 1979, the fully homomorphic encryption (FHE) problem remained open for over 30 years. It was recently solved by Craig Gentry [6], for which he won the 2009 ACM Dissertation award. Although Gentry's cryptosystem is fully homomorphic, and semantically secure, its performance degrades sharply with its security parameter. For a practical degree of security, performance of Gentry's original algorithm has been estimated to be as bad as 10 orders of magnitude worse than the corresponding plaintext operations [4], such that a one second computation would take over three centuries. To address this disparity, in 2011 DARPA initiated the PROCEED program [4]; research on the optimization of FHE is now very active, with several orders of magnitude improvement realized for various portions of FHE (e.g., key generation) [7, 19]; portions of this research have also been released as open source code [9]. However, for the foreseeable future, FHE remains computationally impractical. In addition, an efficient FHE implementation would not immediately enable users to execute conventional queries in a cloud-based PBMS. As the entire DBMS would have to be rewritten as a homomorphic function, a massively complex undertaking. Thus, in the following, we focus on the use of homomorphisms within the context of an existing DBMS.

2.4 Making Practical Tradeoffs

The FHE algorithms in Gentry's thesis illustrate a general principle regarding homomorphic computing. As illustrated in Fig. 2, a three-dimensional space of desirable features exists for homomorphic encryption: *functionality*, *security*, and *efficiency.* Gentry's FHE algorithms provide full computational functionality over plaintext, a very high level of security (i.e., semantic security), but very poor efficiency with respect to the equivalent operations over plaintext.

A cryptosystem with ideal qualities on all three axes does not exist, however, other useful points in this space make tradeoffs differently than Gentry's FHE. The Paillier cryptosystem has similar security to FHE, provides only partial homomorphic functionality (i.e., addition), but is *much* more efficient than FHE (within two orders of magnitude of plaintext addition. Microsoft researchers have recently developed a partially homomorphic cryptosystem [13] which can add integers in about 200 µs per addition (versus 15 µs in Paillier), however, their partially homomorphic functionality is much greater, enabling the computation of statistics like the variance over ciphertexts.

The key insight is that it is not necessary to realize *fully* homomorphic functionality to to provide practical benefits for users today who want to use sensitive data in clouds. It is sufficient to securely and efficiently achieve the functionality required to implement a useful cloud application. For example, most computations in the SQL language can be implemented without requiring full Turing-complete functionality.

2.5 The Database as a Service Architecture

In a groundbreaking 2002 paper [8], Hacigümüş et al. proposed a software architecture for implementing *practical* (i.e., sufficiently efficient, secure, and functional) SQL computations over a remote encrypted database server (e.g., hosted in an outsourced cloud infrastructure). Instead of relying on a single fully homomorphic cryptosystem, this architecture can utilize a carefully-chosen set of partially homomorphic cryptosystems. In other words, this architecture can be used to exploit the individual strengths of *multiple* points in the space of Fig. 2. Plaintext

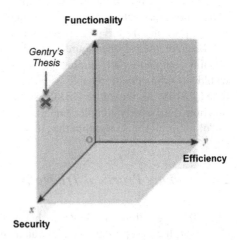

Fig. 2 A three dimensional tradeoff space for homomorphic encryption

SQL operations are translated into the appropriate homomorphic operations, similar to how a compiler translates programming language constructs into the appropriate machine codes.

As shown in Fig. 3, the user's original plaintext SQL query (bottom center) is translated into a query over encrypted data within a trusted client (left side). The correctness of the encrypted query is ensured by translation algorithms which substitute plaintext SQL operations for equivalent homomorphic operations.

The encrypted query is then sent off to a standard relational DBMS at the untrusted server (right side). While the table names, column names, and constants of encrypted query are ciphertext, the query itself remains a syntactically correct SQL query. The untrusted server DBMS thus naively executes it, and produces a set of encrypted results, which are then returned to the client (the temporary results area) and decrypted. In the final step, as discussed in the following section, the query executor applies any necessary *post-processing* to the decrypted results to generate the final correct plaintext answer, which is then returned to the user.

Thus, even though the database is fully encrypted and neither plaintexts nor decryption keys are ever exposed to the server, the end user issues the *same* SQL query and receives the *same* answer as if the database were standard plaintext.

2.6 Current Status and Prototypes

The vision of this paper has grown more compelling with time, as cloud architectures and their need for security has increased in importance, leading to its receipt of the 2012 ACM SIGMOD 10 year *Test of Time* award [1]. A large literature has also resulted from this initial paper, exploring suitable cryptosystems (e.g., varieties of order preserving encryption [2, 3]) and "bucketization" strategies which enable

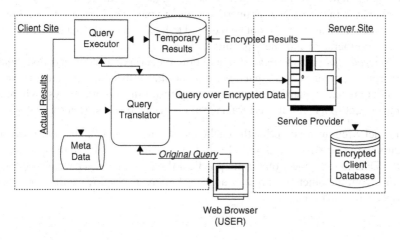

Fig. 3 Database as a service architecture

a tradeoff between the security and efficiency dimensions of the space in Fig. 2. However, as cited in the *Test of Time* award, no practical, commercially available, product which executes queries over encrypted data is available at this time.

Three notable prototyping projects exist, however, which provide valuable insights into the requirements for the practical realization of this technology. The first was developed as part of Hacigümüş' dissertation, and includes a general *planner* for encrypted query execution and introduced the *bucketization* strategy. The second, CryptDB [16] was developed as part of Raluca Popa's dissertation at MIT. CryptDB introduced features like onion encryption, and implemented several novel cryptosystems (e.g., a cryptosystem supporting dynamic joins between tables whose join keys were not previously encrypted with a congruent encryption key, along with algorithms for query processing time re-encryption of join keys). The third system is the MITRE DataStorm project [20], which contributed the IDEA system for generating the encrypted schema, a more detailed system architecture, and whose general focus is identifying and addressing the major barriers to practical computation over encrypted data.

3   Overview of Remainder of Chapter

These projects have yielded valuable insights. In the remaining sections we address three important challenges to the practical realization of this vision of executing database queries over encrypted data:

1. *Unexecutable query operations*: how do we execute query operations which *cannot* be executed over encrypted data? (Sect. 3),
2. *System implementation*: How do we mitigate the complexity of selecting an appropriate set of cryptosystems to apply to a specific user's query workload, using them to create an encrypted database on the server, and setting up a client-server system to service user queries over encrypted data? For this technology to be practical, a user should not be required to have a good understanding of fields like cryptography and query planning. (Sect. 5),
3. *Ciphertext query performance*: In addition to encryption and decryption, homomorphic operations over ciphertexts may be slower than their plaintext versions, and ciphertext expansion of plaintext may result in network delays. Where are the "sweet spots" for the performance of encrypted queries? (Sect. 6).

In each section, we describe the challenge, discuss how it can be addressed, and discuss the prospects for a practical solution. We draw heavily on the experiences of the DataStorm project due to its practical direction, however we also bring in lessons from the other two projects as well. Finally, in Sect. 7, we discuss general prospects for the future.

4   Unexecutable Query Operations

The first challenge is that some user queries may contain operations which, for several different reasons, cannot be executed over a ciphertext database. From the perspective of relational query optimization, we typically desire to *push* selections deeper in the query execution tree, but sometimes cannot. Analogously, here we desire to push operations in the plaintext query into an encrypted execution at the remote cloud server, but for the reasons given below, we cannot.

4.1   Reasons Operations Cannot Be Executed Over Ciphertext

While fully homomorphic encryption (FHE) is a reality, it is not a practical option for cloud users due to its current performance profile. Without the availability of a secure fully homomorphic cipher, we seek to compose a set of partially homomorphic ciphers which will cover the needs of database query operations. So far, we have presented the Paillier cryptosystem as a running example of a partially (additively) homomorphic cipher, but there are many other possibilities. For example, unpadded RSA and ElGamal [12] are multiplicatively homomorphic, and the Goldwasser-Micali cryptosystem is homomorphic with respect to the exclusive-or operation. However, at the present time, the set of operations in SQL is greater than the set for which we have direct translations into partially homomorphic cryptosystems. This is one reason for unexecutable query operations.

Furthermore, ciphers are of course not created equal with respect to their strength and security; in some situations (such as the use of unpadded RSA, which loses semantic security) although a partially homomorphic cipher may provide the desired operation, it not be a reasonable choice because it does not meet the security requirements of an application.

A third type of operation which cannot be executed in ciphertext is one that results in what we call an "encryption type mismatch", an issue first identified in [16]. Consider the < operation in the query segment WHERE age < (SELECT SUM(years) FROM employee). If the input to the SUM() operation (an encryption of the integer year) is a Paillier ciphertext to enable the computation of a summation over ciphertexts, the output will also be a Paillier ciphertext. However, Paillier ciphertexts cannot be used in the ensuing order test, because Paillier is not an order-preserving cryptosystem. Although plaintext operands must only agree with their operator in datatype (e.g., string, integer), ciphertext operands must agree not only in datatype but also in encryption type. In this example, the < order test cannot be executed in ciphertext because its second operand is of the wrong encryption type.

So to summarize, there are three key reasons preventing operations in plaintext queries from being translated into operations which can be executed over ciphertext (i.e., pushed to a cloud).

1. *No available homomorphic operation.* The plaintext operation (e.g. string con-
   catenation, cube roots) simply lacks an appropriate homomorphic ciphertext
   operation.
2. *Insufficiently secure homomorphic operation.* Although homomorphic ciphertext
   operations exist, none have a security profile which meets the requirements of a
   local security policy. For example, an order test in plaintext queries (e.g., WHERE
   age < 21) is directly and efficiently implemented via an order preserving
   cryptosystem. However, such a cryptosystem reveals the order of the encrypted
   plaintexts. If this is the only ciphertext implementation of an order test, and it
   violates local security policy, order tests cannot be executed over ciphertext.
3. *Encryption type mismatches.* A plaintext operation cannot be translated into a
   homomorphic operation whose operands have the required ciphertext type.

If a plaintext query, or a coherent plaintext query workload, contains any
unexecutable operations, encrypted query execution is unavailable without way to
address these operations. In the following we discuss the use of a *post-processing*
architecture to enable the execution of queries and query workloads which contain
unexecutable operations.

4.2   Post-processing

Post-processing is illustrated by the architecture in Fig. 4 (which is representative
of the Hacigümüş and DataStorm prototypes). The data owner initially encrypts
their schema and database instances and installs these on the outsourced server
as the Encrypted DB. During query processing, the user or application submits
a plaintext query Q to a middleware application (developed to enable encrypted
query execution) within its trusted client. The middleware's planner rewrites Q into
a set of queries represented by Q' and Q'' in Fig. 4 which execute: (a) at the server
in the encrypted database, and (b) (for any query components with unexecutable
operations) at the client in the middleware post-processor, over decrypted plaintext
results returned from the encrypted server. A correct plan produces the same results
as running Q against the original plaintext database.

Consider query Q in Fig. 5. Q's WHERE clause contains two parts, one which
is executable over ciphertext and one which is not (due to the SQL LIKE clause).
The planner generates query Q' for execution at the encrypted server. Note that table
names, column names, and constants are all encrypted in Q', however it remains a
well-formed SQL query. The encrypted database sends the results of Q' back to the
middleware where they are decrypted. In the middleware post-processor, query Q''
is executed (in an in-memory DBMS) over the decrypted results, applying the final
portion of the query and returning the final correct answer.

Post-processing thus makes it possible to execute queries containing operations which are unexecutable over ciphertext (e.g., LIKE, cos(), encryption type
mismatches).

4.3 Planning

Query planning can be simple in many cases. If the query contains *no* unexecutable operations, all execution occurs at the server and the post-processing step is skipped. For many more queries, for example *Q* in Fig. 5, a relatively simple "U-shaped" plan is the best choice (i.e., it is correct and no more efficient plan can be found).

However, some queries require a more sophisticated plan. Consider a query to retrieve all 30 year old employees who make less than the average salary:

```
SELECT * FROM emp
WHERE emp.age = 30 AND emp.salary <
SELECT AVG(emp.salary) FROM emp
```

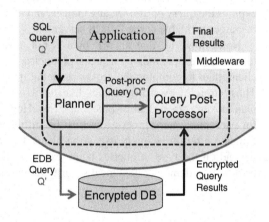

Fig. 4 Post processing architecture

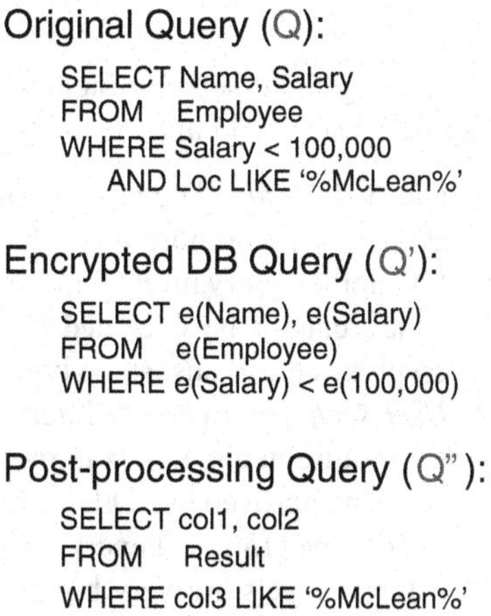

Original Query (Q):

```
SELECT Name, Salary
FROM   Employee
WHERE  Salary < 100,000
       AND Loc LIKE '%McLean%'
```

Encrypted DB Query (Q'):

```
SELECT e(Name), e(Salary)
FROM   e(Employee)
WHERE  e(Salary) < e(100,000)
```

Post-processing Query (Q''):

```
SELECT col1, col2
FROM   Result
WHERE  col3 LIKE '%McLean%'
```

Fig. 5 Query rewriting

Note that the average contains a division. If we encrypt salary with the Paillier cryptosystem, we can compute the sum (and count) at the server over ciphertext, but not the final division, which must be computed back at the client after decryption. However, to execute a simple "U-shaped" execution plan would require us to bring back the *entire* emp table across the network as well to compute the rest of the query, which could be extremely costly for a large table.

A *maximal push* (MP) heuristic, which constructs a better performing plan, is shown in Fig. 6. Starting with a baseline plan that returns everything to the client for post-processing, a maximal push plan is constructed by pushing every possible operation to the server. This heuristic is presented in the original Hacigümüş et al. paper: "we would attempt to rewrite the query tree, such that most of the effort of evaluating the query occurs at the server, and the client does the least amount of work [8]." Not only can the MP plan minimize the server result set size (and the resulting network traffic), pushing every possible operation to the server also exploits the query optimizer, any indices, and likely much more powerful computing resources available at the DBMS server.

Note, however, that an MP plan is not always optimal: it would be cheaper to return the operands of a cross product and compute the cross product at the client, than to compute the cross product at the server and return the entire result! Thus, straightforward heuristics like the U-shaped plan, and the maximal push plan, cover a great deal of practical cases. However, a very general query planner for encrypted query processing must be sufficiently sophisticated to generate and evaluate *alternative* query execution plans. The requirements for a given scenario depend on the type of queries being executed, the size of data tables, and (as the next section demonstrates) local security requirements.

5 System Implementation

A working client-server system which can execute query plans over encrypted data can be a practical challenge to implement, due to:

1. *Query diversity:* The plan for one query might require cryptosystems which are: additively homomorphic, order preserving, and deterministic, whereas the plan for another query might require none of these. And a query might have operations which cannot be executed by any currently available partially homomorphic cryptosystem. Thus, some type of automated query planning is needed.
2. *User scenario diversity:* Interactions with users have shown dramatically different requirements. For example, some users will not use a cryptosystem unless it is on an approved list. Others, realizing they are exposing plaintexts, welcome the use of novel forms of encryption. User priorities may change as well, for example if threat levels are very high. Thus, although a planner is needed, it is difficult

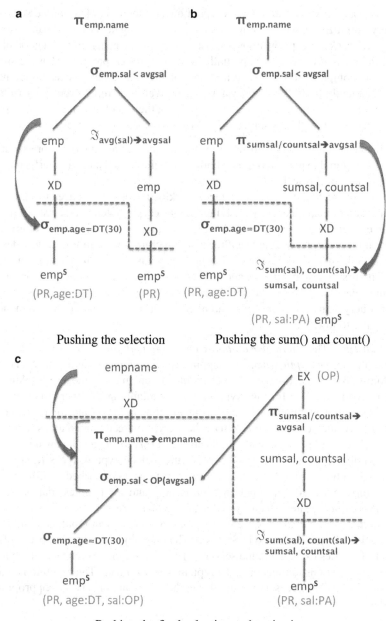

Pushing the selection   Pushing the sum() and count()

Pushing the final selection and projection

Fig. 6 Maximal push query plan

to *automatically* determine an encrypted query execution plan; unlike standard query optimization with its single focus on optimizing query performance, some user feedback about priorities is necessary to guide the generation of a good plan.

3. *Cryptosystem diversity:* Each partially homomorphic cryptosystem has a distinctive and complex profile of security, functionality, and efficiency features. There are frequently *multiple* cryptosystems of a given type (e.g., order preserving), and more are being published every day. Thus, the job of creating the encrypted database which will be installed on the server is a significant challenge.

Ordinary business users who simply want to execute their queries more security cannot be required to possess depth in both cryptography and database performance, or the promise of this technology will never be realized.

Given a plaintext database, and a query workload over it, users need to somehow generate a ciphertext database (involving various cryptosystems) and a set of query plans to execute their query workload over that database. To mitigate the complexity of system implementation, the DataStorm architecture, shown in Fig. 7, includes an intuitive multi-step workflow by which non-specialist users can accomplish these tasks. The first two steps (*design* and *migration*) help the user create an appropriate encrypted database. The third step (*execution*) enables the user to generate and execute query plans in a client-server architecture. These steps are discussed in more detail in the following.

1. *Design Time.* The *interactive database encryption advisor* (IDEA) automatically generates an *encryption map*, a mapping from plaintext columns to encrypted columns based on: (a) the original plaintext schema, (b) the user's plaintext query workload, and (c) the cryptosystems available in the encryption library. IDEA's initial mapping is based on generation of MP plans for each query. Users may interactively override IDEA's encryption recommendations (e.g., due to local security policy constraints), causing IDEA to suggest a new encryption map. IDEA uses a lattice-based visualization of encryption types to simplify interaction for those unfamiliar with cryptosystems, as described in [20].

2. *Migration.* Based on the final encryption map and the plaintext database, the *migration tool* creates the encrypted database on the server.

3. *Execution.* The *planner* takes a user's plaintext query as an input, and builds an execution plan, as described in Sect. 4.3. The plan object produced consists of (a) a set of queries executed at the server, (b) a set of queries executed at the client, and (c) operations to transform, decrypt, and encrypt data. The execution engine traverses the plan tree, sending queries to the client and/or server as appropriate, and assembles the final result.

Although DataStorm's architecture does not consist of commercial grade tools, their use has nonetheless made setting up a working client-server query system much easier.

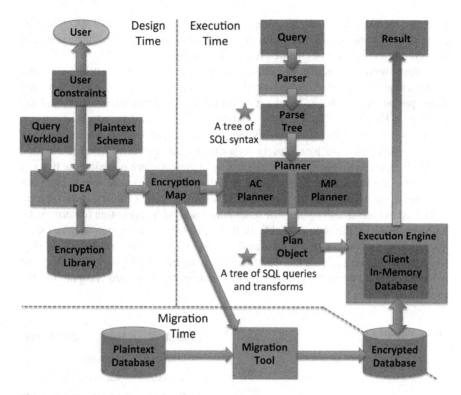

Fig. 7 DataStorm system architecture

6 Ciphertext Query Performance

A basic question potential users of encrypted database queries must ask is: how much does it cost in performance to execute a query over ciphertext, with respect to executing the same query over plaintext?

At a coarse level, there are three major categories of costs to consider:

1. *Client processing:* query planning, decryption of results, and post-processing.
2. *Network:* all transfers, especially returning ciphertext answers to the server.
3. *Server processing:* answering the ciphertext query.

Client processing times can vary widely, and are highly optimizable. For example, Paillier decryptions take a very slow 44 ms per integer. However, optimizations like hardware decryption (e.g., most new chips include AES decryption in their instruction set), and client-side ciphertext caching can speed decryption up significantly.

Network times are heavily impacted by the answer size. Note that this is true for plaintext queries at a remote server as well, however *ciphertext expansion* (the factor by which a ciphertext is larger than its corresponding plaintext) compounds this cost. Network times are also impacted by the network's overall speed and by competition for network bandwidth, but often not in a predictable fashion due to network protocols which dynamically allocate bandwidth.

Despite hard-to-quantify variability, however, for both client processing and network transfers smaller answer sizes are strongly correlated with better overall query performance. This is ideal for a simple and common query like "Find the location of Helicopter 21". Even on a database of many terabytes, the answer size remains small, thus little client processing or network transfer cost is incurred.

In the following, we focus solely on a direct comparison of server processing speeds for plaintexts and ciphertexts. In Fig. 8, we compare a basic equality test query (like the Helicopter 21 query) on an indexed field. Identical server databases were set up in three sizes (10, 100, 1,000 K tuples), one in plaintext and one in ciphertext at each size. The ciphertext database used AES encryption (deterministic AES was used for the indexed field). Both query plans are identical, use the index, and return 4 % of the server database as the answer. To eliminate network variability, both databases were run on *localhost* using a standard Intel laptop with 3.5 GB of RAM running Postgres 9.1.4. After cache warmup, timings were computed as the average of 10 runs.

Fig. 8 Tests on equality query; times in ms

	PT total	CT total	CT/PT ratio
10K	0.6286115	1.0018130	1.59
100K	3.2718125	7.1076260	2.17
1000K	220.8141110	369.9193835	1.67

Figure 8 shows a stable ratio of ciphertext to plaintext execution times (between 1.59 and 2.17); ciphertext being around twice as slow. Decryption and query planning are a negligible fraction of these times. Much of this slowdown is attributable to the increased size of ciphertexts, resulting in more data pages being touched for the same query and data. A two-fold slowdown at the server is acceptable in many cases, especially for queries with a small fixed size answer (e.g., for web queries which populate forms) whose overall cost is dominated by the delay of communicating with a remote server over a network.

Figure 9 shows a similar experiment for a summation query; Paillier encryption was used for the field being summed. The database performed the homomorphic operation, a modular multiplication of ciphertexts, via a user defined aggregate function (UDAF) written in C in about 15 μs. In this case, working with ciphertexts is 67–82 times worse than plaintexts (still much faster than current fully homomorphic encryption algorithms). Note, however, that summation is an "embarrassingly parallel" operation, and commercial clouds make it possible to rent groups of compute servers for parallel computations. Paillier summations are thus an ideal candidate for speedup via cloud parallelism, and this ratio could be substantially reduced, even to unity. In addition, summation is a dramatically data reducing operation: terabytes operands can be reduced to a single answer, which incurs little network delay. Thus, massive summations and the queries that rely on them (e.g., averages, business intelligence aggregates) are promising candidates for encrypted query execution as well.

Fig. 9 Tests on summation query; times in ms

	PT server	CT server	CT/PT ratio
10K	1.498111111	111.9696768	74.74
100K	14.01076768	1153.161051	82.31
1000K	169.0187677	11356.59457	67.19

7 Conclusions

In conclusion, challenges to query execution over encrypted data do exist, including individual query operations which cannot be executed over ciphertext, implementing a working client-server query execution system, and the performance of queries executed over ciphertext. However, as discussed in this chapter, these are well addressed by query planning, tools which assist the user with system implementation, and aiming for performance sweet spots, such as queries retrieving small objects and parallel summation queries.

As new cryptosystems are continually being developed and cloud services (e.g., parallelism on demand) grow, the future of encrypted query processing for cloud security is promising. Synergy between the information management and cryptography research communities, with their differing focus and priorities, is improving and has recently resulted in beneficial research. As that dialogue continues to grow, it will benefit this developing area. Further work is needed to develop commercial grade query planners/optimizers and system implementation tools, and efficient and secure cryptosystems with the partially homomorphic functionality to enable more types of queries to be processed at the server instead of post-processing.

References

1. ACM, *Test of time award*, www.sigmod.org/2012/awards_sigmod.shtml, 2012.
2. Rakesh Agrawal, Jerry Kiernan, Ramakrishnan Srikant, and Yirong Xu, *Order preserving encryption for numeric data*, Proceedings of the 2004 ACM SIGMOD international conference on Management of data (New York, NY, USA), SIGMOD '04, ACM, 2004, pp. 563–574.
3. Alexandra Boldyreva, Nathan Chenette, Younho Lee, and Adam O'Neill, *Order-preserving symmetric encryption*, Advances in Cryptology – EUROCRYPT 2009 (Antoine Joux, ed.), Lecture Notes in Computer Science, vol. 5479, Springer Berlin Heidelberg, 2009, pp. 224–241.
4. DARPA, *The darpa program for programming comutation on encrypted data (proceed)*, http://www.darpa.mil/Our_Work/I2O/Programs/, 2013.

5. Caroline Fontaine and Fabien Galand, *A survey of homomorphic encryption for nonspecialists*, EURASIP Journal on Information Security **1** (2007).

6. Craig Gentry, *A fully homomorphic encryption scheme*, Ph.D. thesis, Stanford University, 2009.

7. Craig Gentry and Shai Halevi, *Implementing gentry's fully-homomorphic encryption scheme*, Advances in Cryptology – EUROCRYPT 2011 (KennethG. Paterson, ed.), Lecture Notes in Computer Science, vol. 6632, Springer Berlin Heidelberg, 2011, pp. 129–148.

8. Hakan Hacigümüş, Bala Iyer, Chen Li, and Sharad Mehrotra, *Executing sql over encrypted data in the database-service-provider model*, Proceedings of ACM SIGMOD (New York, NY, USA), SIGMOD '02, ACM, 2002, pp. 216–227.

9. IBM, *Ibm homomorphic encryption library project on github*, https://github.com/shaih/HElib, 2013.

10. Intel, *Intel advanced encryption standard instructions (aes-ni)*, http://software.intel.com /en-us/articles/intel-advanced-encryption-standard-instructions-aes-ni/, 2011.

11. Witold Litwin, Sushil Jajodia, and Thomas Schwarz, *Privacy of data outsourced to a cloud for selected readers through client-side encryption*, Proceedings of the 10th annual ACM workshop on Privacy in the electronic society (New York, NY, USA), WPES '11, ACM, 2011, pp. 171–176.

12. A.J. Menezes, P.C. van Oorschot, and S.A. Vanstone, *Handbook of applied cryptography*, Discrete Mathematics and Its Applications, Taylor & Francis, 2010.

13. Michael Naehrig, Kristin Lauter, and Vinod Vaikuntanathan, *Can homomorphic encryption be practical?*, Proceedings of the 3rd ACM workshop on Cloud computing security workshop (New York, NY, USA), ACM, 2011, pp. 113–124.

14. Oracle, *Oracle advanced security transparent data encryption best practices*, http://www.oracle.com/technetwork/database/security/twp-transparent-data-encryption-bes-130696.pdf, March 2012.

15. Pascal Paillier, *Public-key cryptosystems based on composite degree residuosity classes*, Advances in Cryptology (EUROCRYPT '99), Lecture Notes in Computer Science **1592** (1999), 223–238.

16. Raluca Ada Popa, Catherine M. S. Redfield, Nickolai Zeldovich, and Hari Balakrishnan, *Cryptdb: protecting confidentiality with encrypted query processing*, Proceedings of the Twenty-Third ACM Symposium on Operating Systems Principles (New York, NY, USA), SOSP '11, ACM, 2011, pp. 85–100.

17. Reuters, *German state ready to buy stolen bank data source*, blogs.reuters.com/financial-regulatory-forum/2010/02/04/german-state-ready-to-buy-stolen-bank-data-source/, 2010.

18. Amazon Web Services, *products page*, aws.amazon.com/products, 2013.

19. N.P. Smart and F. Vercauteren, *Fully homomorphic simd operations*, Designs, Codes and Cryptography (2012), 1–25.

20. Ken Smith, Ameet Kini, William Wang, Chris Wolf, M. David Allen, and Andrew Sillers, *Intuitive interaction with encrypted query execution in datastorm*, 2012 IEEE 28th International Conference on Data Engineering (ICDE), April 2012, pp. 1333 –1336.

21. Colin Tankard, *Advanced persistent threats and how to monitor and deter them*, Network Security **2011** (2011), no. 8, 16 – 19.

22. Yinqian Zhang, Ari Juels, Michael K. Reiter, and Thomas Ristenpart, *Cross-vm side channels and their use to extract private keys*, Proceedings of the 2012 ACM conference on Computer and communications security (New York, NY, USA), ACM, 2012, pp. 305–316.

Privacy-Preserving Keyword Search Over Encrypted Data in Cloud Computing

Wenhai Sun, Wenjing Lou, Y. Thomas Hou, and Hui Li

Abstract Search over encrypted data is a technique of great interest in the cloud computing era, because many believe that sensitive data has to be encrypted before outsourcing to the cloud servers in order to ensure user data privacy. Devising an efficient and secure search scheme over encrypted data involves techniques from multiple domains – information retrieval for index representation, algorithms for search efficiency, and proper design of cryptographic protocols to ensure the security and privacy of the overall system. This chapter provides a basic introduction to the problem definition, system model, and reviews the state-of-the-art mechanisms for implementing privacy-preserving keyword search over encrypted data. We also present one integrated solution, which hopefully offer more insights into this important problem.

1 Introduction

We are in such an information-explosion era that constantly purchasing new hardware, software and training IT personnel is becoming a nightmare for almost every IT practitioner. Fortunately, we are witnessing an enterprise IT architecture shift

W. Sun (✉)
The State Key Laboratory of Integrated Services Networks, Xidian University, Xi'an, Shaanxi, China

Virginia Polytechnic Institute and State University, Blacksburg, VA, USA
e-mail: whsun@xidian.edu.cn

W. Lou • Y.T. Hou
Virginia Polytechnic Institute and State University, Blacksburg, VA, USA
e-mail: wjlou@vt.edu; thou@vt.edu

H. Li
The State Key Laboratory of Integrated Services Networks, Xidian University, Xi'an, Shaanxi, China
e-mail: lihui@mail.xidian.edu.cn

S. Jajodia et al. (eds.), *Secure Cloud Computing*, DOI 10.1007/978-1-4614-9278-8_9,   189
© Springer Science+Business Media New York 2014

to a centralized, more powerful computing paradigm – Cloud Computing, in which enterprise's or individual's databases and applications are moved to the servers in the large data centers (i.e. the cloud) managed by the third-party cloud service providers (CSPs) in the Internet. Cloud computing has been gradually recognized as the most significant turning point in the development of information technology during the past few years. People are fascinated by the benefits it offers, such as ubiquitous and flexible access, on-demand computing resources configuration, considerable capital expenditure savings, etc. Indeed, many companies, organizations, and individual users have adopted the cloud platform to facilitate their business operations, research, or everyday needs [35].

Despite the tremendous business and technical advantages, what we shall always keep in mind is that cloud computing would not be our wonderland until users' outsourced sensitive data could hide from the prying eyes. Privacy concern is one of the primary hurdles that prevent the widespread adoption of the cloud by potential users, especially if the private data of users used to reside in the local storage are to be outsourced to and computed in the cloud. Imagine that CSPs host the services looking into your personal emails, financial and medical records, and social network profiles. Although these sensitive data could be protected by deploying intrusion detection systems, firewalls, or even segmenting data in a virtualized environment, CSP possesses full control of the cloud infrastructure including the system hardware and lower levels of software stack. Privacy breach is still likely to occur owing to the existence of disgruntled, profiteered or curious employees from CSP [25, 37]. Encrypting-then-outsourcing [28,48] provides us strong guarantee that no one could mine any useful information from the ciphertext of users' data. Many people argue that sensitive data has to be encrypted before outsourcing in order to provide user data privacy against the cloud service providers. However, encrypted data makes data utilization a very challenging task. One example is keyword search functions on the documents stored in the cloud. Without those usable data services, the cloud will become merely a remote storage which provides limited value to all parties.

Computation over encrypted data is a challenging task and has drawn significant attention due to the encrypting-then-outsourcing paradigm in cloud computing. It will be remiss if we don't mention fully homomorphic encryption [16], which is considered the Holy Grail of cryptography. Fully homomorphic encryption scheme will allow us to operate directly over ciphertext and generate results matching the computation over plaintext. A theoretical break-through on fully homomorphic encryption took place a few years ago [16]. However, the efficiency of the construction is still far from being practical. Much research work has been focusing on special classes of computation [2, 3, 19, 44]. Search over encrypted data is a fundamental and common form of data utilization service, enabling users to quickly sort out information of interest from huge amount of data, and thus has become a topic of great interest recently. Both public key cryptography (PKC) and symmetric key cryptography (SKC) can be used to build encrypted data search schemes. Generally speaking, PKC-based schemes [7,9,18,20] are more expressive, support more flexible search functions, but more computationally intensive, while

SKC-based schemes [11, 15, 17, 42] are more efficient in searching, but less flexible in the types of search criteria supported.

This chapter aims to provide a general overview of search techniques over encrypted data and their security and privacy objectives, and then elaborate on a scheme that can achieve privacy-preserving multi-keyword search supporting similarity-based ranking, based on [10] and [39]. The chapter is organized as follows. In Sect. 2, we will introduce the encrypted data search problem in terms of its problem formulation and review related works. We will delve into multi-keyword ranked search in Sect. 3, and further improve search result accuracy and search efficiency in Sect. 4. We will conclude this chapter in Sect. 5.

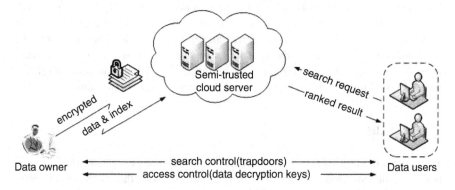

Fig. 1 Architecture of encrypted data search problem (From [10])

2 Overview of Search Over Encrypted Data

2.1 Problem Formulation

In this subsection, we will briefly introduce the general system model of the encrypted data search problem, its threat model and search privacy related requirements in the following.

System Model

The typical participants of a secure search system in the cloud involve the *cloud server*, the *data owner*, and the *data user*, as shown in Fig. 1. The data owner outsources the encrypted dataset and the corresponding secure indexes to the cloud server, where data can be encrypted using any secure encryption technique, such as Advanced Encryption Standard (AES), while the secure index is generated by some particular search-enabled encryption techniques. When a data user wants to query the outsourced dataset hosted on the cloud server, he/she first either generates a trapdoor with the keyword of interest (applied to most PKC-based search schemes), or requests such trapdoor by sending a set of intended keywords to the data owner (in the case of SKC-based search schemes). In the latter case, upon receiving the trapdoor generation request, the data owner constructs the trapdoor, and return it to the user. Then the data user submits the trapdoor to the cloud server. The cloud server will execute the search program with the trapdoor as the input, the search results will be sent back to the user. Note that here we assume there is pre-existing security context between each user and the data owner thus authentication between user and data owner is already in place. The trapdoors can be requested and returned through a secure channel. The management of the decryption keys of the returned files is an orthogonal problem and has been studied separately [28, 48]. Search can be based on certain search criteria and the results be ranked based on certain ranking criteria so that the server returns all the matching documents or only the top-k most relevant ones to the user so as to realise effective and efficient data retrieval functionality, and mitigate the corresponding communication overhead, where k could be predefined by the user at the trapdoor submission time.

Threat Model

The typical threat model that most secure search schemes adopt [6, 10, 27, 39, 43] is to consider the cloud server to be "honest-but-curious", that is the cloud server "honestly" follows the designated protocol specification, but it is "curious" to infer and analyze data (including indexes) in its storage and message flows received during the protocol in order to learn additional information.

Search Privacy

In the literature, many privacy requirements are defined for PKC-based and SKC-based search schemes. We briefly introduce these *search privacy* requirements as follows.

1. **Keyword Privacy:** One of the major privacy concerns is how to protect the keywords of interest in a user's trapdoor against the cloud server. In other words, cloud server is not able to infer what the data user is searching. This fundamental privacy requirement should be satisfied for any valid encrypted data search scheme. Although trapdoor generation can be performed in a cryptographic way to protect the query keywords, the cloud server could identify the searched keywords by other side channel attacks, such as frequency analysis attack [39, 40, 43, 49]. Given the keyword-specific document frequency information (the number of documents containing the keyword) or the keyword frequency (the occurrence count of a keyword in a document) distribution information in a particular dataset, it is sufficient for an attacker to reverse-engineer the keyword in a trapdoor. Notice that this privacy requirement is referred to as *predicate*

privacy in the PKC-based search scenario and it cannot be protected inherently for any asymmetric secure search scheme [34].

2. **Trapdoor Unlinkability:** It is required that the trapdoor should be generated in a random manner. Otherwise, given any two trapdoors, the attacker can easily determine the relationship of them, such as whether they contain the same set of keywords. Therefore, sufficient nondeterminacy should be introduced into the trapdoor generation algorithm. It is worth noting that violation of this privacy requirement can further compromise the keyword privacy in that it allows the cloud server to accumulate frequencies of different search requests with respect to different keyword(s).

3. **Access Pattern:** It is defined to be the sequence of returned documents. Note that protecting access pattern by using private information retrieval technique [12, 21] is extremely expensive since the algorithm has to "touch" the whole dataset outsourced on the cloud server which is inefficient in the large scale cloud system. Thus for efficiency concerns, most of the search over encrypted data schemes do not aim to protect it.

2.2 PKC-Based Search vs. SKC-Based Search

In PKC-based search schemes, different keys are used to generate index and trapdoor, such that a data user is usually free to produce a trapdoor by his/her keywords of interest without interacting with a data owner. Thus, this technique is much more suitable for some dynamic environment, e.g., when multiple data contributors and multiple data users exist in one search system. Otherwise, in SKC-based search, to search datasets from multiple data owners, a data user has to obtain these trapdoors from each individual data owner. This communication cost is definitely cumbersome to the user in such a multi-user and multi-data-contributor scenario. In addition, PKC-based search schemes can achieve more flexible and expressive queries compared with SKC-based schemes in general. For example, range query, subset query, etc., can be easily realised by PKC-based search schemes. In symmetric setting, how to generate trapdoors with similar functionalities is still a challenging problem.

It is worth noting that multi-keyword search can be achieved in both symmetric and asymmetric settings. By incorporating some ranking criteria, a data user is able to enjoy ranked search results by the relevance of documents to the query. Although conjunctive keyword search over encrypted data schemes in public-key setting also provide multi-keyword search function, it often lacks ranking functionality. Moreover, another unparalleled advantage of SKC-based search over PKC-based one is that the overall search process is much more efficient, since asymmetric search usually incurs a lot of time-consumed paring operations. Thus, there has been significant interest in developing efficient SKC-based encrypted data search mechanisms.

In what follows, we review some important related works built from either PKC or SKC technique.

PKC-Based Search

Inspired by identity-based encryption [8], Boneh et al. [7] propose the first PKC-based keyword search scheme with single keyword query, where anyone with public key can write to the data stored on server but only data users with private key can search. Following this work, a lot of PKC-based search schemes have been proposed to enrich the search functionalities. The scheme from [18] supports search queries with conjunctive keywords by explicitly indicating the number of encrypted keywords in an index, that is each keyword within a document is transformed to be a part of the index for this document. When doing query, the server should know which randomized keywords in the index need to be used for match evaluation. This information leakage may raise some privacy concerns. The authors in [20] also present a conjunctive keyword search over encrypted data scheme. They group the queried keywords together in an index to mitigate keyword privacy breach. But this is not flexible, since the data owner has to generate all the possible keyword combinations in one index. In addition, they extend the proposed secure keyword search to multi-user setting, where an encrypted index can be searched by various users holding different private keys. Predicate encryption (PE) [4,9,23,36] is another promising technique to fulfill the expressive search functionality over encrypted data. For example, the proposed scheme in [9] supports conjunctive, subset and range queries, and disjunctions, polynomial equations, and inner products could be realised in [23]. Li et al. [27] use the hierarchical predicate encryption technique to build an authorized keyword search scheme in the cloud. In their design, only authorized data users can be granted search capability, and unauthorized users are not allowed to search the dataset on the cloud server. Nevertheless, these PE-based secure search schemes are generally too computationally intensive to be implemented for practical use.

SKC-Based Search

Curtmola et al. design a symmetric secure search scheme supporting single keyword queries with security guarantees under rigorous definitions [15]. Owing to the adoption of inverted index [31] as the underlying index structure in their scheme, the search process can be extremely efficient. In [40,43,49], the order-preserving techniques are utilized to protect the rank order. By incorporating keyword frequency information and inverted index structure, they can achieve accurate and efficient search at the same time, but only single keyword query is supported. In addition, Kamara et al. [22] propose a dynamic version of [15] with the ability to add and delete files efficiently. In multi-user setting [6,47], the authors separately present an encrypted data search schemes in the enterprise environment. Specifically, the data user must be authorized before he/she can search the dataset, where authorization is enforced by a user list stored and managed by enterprise servers. Note that they differ from the PKC-based work [20] in terms of the allowed number of data contributors. Under the symmetric-key setting, merely one data contributor (enterprise) is allowed in their designs. In [17], the author formulates an IND-CKA security model for indexes, i.e., indistinguishability against chosen keyword attack, and a stronger model IND2-CKA. He also exploits pseudo-random functions and bloom filter to generate a secure index for each file, and its search time is proportional to the number of files in the dataset. The main problem of this scheme is that the final search results inevitably contain false positive due to bloom filter being the underlying index construction technique. Chang et al. [11] present a similar security model to IND2-CKA, and propose a secure search scheme with the index built from pseudo-random functions. Cao et al. [10] propose the first SKC-based encrypted data search scheme supporting multi-keyword ranked search where an index is generated using secure inner product technique. The ranking is realised by similarity measure of coordinate matching. Later, Sun et al. [39] present another secure multi-keyword search scheme in the cloud enabling more accurate search result ranking by using the state-of-the-art similarity measure, i.e., cosine measure in the vector space model, and design a search algorithm over the proposed tree-based index structure to fulfill more efficient search complexity in practice.

2.3   Exact Keyword Search vs. Fuzzy Keyword Search

Unlike the exact keyword search schemes above, it is common that keywords may be entered by a user which contain typos, but the search engine (e.g., Google search) is still capable of tolerating them and returning what the user intends. Thus, *fuzzy keyword search* technique is often used to rectify the mistakes. For the search algorithm to better understand the difference between a correct keyword and its typo, we need a similarity measurement to be supported in the underlying encrypted data search scheme, such that the matching files will be returned when the user's search request exactly matches the keyword in the index or the difference is within some predefined tolerance range.

Li et al. [26] propose a fuzzy keyword search over encrypted data scheme in the cloud. For each keyword, they first construct a wildcard keyword set containing all the variants of the keyword. Upon receipt of the trapdoor, they exploit edit distance to quantify keyword similarity. If the intended keyword is within the fuzzy keyword set, it will be considered a keyword match. By the similar techniques, Liu et al. [29] present another fuzzy keyword search scheme with a size-reduced index. In [13], the authors use a B-tree [14] based index structure to construct a fuzzy keyword search scheme, where although they claim the support of multiple keyword search capability, they only group several keywords together to form a phrase. This is analog to some conjunctive keyword search schemes [20] in public-key setting, which is apparently not flexible in the sense that a data user is not able to query any combination of keywords of his/her choice if this keyword combination is not considered by the data owner at the index generation phase.

2.4   Secure Index-Based Search

Since Song et al.'s seminal work [38], searchable encryption has drawn a lot of attention. Their work enables in-line text search within an encrypted document. Specifically, their scheme encrypts each document word by word and performs full-domain search such that it takes linear operations to cover all the documents. Later, to improve the search efficiency, many secure search schemes have been proposed, where queries can be executed over encrypted indexes (rather than encrypted data themselves) by users who possess proper "trapdoors". This applies to all the encrypted data search schemes mentioned above. To design a keyword search over encrypted data scheme, a series of important factors should be considered as follows.

Index Structure

In general, there are three kinds of index structures often used to construct encrypted data search schemes:

- **Index organized by keywords:** Such index data structure is usually called *inverted index*, or *inverted file* [31]. In this data structure, each keyword is followed by a file list which consists of all the files in the dataset containing this keyword. The advantage of this index structure is to allow significantly efficient text search instead of the full domain text search. But when a file is added to the dataset, it needs increased processing since all the indexes containing the keywords in this file have to be updated. This kind of index structure is widely used in encrypted data search schemes [15,22,40,43,49] due to its extremely fast search process. Note that search schemes with this keyword-based index structure can only realise single keyword query.
- **Index constructed per document:** Another popular index structure adopted by many secure search schemes [10, 11, 17, 20] is to construct an index for each file in the dataset such that one file update usually affects only one corresponding index. The index structure is specific to each document and is generated by all the keywords contained in the target document.
- **Tree-based index structure:** Index structure can also be constructed based on some well-developed tree structures, such as *B*-tree [14], MDB-tree [33], etc. A few existing works [30,39] exploit tree-based structures to design efficient secure search schemes in different scenarios.

Secure Search Algorithm

According to different data structures, search over encrypted data schemes may use different secure search algorithm to do the match. The inverted index structure allows fast direct intended file retrieval, so the search complexity is constant there. For example, the indexed keywords can be hashed and then store the associated file list at a table with its address being the hash value . When a user wants to search a keyword of interest, he/she first hashes it and submits the hash value to the server. Therefore, the server is able to find out the intended files efficiently.

For schemes with index built from each document, the most efficient search algorithm merely enables linear search, i.e., the time for search is linear to the number of documents in the dataset, since the returned search results could not be determined until the search process goes through all the indexes within the document set. This is not desirable when a huge amount of data are present on the server.

By utilizing tree-based structures to construct indexes for encrypted data search schemes, the corresponding secure search algorithm could be devised to achieve more efficient search than the linear search schemes. At the meantime, the same expressive queries as the schemes with index built per document could be realised under this index structure, such as range queries in database scenario [30] and multi-keyword text search with similarity-based ranking [39].

Similarity-Based Ranking

To enhance user searching experience and meet more effective data retrieval need, two fundamental aspects have to be considered when designing a practical encrypted data search scheme. On one hand, most of today's search engines on the Internet (e.g., Google search) allow users to query multiple keywords in one search request instead of only one as the indicator of their search interest. Compared with single keyword query, the main advantage of this multi-keyword search is that it can yield more relevant search results efficiently. On the other hand, ranked search functionality is preferable in the "pay-as-you-go" cloud paradigm. The reason is that cloud server could conduct relevance ranking operation for data user and return the most relevant set of files, rather than directly sending back the undifferentiated search results to data user. As such, the network traffic between cloud server and data user could be dramatically reduced.

By securely incorporating advanced similarity measures into the design of encrypted data search schemes, ranking functionality could be realised during search process with a multi-keyword trapdoor. These adopted similarity measures are borrowed from plaintext information retrieval community, such as coordinate matching, cosine measure in the vector space model [45]. As a result, the constructed encrypted data search schemes enjoys the same flexibility and search result accuracy as the existing multi-keyword search over plaintext.

3   Privacy-Preserving Multi-keyword Ranked Search

Cao et al. [10], for the first time, explore the problem of multi-keyword ranked
search over encrypted cloud data (MRSE), and establish a set of strict privacy
requirements for such a secure cloud data utilization system. They propose two
MRSE schemes based on the similarity measure of coordinate matching while
meeting different privacy requirements in two different threat models. One is *known
ciphertext model*, where the cloud server is supposed to only know encrypted
dataset and searchable index, both of which are outsourced from the data owner.
The other is *known background model*, in which the cloud server could possess
more knowledge than what can be accessed in the known ciphertext model, such as
document frequency information. At the meantime, they execute thorough security
analysis and experiment evaluation on the real world dataset to demonstrate the
privacy and efficiency guarantees of their proposed schemes. In the remaining of
this section, we will discuss this work.

3.1   Technical Overview for MRSE

Coordinate Matching

To support multi-keyword ranked search, the similarity measure, *coordinate matching* [45], is incorporated into the MRSE schemes. This similarity measure counts
the number of query keywords appearing in the documents to quantify the relevance
of that document to the query. The more query keywords that appear in a document,
the more relevant the document to the query. This similarity measure is thought of
as a hybrid intermediate between conjunctive and disjunctive search. Any document
with all or partial keywords matching is considered a part of the search results.
To formalize such similarity measure in practice, they use inner products of the
query vector and a set of document index vectors to reflect the predilection of
the data user for documents. For example, assume that a dictionary is defined as
$\{search, cloud, privacy, network, security\}$. There are two documents A, B in the
dataset. Therefore, set the index vector as a binary vector $D_A = (1, 0, 0, 1, 1)$ for
document A if it only contains keywords $\{search, network, security\}$, where 1 is
used to indicate the existence of some keyword in the document and 0 otherwise. If
the keywords $\{search, cloud, security\}$ appears in the document B, the binary index
vector D_B is defined to be $(1, 1, 0, 0, 1)$. Suppose that the data user has a query with
the intended keywords $\{seach, cloud, privacy\}$. Thus the binary query vector Q is
represented as $(1, 1, 1, 0, 0)$. We can calculate the inner products of the query vector
Q and the index vectors D_A, D_B as the similarity scores of documents A and B:

$$SimilarityScore_A = Q \cdot D_A = (1, 1, 1, 0, 0) \cdot (1, 0, 0, 1, 1) = 1,$$

and

$$SimilarityScore_B = Q \cdot D_B = (1,1,1,0,0) \cdot (1,1,0,0,1) = 2.$$

Therefore, we can deduce that the data user would prefer document B to document A since the similarity score of B is greater than that of A. Also, it yields a ranking $B > A$.

By using the coordinate matching similarity measure, effective multi-keyword ranked search functionality could be realised. Nevertheless, such measure is originally designed for plaintext information retrieval purpose. How to apply it to the encrypted data search without breaching search privacy is a very challenging problem.

Search with Secure Inner Product Evaluation

To use the above mentioned similarity measure in a privacy-preserving way, index vector D_d for each document d, query vector Q and their inner product $D_d \cdot Q$ should not be exposed to the cloud server. In MRSE, the authors propose a secure inner product scheme which is adapted from a secure k-nearest neighbor (kNN) technique [46] to hide these sensitive information.

In database scenario, secure kNN technique can be exploited to select k nearest database records to the query by comparing the Euclidean distance between them. Specifically, each record in the database and the query can be represented by an n-dimensional vectors p_i and q respectively. The secret key consists of one $(n+1)$-dimensional vector S and two $(n+1) \times (n+1)$ invertible matrices M_1 and M_2. Then after vector extension, a new p_i is set as $(p_i, -0.5||p_i^2||)$ and a new query vector q is (rq, r), where $r > 0$ is a random number. As per the splitting indicator S, p_i is split into two vectors as $\{p_i', p_i''\}$ and q is also split into two vectors $\{q', q''\}$ such that p_i and q can be recovered given S, $\{p_i', p_i''\}$ and $\{q', q''\}$. Eventually, the vector pairs $\{p_i', p_i''\}$ and $\{q', q''\}$ are encrypted as $\{M_1^T p_i', M_2^T p_i''\}$ and $\{M_1^{-1} q', M_2^{-1} q''\}$ respectively. At the database search phase, the product of encrypted record vector pair and encrypted query vector pair, i.e., $-0.5r(||p_i||^2 - 2p_i \cdot q)$, is serving as the indicator of Euclidean distance $(||p_i||^2 - 2p_i \cdot q + ||q||^2)$ to select k nearest neighbors. Without prior knowledge of secret key, neither record vector nor query vector, after such a series of processes, can be recovered by analyzing their corresponding ciphertext.

Cao et al. modify this secure kNN technique to measure the inner product similarity instead of the Euclidean distance. In particular, trapdoor vector Q is extended to be (rQ, r, t), where r, t are two random numbers and $r > 0$, such that it is difficult for the cloud server to infer the relationship among the received trapdoors. To obfuscate the document frequency and diminish the chances for re-identifying the keywords, the final similarity scores should be further randomized. Thus some randomness ε_d is introduced into the index vector D_d, and D_d is extended into

$(D_d, \varepsilon_d, 1)$. The encrypted index vector pair $I_d = \{M_1^T D'_d, M_2^T D_d''\}$ and trapdoor vector pair $T = \{M_1^{-1} Q', M_2^{-1} Q''\}$ are generated after applying the vector splitting and matrix multiplication. The final similarity score for document d to the query vector would be:

$$I_d \cdot T = \{M_1^T D'_d, M_2^T D_d''\} \cdot \{M_1^{-1} Q', M_2^{-1} Q''\}$$
$$= D'_d \cdot Q' + D_d'' \cdot Q''$$
$$= (D_d, \varepsilon_d, 1) \cdot (rQ, r, t)$$
$$= r(D_d \cdot Q + \varepsilon_d) + t.$$

By using this equation, the ranked search result can be produced.

This vector encryption method has been proved to be secure in the known ciphertext model [46]. As long as the secret key is kept confidential, the underlying plaintext information in the index vector and trapdoor vector cannot be revealed.

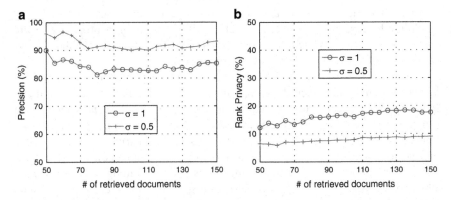

Fig. 2 Tradeoff between (**a**) precision, and (**b**) rank privacy by selecting different standard deviation σ (From [10])

Note that, let ε_d follow a Normal distribution $N(\mu, \sigma^2)$, where the standard deviation σ functions as a flexible trade-off parameter between search accuracy and security. To protect *keyword privacy*, a large σ is selected to introduce more obfuscation into the final similarity score, from which it is difficult for the cloud server to gain statistical information about the original similarity score, but the search result could be less accurate. Thus from the viewpoint of the effective search, small σ is preferable. This is shown in Fig. 2.[1] Due to the splitting process and the random

---

[1] Precision is defined to be the fraction of returned top-k documents that are included in the real top-k list, while rank privacy measures the rank order variation between the returned top-k documents and real top-k documents.

numbers r,t, the trapdoor generation algorithm can output two different trapdoors even for the same search request to guarantee *trapdoor unlinkability*.

To further protect search privacy in the known background model, an enhanced MRSE scheme is proposed. The main modification is to insert more dummy keywords $\sum \varepsilon_d$ instead of only one fixed ε_d into the index vector for each document. The level of search accuracy remains the same with the previous basic MRSE scheme if let $\sum \varepsilon_d$ follow a Normal distribution as well.

Cao et al. for the first time, define and solve the problem of multi-keyword ranked search over encrypted cloud data by combining the efficient similarity measure "coordinate matching" with the adapted secure inner product technique. The proposed schemes can meet various stringent privacy requirements while retaining effective search functionalities.

4 Improvement on Search Accuracy and Efficiency

4.1 Background

Although MRSE can achieve multi-keyword ranked search, there exists a gap between MRSE and the state-of-the-art plaintext information retrieval techniques in terms of search accuracy and search efficiency. On one hand, the similarity measure "coordinate matching" in MRSE has some drawbacks when used to evaluate the document ranking order. First, it takes no account of term[2] frequency such that any keyword appearing in a document will present in the index vector as binary value 1 for that document, irrespective of the number of its appearance. Obviously, it fails to reflect the importance of a frequently appeared keyword to the document. Second, it takes no account of term scarcity. Usually a keyword appearing in only one document is more important than a keyword appearing in several ones. In addition, long documents with many terms will be favored by the ranking process because they are likely to contain more terms than short documents. Hence, due to these limitations, the heuristic ranking function, "coordinate matching", is not able to produce more accurate search results. More advanced similarity measure should be adopted from plaintext information retrieval community, such as *cosine measure* in the *vector space model* [45]. On the other hand, the search complexity of MRSE is linear to the number of documents in the dataset, which becomes undesirable and inefficient when a huge amount of documents are present, while many efficient index structures exist in the plaintext information retrieval techniques, e.g., B-tree [14], inverted index [31], etc.

Sun et al. [39] present a privacy-preserving multi-keyword text search (MTS) scheme in the cloud supporting similarity-based ranking to address the challenge of

---

[2]We do not differentiate *term* and *keyword* hereafter.

constructing more accurate, practically efficient and flexible encrypted data search
functionalities. Specifically, the index vector for each document is generated based
on the cosine measure in the vector space model to support multi-keyword query
and search result ranking functionality, and utilize the "term frequency (TF) ×
inverse document frequency (IDF)" weight to achieve high search result accuracy.
By incorporating the state-of-the-art information retrieval technique, the proposed
MTS schemes enjoy the same flexibility and search result accuracy as the existing
state-of-the-art multi-keyword ranked search over plaintext. In order to improve
the search efficiency, they propose a tree-based index structure, where each value
in a node is a vector of term frequency related information. Furthermore, an
efficient search algorithm is presented to realise more efficient search functionality
compared with [10]. To satisfy various search privacy requirements, two secure
index schemes for multi-keyword text search with similarity-based ranking are
devised. The basic scheme (BMTS) is secure under the known ciphertext model,
and the other enhanced secure index scheme (EMTS) is constructed against sensitive
frequency information leakage to meet more stringent privacy requirements under
the stronger threat model, i.e., known background model.

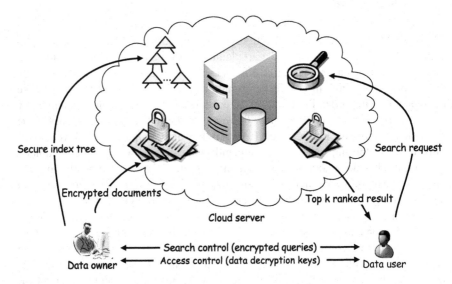

Fig. 3 Framework of MTS (From [39])

4.2 Technical Overview of MTS

The system framework in [39] is analog to [10] as shown in Fig. 3, wherein three
participants, i.e., the data owner, the data user and the cloud server, are defined. Note
that the index vectors are organized as a secure index tree instead of each individual
vector before outsourced to the cloud server. Assume the cloud server still acts in an

"honest-but-curious" manner. Since the term frequency information is incorporated into the ranking function, in the known background model the attacker may extract such statistical information from a known comparable dataset of the similar nature to the target dataset, e.g., the TF distribution information of a specific keyword. Given such statistical information, the cloud server is able to launch statistical attack to deduce/identify particular keywords in the query [40, 43, 49].

Vector Space Model

Vector space model is one of the most popular similarity measures in the plain-text information retrieval community, supporting both conjunctive and disjunctive search. The ranking order for a particular document set is determined by comparing the deviation of angles, i.e., cosine values, between each document vector and the query vector. The cosine measure allows accurate ranking due to the "TF×IDF rule", where TF denotes the occurrence count of a term within a document,[3] and IDF is obtained by dividing the total number of documents in the collection by the number of documents containing the term.[4] Thus, unlike the coordinate matching, each dimension of an index vector in MTS is a TF weight $w_{d,t}$, and a query vector is comprised of IDF weights $w_{q,t}$, where d,t denote a specific document in the dataset and a term in the dictionary respectively. The ranked search functionality can be achieved by the following similarity function:

$$Cos(D_d, Q) = \frac{1}{W_d W_q} \sum_{t \in Q \cap D_d} w_{d,t} \cdot w_{q,t},$$

where $W_d = \sqrt{\sum_{t \in Q \cap D_d} w_{d,t}^2}$, $W_q = \sqrt{\sum_{t \in Q \cap D_d} w_{q,t}^2}$. Thus, the index vector D_d and query vector Q are both unit vectors.

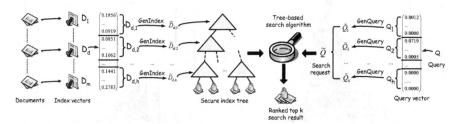

Fig. 4 Overview of secure index scheme (From [39])

---

[3]It is used to measure how important a specific term is to a particular document.

[4]It implies that this frequency of a term tends to be inversely proportional to its ranking.

Secure Index Scheme

To construct the index tree structure, the original long document index vector D_d has to be divided into multiple sub-vectors such that each sub-vector $D_{d,i}$ represents a subset of keywords, and becomes a part of the i-th level of the index tree, as shown in Fig. 4. Similarly, let Q_i be the query sub-vector at the i-th level. As such, the final similarity score for document d can be obtained by summing up the scores from each level. Based on these similarity scores, the cloud server determines the relevance of document d to the query Q and sends the top-k most relevant documents back to the user. The similar secure inner product scheme [10] is adopted here but applied to each level of the index tree. In addition, they do not use the dimension extension technique for BMTS in the known ciphertext model. The similarity score at the i-th level is computed as follows:

$$Cos(\widetilde{D_{d,i}}, \widetilde{Q}_i) = \{M_{1,i}^T D_{d,i}{}', M_{2,i}^T D_{d,i}{}''\} \cdot \{M_{1,i}^{-1} Q_i{}', M_{2,i}^{-1} Q_i{}''\}$$
$$= D_{d,i}{}' \cdot Q_i' + D_{d,i}{}'' \cdot Q_i''$$
$$= D_{d,i} \cdot Q_i,$$

where $\widetilde{D_{d,i}}$ and $\widetilde{Q}_i$ represent the encrypted forms of index vector and query vector at the i-th level respectively. Hence, the final similarity score for document d is $\sum_{i=1}^{h} D_{d,i} \cdot Q_i = D_d \cdot Q$ by assuming that the index tree has h levels in total.

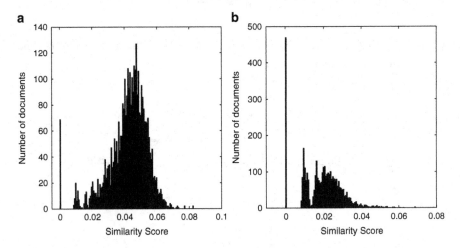

Fig. 5 Distribution of similarity score when a single keyword in a query vector with BMTS. (**a**) For keyword "network". (**b**) For keyword "search" (From [39])

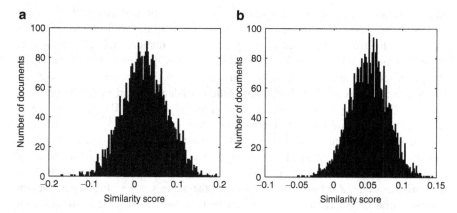

Fig. 6 Obfuscation to distribution of similarity score for keyword "network" with different standard deviations in EMTS. (**a**) $\sigma = 0.05$. (**b**) $\sigma = 0.03$ (From [39])

In BMTS, index and query confidentiality can be well protected by the secure inner product technique. Due to the non-deterministic property of the encryption method, the trapdoor unlinkability can be preserved similar to [10]. As assumed in the defined known background model, the cloud server may have the knowledge of the TF distributions, or normalized ones of some sensitive keywords from a known comparable dataset. It is worth noting that these distributions are keyword specific, as shown in Fig. 5.[5] Therefore, to further prevent this sensitive information from being disclosed to the server, the authors insert phantom terms into the query vector in EMTS so as to obfuscate the final similarity scores while maintaining effective search functionalities, as shown in Fig. 6. The larger σ is selected, the better the TF distribution can be protected. This technique can achieve the same privacy preserving functionality as MRSE, and the selection of σ reflects the user's preference for privacy preservation or search accuracy. On the other hand, this query-side randomization technique significantly differs from [10] in the sense that randomization in [10] is applied to the index vector and is not possible to be calibrated by users as an effective privacy-preserving parameter.

Efficient Tree-Based Search Algorithm

In database community, query process could complete in logarithmic time by using B-tree, B^+-tree, etc. These tree-based structures are not only used in the plaintext database search, but also can be used in the encrypted database scenario [30] to realise efficient range query. Nevertheless, they are not applicable to text search. The similarity score is a dynamic value depending on the query and has to be evaluated

---

[5]The background dataset is collected from the recent 10 years' IEEE INFOCOM publications.

in the runtime, which makes the fixed tree structure, such as B-tree or B^+-tree, not suitable here. Inverted index [31] is the most efficient and well-developed index structure which is widely used in the plaintext information retrieval community. In the literature, however, a few works [15, 40, 43, 49] employ this technique to design efficient search algorithm but only for single keyword query. Sun et al. propose a tree-based search algorithm, which is adapted from multi-dimensional B-tree (MDB-tree) [33] based multi-dimensional algorithm (MD-algorithm) [32], to enable efficient multi-keyword ranked search.

The MD-algorithm is used to find the k-best matches in a database that is structured as an MDB-tree, as shown in Fig. 7. Each attribute domain in the database constitutes one level of the MDB-tree and each attribute in that domain is assigned an attribute value. All the attributes sharing the same value in the upper domain forms a child node. As such, a set of objects is allowed to be indexed in one data structure. An important search parameter, the prediction threshold value $\hat{P}_i$ for each level i, is obtained from the maximum attribute value P_i at each level, for example, in Fig. 7, $\hat{P}_i = P_i = 1.0$.

In a depth-first manner, MD-algorithm starts from the root node with a recursive procedure upon this tree. Specifically, search process selects the unused maximum attribute value when it enters a node, and based on $\hat{P}_i$'s below this level, predicts the maximum possible final score to be obtained. The criteria for node selection is that if this predicted final score is less than or equal to the minimum score of the top-k objects which have been selected, search process returns to the parent

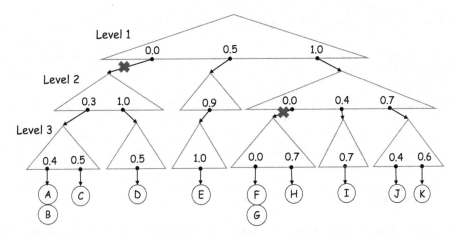

Fig. 7 Illustration of MD-algorithm on MDB-tree (From [39])

node, otherwise, it goes down to the child node at the next level. This procedure is executed recursively until the objects with top-k scores are selected.

The search can be done very efficiently due to the relatively accurate final score prediction, and thus only part of the objects in the tree are accessed. Figure 7 shows an example that, when $k = 3$, the set of objects, E, K, and J, are returned to the user and the cross signs in the figure indicate that it is not necessary to access the nodes below. More details of the MD-algorithm and MDB-tree can be found in [32].

The MD-algorithm is originally designed for plaintext database search. In the case of privacy-preserving similarity-based multi-keyword ranked text search, it cannot be applied in a straightforward manner. Instead of a numerical "attribute value" for each attribute in the MDB-tree, the index tree structure has to be built on vectors. Another remarkable difference between the proposed search algorithm and MD-algorithm is that it is not possible to set $\hat{P}_i$ to P_i as running the MD-algorithm in database scenario, since P_i varies for queries and has to be securely evaluated in the runtime.

Search Efficiency Improvements

During the evaluation of the MD-algorithm on the proposed secure index tree, three important efficiency-improving factors are identified by the authors. Next, we will briefly elaborate on those observations.

1. **Impact of Prediction Threshold Value:** By observation, they found that the smaller the predication threshold value, the faster the search algorithm is terminated, which means the search process can be terminated earlier without going into unnecessary nodes. As such, at each level, $\hat{P}_i$ should decreasingly approach P_i as close as possible.

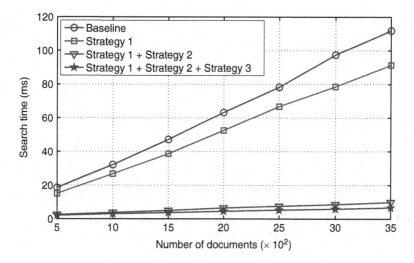

Fig. 8 Comparison of search efficiency with different efficiency-improving strategies (From [39])

2. **Impact of Intended Keyword Position:** Another observed efficiency-improving factor is that the search efficiency is significantly dependent on the position of the intended keywords on the index tree. Indeed, people usually complete a search with a query only consisting of a few keywords [1], which is different from using the MD-algorithm in database scenario. Typically, to find out the object of interest, all the attributes are utilized to query the database. It is apparently inefficient since the search process needs to go to the bottom level of the index tree where the intended attribute resides.

3. **Impact of Index Vector Clustering:** The last search efficiency related observation is that "similar" vector index could be clustered together to reduce the number of accessed nodes in the index tree at the expense of lower search precision.

Based the these key observations, the authors propose the corresponding effective strategies to improve the practical search efficiency with vector indexes while not introducing new privacy vulnerabilities. Compared with the original MD-algorithm, the experimental result[6] shows the much more improved search efficiency in Fig. 8.[7] Furthermore, Fig. 9a shows the search time for BMTS and EMTS with the proposed efficiency-improving strategies, compared with [10] and baseline search with respect to the size of document set. Due to the proposed search algorithm and tree-based index structure, the baseline search is far efficient than [10]. Note that the time cost of BMTS and EMTS is more efficient than [10] and the baseline search. Besides, the two proposed schemes enjoy almost the same and nearly constant search time. Figure 9b shows that the proposed secure search schemes are still extremely efficient in the case of more documents are required to be returned.

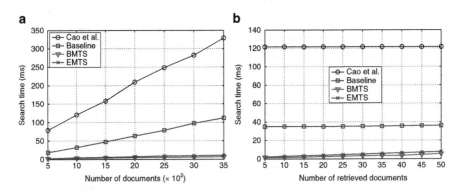

Fig. 9 Comparison of search efficiency with the same 10 keywords of interest. (**a**) For the different size of document set. (**b**) For the different number of retrieved documents (From [39])

---

[6]All the experimental results in [39] are obtained from implementation of the proposed secure search system using JAVA on a Linux Server with Intel Core i3 Processor 3.3 GHz.

[7]The baseline search is with respect to the original MD-algorithm. The strategies 1 is proposed from the observation 1. Likewise, the strategy 2 is from the observation 2 and the strategy 3 from the observation 3.

5 Conclusion

With the advent of cloud computing, more and more sensitive data are outsourced to the cloud server to reduce the management cost and enjoy the ubiquitous access. However, this novel computing paradigm introduces serious privacy challenges in that users' data are no longer locally possessed but stored on the remote server which belongs to a different trust domain compared with the data users'. In this chapter, we focus on the privacy concerns in the secure search function performed over encrypted cloud data. We first provide a brief introduction to the background knowledge of encrypted data search techniques that have been proposed in the literature and dedicated to address the secure search problem in the computation outsourcing model. Then we elaborate on a state-of-the-art secure search scheme in the text search scenario, and show that they can achieve flexible/expressive search functionalities, i.e., multi-keyword ranked search. In addition, the same search accuracy as the plaintext information retrieval can be realised using the state-of-the-art similarity measure while search privacy is well protected. Finally, with the proposed search algorithm, the discussed secure search system is efficient enough to be deployed in practice.

While continued research is necessary to further enrich the search functionality and improve the efficiency and scalability of search schemes, another very interesting direction is on virtualization security that tries to secure the execution environment (i.e., virtual machines) in the cloud server. This will require a slight change in the security model – instead of an honest-but-curious server model which does not trust the server, we may choose to place minimum trust on the server, for example, trust the bare hardware on the server, and design the secure operating system to protect the virtual machine against the software-based attacks, be it from other virtual machines running on the same physical machine or the hosting machine's operating system. We argue that the data should be stored in the cloud in the encrypted form. However, after they are loaded to the users' secure execution environment, they can be in the plaintext form in order to enable effective computation, such as search. Research along this line includes [5, 24, 41, 50] and it aims to provide a more general solution to the secure computation on the untrusted cloud server problem. We believe both research directions are interesting and call for more effort from the research community.

Acknowledgments This work was supported in part by the NSFC 61272457, the FRFCU K50511010001, the PCSIRT 1078, the National 111 Project B08038, and the U.S. NSF grant CNS-1217889.

References

1. Keyword and search engines statistics. http://www.keyworddiscovery.com/keyword-stats.html?date=2013-01-01 (2013)
2. Atallah, M.J., Frikken, K.B.: Securely outsourcing linear algebra computations. In: Proceedings of the 5th ACM Symposium on Information, Computer and Communications Security, pp. 48–59. ACM (2010)
3. Atallah, M.J., Li, J.: Secure outsourcing of sequence comparisons. International Journal of Information Security 4(4), 277–287 (2005)
4. Attrapadung, N., Libert, B.: Functional encryption for inner product: Achieving constant-size ciphertexts with adaptive security or support for negation. In: Public Key Cryptography–PKC 2010, pp. 384–402. Springer (2010)
5. Azab, A.M., Ning, P., Zhang, X.: Sice: a hardware-level strongly isolated computing environment for x86 multi-core platforms. In: Proceedings of the 18th ACM conference on Computer and communications security, pp. 375–388. ACM (2011)
6. Bao, F., Deng, R.H., Ding, X., Yang, Y.: Private query on encrypted data in multi-user settings. In: Information Security Practice and Experience, pp. 71–85. Springer (2008)
7. Boneh, D., Di Crescenzo, G., Ostrovsky, R., Persiano, G.: Public key encryption with keyword search. In: Advances in Cryptology-Eurocrypt 2004, pp. 506–522. Springer (2004)
8. Boneh, D., Franklin, M.: Identity-based encryption from the weil pairing. In: Advances in Cryptology – CRYPTO 2001, pp. 213–229. Springer (2001)
9. Boneh, D., Waters, B.: Conjunctive, subset, and range queries on encrypted data. In: Proceedings of the 4th conference on Theory of cryptography, pp. 535–554. Springer-Verlag (2007)
10. Cao, N., Wang, C., Li, M., Ren, K., Lou, W.: Privacy-preserving multi-keyword ranked search over encrypted cloud data. In: Proceedings of IEEE INFOCOM, pp. 829–837 (2011)
11. Chang, Y.C., Mitzenmacher, M.: Privacy preserving keyword searches on remote encrypted data. In: Applied Cryptography and Network Security, pp. 442–455. Springer (2005)
12. Chor, B., Kushilevitz, E., Goldreich, O., Sudan, M.: Private information retrieval. Journal of the ACM 45(6), 965–981 (1998)
13. Chuah, M., Hu, W.: Privacy-aware bedtree based solution for fuzzy multi-keyword search over encrypted data. In: Distributed Computing Systems Workshops (ICDCSW), 2011 31st International Conference on, pp. 273–281. IEEE (2011)
14. Comer, D.: Ubiquitous b-tree. ACM computing surveys 11(2), 121–137 (1979)
15. Curtmola, R., Garay, J., Kamara, S., Ostrovsky, R.: Searchable symmetric encryption: improved definitions and efficient constructions. In: Proceedings of the 13th ACM conference on Computer and communications security, pp. 79–88. ACM (2006)
16. Gentry, C.: A fully homomorphic encryption scheme. Ph.D. thesis, Stanford University (2009)
17. Goh, E.J.: Secure indexes. Cryptology ePrint Archive. http://eprint.iacr.org/2003/216 (2003)
18. Golle, P., Staddon, J., Waters, B.: Secure conjunctive keyword search over encrypted data. In: ACNS 04: 2nd International Conference on Applied Cryptography and Network Security, pp. 31–45. Springer-Verlag (2004)
19. Hohenberger, S., Lysyanskaya, A.: How to securely outsource cryptographic computations. In: Theory of Cryptography, pp. 264–282. Springer (2005)
20. Hwang, Y.H., Lee, P.J.: Public key encryption with conjunctive keyword search and its extension to a multi-user system. In: Pairing-Based Cryptography–Pairing 2007, pp. 2–22. Springer (2007)
21. Ishai, Y., Kushilevitz, E., Ostrovsky, R., Sahai, A.: Cryptography from anonymity. In: the 47th Annual IEEE Symposium on Foundations of Computer Science, pp. 239–248. IEEE (2006)
22. Kamara, S., Papamanthou, C., Roeder, T.: Dynamic searchable symmetric encryption. In: Proceedings of the 2012 ACM conference on Computer and communications security, pp. 965–976. ACM (2012)
23. Katz, J., Sahai, A., Waters, B.: Predicate encryption supporting disjunctions, polynomial equations, and inner products. In: Advances in Cryptology–EUROCRYPT 2008, pp. 146–162. Springer (2008)

24. Keller, E., Szefer, J., Rexford, J., Lee, R.B.: Nohype: virtualized cloud infrastructure without the virtualization. In: ACM SIGARCH Computer Architecture News, vol. 38, pp. 350–361. ACM (2010)
25. Krebs, B.: Payment processor breach may be largest ever. http://voices.washingtonpost.com/securityfix/2009/01/payment_processor_breach_may_b.html (2009)
26. Li, J., Wang, Q., Wang, C., Cao, N., Ren, K., Lou, W.: Fuzzy keyword search over encrypted data in cloud computing. In: INFOCOM, 2010 Proceedings IEEE, pp. 1–5. IEEE (2010)
27. Li, M., Yu, S., Cao, N., Lou, W.: Authorized private keyword search over encrypted data in cloud computing. In: Distributed Computing Systems (ICDCS), 2011 31st International Conference on, pp. 383–392. IEEE (2011)
28. Li, M., Yu, S., Zheng, Y., Ren, K., Lou, W.: Scalable and secure sharing of personal health records in cloud computing using attribute-based encryption. IEEE Transactions on Parallel and Distributed Systems **24**(1), 131–143 (2013)
29. Liu, C., Zhu, L., Li, L., Tan, Y.: Fuzzy keyword search on encrypted cloud storage data with small index. In: Cloud Computing and Intelligence Systems (CCIS), 2011 IEEE International Conference on, pp. 269–273. IEEE (2011)
30. Lu, Y.: Privacy-preserving logarithmic-time search on encrypted data in cloud. In: 19th Annual Network and Distributed System Security Symposium (NDSS Symposium'12) (2012)
31. NIST: NIST's dictionary of algorithms and data structures: inverted index. http://xlinux.nist.gov/dads/HTML/invertedIndex.html
32. Ondreička, M., Pokorný, J.: Extending fagin's algorithm for more users based on multidimensional b-tree. In: Advances in Databases and Information Systems, pp. 199–214. Springer (2008)
33. Scheuermann, P., Ouksel, M.: Multidimensional b-trees for associative searching in database systems. Information systems **7**(2), 123–137 (1982)
34. Shen, E., Shi, E., Waters, B.: Predicate privacy in encryption systems. In: Theory of Cryptography, pp. 457–473. Springer (2009)
35. Sheridan, J., Cooper, C.: Defending the cloud. http://www.reactionpenetrationtesting.co.uk/Defending%20the%20Cloud%20v1.0.pdf (2012)
36. Shi, E., Bethencourt, J., Chan, H., Song, D., Perrig, A.: Multi-dimensional range query over encrypted data. In: Proceedings of IEEE Symposium on Security and Privacy, pp. 350–364 (2007)
37. Slocum, Z.: Your google docs: Soon in search results? http://news.cnet.com/8301-17939_109-1035713%207-2.html (2009)
38. Song, D., Wagner, D., Perrig, A.: Practical techniques for searches on encrypted data. In: Proceedings of IEEE Symposium on Security and Privacy, pp. 44–55 (2000)
39. Sun, W., Wang, B., Cao, N., Li, M., Lou, W., Hou, Y.T., Li, H.: Privacy-preserving multi-keyword text search in the cloud supporting similarity-based ranking. In: Proceedings of the 8th ACM SIGSAC symposium on Information, computer and communications security, pp. 71–82. ACM (2013)
40. Swaminathan, A., Mao, Y., Su, G.M., Gou, H., Varna, A.L., He, S., Wu, M., Oard, D.W.: Confidentiality-preserving rank-ordered search. In: Proceedings of the 2007 ACM Workshop on Storage Security and Survivability, pp. 7–12 (2007)
41. Szefer, J., Keller, E., Lee, R.B., Rexford, J.: Eliminating the hypervisor attack surface for a more secure cloud. In: Proceedings of the 18th ACM conference on Computer and communications security, pp. 401–412. ACM (2011)
42. Van Liesdonk, P., Sedghi, S., Doumen, J., Hartel, P., Jonker, W.: Computationally efficient searchable symmetric encryption. In: Secure Data Management, pp. 87–100. Springer (2010)
43. Wang, C., Cao, N., Ren, K., Lou, W.: Enabling secure and efficient ranked keyword search over outsourced cloud data. IEEE Transactions on Parallel and Distributed Systems **23**(8), 1467–1479 (2012)
44. Wang, C., Ren, K., Wang, J.: Secure and practical outsourcing of linear programming in cloud computing. In: INFOCOM, 2011 Proceedings IEEE, pp. 820–828. IEEE (2011)

45. Witten, I.H., Moffat, A., Bell, T.C.: Managing gigabytes: Compressing and indexing documents and images. Morgan Kaufmann Publishing, San Francisco, May 1999
46. Wong, W.K., Cheung, D.W.l., Kao, B., Mamoulis, N.: Secure knn computation on encrypted databases. In: Proceedings of the 2009 ACM SIGMOD International Conference on Management of data, pp. 139–152. ACM (2009)
47. Yang, Y., Lu, H., Weng, J.: Multi-user private keyword search for cloud computing. In: Cloud Computing Technology and Science (CloudCom), 2011 IEEE Third International Conference on, pp. 264–271. IEEE (2011)
48. Yu, S., Wang, C., Ren, K., Lou, W.: Achieving secure, scalable, and fine-grained data access control in cloud computing. In: Proceedings of IEEE INFOCOM, pp. 1–9 (2010)
49. Zerr, S., Olmedilla, D., Nejdl, W., Siberski, W.: Zerber+ r: Top-k retrieval from a confidential index. In: Proceedings of the 12th International Conference on Extending Database Technology: Advances in Database Technology, pp. 439–449. ACM (2009)
50. Zhang, N., Li, M., Lou, W., Hou, Y.T.: Mushi: Toward multiple level security cloud with strong hardware level isolation. In: MILITARY COMMUNICATIONS CONFERENCE, 2012-MILCOM 2012, pp. 1–6. IEEE (2012)

Towards Data Confidentiality
and a Vulnerability Analysis Framework
for Cloud Computing

**Kerim Y. Oktay, Mahadevan Gomathisankaran, Murat Kantarcioglu,
Sharad Mehrotra, and Anoop Singhal**

Abstract This chapter explores two related challenges in the context of secure processing in cloud computing. The first is the concern of "loss of control" that results from outsourcing data and computation to the clouds. While loss of control has multiple manifestations, the chapter focusses on the potential loss of data privacy and confidentiality when cloud providers are untrusted. Instead of using a well studied (but still unsolved) approach of encrypting data when outsourcing it and computing on the encrypted domain, the paper advocates risk-based processing over a hybrid cloud architecture as a possible solution. Hybrid clouds are a composition of two or more distinct cloud infrastructures (private, community, or public) that remain unique entities, but are bound together by standardized or proprietary technology that enables data and application portability. Hybrid clouds offer an opportunity to selectively outsource data and computation based on the level of sensitivity involved. The paper postulates a risk-aware approach to partitioning computation over hybrid clouds that provides an abstraction to address secure cloud data processing in a variety of system and application contexts. Solutions to the workload partitioning problem are sketched in two example settings such as

K.Y. Oktay (✉) • S. Mehrotra
Department of Computer Science, University of California, Irvine, CA, USA
e-mail: koktay@uci.edu; sharad@ics.uci.edu

M. Gomathisankaran
Department of Computer Science and Engineering, University of North Texas,
Denton, TX, USA
e-mail: mgomathi@unt.edu

M. Kantarcioglu
Department of Computer Science, University of Texas at Dallas, Richardson, TX, USA
e-mail: muratk@utdallas.edu

A. Singhal
Computer Systems Division, National Institute of Standards and Technology,
Gaithersburg, MD, USA
e-mail: anoop.singhal@nist.gov

S. Jajodia et al. (eds.), *Secure Cloud Computing*, DOI 10.1007/978-1-4614-9278-8_10,
© Springer Science+Business Media New York 2014

partitioning database workloads and distributing map reduce task across public and private machines. The paper also explores a related challenge of developing vulnerability assessment frameworks for cloud computing environments. Preliminary work on an ontology driven framework for vulnerability assessment is described. The proposed framework addresses the challenges introduced by the complexity of running software on the cloud environment where the exact infrastructure used is not known or constrained prior to execution and applications/services could be composed to form additional services.

1 Introduction

Fueled by the advances in virtualization and high-speed network technologies, cloud computing is emerging as a dominant computing paradigm for the future. Cloud computing can roughly be summarized as "X as a service" where X could be a virtualized infrastructure (e.g., computing and/or storage), a platform (e.g., OS, programming language execution environment, databases, web servers), software applications (e.g., Google apps), a service, or a test environment, etc. A distinguishing aspect of cloud computing is the utility computing model (aka pay-as-you-go model) where users get billed for the computers, storage, or any resources based on their usage with no up-front costs of purchasing the hardware/software or of managing the IT infrastructure. The cloud provides an illusion of limitless resources which one can tap into in times of need, limited only by the amount one wishes to spend on renting the resources.

Despite numerous benefits, organizations, especially those that deal with potentially sensitive data (e.g., business secrets, sensitive client information such as credit card and social security numbers, medical records), hesitate to embrace the cloud model completely. One of the main impediments is the sense of "loss of control" over ones data wherein the end-users (clients) cannot restrict the access to potentially sensitive data by other entities, whether they be other tenants to the common cloud resources or privileged insiders who have access to the cloud infrastructure. The key operative issue here is the notion of trust. Loss of control, in itself, is not as much of an issue if clients/users could fully trust the service provider. In a world where service providers could be located anywhere, under varying legal jurisdictions; where privacy and confidentiality of ones data is subject to policies and laws that are at best (or under some circumstances) ambiguous; where policy compliance is virtually impossible to check, and the threat of "insider attacks" is very real – trust is a difficult property to achieve. Loss of control over resources (by migrating to the cloud) coupled with lack of trust (in the service provider) poses numerous concerns about data integrity (will service provider serve my data correctly? Can my data get corrupted?), availability (will I have access to my data and service at any time?), security, privacy and confidentiality (will sensitive data remain confidential? Will my data be vulnerable to misuse? By other tenants? By service provider?) to name a few.

In this position paper, we focus on two complementary challenges in the context of cloud computing: First, we explore the challenge of privacy and confidentiality aspects of data processing in public cloud environments. An obvious approach to achieving confidentiality and privacy is to appropriately encrypt data prior to storing it on the cloud. This way, data remains secure against all types of attacks, whether they be due to using shared systems & resources also accessible to others, insider attacks, or data mining attacks leading to information leakage. While encrypting data mitigates many of the confidentiality concerns, it poses a new challenge – how does one continue to process encrypted data in the cloud? Over the past few decades, numerous cryptographic approaches as well as information hiding techniques have been developed to support basic computations over encrypted data [13–15]. For instance, a variety of semantically secure searchable encryption techniques that can support various forms of keyword search as well as range search techniques have been proposed. Likewise, work in the area of database as a service [16] has explored support for SQL style queries with selections/projections/joins etc. Many such approaches offer sliding scale confidentiality wherein higher confidentiality can be achieved, albeit extra overheads. While significant progress has been made in designing solutions that offer viable approaches when the computation to be performed on encrypted data is suitably constrained, a general solution that is efficient enough to be of practical use is, however, seems unlikely to emerge in the near future.

To address privacy and confidentiality challenge, instead of opting for solutions that completely eliminate the possibility of attacks (e.g., by devising appropriate mechanisms to compute on the encrypted representations directly), we promote an alternate/complementary risk-based view to secure database query processing that instead of preventing loss of sensitive data, controls how data is stored and processed in the cloud so as to limit the exposure of sensitive data on public cloud. We focus the discussion to our ongoing work in the Radicle Project (http://radicle.ics.uci.edu) on risk-based computing in hybrid cloud setting wherein in-house systems may offload part of their work during peak demand to the public cloud infrastructures (e.g., Amazon EC2, Microsoft Azure). Such a hybrid cloud creates a mixed security environment for data processing – while organizations can control (to a degree) security on their own infrastructure, the public infrastructure is susceptible to myriad of security concerns, including information leakage through "excessive privilege abuse" (aka insider attack which has been identified as amongst most important database security threat by numerous practitioners). A risk-based approach controls what data and computation is offloaded to the public cloud and how such data is represented, in order to control the risk of data exposure. Different ways to steer data through the public and private clouds exhibit different levels of risks and expose a tradeoff between exposure risks and performance. Given such a tradeoff, the goal of the risk aware computing changes from purely attempting to minimize costs (and hence maximize performance) to that of achieving a balance between performance and sensitive data disclosure risk.

Developing such a risk-based strategy opens multiple challenges. First and foremost, given different ways in which data can be partitioned, represented (e.g., in plain text, encrypted using searchable encryption techniques, deterministic encryption, non-deterministic encryption), exposed at the public machines for different periods of times, and different levels of trust a user may have in the public infrastructure, we need principled ways of assessing risk of data loss with the diverse choices. Given the risk model, the next challenge is to model the tradeoff problem as a multi-criteria optimization that achieves a balance between performance and exposure risk. Two specific settings of such multi-criteria problems can be (a) optimize for performance while ensuring that exposure risks are constrained, or alternatively, (b) constrain the additional overhead of the strategy, while minimizing the risk of data loss. Solution to such a multi-criteria optimization will allow us to determine how data should be stored and computation partitioned such that the proposed system maintains the performance while limiting/minimizing loss of sensitive data.

The second major challenge we address in the paper is that of assessing security of software services on clouds. Security on the clouds (e.g., from cyber attacks) depends upon the vulnerability of the infrastructure, platforms, and services. In many cloud-based solutions, the platform or the infrastructure on which software may run is now known or guaranteed a priori. Furthermore, the cloud and service oriented architectures (SoA) support service level compositions, whereby new services can be created rapidly by composing existing services. Vulnerability assessment in such environments opens new challenges since security of the software service must be assured regardless of the underlying infrastructure or platform and must be tested across diverse service compositions requiring a large number of combinations.

The outline of the rest of the paper is as follows: the paper first focuses on the privacy and confidentiality challenge. In Sect. 2, we begin by further discussing the hybrid cloud model highlighting the challenges in developing a risk-based approach for data processing in such an environment. Section 3 describes preliminary ideas on risk-based data processing in hybrid clouds. In particular, we postulate the workload partitioning problem that explore the tradeoff between risks and exposure. We further illustrate a solution to the partitioning problem for two cases of hybrid cloud: first is the task of assigning queries between private and public machines in ways that minimize either performance overhead or risk, and the second considers distributing workloads consisting of map-reduce jobs in hybrid clouds. We then shift our attention to vulnerability modeling for cloud environments in Sect. 4. Then, we describe our ongoing work on developing the Vulnerability Assessment framework for Cloud Computing (VULCAN). Finally, we conclude the paper in Sect. 5.

2 Hybrid Cloud

A hybrid cloud is a composition of two or more distinct cloud infrastructures (private, community, or public) that remain unique entities, but are bound together by standardized or proprietary technology that enables data and application portability [5]. The emergence of the hybrid cloud paradigm has allowed end-users to seamlessly integrate their in-house computing resources with public cloud services and construct potent, secure and economical data processing solutions. A growing number of organizations have turned to such a **hybrid cloud model** [1,2] since they offer flexibility on the tasks that can be offloaded to public clouds thereby offering the advantages of increased throughput, reduced operational cost while maintaining high levels of security.

A risk-based data processing approach explores how risk of information exposure can be controlled in hybrid clouds where organizational data (both sensitive and non-sensitive) and computation spans both (relatively) secure as well as non-secure (public) nodes. The setting is reminiscent of the previous work on Database as a Service [11] in the data management literature in which the data is stored on the server side in an encrypted form and query processing is done on encrypted domain. When processing could not continue on the encrypted domain, the data is transferred to the secure client, which could then decrypt the data and continue the computation. The goal in such processing is to minimize the client side work, while simultaneously minimizing data exposure. In our previous work [11], we outlined how an SQL query can be split to be executed partly on the server and partly on the client to compute the final answer.

In the cloud setting, however, there are many fundamental differences.

- Unlike DAS, where the resources were assumed to be very limited on the client-side, in the cloud setting organizations may actually possess significant resources that meets majority of their storage and query processing needs. For instance, in the cloud setting data may only be partially outsourced, e.g., only non-sensitive part of the data may be kept on the cloud. Also, it is only at peak query loads that the computation needs to be offloaded to the cloud. This has implications from the security perspective since much of the processing involving sensitive data can be done in the private side, e.g., if query primarily touches sensitive data, it could be executed on the private side.

- In DAS, since the goal was to fully outsource the data and computation, the focus of the solutions was on devising mechanism to compute on the encrypted representation (even though such techniques may incur significant overhead). In contrast, since in the hybrid cloud environments, since local machines may have significant computational capabilities, solutions that incur limited amount of data exposure of sensitive data (possibly at a significant performance gain) become attractive.

- While DAS work has primarily dealt with database query workload (and text search [14]), in a cloud setting, we may be interested in more general computation mechanisms (i.e. not only database workloads). For instance, map-reduce (MR) frameworks are used widely for large-scale data analysis in the cloud. We may, thus, be interested in secure execution of MR jobs in the context of hybrid clouds.

While there are significant new challenges and opportunities in secure processing of data in cloud environments, the techniques for query processing/search in mixed security environments developed in the literature to support the DAS model (e.g., techniques for various types of search over encrypted data, techniques to limit data exposure by splitting computation between public and private sides, cooperatively implementing database operators/search in ways that limit exposure of cleartext at the public-side, etc.) provide a solid foundation over which risk-aware processing in hybrid clouds can be explored. In the following section, build towards such a risk-aware processing architecture for hybrid clouds.

3   Risk Aware Data Processing Over Hybrid Clouds

In our discussion, we will differentiate between three distinct hybrid cloud settings that target different usage scenarios and pose different tradeoffs:

- *Outsourcing* scenario, where an organization relies on a public cloud to fulfill their IT requirements, and uses their limited private cloud to perform supplementary tasks such as filtering incorrect results or decrypting encrypted results. This is similar to the DAS model studied in the literature.
- *Cloudbursting* setting, where an organization uses their private cloud to develop, test and deploy applications, and depends on a public cloud to mitigate sudden spikes of activity in an application that arise due to unforeseen circumstances.
- *Fully Hybrid* scenario, the companies consider the entire hybrid cloud as one big cluster of machines and are willing to keep the load imbalance across the hybrid cloud as little as possible in order to obtain the best performance. While achieving this, they prefer to handle sensitive computations within the private cloud, whereas the public side executes mostly the workload's non-sensitive portion.

While specific techniques and solutions to achieve risk-aware processing in each of the above depend upon the specific instantiation of the problem, fundamental to each approach is the underlying challenge of workload and data partitioning. We illustrate the workload partitioning challenge with following two examples.

Consider a sequence of MapReduce (MR) job. In MR, a programming model for processing large data sets with a parallel, distributed algorithm on a cluster, input files can be stored across hybrid cloud and MR jobs can be defined to run on both public and private machines. The first challenge is then how to distribute files in such a way that risk is limited. For instance, we may limit sensitive data exposure and only store non-sensitive data on public machines. This, however, does not fully address the problem, since during execution sensitive data may need to be shuffled to the public side thereby posing exposure possibility. The goal then is to partition the MR jobs in ways that such data distribution into file chunks as well as later shuffling during execution does not cause unconstrained exposure.

As another example, consider now a data management workload with a set of database queries which one would like to periodically execute with some timing guarantees. The workload may be too large for a given private infrastructure and the option might be to shift some queries to public side. Even within such a architecture there may be multiple choices. Either shift entire query to public side

– of course, this necessitate the corresponding data for query execution to also be shifted and stored on public side. Or alternatively, one could use DAS style query operator implementation whereby the public and private sides split the task of query execution cooperatively. In either case, the above leads to workload distribution challenge that prevents unconstrained data exposure.

3.1 Criteria for Workload Distribution

Before we explore a risk-based framework for data processing in hybrid clouds, we first identify the key criteria of importance in designing hybrid cloud solutions. These design criteria will form the basis of postulating the risk-based strategy as will become clear later.

Performance: Consider a workload W. Let the execution of W be distributed in private and public side and the corresponding computations be denoted by W_{priv} and W_{pub} respectively. Note that the execution of W_{priv} and W_{pub} together achieves W. Further, let the dataset R needed for the workload W be partitioned as R_{pub} and R_{priv} which represents partitioning of data amongst public and private machines (note that R_{pub} and R_{priv} may not strictly correspond to a partitioning and may overlap). The partitioning of data is such that R_{priv} (R_{pub}) includes all the data needed by the workload W_{priv} (W_{pub}). The performance of an data processing architecture in hybrid cloud is directly proportional to overall running time of W with given W_{pub} and W_{priv}. We use the notation $ORunTime(W, W_{pub})$ to express the performance factor. Estimating the expected total running time depends upon variety of factors such as characteristics of the workload W, control flow between W_{priv} and W_{pub} (e.g., do they need to run sequentially or can be executed in parallel), the speeds of machines/infrastructure, the network throughput in case data needs to be shuffled between public and private machines, the underlying representation of data R_{pub}, etc.

Data Disclosure Risk: $Risk(R_{pub})$ estimates the risk of disclosing sensitive data to a public cloud service provider based on the data outsourced to public cloud or exposed during processing. Disclosure risks depend upon a variety of factors: it is directly proportional to the number of sensitive data items that R_{pub} includes. Larger the sensitive data items in R_{pub}, higher is the $Risk(R_{pub})$; it depends upon the representation format (e.g., encryption level) used to store R_{pub} – using a less secure encrpytion technique incurs higher risk; it could depend upon the duration of time for which sensitive data is exposed in R_{pub}; it depends upon the vulnerability of the public cloud against the outsider attacks – the more vulnerable the system, the higher the exposure risk will be.

Resource Allocation Cost: Resource allocation cost, $Pricing(R_{pub}, W_{pub})$, is associated with storing data on public infrastructure and processing taken place over the public machines. This criterion measures the financial cost (in terms of $)

engendered by the incorporation of some type of public cloud services into hybrid cloud models. The cost can be classified into the following two broad categories:

- *On-premise Costs*: This category measures the cost incurred in acquiring and maintaining a private cloud.
- *Cloud Costs*: This category can be further sub-divided as follows: (a) *Elastic costs*: A user is charged only for the services they use (pay-as-you-use). (b) *Subscription costs*: A user is charged a decided fee on a regular basis (fixed).

The financial cost of an end-user's hybrid cloud model implementation is dependent on several factors such as the data model/query language, storage representation, etc. In general, the larger the R_{pub} and W_{pub} are, the higher the cost will be.

The above three factors – performance, risks, and costs – provide the main criteria along which different solutions of risk based processing in hybrid clouds can be compared. It is not surprising that spectrum of possible solutions represent tradeoffs between these factors. For instance, solutions that indiscriminately distribute work to the public machines in an unconstrained way may optimize performance but they will be suboptimal from the perspective of risks. Likewise, a solution that minimizes risk by performing any operation that may leak sensitive data on private machines may either suffer significantly from the performance perspective, or require a heavy investment in private infrastructure to meet applications timeliness goals thus not leveraging the advantages of the cloud based model.

A risk-based approach to hybrid cloud processing allows users to explore the above tradeoffs in a principled manner thereby enabling users to effectively realize their performance, security, and financial constraints. For instance, given an existing private cloud, a user may specify the dollar costs they are willing to incur for using public resources and the maximum disclosure risks they are willing to incur. A risk-based approach may then attempt to optimize the performance given such constraints specified by the user. An alternate formulation may be minimize the disclosure risks given desirable performance and cost constraints (assuming a feasible solution exists for such an optimization).

Two main issues in designing such a risk-based approach are: (a) identifying metrics for the above three criteria (performance, risks, costs) in terms of parameters that can be modified by the risk-based approach, e.g., workload distribution, data partitioning, cost constraints for acquiring cloud services (and/or private machines) a user may have, etc. (b) designing a principled approach to determine the optimal instantiation of the parameters that meet the performance, cost and risk constraints of the user.

Both of these issues pose significant challenges. Estimating factor such as cost and performance is relatively easier in our view. For instance, the resource allocation cost is contingent on the cloud vendor and type of services being commissioned and existing models supported by various cloud vendors provide a good mechanism for estimating such costs. Furthermore, a recent paper [41] has extended performance-estimation mechanisms for SQL query processing to HIVE queries over Hadoop. Such techniques provide a starting point for modeling workload performance. In contrast, modeling risks due to data exposure given data representation seems significantly more complex. In general, it may require us to model how useful is the information to the adversary, what will it enable the adversary to do, and/or model the loss to data owner (e.g., economic loss) as a result of information being leaked. While such risk modeling represents an interesting question, we limit our model to relatively simple metrics of rid such as the number of sensitive cells exposed, the duration of such exposure [4] or a bit more complex analytical [6] or entropy-based [7] techniques. We focus our discussion in the next section on how the workload partitioning problem can be specified with the given metrics for performance, risk, and costs. When we offer a concrete instantiation of the workload distribution problem in the context of distributed database query workload, we will show how these metrics can be computed in the context of the problem we study.

3.2 Workload Partitioning Problem (WPP)

WPP varies upon whether one aims to use hybrid cloud in cloudbursting, outsourcing or fully-hybrid setting. This paper states the formal definition of WPP for each hybrid cloud model and provides an efficient dynamic programming oriented solution to the one in fully-hybrid model.

Given the three factors – performance, risks, resource allocation costs, discussed in the previous section, we can now formalize the workload partitioning problem as a multi-criteria optimization problem that chooses the system parameters such as workload and data partitioning so as to simultaneously optimize the three metrics. We model the problem as a constrained optimization problem, wherein one of the metrics is optimized while ensuring that the solution is feasible with respect to the constraints specified by the user on the other metrics. In general, in a WPP, a user may specify the three constraints: $TIME\_CONST$, $DISC\_CONST$ and PRA_CONST, where $TIME\_CONST$ corresponds to the maximum amount of time that the workload W needs to be completed in, PRA_CONST acts as an upper bound on the maximum allowable monetary cost that can be expended on storing and processing data on a public cloud, and $DISC\_CONST$ denotes the maximum permissible data disclosure risk that can be taken while storing the sensitive data on public cloud. WPP can thus be specified as that of distributing a workload W (and implicitly a dataset R) over a hybrid cloud deployment such that one of the three factors is minimized subject to constraints on the remaining two. Let us next explore the problem formulation for the three different cloud settings we had introduced earlier:

WPP Definition for outsourcing model: Organizations using hybrid cloud in outsourcing mode mostly rely on the public cloud, since their private resources are very limited. In the context of risk aware data processing, the purpose of outsourcing model is to push as much sensitive computation as possible to the private side while meeting specified overall running time and monetary cost limit. Thereby, WPP in outsourcing setting can be defined as follows: Given a dataset R and a workload W, WPP is an optimization problem whose goal is to find subsets $W_{pub} \subseteq W$ and $R_{pub} \subseteq R$ such that the total disclosure risk, $Risk(R_{pub})$, is minimized.

$$\text{minimize} \quad Risk(R_{pub})$$
$$\text{subject to} \quad (1)\ ORunT(W, W_{pub}) \leq TIME\_CONST$$
$$(2)\ Pricing(R_{pub}, W_{pub}) \leq PRA\_CONST$$

WPP Definition for cloudbursting model: In the cloudbursting model, the end-user more likely wants to finish the given workload less than a speicified time limit by paying the minimum cost. Also, while meeting these requirements, one may want to formalize WPP as follows: Given a dataset R and a workload W, WPP is an optimization problem whose goal is to find subsets $W_{pub} \subseteq W$ and $R_{pub} \subseteq R$ such that the total monetary cost, $Pricing(R_{pub}, W_{pub})$, that arises to exetute W is minimized.

$$\text{minimize} \quad Pricing(R_{pub}, W_{pub})$$
$$\text{subject to} \quad (1)\ ORunT(W, W_{pub}) \leq TIME\_CONST$$
$$(2)\ Risk(R_{pub}) \leq DISC\_CONST$$

WPP Definition for fully hybrid model: In fully hybrid setting, as stated earlier, the primary goal is to maximize the performance. Besides, the end-user may want to put an upper limit on the disclosure risk and the monetary cost while distributing the computation across the cluster. Given these criteria, WPP definition in can be given as follows: Given a dataset R and a workload W, WPP can be modeled as an optimization problem whose goal is to find subsets $W_{pub} \subseteq W$ and $R_{pub} \subseteq R$ such that the overall execution time of W is minimized.

$$\text{minimize} \quad ORunT(W, W_{pub})$$
$$\text{subject to} \quad (1)\ Risk(R_{pub}) \leq DISC\_CONST$$
$$(2)\ Pricing(R_{pub}, W_{pub}) \leq PRA\_CONST$$

WPP definition in each of these settings depends upon mechanisms to appropriately estimate the runtime, monetary costs, and risks associated with a given workload/data partitioning. Below we specify a possible approach to how such factors can be estimated.

Overall Workload Execution Time: It is denoted as $ORunT(W, W_{pub})$, as an indicator of performance. Consequently, WPP variants either aim to minimize the overall execution time of a given task workload W or try to keep it under a threshold. The execution time of tasks in W over a hybrid cloud, given that tasks in W_{pub} are executed on a public cloud can be represented as follows:

$$ORunT(W, W_{pub}) = \max \begin{cases} \sum_{t \in W_{pub}} runT_{pub}(t) \\ \sum_{t \in W - W_{pub}} runT_{priv}(t) \end{cases}$$

where, $runT_x(t)$ denotes the estimated running time of task $t \in T$ at site x where x is either a public ($x = pub$) or private ($x = priv$) cloud. The running time of a task on public/private machines, in itself, depends upon the machine characteristics and the task. Models for estimating these have been widely developed for database workloads in the literature and more recently for HIVE queries in the context of cluster computing [41]. We have further developed similar cost-estimation models for SPARQL queries over RDF stores.

Data Disclosure Risk: The disclosure risk that is associated with storing the public side partition of data, namely R_{pub}, is estimated as follows:

$$Risk(R_{pub}) = \sum_{R_i \in R_{pub}, s} sens(R_i, s),$$

where $sens(R_i, s)$ is the number of sensitive values contained in a data item $R_i \in R_{pub}$, which are stored on a public cloud. We are, of course, using a simple measure – viz. number of sensitive data exposed – as a measure of risk in the above formulation.

Resource Allocation Cost: It estimates the financial cost of utilizing public cloud services as follows:

$$Pricing(R_{pub}, W_{pub}) = store(R_{pub}) + \sum_{t \in W_{pub}} freq(t) \times proc(t),$$

where $store(R_{pub})$ represents the monetary cost of storing a subset $R_{pub} \subseteq R$ on a public cloud, $freq(t)$ denotes the access frequency of task $t \in W$, and $proc(t)$ denotes the monetary cost associated with processing t on a public cloud. Such monetary costs for storing and executing tasks on the public cloud depend upon the pricing models of current cloud vendors. In our experiments given later, we will use the Amazon's pricing model to compute such monetary costs.

3.3 WPP Solution for Fully Hybrid Setting

Above, we have discussed the WPP abstractly for various hybrid cloud settings. To make the discussion concrete, in this section, we sketch a solution based on dynamic programming for one such instantiation of the WPP problem. Specifically, we consider a fully-hybrid cloud deployment which has to be used to compute a workload of database queries. Furthermore, in the solution, we will make simplifying assumption that data is stored unencrypted both on the private and public machines. Thus, exposure risks can be directly computed as the number of sensitive data outsourced to the public machines. As we stated earlier, the WPP in fully-hybrid deployment model attempts to find a subset of the given dataset and workload that can be shipped to the public cloud. The WPP problem tries to achieve this goal by aiming to minimize the total processing time of the workload across the hybrid cloud under several constraints.

Nevertheless, WPP can be simplified to a more trivial version in which the problem only attempts to find W_{pub}, since R_{pub} can be considered as being equivalent to ($\bigcup_{t \in W_{pub}} baseData(t)$) where $baseData(t)$ denotes the minimum set of data items to execute task t accurately. In other words, any other solution R' that minimizes the overall performance should be a superset of $\bigcup_{t \in W_{pub}} baseData(t)$ and, yet, the solution $\bigcup_{t \in W_{pub}} baseData(t)$ is the one with the least sensitive data exposure and monetary cost. As a result, WPP can be considered to be a problem that aims to find the subset of the query workload that minimizes the workload execution time without violating the given constraints.

To represent WPP along with its inputs and constraints, we use the following notation: $WPP(W, PRA\_CONST, DISC\_CONST)$. We also assume that the query workload, W, and the constraints, PRA_CONST and $DISC\_CONST$ are all given beforehand.

Dynamic Programming Approach to Solve WPP

Given the exponential number of query workload subsets, we use a dynamic programming approach to find the best one. We now present Algorithm 1 that produces a set of queries W_{pub} as a solution to $WPP(W, PRA\_CONST, DISC\_CONST)$.

Algorithm 1 uses a data structure $pubW$ and frequently calls a method labeled as $checkConstr$. The purpose of these constructs is as follows:

- **pubW[i][j][k]**: This data structure maintains the set of public side tasks for $WPP(W^i, j, k)$ where $W^i = \{t_1, t_2, \ldots, t_i\}$. Given that the maximum admissible monetary cost and the maximum disclosure risk are equal to j and k respectively, this data structure stores the queries from amongst the first i tasks that are selected to be processed over the public cloud so as to minimize the overall response time of the first i tasks. Notice that $pubW[i][j][k] \subseteq W^i$.
- **checkConstr(W', j', k')**: This method returns whether monetary cost bound j' and disclosure risk limit k' are satisfied when the queries in W' are executed on the public side. In particular, the method checks if $store(\bigcup_{t \in W'} baseData(t)) +$
$\sum_{t \in W'} (freq(t) \times proc(t)) \leq j'$ and $sens(\bigcup_{t \in W'} baseData(t)) \leq k'$.

To make it easily understandable for readers, we present the notion behind our dynamic programming algorithm. Intuitively, $WPP(W^n, PRA\_CONST, SENS\_CONST)$ can be generalized as $WPP(W^i, j, k)$. As the solution to this general problem will be a subset of W^i, there are two possible assignments for the last task t_i in W^i. The task t_i is either in the solution to $WPP(W^i, j, k)$ or is not. Therefore, both cases should be investigated carefully. Before expanding on both cases, let us illustrate how our algorithm works with an example. Assume that our workload W consists of three tasks (i.e. $W = \{t_1, t_2, t_3\}$) and $WPP(W^3, j, k)$ needs to be solved. The detailed information about these three queries is given below.

W	$proc(t)$	$store(baseData(t))$	$sens(baseData(t))$
t_1	\$10	\$15	20
t_2	\$20	\$10	10
t_3	\$15	\$10	20

Before investigating the two different cases in further details, we need to check whether assigning t_3 to the public side violates any constraints (line 17). If we ship t_3 to the public side, then the overall monetary cost and the overall disclosure risk will be at least \$25 and 20 sensitive cells respectively (assume that $\forall 1 \leq i \leq 3\ freq(i) = 1$). If $j < 25$ or $k < 20$, then any solution considering t_3 as a public side query will not be a feasible one, and in turn $WPP(W^3, j, k) = WPP(W^2, j, k)$ (line 30). Note that, since executing any query on the private side does not cause a violation of any constraints, this case essentially does not require a feasibility analysis. Now, we can go into the details of each case.

Case 1: If t_3 runs on the public side, then there will be more than 1 WPP subproblems that need to be investigated. This is due to the fact that the possible execution of t_3 on the public side will bring at least \$15 and at most \$25 into the overall monetary cost value. In terms of disclosure risk, the numbers will be between 0 and 20 sensitive cells. The reason is that a portion of (or the entire) $baseData(t_3)$ could already be partially included in the solution, W_s, to some $WPP(W^2, j', k')$, and in turn storing $baseData(t_3)$ in addition to $\bigcup_{t \in W_s} baseData(t)$ may not bring as much monetary cost and disclosure risk as is represented in the table above. Consequently, $WPP(W^2, j', k')$ where $j - 25 \leq j' \leq j - 15$ and $k - 20 \leq k' \leq k$ should be investigated in order to solve $WPP(W^3, j, k)$ optimally (lines 18–26). However, every candidate set of queries formed by taking the union of t_3 with the solution of $WPP(W^2, j', k')$ should be tested to ensure that it does not violate any constraint and it is the best solution in terms of performance from amongst all solutions obtained in *Case 1* (line 21). If it does produce the best solution, it will be one of the solution candidates with the one coming from *Case 2* (lines 21–24).

Case 2: In case query t_3 runs on the private side, then $WPP(W^3, i, j) = WPP(W^2, i, j)$ (line 28).

Algorithm 1 Dynamic programming()

Input: W, PRA_CONST, $DISC\_CONST$ **Output:** W_{pub}

1: initialize $pubW[\,][\,][\,]$
2: **for** $i = 1 \rightarrow W.size$ **do**
3:     $procCost \leftarrow proc(t_i)$
4:     $totCost \leftarrow procCost + store(baseData(t_i))$
5:     $disc \leftarrow sens(baseData(t_i))$
6:     **for** $j = 0 \rightarrow PRA - CONST$ **do**
7:         **for** $k = 0 \rightarrow DISC - CONST$ **do**
8:             **if** $i = 1$ **then**
9:                 **if** $checkConstr(\{t_1\}, j, k)$
                    AND $ORunT(W^1, W^1) < ORunT(W^1, \emptyset)$ **then**
10:                     $pubW[i][j][k] \leftarrow \{t_1\}$
11:                 **else**
12:                     $pubW[i][j][k] \leftarrow \emptyset$
13:                 **end if**
14:             **else**
15:                 $pubCaseOT \leftarrow \infty$
16:                 $(j', k') \leftarrow (NaN, NaN)$
17:                 **if** $checkConstr(\{t_i\}, j, k)$ **then**
18:                     **for all** $j - totCost \leq iC \leq j - procCost$ **do**
19:                         **for all** $k - disc \leq iD \leq k$ **do**
20:                             $tmpSet \leftarrow pubW[i][iC][iD] \cup q_i$
21:                             **if** $checkConst(tmpSet, iC, iD)$ AND $ORunT(W^i, tmpSet) < pubCaseOT$
                                then
22:                                 $pubCaseOT \leftarrow ORunT(W^i, tmpSet)$
23:                                 $(j', k') \leftarrow (iC, iD)$
24:                             **end if**
25:                         **end for**
26:                     **end for**
27:                 **end if**
28:                 $privCaseOT \leftarrow ORunT(W^i, pubW[i-1][j][k])$
29:                 **if** $privCaseOT \leq pubCaseOT$ **then**
30:                     $pubW[i][j][k] \leftarrow pubW[i-1][j][k]$
31:                 **else**
32:                     $pubW[i][j][k] \leftarrow pubW[i-1][j'][k'] \cup \{t_i\}$
33:                 **end if**
34:             **end if**
35:         **end for**
36:     **end for**
37: **end for**
38: **return** $pubW[W.Size - 1][PRA\_CONST][DISC\_CONST]$

After computing the best solution candidate for both cases, our algorithm compares the overall expected running times of both solutions and picks the minimum one as the solution to $WPP(W^3, j, k)$ (lines 29–33).

The algorithm above requires us to determine various costs (viz., disclosure, monetary, and query execution) for a given workload W and the arbitrary data partitions. We note that the incurred disclosure risk, in our model, is dependent only on the public-side partition R_{pub}, which in turn is implicitly defined using the given query workload. Determining query execution times and monetary costs, however, depends upon the query workload. They can both be estimated as the sum of costs of the individual queries.[1]

Experimental Results

For all our experiments, we have used the TPC-H benchmark with a scale factor 100 in our experiments. We used a query workload of 40 queries containing modified versions of TPC-H queries Q1, Q3, Q6 and Q11. In particular, we do not perform grouping and aggregate operations in any query because of the high complexity of estimating overall I/O size for these types of operators in Hive. Further, we assumed that each query was equally likely in the workload. The predicates in each of the queries are randomly modified to vary the range (as mandated by TPC-H) of the data that is accessed.

We first computed the running time of the query workload when all computations are performed on the private cloud (Private). The experiments subsequently use this case as a baseline to determine the performance of the dynamic programming approach that was proposed earlier to solve the WPP problem.

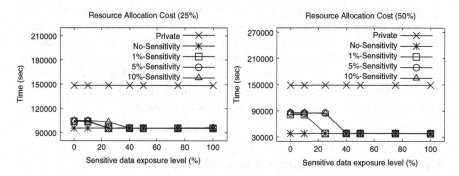

Fig. 1 Performance of the dynamic programming approach towards solving the WPP problem

Experiments for Dynamic Programming approach: The goal of these experiments is to measure the performance of the dynamic programming approach that was proposed earlier for solving the WPP. To perform these experiments, we varied all parameters under consideration in the following way: (i) Resource allocation cost: The resource allocation cost was varied between 25 and 50 % of the maximum cost value that can occur along the workload execution. Given the above cost metric definition, the maximum cost incurs when the dataset R is completely stored over

---

[1]Recent work has explored techniques such as shared scans in the context of executing queries over MapReduce frameworks [8], which can reduce costs of query workloads. We, however, do not consider such optimizations in developing our partitioning framework in this paper.

public cloud and the entire query workload is executed on public machines. (ii) We defined four different overall sensitivity levels as, No-Sensitivity (the entire dataset is non-sensitive), 1 %-Sensitivity, 5 %-Sensitivity and 10 %-Sensitivity (1, 5 and 10 % of the tuples of the *lineitem* table are made sensitive). (iii) We defined seven different sensitive data exposure levels as 0 % (none of the sensitive data is exposed), 10, 25, 40, 50, 75 and 100 % (all of the defined sensitive data may be exposed).

We then computed the overall performance of the query workload for different combinations of these three parameters, the results of which are presented in Fig. 1. One of the first observations that can be made from Fig. 1 is that when a user is willing to take additional risks by storing more sensitive data on the public side, they can gain a considerable speed-up in overall execution time (even greater than 50 %). On the other hand, Fig. 1 also shows that the monetary expenditure on public side resources is substantially low even when a user takes additional risks by storing increasing amounts of sensitive data on the public cloud (graph for 50 % resource allocation cost show that even when more money is allowed to be spent on public side resources the overall performance is relatively the same for these cases suggesting that a budget of only about 50 % of *PRA_CONST* is sufficient to boost the performance savings by upto 50 %).

Figure 1 also shows that when a user invests more capital towards resource allocation, a considerable gain in overall workload performance (even greater than 50 %) can be achieved. This is expected since when more resources are allocated on the public side, we are better able to exploit the parallelism that is afforded by a hybrid cloud. Thus, the intuition that a hybrid cloud improves performance due to greater use of inherent parallelism is justified. Finally, from Fig. 1, we also notice that we can achieve a considerable improvement in query performance ($\approx$50 %) for a relatively low risk ($\approx$40 %) and resource allocation cost ($\approx$50 %).

3.4   Risk-Aware MapReduce Over Hybrid Clouds

As another example of risk-based data processing in hybrid clouds, let us consider a mapreduce job which may access sensitive data. MR frameworks such as Hadoop are widely popular for large scale data analysis [9, 10]. MR programming model uses two functional operators in order to process data:

$$map : (k_1, v_1) \rightarrow list(k_2, v_2)$$

$$reduce : (k_2, list(v_2)) \rightarrow list(v_3)$$

MapReduce systems use a Distributed File System (DFS) as its underlying storage mechanism (HDFS for Hadoop). A *master* node manages the entire file system by keeping track of how blocks of files are distributed over all *slave* nodes. On the other hand, a process running on every slave node manages the storage infrastructure for that node. This architecture then uses the MR paradigm to process data stored in the DFS in a parallelized fashion over a cluster of nodes. The MR framework typically consists of a single master and several slaves. The master is responsible for scheduling an MR job among the slaves while a slave node is responsible for executing the given sub-task. By labeling one of the nodes as master and the remaining ones as slave nodes, MR paradigm can be made to work on hybrid clouds.

Map operations are usually distributed across a cluster by automatically partitioning the input to possibly equivalent sized blocks (in default 64 MB), which can then be processed in parallel by separate machines. Once a map operation completes on a slave, the intermediate key-value pairs are stored as partitions (hash partitioning) in local disks on that slave. The intermediate partitions are then shuffled to different nodes based on their partition-id to the right reducers.

In MR setting, sensitive data leakage can happen in multiple ways. It could occur either while storing data over DFS or during MR processing. For instance, when an input block that contains sensitive data is assigned to a map task running on the public cloud, those sensitive data items will be directly exposed to the public side. Alternatively, if a reducer whose input partition contains sensitive information is assigned to public nodes then that sensitive information would be leaked. Mechanisms to prevent disclosure by using encrytped computing while interesting are not generally applicable.

Recent efforts have explored secure map reduce techniques on hybrid clouds. One of the popular methods is *Sedic*, proposed in [12], that prevents leakage by doing two things:

- Sensitivity aware data distribution that guarantees no sensitive data out to public machines in turn the map tasks that touch sensitive data to be limited to private side only, and
- Constraining reducers to run exclusively on the private side.

To overcome the performance degradation during the reduce phase, Sedic attempts to use *combiners* to shift some of the work done during the reduce phase to the public side without causing any exposure. Nonetheless, combiners cannot be applied for many important data analysis tasks such as joining two tables. Therefore, Sedic has performance limitations for the tasks that require reducers wherein cannot be executed by using combiners.

One could potentially use a risk-based approach to resolve this performance issue. Consider that the user is tolerant to some risks. In this case, some reducers (specially ones with low level of sensitive data exposure can be assigned to public machines). This will increase data exposure risks but will allow better performance and load balancing across the hybrid cloud sides. Such a technique reflects a tradeoff between risk and performance (i.e., load balancing of MR jobs). At one extreme, there is Sedic which can be regarded as 0 % risk; and at another extreme, original MR can may result in unconstrained leakage of sensitive data to public cloud for performance purposes, namely full-exposure (100 % risk). However, we can limit the partitions that are assigned to public machines to achieve a performance vs. risk tradeoff, similar to the one presented in the context of workload partitioning earlier in the section.

While the risk-aware MR workload partitioning is relatively straightforward to formalize, there are many complexities. For instance, in original MR setting, the assignment of partition to reduce tasks is done when the job is initialized (deployed) and reducer to machine assignment is done based on a policy such as FIFO. Controlling disclosure in such a setup requires us to track what data is sensitive in each map output partition so that we can then assign them to the right machines based on given risk threshold (i.e., risk aware partition assignment). Such a tracking should not be too costly so as to nullify the performance advantages obtained by using public side for some reduce tasks. Another complexity is that if the partitioning criteria used for assigning work to reducers is completely randomized (as is generally the case for load balancing purposes), then the sensitive data may also be randomly distributed across the partitions. In such a case, the number of partitions that can be offloaded to the public side will be limited to that dictated by the risk tolerance. Designing appropriate partitioning strategies and scheduling of reduce task is a substantial challenge.

4   Software Vulnerability Assessment on the Cloud

Assessing the security of software services in clouds is challenging because of vulnerabilities in the infrastructure, platform and applications. The recent denial of service cyber attacks on the websites of banks clearly shows the importance of security risk analysis for cloud computing. It was discovered that various cloud services and public Web hosting services were infected by malware that has existed for years. A security risk analysis framework can be used to discover existing vulnerabilities and help organizations to protect themselves from cyber attacks. Such a framework in the context of cloud computing opens several challenges. Complexity arises since in the cloud setting, the platform or the infrastructure on which the software can actually run may not be known or guaranteed. This implies that the security of the software service must be assured regardless of the underlying infrastructure or platform, requiring a large number of combinations. Another common trend in Cloud and Service oriented Architecture (SoA) environments is Service composition, whereby new services can be created rapidly by composing existing services. Once again, the component services must be tested for security levels on a large number of platform and infrastructure combinations. In this section, we briefly describe a novel vulnerability assessment framework, entitled VULCAN, for cloud computing systems. Our framework is designed to empower analysts with the ability to answer questions such as "I developed this cloud product as a service, is it vulnerable?". Or "I want to host this software application in this cloud environment, what security vulnerabilities I should watch out for?". One of VULCAN's main design features is an easy-to-use interface that can be used to assess security vulnerabilities of cloud-based system deployments. Another important feature is extensibility. Different components of the VULCAN framework (viz., Ontological vulnerability assessment, component, Ontology knowledge base, semantic natural language processors, vulnerability class index, etc.) can be integrated into any existing assessment frameworks (e.g., Metasploit [21]). Likewise, any additional security vulnerability analysis components can be integrated into VULCAN. VULCAN effectively supports:

- Software vulnerabilities modeling
- Analysis of vulnerabilities for cloud computing and mobile environments
- Software penetration tool environment
- Discovery of new vulnerabilities from the known one via the use of reasoning tasks on our ontology knowledge base

Before we provide a technical overview of VULCAN components and design, we briefly review the state of the art in vulnerability assessment techniques and frameworks developed in the literature.

4.1 Vulnerability Assessment Techniques and Tools

Vulnerability Assessment Framework is a structure supporting a set of tools that allows security practitioners to create and deploy exploits to find vulnerabilities. For example, Mercury [17] is one such assessment framework for Android based systems. Mercury is a framework that provides an interactive tool that allows for dynamic interactions with the target applications running on a device. Using Mercury, it is possible to realize some of the attacks illustrated in Vidas et al. [31] survey of current android attacks against android security.

Previous research on vulnerability assessment has yielded some solutions such as: the development of penetration testing tools, taxonomies and ontologies of vulnerabilities, and assessment frameworks that allows integration of other components. Steele's [18] work on ontological vulnerability assessment shows that taking an ontological approach results in improved identification of complex vulnerabilities. Guo and Wang [22] work present an ontology-based approach to model security vulnerabilities listed in Common Vulnerabilities and Exposures (CVE), providing machine understandable CVE vulnerability knowledge and reusable security vulnerabilities interoperability. The ontology for Vulnerability Management (OVM) [23] captures important concepts and relations for describing vulnerabilities in the context of software and system security. Paul et al. [24] recommend the use of ontology to capture evolving requirements like in high assurance systems. Wang et al. [25] propose an ontology-based approach to analyze and assess the security posture for software products. Normally, given a knowledge base of security vulnerability, you could retrieve currently known vulnerabilities of given target. Xiao et al. [27] proposed a solution to overcome the tedious manual work on extracting Access Control Policies (ACP) from Natural Language (NL) documents. They proposed a solution 'Text2Policy', to automatically extract ACPs from NL software documents. This work is related to VULCAN which attempts to automate ontology generation from vulnerability data sources. The state of the art automatic ontology generation [29] defines its life cycle as a process composed of Extraction (acquisition of information needed to generate the ontology), Analysis (focuses on the matching of retrieved information and/or alignment of two or more existing ontology, depending on the use case), Generation (Ontology generation), Validation (Authenticate whether the generated ontology is correct or not), and Evolution (adapt to the ontology changes). Our goal is to come up with techniques to implement various components of the system for automatic ontology generation and population from multiple sources of vulnerabilities. In Meunier's [21] work, their contribution is a survey of currently known attempts to classify vulnerabilities and attacks. They illustrate how the current classifications fail to come up with one unified classification schema of all vulnerabilities and attacks. A recommended approach is to use ontology for vulnerabilities conceptualization. Because it is capable of adopting all kinds of vulnerabilities regardless of which sub categories they belong too. Our Ontology proves that the recommended approach to be essentials when developing a vulnerability analysis assessment framework.

Amongst the most important techniques for vulnerability analysis is the concept of attack graphs that depict Attack graphs [32] depict ways in which an adversary exploits system vulnerabilities to achieve a desired state. Sheyner and Wing [33] proposed a tool useful for generating and analyzing attack graphs. Our work on VULCAN uses the ontology as a root node to discover known vulnerabilities of the target system, then initializes the attack graph generation for it. Security vulnerabilities are conceptualized in ways similar to Heberlein et al. [34] work on establishing a taxonomic foundation for comparing and contrasting attack-graph approaches.

4.2 Vulcan: Vulnerability Assessment Framework for Cloud Computing

The main purpose of our assessment framework VULCAN is to provide complete vulnerability assessment for the cloud environment. VULCAN is based on onto-logical Vulnerability Assessment [18]. Using our Ontology Vulnerability Database (OVDB) [19], suitably extended with definitions for cloud computing, we provide two vital features to our framework. First feature, is the access to a conceptualized set of current known vulnerabilities listed in the National Vulnerabilities Database (NVD) [20]. The next feature, is using powerful ontology reasoning capabilities to search our knowledge base of vulnerabilities. And also, the ability to discover new vulnerabilities from the known existing one for a particular target system. Vulcan embodies an automated process to create ontology knowledge base from NVD data sources. To use most updated information on the current known vulnerabilities, we automate the process of discovering, extracting them and populating our OVDB. Our vulnerability data sources comes from different repositories and sources such as NVD and web searches. Our framework allows us to do penetration testing as well. We use an approach of mapping our OVDB with attack exploits database such as Metasploit Auxiliary Module and Exploit Database [21]. Within the framework, both vulnerabilities and their exploits are mapped together, this provides a complete penetration testing environment.

Below we briefly discuss the different components of VULCAN depicted in the figure below (VULCAN Architecture figure).

- **NVD:** National Vulnerability Database (NVD) is a SCAP [35] compliant vulnerability database. The NVD database collects vulnerability information from various interrelated vulnerability databases like CVE [36], CWE [37], CPE [38], CVSS [39] etc. and compiles the information into a single database. A typical vulnerability entry in the NVD database has the vulnerability identifier, description of the vulnerability, list of software and their versions in which this vulnerability is found in, vulnerability severity score (CVSS) etc. collected from appropriate vulnerability databases. These vulnerability databases are industry standard databases maintained by MITRE. VULCAN uses NVD as the source to populate vulnerability information into the ontology knowledge base.

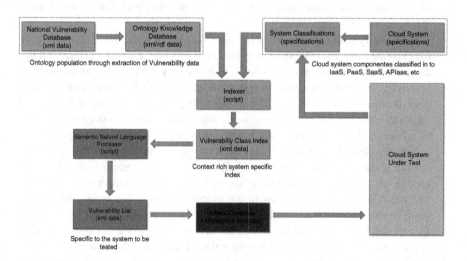

Fig. 2 The Vulcan architecture

- **OKB:** Ontology Knowledge Base is the ontological database of vulnerability information from the NVD database. NVD provides the vulnerability database in a XML feed. We extract the vulnerability information from the XML feed and populate ontology knowledge base. The vulnerability information in the NVD XML feed is present in various tags. All the information in these tags are mapped to various classes and properties defined in the ontology.

- **System Classifiers:** System Classifiers are dynamic inputs provided to the Indexer which will classify the classes in the ontology knowledge base. An example classification includes various vendors in the cloud computing domain and various software or hardware components in each service level of cloud computing services. As shown in the figure above, cloud computing domain is classified into IaaS, PaaS, SaaS etc. sub domains. In each of these domains we will include software and hardware components used in popular cloud computing vendors like Xen hypervisor in IaaS sub-domain, Google App Engine in PaaS sub-domain and Salesforce CRM in SaaS sub-domain. We can provide the system classifiers to whatever detail and depth we want to. The indexer takes these system classifiers as input and crawls through the ontology knowledge base and creates an index. The index consists of vulnerabilities grouped according to the system classifiers provided by us. The changes in software or hardware in any domain or vendor would require updating the system classifiers and re-indexing the ontology knowledge base.
- **Indexer:** Indexer is the software responsible for crawling through the ontology knowledge base to create an index. This index will in turn be used by the SNLP module to search the ontology knowledge base depending on the user query. The indexer is set to run every time the ontology knowledge base and/or system classifiers change. The indexer identifies all the vulnerabilities that are related to software or hardware components listed in the system classifiers and groupe them accordingly in the index.
- **Vulnerability Class Index:** Vulnerability Class Index is the list of all vulnerabilities grouped into the categories provided by the system classifiers. These groups are called as "Vulnerability Classes". Vulnerability classes will assist users to search for vulnerabilities within a specific domain or sub-domain. At the top level there is cloud computing class. Cloud computing has a sub class called PaaS and the PaaS class has Xen hypervisor as it's sub class. In the Xen class we have list of vulnerabilities extracted by the indexer from the ontology knowledge base.

    SNLP: Semantic Natural Language Processor enables users to search and reason about vulnerabilities. It includes various sub components which are capable of doing pattern matching, keyword search, and reason over properties and relationships of the classes in the ontology knowledge base. SNLP takes input from user and tries to understand what the user is asking for. Then based on the input, it provides him a list of vulnerabilities for the requested product and/or class. SNLP is capable of looking up vulnerabilities for the requested product and listing vulnerabilities in a particular class or product across various vendors. It also can reason and list vulnerabilities for the technology or framework used in the user's application.
- **Other Components:** The main components and modules of VULCAN are detailed above, the rest parts of its architecture as shown in Fig. 2 are the customizable features that provide means to our framework for Cloud System testing purposes. The Vulnerability List is generated from the SNLP component after processing the user natural language query. Moreover, the Attack Database is an independent source of attack modules where we utilize Metasploit Modules

for testing purposes in our case study. Then, we have our target Cloud System which is being assessed whether it is vulnerable to the discovered vulnerabilities in the previous phase.

We have implemented our VULCAN via a set of interconnected components as described above. In our implementation of OKB we extract NVD data and store them in a graph database which is realized via Resource Description Framework (RDF) triples. With our graph database, we generate an ontology that enable us to do some reasoning tasks which are useful for vulnerability assessment within our VULCAN. The three componets: classifiers, indexers, and vulnerability class indexers Together achieve dynamic vulnerability assessment for Cloud Computing. In our SNLP implementation, we rely on our Ontology Knowledge Base for information and the capabilities of our modules to properly fetch the cloud computing relevant search results.

We envision that cloud computing users, providers, security analysts can use VULCAN features to perform different type of assessment of their cloud environment. Also, our framework is flexible that developers can extend it by creating and adding new modules and components as they see fit. In addition, users can integrate our VULCAN's capabilities into any other compatible mobile, desktop or cloud security assessment frameworks. Ultimately, VULCAN should be able to mitigate current threats that cloud environment can face via its known vulnerabilities. Our framework is capable of exposing those vulnerabilities individually and also for a given cloud system target, we should be able to discover new possible vulnerabilities by performing reasoning tasks.

A typical use case scenario of using VULCAN components and modules to assess vulnerabilities for an android device using Mercury Framework goes like this:

1. A User provides both dynamic inputs for example Android (this data is provided to the System Classifiers module of our VULCAN framework), and a natural language query for example Assess for weaknesses that could allow an unauthorized access to my device? (this query is processed within our VULCAN Semantic Natural Language Processor – SNLP).

2. The System Classifiers generate possible android based solutions and feed them to the Indexer module. Then, the Indexer creates relevant vulnerabilities indexes which are used to produce vulnerabilities groups from the Vulnerability Class Index module. A sample created vulnerabilities group named Root Access contains indexed data of these CVE-IDs: CVE-2011-3874, CVE-2011-1823 and CVE-2009-2692.

3. The SNLP component, will do reasoning tasks on the user query and using the created vulnerabilities group data. It will return to the user via a dialogue agent interface relevant results such as the IT Products that have vulnerabilities and other necessary information that comply with the user query.

4. Using our Middle-ware application, we map the found IT Products to a Mercury framework [17] module called Test for vulnerabilities that allow a malicious application to gain root access to launch attacks on the products within our targeted android user device.

5. Then, VULCAN traces the deployment of the module payloads and report whether the attacks were successful on the device or not and if the tested vulnerabilities are still present or fixed for those IT Products.

5 Conclusion

In this position paper, we explored two challenges in the context of secure processing on the cloud. While cloud computing offers new opportunities and is becoming increasingly ubiquitous. As individuals, services and organizations shift to using cloud resources, they face a fundamental challenge of loss of control over their data. Furthermore, the key decision of moving processing to the cloud depends upon the vulnerability of the cloud infrastructure itself. The paper describes our preliminary work on developing vulnerability assessment tools for cloud computing. Challenges related to service composition and partial knowledge of infrastructure on which software will execute is explored. To address the issues due to loss of control, the paper explores a risk aware processing model in the context of hybrid clouds. A hybrid cloud is a composition of two or more distinct cloud infrastructures (private, community, or public) that remain unique entities, but are bound together by standardized or proprietary technology that enables data and application portability. Hybrid cloud offers a new opportunity for secure processing in the cloud environment such that processing of sensitive data on public machines can be controlled. This raises the fundamental challenge of workload and data partitioning across private and public machines. The paper formalizes such a challenge as a multi-criteria optimization problem and instantiates it in a variety of hybrid cloud settings. Furthermore, the paper sketches the solution approaches in two distinct settings: (a) a fully hybrid model where the goal is to partition workload to meet risk and cot requirements by paying the minimum performance overheads. (b) A new risk aware MR architecture over the hybrid cloud which allows to take risks while executing a single MR job in order to increase the performance.

The paper focuses on introducing a new approach to processing computation in a hybrid cloud model and identifies challenges that need to be addressed in developing an effective solution.

References

1. M. Lev-Ram. Why Zynga loves the hybrid cloud. http://tech.fortune.cnn.com/2012/04/09/zynga-2/?iid=HP_LN, 2012.
2. L. Mearian. EMC's Tucci sees hybrid cloud becoming de facto standard. http://www.computerworld.com/s/article/9216573/EMC_s_Tucci_sees_hybrid_cloud_becoming_de_facto_standard, 2011.
3. K. Zhang, X–y. Zhou, Y. Chen, XF. Wang, and Y. Ruan. Sedic: privacy-aware data intensive computing on hybrid clouds. In *ACM Conference on Computer and Communications Security*, pages 515–526, 2011.

4. K. Y. Oktay, V. Khadilkar, B. Hore, M. Kantarcioglu, S. Mehrotra, and B. Thuraisingham. Risk-Aware Workload Distribution in Hybrid Clouds. In *IEEE CLOUD*, pages 229–236, 2012.
5. Hybrid Cloud. The NIST Definition of Cloud Computing. *National Institute of Science and Technology, Special Publication, 800-145*, 2011.
6. M. R. Fouad, G. Lebanon, and E. Bertino. ARUBA: A Risk-Utility-Based Algorithm for Data Disclosure. In *Secure Data Management*, pages 32–49, 2008.
7. S. Trabelsi, V. Salzgeber, M. Bezzi, and G. Montagnon. Data disclosure risk evaluation. In *CRiSIS*, pages 35–72, 2009.
8. Tomasz Nykiel, Michalis Potamias, Chaitanya Mishra, George Kollios, and Nick Koudas. 2010. MRShare: sharing across multiple queries in MapReduce. Proc. VLDB Endow. 3, 1–2 (September 2010), 494–505.
9. Jeffrey Dean and Sanjay Ghemawat. 2008. MapReduce: simplified data processing on large clusters. Commun. ACM 51, 1 (January 2008), 107–113.
10. Apache Hadoop. http://hadoop.apache.org/.
11. H. Hacigümüş, B. R. Iyer, C. Li, and S. Mehrotra. Executing SQL over encrypted data in the database-service-provider model. In *SIGMOD*, pages 216–227, 2002.
12. Kehuan Zhang, Xiaoyong Zhou, Yangyi Chen, XiaoFeng Wang, and Yaoping Ruan. 2011. Sedic: privacy-aware data intensive computing on hybrid clouds. In Proceedings of the 18th ACM conference on Computer and communications security (CCS '11). ACM, New York, NY, USA, 515–526.
13. Bijit Hore, Sharad Mehrotra, Hakan Hacigümüç, Managing and querying encrypted data, Handbook of Database Security, Editors: Michael Gertz and Sushil Jajodia, Pages 163–190, Publisher, Springer US 2008/1/1
14. Ali Bagherzandi, Bijit Hore, Sharad Mehrotra, Search over Encrypted Data, In Encyclopedia of Cryptography and Security, Springer 2011
15. Hakan Hacigumus, Bijit Hore, Sharad Mehrotra, Privacy of Outsourced Data In Encyclopedia of Cryptography and Security, Springer 2011
16. Hakan Hacigumus, Bala Iyer, Sharad Mehrotra, Providing Database as a Service, IEEE International Conference in Data Engineering, 2002
17. T. Erasmus. The heavy metal that poisoned the droid. Tech. rep. MWR Info Security, 2012. URL: http://labs.mwrinfosecurity.com/tools/2012/03/16/mercury/documentation/white-paper/.
18. Aaron Steele. Ontological Vulnerability Assessment. In: Web Information Systems Engineering WISE 2008 Workshops. Ed. by Sven Hartmann, Xiaofang Zhou, and Markus Kirchberg. Vol. 5176. Lecture Notes in Computer Science. Springer Berlin Heidelberg, 2008, pp. 24–35. ISBN: 978-3-540-85199-8. URL: http://dx.doi.org/10.1007/978-3-540-85200-15.
19. Srujan Kotikela, Krishna Kavi, and Mahadevan Gomathisankaran. Vulnerability Assessment in Cloud Computing. In: The 2012 International Conference on Security Management (SAM 2012). Ed. by Kevin Daimi and Hamid R Arabnia. WORLDCOMP 2012. July 16–19, 2012, Las Vegas, Nevada, USA: CSREA Press, 2012, pp. 67–73.
20. National Vulnerability Database. NIST. 2012. URL: http://nvd.nist.gov/.
21. Metasploit Auxiliary Module and Exploit Database (DB). Metasploit.
22. M. Guo and J.A. Wang. An Ontology-based Approach to Model Common Vulnerabilities and Exposures in Information Security. In: ASEE Southest Section Conference. 2009.
23. Ju An Wang and Minzhe Guo. OVM: an ontology for vulnerability management. In: Proceedings of the 5th Annual Workshop on Cyber Security and Information Intelligence Research: Cyber Security and Information Intelligence Challenges and Strategies. CSIIRW 09. Oak Ridge, Tennessee: ACM, 2009, 34:1–34:4. ISBN: 978-1-60558-518-5. URL: http://doi.acm.org/10.1145/1558607.1558646.
24. R. Paul, I.L. Yen, F. Bastani, J. Dong, W.T. Tsai, K. Kavi, A. Ghafoor, and J. Srivastava. An Ontology-Based Integrated Assessment Framework for High-Assurance Systems. In: Semantic Computing, 2008 IEEE International Conference on. IEEE. 2008, pp. 386–393.

25. Ju An Wang, Minzhe Guo, Hao Wang, Min Xia, and Linfeng Zhou. Ontology-based security assessment for software products. In: Proceedings of the 5th Annual Workshop on Cyber Security and Information Intelligence Research: Cyber Security and Information Intelligence Challenges and Strategies. CSIIRW 09. Oak Ridge, Tennessee: ACM, 2009, 15:1–15:4. ISBN: 978-1-60558-518-5. URL: http://doi.acm.org/10.1145/1558607.1558625.
26. Anoop Singhal and Duminda Wijesekera. Ontologies for modeling enterprise level security metrics. In: Proceedings of the Sixth Annual Workshop on Cyber Security and Information Intelligence Research. CSIIRW 10. Oak Ridge, Tennessee: ACM, 2010, 58:1–58:3. ISBN: 978-1-4503-0017-9. URL: http://doi.acm.org/10.1145/1852666.1852731.
27. Xusheng Xiao, Amit Paradkar, Suresh Thummalapenta, and Tao Xie. Automated extraction of security policies from natural-language software documents. In: Proceedings of the ACM SIGSOFT 20th International Symposium on the Foundations of Software Engineering. FSE 12. Cary, North Carolina: ACM, 2012, 12:1–12:11. ISBN: 978-1-4503-1614-9. URL: http://doi.acm.org/10.1145/2393596.2393608.
28. Nora Yahia, Sahar A. Mokhtar, and AbdelWahab Ahmed. Automatic Generation of OWL Ontology from XML Data Source. In: CoRR abs/1206.0570 (2012).
29. I. Bedini and B. Nguyen. Automatic ontology generation: State of the art. In: PRiSM Laboratory Technical Report. University of Versailles (2007).
30. P. Meunier. Classes of vulnerabilities and attacks. In: Wiley Handbook of Science and Technology for Homeland Security (2008).
31. Timothy Vidas, Daniel Votipka, and Nicolas Christin. All your droid are belong to us: a survey of current android attacks. In: Proceedings of the 5th USENIX conference on Offensive technologies. WOOT11. San Francisco, CA: USENIX Association, 2011, pp. 10–10. URL: http://dl.acm.org/citation.cfm?id=2028052.2028062.
32. A. Singhal and X. Ou. Security Risk Analysis of Enterprise Networks Using Probabilistic Attack Graphs. In: NIST InterAgency Report (2011).
33. O. Sheyner and J. Wing. Tools for generating and analyzing attack graphs. In: Formal methods for components and objects. Springer. 2004, pp. 344–371.
34. T. Heberlein, M. Bishop, E. Ceesay, M. Danforth, CG Senthilkumar, and T. Stallard. A Taxonomy for Comparing Attack-Graph Approaches. Tech. rep. Submitted to ARDA. Net Squared, Inc., 2004. URL: http://www.netsq.com/Documents/AttackGraphPaper.pdf.
35. Security Content Automation Protocol. NIST. 2012. URL: http://scap.nist.gov/.
36. Common Vulnerabilities and Exposures. MITRE. 2012. URL: http://cve.mitre.org/.
37. Common Weakness Enumeration. MITRE. 2012. URL: http://cwe.mitre.org/.
38. Common Platform Enumeration. MITRE. 2012. URL: http://cpe.mitre.org/.
39. Common Vulnerability Scoring System. FIRST. 2012. URL: http://www.first.org/cvss.
40. SPARQL Query Language for RDF. W3C. 2012. URL: http://www.w3.org/TR/rdf-sparql-query/.
41. Sai Wu, Feng Li, Sharad Mehrotra, Beng Chin Ooi, Query Optimization for massively parallel data processing, SoCC 2011

Securing Mission-Centric Operations in the Cloud

Massimiliano Albanese, Sushil Jajodia, Ravi Jhawar, and Vincenzo Piuri

Abstract Recent years have seen a growing interest in the use of Cloud Computing facilities to execute critical missions. However, due to their inherent complexity, most Cloud Computing services are vulnerable to multiple types of cyber-attacks and prone to a number of failures. Current solutions focus either on the infrastructure itself or on mission analysis, but fail to consider the complex interdependencies between system components, vulnerabilities, failures, and mission tasks. In this chapter, we propose a different approach, and present a solution for deploying missions in the cloud in a way that minimizes a mission's exposure to vulnerabilities by taking into account available information about vulnerabilities and dependencies. We model the mission deployment problem as a task allocation problem, subject to various dependability constraints, and propose a solution based on the A^* algorithm for searching the solution space. Additionally, in order to provide missions with further availability and fault tolerance guarantees, we propose a cost-effective approach to harden the set of computational resources that have been selected for executing a given mission. Finally, we consider offering fault tolerance as a service to users in need of deploying missions in the Cloud. This approach allows missions to obtain required fault tolerance guarantees from a third party in a transparent manner.

M. Albanese (✉) • S. Jajodia
Center for Secure Information Systems, George Mason University,
Fairfax, VA 22030-4422, USA
e-mail: malbanes@gmu.edu; jajodia@gmu.edu

R. Jhawar • V. Piuri
Department of Computer Science, Università degli Studi di Milano, Crema, Italy
e-mail: ravi.jhawar@unimi.it; vincenzo.piuri@unimi.it

S. Jajodia et al. (eds.), *Secure Cloud Computing*, DOI 10.1007/978-1-4614-9278-8_11,
© Springer Science+Business Media New York 2014

1 Introduction

In recent years, individuals and organizations are increasingly resorting to Cloud-based services for storage, processing, and management of their data and applications. This practice offers several advantages to application and data owners – users, in general – with respect to traditional in-house management. First, users are relieved from buying expensive hardware and software licenses, and recruiting skilled personnel to administer and maintain their computing resources, thus providing significant economic savings. Second, users can access their applications using any device providing Internet connectivity. Third, even individuals with little or no IT background can take advantage of Cloud-based services to develop applications with very high scalability and elasticity requirements. These benefits are also providing an incentive for users to leverage Cloud-based solutions to deploy mission-critical applications.

A Cloud computing infrastructure is typically built by inter-connecting massive amounts of hardware according to well-defined design patterns, resulting in large-scale data centers that can elastically deliver computing resources to the users through virtualization. The main problem of adopting such Cloud-based Infrastructure-as-a-Service (IaaS) model is that the data centers, due to their very high complexity, may be vulnerable to various cyber-attacks and subject to a large number of failures, which are not within the control scope of the users, thus increasing users's security and fault tolerance concerns [1]. We identify two primary reasons why state-of-art techniques are unable to suitably address such concerns:

- Most security solutions either design data centers integrating tools such as intrusion detection systems and firewalls, or develop strategies to implement applications using techniques such as data obfuscation and memory management. However, interdependencies between the infrastructure, applications, and residual vulnerabilities are not taken into account.
- Fault tolerance methods are generally applied at application procurement and development time. This approach requires users to build their applications by considering environment specific parameters. However, it is infeasible to combine failure behavior and system architecture in Cloud computing due to the limited information about the infrastructure that providers release to the users.

The goal of this chapter is to provide an overview of approaches that can address the aforementioned problems. We discuss the inherent challenges, possible solutions, and relevant open issues. In particular, as an approach to address the security issues, we describe a solution that considers the current vulnerability status of the infrastructure and deploys mission-critical applications (or simply, *missions*) so as to minimize their exposure to existing network vulnerabilities. Once a mission is deployed, the proposed solution then protects the resources (computational hosts and network links) used by the mission to ensure high levels of security during mission execution (Sects. 3 and 4). Note that this approach is mission-centric and aims at providing maximum security for missions, given the current state of the infrastructure. To address the fault tolerance issues, we discuss a scheme that can help design fault tolerance solutions based on users' requirements at runtime and apply it to missions in a transparent manner. The latter approach can be integrated within the overall framework for delivering fault tolerance as a service to users' applications or missions (Sect. 5).

2 Background

In this section, we present some preliminary concepts and our assumptions about the Cloud infrastructure and the missions. We discuss the vulnerability behavior and failure characteristics of typical Cloud infrastructures, and the requirements for satisfying a mission's dependability goals.

2.1 Cloud Infrastructure

A Cloud computing infrastructure is typically built by inter-connecting large-scale, geographically distributed, data centers. Each data center consists of thousands of hosts that are organized into racks and clusters, and each host contains multiple processors, storage disks, memory modules and network interfaces. Physical hosts are first connected via high-speed rack switches, which are in turn connected to aggregation switches (AggS), forming a subsystem that can be viewed as a cluster. A cluster groups hosts with similar resource characteristics or administrative parameters. An AggS connects tens of racks to redundant access routers (AccR) that finally connects different data centers via the Internet backbone. Typically, data centers also deploy security services (e.g., firewalls, intrusion detection systems) to protect network elements from potential threats, and install hypervisors on physical hosts so that VMs with desired size and software stack can be instantiated and delivered to the users upon request.

Vulnerability characteristics. Despite careful security engineering, a number of vulnerabilities remain in the network and allow malicious adversaries to launch different types of cyber-attacks. For example, an attacker may exploit vulnerabilities in services such as *ftp*, *rsh*, and *sshd* to gain desired access privileges on a given host. Such exploits can be used to compromise users' applications or missions deployed in the system. Vulnerabilities and attack paths in the network can be analyzed using vulnerability scanners, and approaches based on attack graphs, dependency graphs, and attack surfaces (e.g., [2–5]). Analysis tools can also be extended with probabilistic schemes and ranking methods to quantify the vulnerability level of individual hosts. For simplicity, in this chapter, we assume that a vulnerability value V_h is pre-computed for each host $h \in \mathcal{H}$ in the infrastructure by adopting one of the existing techniques.

A physical host $h \in \mathcal{H}$ in the infrastructure can be characterized using a vector $\overrightarrow{h} = (h[1], h[2], \ldots, h[d], h[d+1])$, where the first d dimensions represent the host's residual capacity for each resource type (e.g., CPU, memory). The $d+1$th dimension represents the host's vulnerability value V_h. The residual resource capacities and the vulnerability level of each host are represented using normalized values in $[0,1]$. For example, $\overrightarrow{h} = (cpu, mem, V_h) = (1,1,1)$, where $cpu = 1$ and $mem = 1$, implies that both resources are fully available, whereas $V_h = 1$ means that the host is extremely vulnerable.

Failure behavior. Due to their high complexity, infrastructure components are subject to a large number failures that may prevent the system from fulfilling its intended functionality. Research on a system's failure characteristics is necessary because infrastructure failures may have a significant impact on the applications deployed in the Cloud. Several researchers54 [6, 7] used data mining techniques to understand the failure behavior of data center components. Examples of key observations from these studies are as follows:

- The annual failure rate for servers is around 8 %. The average number of repairs is 2 per machine (e.g., 20 repair or replacement events in 9 machines were identified over a 14 months period).
- Hard disks are the most failure-prone hardware components and the most significant reason behind server failures (about 78 % of total faults or replacements affected hard disks).
- Among network devices, top-of-rack switches are most reliable (failure rate less than 5 %) and load balancers are least reliable (failure probability of 1 in 5). Load balancers mainly fail due to software bugs and configuration errors, and experience short but frequent failures.

The failure behavior of various server and network components can also be analyzed using analytical models such as fault trees and Markov chains [8, 9]. Such modeling techniques, as discussed in Sect. 5, can be used to analyze the impact of component failures on users' applications.

2.2 Missions

We consider a mission M to be a composition of a set of tasks $M = \{\tau_1, \ldots, \tau_m\}$. This model-independent definition allows us to consider different software architectures for the mission (e.g., web services, business processes, scientific applications) as well as different formalisms (e.g., Petri Nets, work flows). For example, a mission can be a three-tier web application realizing an e-Commerce service or a scientific tool with tasks performing graph theoretical calculations on geographical maps. Intuitively, a mission is successful if (i) all the tasks start from a correct initial state, perform their operations, and generate the correct output in a specified amount of time, and (ii) the protocol that composes the information from individual tasks can justifiably be trusted. Each task in the mission can be associated with a tolerance value *tol* when it is implemented using some security mechanisms (e.g., memory management guards to protect from buffer overflow attacks). Intuitively, the *tol* value provides an estimate of the maximum level of vulnerability that the task can be exposed to without compromising its successful completion. Each mission task may also be replicated to tolerate failures. In fact, we create a set of task replicas $R_k = \{\tau_k^1, \ldots, \tau_k^{|R_k|}\}$ for each task, and the overall mission becomes a composition of the set of replicated task sets $T = \{t_i\} = \bigcup_{\tau_k \in M} R_k$. We treat task replicas as independent tasks for the purpose of mission deployment.

Similarly to physical hosts, we characterize each mission task using a vector $\overrightarrow{t} = (t[1], t[2], \ldots, t[d], t[d+1])$, where the first d dimensions represent the task's requirements for specific computing resources (e.g., CPU, memory) and the $d+1$th dimension is the task's maximum vulnerability tolerance value *tol*. Resource requirements and vulnerability tolerance are also represented using normalized values in $[0, 1]$, e.g., $\overrightarrow{t} = (cpu, mem, tol) = (0.5, 0.6, 0.6)$.

Security of the mission. A number of aspects must be considered to securely operate a given mission in a Cloud infrastructure. In this chapter, instead of considering traditional approaches based on network hardening or applying software security techniques, we study the following aspects:

- *Secure mission deployment*: Given a mission and the current vulnerability state of the infrastructure, deploy the mission's tasks in the network using the resources (hosts and network links) that are most suitable for successfully executing the mission. We formulate this problem as a task allocation problem that minimizes the mission's exposure to existing vulnerabilities. We consider both dynamic and static versions of this problem by modeling missions ignoring or considering temporal aspects respectively (see Sect. 3).
- *Static and dynamic resource protection*: Given a mission and the resources it uses (after it has been deployed), harden these resources in a way that is optimal with respect to a given cost function, in order to ensure high levels of security to the mission during execution. The static version of the problem protects resources for the entire duration of the execution whereas the dynamic version protects only the resources still to be used for execution (see Sect. 4).

Both these aspects should be addressed for any given mission in order to ensure that it achieves high levels of security in the Cloud. Note that the application of the resource protection scheme does not change the solution space of the mission deployment scheme. Therefore, the above two aspects generate independent, yet complementary, results that together allow the mission's execution in the Cloud infrastructure in a way that minimizes its exposure to vulnerabilities and the impact of exploits.

Fault tolerance of the mission. Implementing a fault tolerant mission using traditional approaches may be infeasible since the system's architectural details are not widely available to Cloud computing users. As a consequence, a new approach to address fault tolerance issues of missions is necessary. In this chapter, we discuss an approach where missions can obtain required fault tolerance properties *as a service* from a third-party *fault tolerance service provider*. In particular, we study the following aspect:

- *Fault tolerance management*: Given a mission and its fault tolerance requirements, apply a comprehensive fault tolerance solution to the mission and ascertain users' requirements at runtime. We present a scheme that realizes general fault tolerance mechanisms as independent modules that can transparently function on the missions, and based on user's requirements, appropriate modules are selected and composed in a specified manner to form a comprehensive solution (see Sect. 5).

3 Secure Mission Deployment

The first step to securely execute a given mission is to deploy the mission tasks in the Cloud such that their exposure to vulnerabilities is minimized. Since requests for mission deployment may arrive at any time, we develop a deployment strategy that considers the current resource allocation and vulnerability status of the Cloud. When a request is received, the allocation for the new mission is computed based on the availability of currently unused resources. Once the mission is deployed, resource allocation and vulnerability status are updated accordingly. In this section, we present a detailed problem formulation, and an approach to solve the mission deployment problem. We also discuss the challenges that still need to be addressed.

Problem formulation. To focus on the deployment problem, we assume that a virtual machine containing required resources and services is instantiated for each task in the mission. This assumption reduces mission deployment to a task allocation problem that can be characterized as a function $a : T \rightarrow \mathscr{H}$ which maps each mission task $t_i \in T$ to a physical host $h_j \in \mathscr{H}$ in the infrastructure. The binary variable a_{ij} denotes the truth value of $a(t_i) = h_j$, that is,

$$(\forall t_i \in T, h_j \in \mathscr{H}) \quad a_{ij} = \begin{cases} 1 & \text{if} a(t_i) = h_j \\ 0 & \text{otherwise} \end{cases}$$

Every time a task t_i is allocated on host h_j, the vulnerability score of host h_j may increase by $\Delta V_{t_i,h_j}$ since new vulnerabilities are potentially introduced on the host. Note that, although multiple hosts may have similar configurations and, consequently, similar vulnerability scores, their vulnerability scores may vary significantly at run time, as tasks are dynamically allocated and deallocated. Let $V^*_{h_j}$ denote the vulnerability score of host h_j after mission deployment. Our objective is to find, among all possible allocations $a \in \mathscr{A}$, the allocation that minimizes the largest $V_{h_j}^*$ amongst all the hosts involved in the mission, that is

$$\min_{a \in \mathscr{A}} \quad \max_{h_j \in \mathscr{H} | \exists t_i \in T, a(t_i) = h_j} \quad V_{h_j}^* \tag{1}$$

Note that, ideally, the mission's exposure to vulnerabilities in the system after allocation should be zero. In practice, the effectiveness of task allocation must be measured in terms of the deviation from the ideal behavior. Furthermore, note that this formulation focuses on optimizing the security and workload of the mission. The fault tolerance aspects of the mission are integrated in the optimization problem in the form of constraints on the placement of each mission task in the Cloud infrastructure (e.g., the distribution constraint described below). We provide a detailed discussion on fault tolerance constraints, and a method to derive them, in Sect. 5.

Each allocation $a \in \mathscr{A}$ should satisfy the following constraints to ensure the dependability of the mission.

- *Consistent allocation*: This constraint specifies two conditions that must be satisfied across all the hosts in the infrastructure at all times.

$$(\forall t_i \in T) \quad \sum_{h_j \in \mathscr{H}} a_{ij} = 1 \tag{2}$$

$$(\forall h_j \in \mathscr{H})(\forall x \in [1,d]) \quad \sum_{t_i \in T} a_{ij} \cdot t[x] \leq h[x] \tag{3}$$

Equation 2 specifies that each mission task must be allocated only on a single physical host. Equation 3 implies that the amount of resources consumed by all the tasks mapped on a single host cannot exceed the total capacity of that host in any dimension.

- *Distribution*: Equation 4 specifies that the allocation function $a : T \rightarrow \mathscr{H}$ must map all the replicas of a task on different hosts to avoid single points of failure.

$$(\forall \tau_k \in M)(\forall \tau_k', \tau_k'' \in R_k) \quad a(\tau_k') \neq a(\tau_k'') \tag{4}$$

- *Vulnerability tolerance*: To protect the tasks from being compromised due to the vulnerabilities on the hosts on which they are allocated, this constraint specifies that a task can be mapped only to the hosts whose vulnerability value V is less than the vulnerability tolerance *tol* of that task, that is,

$$(\forall h_j \in \mathscr{H})(\forall t_i \in T) \quad t_i[d+1] \geq a_{ij} \cdot h_j[d+1] \tag{5}$$

An attacker can exploit the vulnerabilities on a given host h_j and compromise the mission if a task $t_i \in T$ is placed on host h_j having vulnerability value higher than the tolerance level of the task.

Mission deployment solution. Modeling secure mission deployment as an optimization problem has not been well-studied in the literature. Given the NP-hardness of the general allocation problem, existing solutions typically adopt heuristics, meta-heuristics, and mathematical programming based approaches. In general, such approaches either have scalability issues or relax the optimality goals. In our context, we need an approach that solves the mission deployment problem in a time-efficient manner and provides acceptable sub-optimal results. One possible solution is based on the A^* state-space search method discussed in [10]. Here, we provide a detailed description of this approach.

To enable A^* exploration, the overall state-space is represented as a tree. We start by describing the data structure supporting the exploration of the solution using the A^* algorithm:

- A *state* s is a possible choice for allocating task t_i on host h_j. A state is represented by the pair (t_i, h_j).
- The *root state* represents is the initial state from which the algorithm starts, with no task being allocated yet.
- An *operation* of the A^* algorithm generates the set of feasible child states for a given state s.
- The *solution path* is the path from the root state to the first leaf state that is reached during state-space exploration.
- The *goal state* is a state in which all the tasks have been allocated. A leaf state corresponds to a complete allocation.

To generate the search tree from the root state, the set T of tasks is initially sorted in increasing order of vulnerability tolerance *tol* and considered for allocation in this order. The ith task in the sorted list corresponds to the ith level in the state-space tree. Given a state $s = (t_i, h_j)$, the next task t' from the sorted list is chosen, and all the hosts $h_j \in \mathcal{H}$ that satisfy the dependability constraints (consistent allocation, distribution, and vulnerability tolerance constraints) with respect to t' are shortlisted. The successors of state s are all the states mapping t' to one of the shortlisted hosts.

The evaluation function for state s in the state-space tree is as follows:

$$f_{vul}(s) = g_{vul}(s) + h_{vul}(s) \tag{6}$$

where $g_{vul}(s)$ is the aggregate vulnerability score associated with the allocation path from the root state to the current state s, and $h_{vul}(s)$ estimates the minimum

---

Algorithm 1 Estimate cost

1: Repeat steps 2 through 4 until a goal state is reached.
2: Use the A^* *operation* to obtain the set S of feasible successors of the current state.
3: Calculate $(V_{h_j} + \Delta V_{t_i,h_j})$ for each state in S.
4: Select the state with minimum $(V_{h_j} + \Delta V_{t_i,h_j})$ value and temporarily mark it as the current state s. {Note that we choose the state with minimum value to keep the value of $h_{vul}(s)$ as the lower bound.}

Algorithm 2 State-space tree traversal scheme

1: Push the root state in OPEN and execute steps 2–5 until either a complete allocation is obtained or OPEN becomes empty.
2: Pop the state s with minimum $f_{vul}(s)$ from OPEN.
3: If state s corresponds to the goal state, construct the final solution by traversing the tree in the reverse order from the goal state to the root state; else, generate the successors of s using the A^* *operation*.
4: For each successor s^* of s

   (i) Calculate new_g_{vul}, the aggregate vulnerability from the root state to state s^*.
   (ii) If the entry corresponding s^* already exists in either OPEN or CLOSE and its real cost is less than that of the current successor, drop the current successor since the same state has already been reached with lower cost. Otherwise, continue with the next step.
   (iii) Estimate the lower bound $h_{vul}(s^*)$ and compute $f_{vul}(s^*) = g_{vul}(s^*) + h_{vul}(s^*)$.
   (iv) Push the successor s^* and its $f_{vul}(s^*)$ value in OPEN since state s^* has been successfully generated and its cost computed.

5: Push the parent state s in CLOSE since it has been visited.

---

additional vulnerability associated with completing the allocation from state s to a goal state. The value of $g_{vul}(s)$ is computed as follows:

$$g_{vul}(s) = g_{vul}(parent(s)) + V_{h_j} + \Delta V_{t_i,h_j} \tag{7}$$

where $g_{vul}(parent(s))$ denotes the aggregate vulnerability score associated with the allocation path leading to the parent state of s and $(V_{h_j} + \Delta V_{t_i,h_j})$ denotes the updated vulnerability score of host h_j after allocation of task t_i. The $gvul(s)$ value for the root state is initialized to 0.

If we consider a uniform cost search, the lower bound estimate for each state must be considered zero, that is, $h_{vul}(s) = 0$. The A^* algorithm, in this case, obtains an optimal solution but expands a higher number of states (as shown in Example 1). Therefore, a heuristic is necessary to estimate h_{vul}. Algorithm 1 outlines an approach to realize the *estimateCost* function. In this case, h_{vul} is computed as the total vulnerability value along the traversed path. This algorithm significantly improves the performance of the traversal scheme when compared to a uniform cost search without influencing the final result.

The state-space tree traversal scheme provides the solution path that minimizes the mission's exposure to the vulnerabilities in the system. The traversal scheme dynamically generates the state-space tree based on the states that are expanded and visited. The tree expansion starts from the root state and stops at the goal state, where it obtains a near-optimal allocation. Two data structures OPEN and CLOSE are used for making the traversal decisions. OPEN contains the set of states that are generated using the A^* *operation* but not yet visited, and CLOSE contains the states that are already visited. Each entry in OPEN and CLOSE contains a state s and its corresponding $f_{vul}(s)$ value. Algorithm 2 outlines the traversal scheme using (i) the A^* *operation* which, given a state s, generates the set of feasible child states or successors, and (ii) the *estimateCost* heuristic that calculates the lower bound vulnerability value h_{vul} of each successor.

Table 1 Example scenario for mission deployment

Infrastructure		Mission	
Host	Residual CPU capacity, vulnerability level	Task	CPU requirement, vulnerability tolerance
$h_j \in \mathcal{H}$	$\vec{h}(cpu, V)$	$t_i \in T$	$\vec{t}(cpu, tol)$
h_1	0.5, 0.2	t_1	0.4, 0.2
h_2	0.3, 0.2	t_2	0.4, 0.2
h_3	0.7, 0.1	t_3	0.3, 0.4
h_4	0.5, 0.3		

Table 2 Increase in vulnerability scores

$\Delta V_{t_i, h_j}$	h_1	h_2	h_3	h_4
t_1	0.2	0.1	0.1	0.3
t_2	0	0.1	0.2	0.1
t_3	0.1	0.1	0.2	0

Example 1. Consider an infrastructure with four hosts $\mathcal{H} = \{h_1, \ldots, h_4\}$ and a mission with two tasks $M = \{\tau_1, \tau_2\}$, where $\mathcal{R}_1 = \{\tau_1^1, \tau_1^2\}$ and $\mathcal{R}_2 = \{\tau_2^1\}$. Mission deployment is driven by $a : \{t_1, t_2, t_3\} \rightarrow \{h_1, h_2, h_3, h_4\}$, and distribute constraint holds for tasks t_1 and t_2. For simplicity, consider only a single resource dimension for hosts and tasks (say CPU). Table 1 outlines available CPU capacity and vulnerability level of each host, and CPU requirements and vulnerability tolerance threshold of each task. Table 2 provides details on the increase in the vulnerability scores.

Figure 1a illustrates the state-space tree generated by our algorithm during mission deployment. The algorithm starts from the *root state* by generating the states for the first level in the tree. The *operation* considers task t_1, discards hosts h_2 and h_4 since they violate the capacity and vulnerability threshold constraints respectively, and generates states (t_1, h_3) and (t_1, h_1). The $f_{vul}(s)$ values for the two states are calculated as 0.7 and 1.0 respectively and pushed into OPEN.

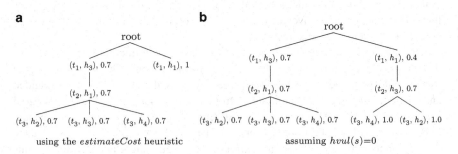

Fig. 1 State-space tree expanded using the A^* traversal scheme

Since state (t_1, h_3) has the smallest $f_{vul}(s)$ value, it is extracted from OPEN and marked as the current state. Its successors are then generated and f_{vul} values calculated. In this case only state $s = (t_2, h_1)$ with $fvul(s) = 0.7$ is returned and pushed into OPEN. In particular, after calculating $g_{vul}(s) = 0.4$, the *estimateCost* function is used to estimate the vulnerability value $h_{vul}(s)$ along this path. In this case, feasible states corresponding to task t_3 are considered, and the state with minimum $g_{vul}(s)$ value (0.3) is returned since states corresponding to task t_3 are leaf nodes.

At this point, state (t_2, h_1) is the entry with the lowest $fvul(s)$ value in OPEN. This state is marked as the current state and its successors (t_3, h_4), (t_3, h_3) and (t_3, h_2) are generated. The $fvul(s)$ value of all these states are calculated and pushed in OPEN. The state (t_2, h_1) is now pushed in CLOSE. The states corresponding to the task t_3 are similarly expanded and visited. The state-space search has now reached the goal state and found the complete task allocation. The algorithm pushes (t_3, h_4) in CLOSE, and returns $a(t_1) = h_3$, $a(t_2) = h_1$ and $a(t_3) = h_4$ as the complete allocation solution.

When uniform cost is assumed (i.e., $(\forall s) h_{vul}(s) = 0$) and this heuristic is not used, nine states are expanded to perform task allocation, as shown in Fig. 1b, while our algorithm expands only six states.

Open issues. Based on the above formulation of the mission deployment problem, we identify that three main challenges still need to be addressed.

- *VM images selection*: For each task, we need to instantiate a virtual machine containing all the resources and the services required to successfully execute that task. Hence, during mission deployment, we must first map each task to an available VM image and then to a physical host.

  Existing Cloud computing services usually require users to manually select VM images from a repository. Typically, users can also upload and share their VM images with other customers. This feature exacerbates the security problems in public Cloud services, and such problems cannot be identified by the users in a straightforward manner during image selection. For example, Balduzzi et al. [11] studied the vulnerability issues in Amazon EC2 service[1] by analyzing over 5,000 public images; using the Nessus vulnerability scanner, they identified that 98 % of Windows AMIs (Amazon Machine Images) and 58 % of Linux AMIs had software with critical vulnerabilities. This implies that an automated security-driven search scheme is required to deploy mission tasks. In other words, a task allocation function $a^{image} : T \to \mathscr{I}$ which maps each task $t \in T$ to a VM image $I \in \mathscr{I}$ based on security requirements needs to be defined.

- *Dynamic mission deployment*: Instead of allocating resources to tasks for the entire duration of a mission, we must consider the execution time of each task and perform allocation only for necessary periods of time while minimizing its exposure to the vulnerabilities.

  The mission model must be extended to include the start time and a deadline for each task. This extension allows us to generate the target execution timeline of the mission and obtain an enhanced mission model. This mission model is a

---

[1] http://aws.amazon.com/ec2/

special kind of labeled graph $M = (S, T, \rho)$, where S is a set of nodes representing the state of the computation, T is a set of edges representing tasks, and $\rho : T \to 2^R$ is a function mapping each task to the pool of resource types required to complete the task. Additionally, edges are labeled with task durations. Similar to the mission deployment approach discussed in this section, scalable solutions that can efficiently schedule mission tasks are required to address this challenge.

- *Incremental vulnerability analysis*: Each allocation introduces a set of new services on a host and increases its vulnerability level. We need a function $v : \mathscr{H} \times T \to \mathbb{R}$ that can estimate the increase in the vulnerability level $\Delta V_{t_i, h_j}$ to facilitate the "what-if" analysis. One possible approach to vulnerability assessment is by means of attack graphs, and a naive method to estimate $\Delta V_{t_i, h_j}$ is to discard the original attack graph and perform re-computation from scratch using the new data. However, such re-computation is wasteful since typically the changes are small, resulting in information that is not very different from the original one. Therefore, we need to take an incremental approach that (i) identifies the portions of the attack graph that have changed due to an event, (ii) re-computes the vulnerability information only in the changed portion, and (iii) combines the new and original information to provide updated results.

4 Mission Protection

The second step to securely execute a mission is to protect the hosts and network links used by the mission from possible cyber-attacks. In this section, we formulate the hardening problem and the cost model, and discuss the approach presented in [2] to solve the problem using attack graphs.

Problem formulation. A network hardening strategy is a set of atomic actions that can be taken to guard various resources in the network. For instance, an action may consist in stopping the *ftp* service on a given host. We start by introducing the notion of attack graphs that represent prior knowledge about vulnerabilities, their dependencies, and network connectivity. Given a set E of exploits, a set of security conditions C (e.g., existence of a vulnerability on a host or connectivity between two hosts), a require relation $R_r \subseteq C \times E$, and an imply relation $R_r \subseteq E \times C$, an *attack graph* is a directed graph $G = (E \cup C, R_r \cup R_i)$, where $E \cup C$ is the vertex set and $R_r \cup R_i$ is the edge set [2]. The term *Initial conditions* refers to the subset of conditions $C_i = \{c \in C \mid \nexists e \in E \text{ s.t. } (e, c) \in R_i\}$, whereas other conditions, which are usually consequences of exploits, are referred to as intermediate conditions.

Example 2. In Example 1, mission tasks are allocated on hosts h_3, h_1 and h_4. Assume that our objective is to prevent the attacker from gaining root privileges on host h_4, i.e., we want to avoid reaching condition $root(h_4)$ so as to protect task t_3.

Figure 2 illustrates an example attack graph in which exploits are represented using rectangles and conditions using ovals. The dashed ovals are the initial

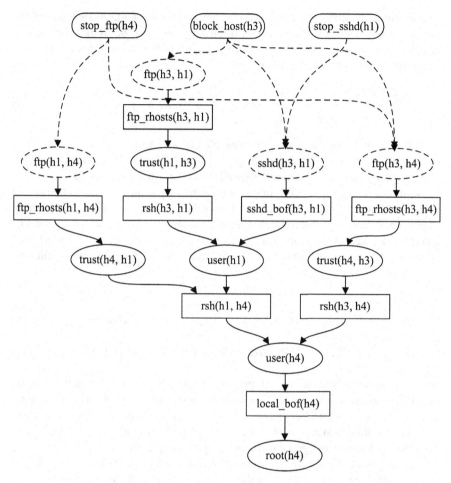

Fig. 2 Example of an attack graph including possible hardening actions, initial conditions, intermediate conditions, and exploits

conditions and other ovals represent intermediate conditions. The attack graph is simplified in several ways. For example, a single condition $ftp(h_s, h_d)$ is used to denote transport-layer ftp connectivity between two hosts h_s and h_d, physical-layer connectivity, and existence of the ftp daemon on host h_d. The attack graph depicts a simple scenario, with hosts h_3, h_1 and h_4, and four types of vulnerabilities: ftp_rhosts, rsh, $sshd\_bof$, and $local\_bof$. An example of attack path is the one where the attacker starts by establishing a trust relationship with host h_4 (condition $trust(h_4, h_3)$) by exploiting an ftp vulnerability on host h_4 ($ftp\_rhosts(h_3, h_4)$). The attacker can then gain user privileges on host h_4 (condition $user(h_4)$) with an rsh login, and achieve the goal condition $root(h_4)$ using a local buffer overflow attack.

An allowable *hardening action* is any subset of initial conditions such that all the conditions can be jointly disabled in a single step, and no other initial condition is disabled as a consequence. The rounded rectangles in the attack graph in Fig. 2 are examples of allowable hardening actions:

- $stop\_ftp(h_4) = \{ftp(h_1,h_4), ftp(h_3,h_4)\}$
- $block\_host(h_3) = \{ftp(h_3,h_1), sshd(h_3,h_1), ftp(h_3,h_4)\}$
- $stop\_sshd(h_1) = \{sshd(h_3,h_1)\}$

Given an attack graph, a set A of allowable actions and a set of target conditions $C_t = \{c_1,\ldots,c_n\}$, a *hardening strategy* S is a set of hardening actions such that conditions in C_t cannot be reached after all the actions in S are applied.

Note that removing specific initial conditions may require to take actions that disable additional conditions (e.g., conditions that are not part of any attack path). Therefore, in order to obtain a cost-effective *hardening strategy*, we need to define a cost model that takes the impact of hardening actions into account. A *hardening cost function* is any function $cost : \mathscr{S} \to \mathbb{R}^+$ that satisfies the following conditions:

$$cost(\emptyset) = 0 \tag{8}$$

$$(\forall S_1, S_2 \in \mathscr{S})(C(S_1) \subseteq C(S_2) \implies cost(S_1) \leq cost(S_2)) \tag{9}$$

$$(\forall S_1, S_2 \in \mathscr{S})(cost(S_1 \cup S_2) \leq cost(S_1) + cost(S_2)) \tag{10}$$

where $\mathscr{S}$ denotes the set of all possible strategies and $C(S)$ denotes the set of all conditions disabled under strategy S. Note that many different cost functions can be defined. For example, a basic cost function could simply count the number of initial conditions that are removed under a hardening strategy. Two possible hardening strategies for the attack graph Fig. 2 are $S_1 = \{stop\_ftp(h_4)\}$ and $S_2 = \{block\_host(h_3)\}$. If we assume that $cost(\{stop\_ftp(h_4)\}) = 20$ and $cost(\{block\_host(h_3)\}) = 10$, then the optimal strategy with respect to $root(h_4)$ is $S_2 = \{block\_host(h_3)\}$.

Mission protection solution. Most hardening techniques starts from the target conditions and move backwards through the attack graph to make logical inferences. Such backward search schemes typically face combinatorial explosion issues. Therefore, we must define a scalable scheme to build hardening strategies.

Starting from initial conditions, the hardening scheme in [2] traverses the attack graph forward. A key advantage of traversing the attack graph forward is that in a single pass, the algorithm can compute hardening strategies with respect to any condition. More importantly, forward traversal enables us to prune the search space, as briefly discussed below. The hardening algorithm first performs a topological sort of the nodes in the attack graph, and pushes them into a queue, with initial conditions at the front of the queue. Each node q in the queue is then analyzed and a set $\sigma(q)$ of possible hardening strategies w.r.t. to q is determined. Based on the nature of q (exploit or security condition), different steps are taken to compute $\sigma(q)$, as described in the following.

- If q is an *initial condition*, it is associated with a set of strategies $\sigma(q)$ such that each strategy contains one and only one of the allowable actions that disable q.
- If q is an *exploit*, it is associated with a set of strategies $\sigma(q)$ that is the union of the sets of strategies for each condition c required by q. In fact, an exploit can be prevented by disabling at least one of its required conditions.
- If q is an *intermediate condition*, it is associated with a set of strategies $\sigma(q)$ such that each strategy is the union of a strategy for each of the exploits that imply q. In fact, in order to prevent the attacker from reaching an intermediate condition, all the exploits that imply it must be prevented

In order to prevent the combinatorial explosion of the search space, the algorithm only maintains the k best solution w.r.t. cost for each intermediate node. Setting $k = 1$ will result in very fast execution, but will provide more expensive solutions. Higher values of k will increase execution times but will result in solutions that are closer to the optimal one. This scheme, under reasonable assumptions, provides an approximation ratio that, for $k = 1$, is bounded by $n^{d/2}$, where n is the maximum in-degree of nodes in the graph and d is the depth of the graph. Additionally, experiments reported in [2] show that, in practice, the approximation ratio is much lower than its theoretical upper bound.

Example 3. Consider again the attack graph of Fig. 2, and assume that the cost of actions $stop\_ftp(h_4)$, $block\_host(h_3)$, and $stop\_sshd(h_1)$ is 20, 10, and 15 respectively. After executing the topological sort and examining initial conditions, using $k = 1$, we obtain the following intermediate results:

- $\sigma(ftp(h_1, h_4)) = \{\{stop\_ftp(h_4)\}\}$
- $\sigma(ftp(h_3, h_1)) = \{\{block\_host(h_3)\}\}$
- $\sigma(sshd(h_3, h_1)) = \{\{block\_host(h_3)\}\}$
- $\sigma(ftp(h_3, h_4)) = \{\{block\_host(h_3)\}\}$

When the algorithm examines the exploit $rsh(h_1, h_4)$, before pruning we obtain $\sigma(rsh(h_1, h_4)) = \{\{stop\_ftp(h_4)\}, \{block\_host(h_3)\}\}$. After pruning, we obtain $\sigma(rsh(h_1, h_4)) = \{\{block\_host(h_3)\}\}$. Similarly, it is easy to show that the algorithm finally returns $\sigma(root(h_4)) = \{\{block\_host(h_3)\}\}$ as the recommended hardening strategy, which in this case coincides with the optimal solution.

Open issues. The dynamic version of the problem where we must take into account information about ongoing attacks remains an open issue. This will require the additional capability of detecting and tracking cyber attacks in real time as well as assessing and mitigating their potential impact on deployed missions. That is, given a mission, the set of hosts and links used to deploy the mission, and a stream of security alerts, we must find a cost-optimal time-varying strategy to harden, at any point in time, only the subset of resourced not used yet. A solution to this problem will help minimize the disruption that network hardening may cause to legitimate users.

5 Fault Tolerance Management

Fault tolerance is a critical and highly desirable property for mission deployed in the Cloud, given that large Cloud installations may be subject to a large number of failures. In this section, we adopt the perspective discussed in [12], where mission tasks can acquire desired fault tolerance properties as a service from a third-party (the fault tolerance *service provider*). The service provider must perform the following activities in order to realize this perspective.

- Defining an approach to implement general fault tolerance mechanisms as independent modules such that each module can transparently function on mission tasks.
- Analyzing the fault tolerance properties of each module by taking into account the failure behavior and system architecture. This sub-problem allows the service provider to select appropriate low-level modules based on the users' high-level goals.
- Defining a scheme to deliver a holistic fault tolerance solution to mission tasks by combining the set of selected modules.

Realizing fault tolerance modules. To offer fault tolerance as a service, the service provider must define general fault tolerance mechanisms in a way that they can transparently function on mission tasks deployed on virtual machines. This requirement can be satisfied by applying fault tolerance mechanisms at the virtualization layer [13]. We use ft_unit to denote the fundamental module that applies a coherent fault tolerance mechanism at the granularity of a VM instance. For instance, an ft_unit may replicate the entire VM instance on multiple physical hosts or an ft_unit may detect server crashes using well-known failure detection algorithms (e.g., by running the heartbeat protocol in the VM independently of mission tasks). In this manner, replication and failure detection can be performed without making any changes to the mission's source code, and the impact of hardware failures on the mission can be handled transparently.

Since different fault tolerance units realize different mechanisms, they offer a unique set of fault tolerance properties. Such properties can be characterized using their functional, operational, and structural attributes. The fault tolerance property p of an ft_unit can be denoted as $p = (u, \hat{p}, A)$ where u represents the ft_unit, $\hat{p}$ is the abstract property (e.g., availability, reliability), and A is a set of attributes that refers to the granularity at which u can handle failures, benefits and limitations of using u, and quality of service parameters. An order relationship can be defined on the domain of each attribute $a \in A$. Therefore, by looking at the attributes set A associated with an ft_unit, the service provider can evaluate fault tolerance properties that can be achieved with its use. An example of fault tolerance property for an ft_unit u^* is $p = (u^*, availability = 98\%, \{mechanism = active\_replication, no\_of\_replicas = 4, fault\_model = \text{node\_crashes}\})$.

Analyzing the effectiveness of a fault tolerance module. The effectiveness of an ft_unit can be evaluated in terms of the level of reliability and availability that can be obtained with its use. This analysis requires the service provider to (i) evaluate different configurations of modules, and (ii) quantify the reliability and availability obtained with each *ft_unit* by taking into account the failure characteristics of the system. We briefly discuss each of these two aspects in the following.

Evaluating the configuration of fault tolerance modules. A fault tolerance module *ft_unit* may have different configurations. For example, the *ft_unit* realizing replication schemes may have three configurations, namely, semi-active, semi-passive, and passive. These configurations represent the majority of fault tolerance implementations that are currently being used, and each configuration provides a different set of properties. One approach to characterize the effectiveness of an *ft_unit*, in a specific configuration, is to use Markov chains. As an example, we discuss Markov modeling for semi-active replication. Other models can be generated in a similar manner [8].

In semi-active replication, the input is either provided to all the replicas or state information of the primary replica is frequently sent to backup replicas. All the replicas (primary as well as backup replicas) execute all the instructions. However, only the output generated by the primary replica is made available to the user, and output messages from the backup replicas are logged. When the primary replica fails, one of the backup replicas can resume execution from a correct state.

Fig. 3 Example of a Markov model for semi-active replication

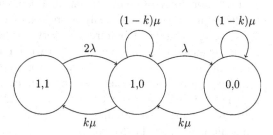

Figure 3 illustrates the Markov model of an *ft_unit* that realizes a semi-active replication scheme with two replicas. Each state is represented as (x, y) where $x = 1$ implies that the primary replica is working and $x = 0$ implies that it failed. Similarly, y represents the state of the backup replica. Normal execution starts in state $(1, 1)$ and remains in this state as long as both replicas are available. When either the primary replica or the backup replica fails, the system moves to state $(0, 1)$ or $(1, 0)$ accordingly, and the other replica continues the execution. From the mission's perspective, states $(0, 1)$ and $(1, 0)$ are equivalent, thus, they are represented using a single state. In state $(0, 1)$ or $(1, 0)$, the recovery mechanism is initiated, and the system moves to state $(1, 1)$ if the recovery is successful. Otherwise, if the current replica fails, the system transitions to state $(0, 0)$ and the service becomes unavailable. In the figure, λ denotes the failure rate and μ denotes the recovery rate.

Deployment contexts for a fault tolerance module. If all the replicas generated through an *ft_unit* are deployed on the same physical host, the host failure may result in the failure of the mission. This implies that the location of each replica is also critical to the fault tolerance of the mission. We analyze how the fault tolerance property of a given ft_unit changes across three different deployment contexts.

- *Different physical hosts within a cluster.* Replicas of a mission task are assigned to different hosts that are connected in a LAN. This deployment provides benefits in terms of low latency and high bandwidth but offers very fault tolerance. For example, a single switch failure may prevent the replicas from communicating with one other, and as a consequence, the consistency protocol cannot be executed.
- *Different clusters within a data center.* Replicas of a mission task are assigned to hosts that belong to different clusters within the same data center. This deployment provides moderate benefits in terms of latency and bandwidth, and offers higher fault tolerance.
- *Multiple data centers.* Replicas of a mission task are assigned to hosts that belong to different data centers. This deployment reduces the performance of the mission with respect to network latency, but offers a very high level of fault tolerance.

As the values of most low-level parameters (e.g., MTBF, MTTR) of hardware and system software are normally vendor-confidential, the work presented in [8] uses the data published in [14, 15] to determine the overall *availability* provided by various ft_unit's for different configurations and deployment schemes. In particular, the results from Markov model analysis are combined with the notion of deployment levels using hierarchical fault trees for server failures. We observe from the results that the availability of missions is higher when replicas are placed in two different data centers. The value is slightly lower for the deployment level where replicas are placed in different clusters within a data center and still lower when replicas are placed inside the same cluster. The overall availability obtained by semi-active replication is slightly higher than semi-passive replication, whereas passive replication appears to be the worst.

This analysis allows a service provider to identify the placement conditions inherent to each ft_unit. Such conditions can be specified in the form of fault tolerance constraints, that are then taken into account while deploying mission tasks in the infrastructure (e.g., using the technique in Section 3). Examples of fault tolerance constraints are as follows [16].

- *Restriction.* The service provider may require that task replicas be located within a subset of hosts in the infrastructure (e.g., a cluster or data center). Such requirement naturally arises when a deployment context is chosen (e.g., place two replicas of a task in different clusters within a data center). To satisfy such requirements, the service provider can use a restriction constraint that limits a task $t_i \in T$ to being allocated only on a specified group of physical hosts $H \subset \mathcal{H}$. When the set $Restrict = \{(t_i, H_j) \mid t_i \in T \wedge H_j \subset \mathcal{H}\}$ is defined, the allocation function $a : T \rightarrow \mathcal{H}$ must ensure the following:

$$\left(\forall t_i \in T, H_j \in 2^{\mathcal{H}}\right) \ ((t_i, H_j) \in Restrict \implies a(t_i) \in H_j) \qquad (11)$$

- *Forbid.* The service provider may need to specify that the allocation function must not deploy a given task on a subset of hosts. For example, if tasks t_1 and t_2 must be allocated on two different clusters C_1 and C_2, it is sufficient to restrict one task to one of the two clusters and forbid the other task from being deployed in the same cluster. Therefore, when the service provider defines a set $Forbid = \{(t_i, H_j) \mid t_i \in T \land H_j \subset \mathscr{H}\}$ specifying that task t_i must be forbidden from being allocated on hosts in H_j, the allocation function must satisfy the following:

$$\left(\forall t_i \in T, H_j \in 2^{\mathscr{H}}\right) \; (t_i, H_j) \in Forbid \implies (a(t_i) \notin H_j) \qquad (12)$$

- *Network latency threshold.* To balance the performance of the mission, the service provider may want to allocate task replicas $t_i, t_j \in T$ such that the network latency between them is below a given threshold δ. In this case, the service provider can define a set $Latency = \{(t_i, t_j, \delta) \mid t_i, t_j \in T) \land \delta \in \mathbb{R}^+\}$, and the allocation function $a : T \to \mathscr{H}$ must satisfy the following:

$$(\forall t_j \in T, t_j \in T) \; ((t_i, t_j, \delta) \in Latency \implies latency(a(t_i), a(t_j)) \leq \delta) \qquad (13)$$

We assume that the service provider realizes a range of fault tolerance mechanisms as ft_unit's and estimates the overall reliability and availability that can be achieved using each ft_unit with different configurations and deployment schemes. Let U be the set of possible ft_unit's applicable to the system. For a given user request, first, the set $U' \subseteq U$ of ft_unit's that satisfy the abstract property requirements is derived. Any $u \in U'$ can be used to deliver the desired fault tolerance properties if there are no additional constraints on cost or performance. However, since users may specify constraints on attributes in A, a second set $U'' \subseteq U'$ of modules is defined by only including those modules in U' that satisfy the additional constraints. For instance, a user may specify that the value of a given attribute $a \in A$ must be above a given threshold. Finally, modules in U'' are ordered with respect to users' requirements. The first ft_unit in the ordered set U'' can be selected as the most appropriate fault tolerance module.

Delivering comprehensive fault tolerance solutions. Although an ft_unit can serve as the fundamental fault tolerance module, a comprehensive solution ft_sol can be obtained by combining a set of ft_unit's in a specific execution logic. For example, a heartbeat test (ft_unit_1) can be applied only after a mission task is replicated on multiple hosts (ft_unit_2), and a recovery mechanism (ft_unit_3) can be applied only after a failure is detected. Therefore, using the above matching process, the service provider first designs a comprehensive fault tolerance solution ft_sol and applies it to the mission tasks. Note that by using ft_unit's to deliver a comprehensive solution, the extent of the fault tolerance support can be changed dynamically. In other words, the fault tolerance properties applied on a mission task can be dynamically changed based on the business needs. For instance, a robust failure detection mechanism can be replaced with a less robust one. Furthermore, by designing an *ft_unit* to be configurable at runtime, resource consumption and costs can be controlled.

The service provider starts monitoring the service once an *ft_sol* is applied to a mission. Runtime monitoring is critical for efficient service delivery since the context and attribute values of a fault tolerance solution may change at runtime due to the dynamic nature of the Cloud computing environment. To achieve this, the service provider first defines a set of rules over attributes $a \in A$ such that the validity of every rule establishes that property p is supported by the fault tolerance solution. For instance, given an *ft_sol* s_1 that satisfies property $p_1 = (s_1, availability = 98\%, \{mechanism = \text{active\_replication}, failure\_detection = \text{heartbeat\_test}, max\_recovery\_time = 25\text{ms}, level = 3\})$, the set of rules that can test the validity of p_1 can be defined as:

- $r_1 : no\_of\_server\_instances \geq 3$
- $r_2 : heartbeat\_test\_frequency = 5ms$
- $r_3 : recovery\_time \leq 25ms$

In this context, the task of the service provider is to monitor the attribute values of each *ft_sol* at runtime, and verify the corresponding set of rules to ensure that missions requirements are satisfied.

6 Conclusions

In this chapter, we highlighted that existing solutions do not suitably address users' security and fault tolerance concerns in the Cloud computing scenario. We then showed how our work can address some of these limitations, although some issues still remain open.

Specifically, we formulated the mission deployment problem as a security-oriented task allocation problem, and proposed a solution aimed at minimizing a mission's exposure to vulnerabilities. In order to define a more comprehensive solution, and provide better availability and fault tolerance guarantees to missions, we discussed an efficient approach to effective network hardening. Finally, we discussed how to offer fault tolerance as a service to missions.

In addition to the open issues already discussed throughout the chapter, another important issue that needs to be addressed is the ability to automatically respond to incidents at runtime in order to salvage missions that may have already been compromised by those incidents.

Acknowledgements The work presented in this chapter has been supported in part by the Office of Naval Research under award number N00014-12-1-0461, by Italian Ministry of Research within PRIN project "GenData 2020" (2010RTFWBH), and by the European Union under Integrated Project FP7-SEC-2012-312797 ABC gates for Europe.

References

1. P. Samarati and S. De Capitani di Vimercati, "Data protection in outsourcing scenarios: Issues and directions," in *Proceedings of the 5th ACM Symposium on Information, Computer and Communications Security (ASIACCS 2010)*, Beijing, China, April 2010, pp. 1–14.
2. M. Albanese, S. Jajodia, and S. Noel, "Time-efficient and cost-effective network hardening using attack graphs," in *Proceedings of the 42nd Annual IEEE/IFIP International Conference on Dependable Systems and Networks (DSN 2012)*, Boston, MA, USA, June 2012.
3. V. Mehta, C. Bartzis, H. Zhu, E. Clarke, and J. Wing, "Ranking attack graphs," in *Proceedings of the 9th International Symposium On Recent Advances In Intrusion Detection (RAID 2006)*, ser. Lecture Notes in Computer Science, vol. 4219, Hamburg, Germany, September 2006, pp. 127–144.
4. P. K. Manadhata and J. M. Wing, "An attack surface metric," *IEEE Transactions on Software Engineering*, vol. 37, no. 3, pp. 371–386, May 2011.
5. G. Jakobson, "Mission cyber security situation assessment using impact dependency graphs," in *Proceedings of the 14th International Conference on Information Fusion (FUSION)*, Chicago, IL, USA, July 2011.
6. K. V. Vishwanath and N. Nagappan, "Characterizing cloud computing hardware reliability," in *Proceedings of the 1st ACM Symposium on Cloud Computing*, Indianapolis, IN, USA, 2010, pp. 93–204.
7. P. Gill, N. Jain, and N. Nagappan, "Understanding network failures in data centers: Measurement, analysis, and implications," in *Proceedings of the ACM SIGCOMM 2011*, Toronto, ON, Canada, August 2011, pp. 350–361.
8. R. Jhawar and V. Piuri, "Fault tolerance management in iaas clouds," in *Proceedings of the IEEE First AESS European Conference on Satellite Telecommunications (ESTEL 2012)*, Rome, Italy, October 2012.
9. D. S. Kim, F. Machida, and K. S. Trivedi, "Availability modeling and analysis of a virtualized system," in *Proceedings of the 15th IEEE Pacific Rim International Symposium on Dependable Computing (PRDC 2009)*, Shanghai, China, November 2009, pp. 365–371.
10. M. Albanese, S. Jajodia, R. Jhawar, and V. Piuri, "Reliable mission deployment in vulnerable distributed systems," in *Proceedings of the 43rd IEEE/IFIP International Conference on Dependable Systems and Networks Workshops (DSN-W 2013)*, Budapest, Hungary, June 2013.
11. M. Balduzzi, J. Zaddach, D. Balzarotti, E. Kirda, and S. Loureiro, "A security analysis of amazon's elastic compute cloud service," in *Proceedings of the 27th Annual ACM Symposium on Applied Computing (SAC 2012)*, 2012, pp. 1427–1434.
12. R. Jhawar, V. Piuri, and M. Santambrogio, "Fault tolerance management in cloud computing: A system-level perspective," *IEEE Systems Journal*, vol. 7, no. 2, pp. 288–297, June 2012.
13. B. Cully, G. Lefebvre, D. Meyer, M. Feeley, N. Hutchinson, and A. Warfield, "Remus: High availability via asynchronous virtual machine replication," in *Proceedings of the 5th USENIX Symposium on Networked Systems Design and Implementation (NSDI 2008)*. San Francisco, CA, USA: USENIX Association, 2008, pp. 161–174.
14. W. E. Smith, K. S. Trivedi, L. A. Tomek, and J. Ackaret, "Availability analysis of blade server systems," *IBM Systems Journal*, vol. 47, no. 4, pp. 621–640, 2008.
15. A. Undheim, A. Chilwan, and P. Heegaard, "Differentiated availability in cloud computing slas," in *Proceedings of the 12th IEEE/ACM International Conference on Grid Computing (GRID 2011)*, Lyon, France, September 2011, pp. 129–136.
16. R. Jhawar, V. Piuri, and P. Samarati, "Supporting security requirements for resource management in cloud computing," in *Proceedings of the 15th IEEE International Conference on Computational Science and Engineering (CSE 2012)*, Paphos, Cyprus, December 2012, pp. 170–177.

Computational Decoys for Cloud Security

Georgios Kontaxis, Michalis Polychronakis, and Angelos D. Keromytis

Abstract Cloud-based applications benefit from the scalability and efficiency offered by server consolidation and shared facilities. However, the shared nature of cloud infrastructures may introduce threats stemming from the co-location and combination of untrusted components, in addition to typical risks due to the inevitable presence of weaknesses in the infrastructure itself. As a result, adversaries may be able to place themselves in monitoring proximity to high-value targets and gain unauthorized access to sensitive data. In this paper we present DIGIT, a system that employs *decoy computation* to impede the ability of adversaries to take advantage of unauthorized access to sensitive information. DIGIT introduces uncertainly as to which data and computation is legitimate by generating a mix of real and decoy activity within a cloud application. Although DIGIT may not impede intruders indefinitely, it prevents them from determining whether a captured system is handling actual or bogus processing within a reasonable amount of time. As adversaries cannot easily distinguish between real and decoy activity, they have to either risk triggering beacon-bearing data that can be traced back to them, or expend significant effort to pinpoint any actual data of interest, forcing them to reveal their presence.

1 Introduction

The multifaceted benefits of cloud computing have led to its rapid adoption for the deployment of online services and applications. As businesses and individuals increasingly rely on the cloud, the threat of unauthorized data access or full compromise of cloud services becomes more pertinent. The recent spate of security breaches in major online services [1–3, 6, 13, 25, 29] is indicative, and shows that

G. Kontaxis (✉) • M. Polychronakis • A.D. Keromytis
Network Security Laboratory, Columbia University, New York, NY, USA
e-mail: kontaxis@cs.columbia.edu; mikepo@cs.columbia.edu; angelos@cs.columbia.edu

S. Jajodia et al. (eds.), *Secure Cloud Computing*, DOI 10.1007/978-1-4614-9278-8_12,
© Springer Science+Business Media New York 2014

despite major advances in security research and engineering, vulnerabilities in software components, protocol design, system configuration, operational procedures, and other aspects of complex systems will continue to put cloud-based applications at risk.

The increasing sophistication of attack methods and exploitation techniques has shown that even the latest protection techniques can be bypassed, and the most up-to-date detection systems can be evaded. The added need of defending against tenants who have legitimate access but behave maliciously against other users of the same cloud service increases the complexity of the problem [23]. This situation necessitates the implementation of domain-specific "defense in depth" strategies that combine multiple and diverse security measures. Prior research on cloud security has focused on various aspects of cloud infrastructures, including data and network isolation [20], software attestation [11], and data availability [10, 16]. Although most research efforts have focused on systems and methods for hardening cloud-based systems and enabling the detection and prevention of security incidents, less attention has been given to "second-line" defenses for hindering attackers that have managed to gain access to parts of a system, or insider threats.

In this work we propose the concept of *computational decoys*, a novel approach that encompasses deceptive information and "throw-away" computation to impede the ability of an adversary to take advantage of any initial success they may have in compromising a system. The main goal of our approach is to introduce uncertainty as to the validity and authenticity of data captured by an adversary after gaining unauthorized access in one or more hosts, and in some scenarios, reveal the presence of the adversary.

We have applied this approach in *DIGIT*, a deceptive information generation, injection, and tracking system aimed at detecting and confusing adversaries in cloud settings. The system is based on a large number of application replicas, some of which (the "deception set") are provided with fake inputs. An adversary controlling a malicious or compromised replica will be uncertain as to the validity of any captured data. The whole process is orchestrated by an application-level proxy that mixes and dispatches real and fake requests to primary and decoy application replicas, respectively. Primary and decoy replicas can be swapped at any time simply by changing the source of inputs, increasing the confusion to potential adversaries.

A key aspect of the proposed mechanism is the believability of the generated decoy traffic, and consequently the fidelity of the evoked computation on a decoy replica. Enticing decoy traffic is generated automatically based on real client traffic using context-aware protocol field randomization. The generated inputs can contain specially crafted data whose misuse by an adversary can be subsequently detected. Examples of such enticing bait information include documents with built-in "beacons," URLs or credentials to honeypots or sites whose access can be directly or indirectly monitored, credit card and bank account numbers with triggers, and so on [8,9]. Other types of decoy information that we propose to use include deceptive documents in the file system and entries in database tables (or entire databases)—the exact type of bait used depends on the application. Besides application-level protocols, deceptive computation can be introduced at different levels, e.g., by simulating user activity at a higher level through the generation of key strokes and mouse input operations.

2 Threat Model

Our threat model revolves around a cloud computing environment where partitioned applications handle data-oriented user requests. We consider adversaries that have infiltrated one or more but not all server instances or modules of a cloud application, and have the ability to monitor the execution of the server program as well as its data flows, including user requests and program responses. We assume that, in case more than one cloud instances have been breached, adversaries may correlate information received from different back-end points. However, adversaries do not have the ability to simultaneously monitor network traffic both inside and at the edges of the cloud. This means that adversaries cannot determine whether a specific connection comes directly from the outside, or originates from a cloud-local proxy.

Finally, we consider that the amount of data collected in a production environment prohibits efficient analysis by humans within a realistic time frame. Therefore, we assume that an adversary's efforts to verify the quality of captured information are automated and rely on behavioral heuristics as well as grammatical and statistical analysis of the data rather than human interpretation of the content and context of the collected information. Note that server instances are oblivious to the use of computational decoys, and thus cannot hint an attacker as to their existence. Any access of decoy information by an attacker will lead to an alert signaling the breach, as well as to the immediate identification of the breached instance, as decoys are unique to the environment in which they have been deployed and their recipient.

3 Design

In this section we present the design of our application-level system that uses computational decoys to deceive an infiltrating adversary stealing information. Our design can be overlaid on top of existing infrastructures without rearranging the production environment. Figure 1 illustrates the modular structure of our proposed system and presents the data relationships within the system itself, as well as the exchange of flows within a cloud-computing setup.

A set of application replicas with identical functionality as the original application servers and components receives decoy requests. All requests to application replicas are handled normally, as if they were real, resulting in decoy computation and system activities indistinguishable from those of real application instances. The main component of DIGIT is placed at the edge of the cloud where a typical SSL terminator or load balancer typically terminates user connections.

This choice is made for two main reasons: first, the system must be interposed in the communication of clients with the cloud, and second, this placement enables the system to acquire a high-level view of the application instances operating at any given time. The overall operation of the system consists of four stages: incoming traffic interception and classification, decoy generation, decoy dissemination, and outgoing traffic reconciliation.

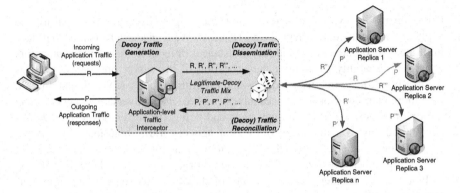

Fig. 1 High-level overview of DIGIT's architecture. DIGIT is designed as an overlay on top of existing cloud infrastructures, and consists of an application-level traffic interception and decoy generation system, and application replicas with identical functionality as the original application servers and components. The modular design of the system allows it to be easily extended with support for more applications (application-level traffic interception) and evolve the quality of the decoys (decoy generation)

Initially, the system intercepts and identifies the type of incoming application traffic. The type is defined as the combination of application protocol (e.g., HTTP) and target application (e.g., messages targeting the end points of an e-commerce site). Recognizing the type of incoming traffic is necessary for proceeding with traffic analysis and the generation of decoys tailored to the particular application. Traffic interception, shown in the center part of Fig. 1, is organized around a series of application-specific modules that register traffic filters with the core interceptor module. Upon a match with one of these filters, the appropriate module is called and the system forwards any related incoming traffic to the analysis module.

That analysis module is aware of the application protocol and identifies specific messages to provide the necessary context to the decoy generation modules. The analysis phase takes into account context-specific information such as client sessions. The output of the analysis phase consists of an application and message specific template which will be used for decoy generation. Although we aim at producing such templates in real time, an administrator can provide them based on protocol specifications of a specific application. In that case, the output of the analysis phase is a reference containing a specific template for use towards the decoy generation component.

The decoy generation component receives message templates (and optionally context-related information) and produces decoy messages that are required to be indistinguishable from the original message when they reach an application server instance. To do so it follows a generation-evaluation cycle that can be extended to be reactive to feedback from the evaluation phase.

The decoy dissemination component follows decoy generation and utilizes knowledge about the setup of a cloud environment to distribute decoys and legitimate messages among the instances of an application server. It makes no assumptions about the status of an application, e.g., whether it is compromised or not. It may take into account information from the load balancer so as to distribute decoys and legitimate messages in a manner similar to the load balancer's intended behavior.

Finally, the decoy reconciliation component receives responses to the decoy and legitimate requests from the application instances, discards the decoy responses, and forwards the legitimate responses to the client. Optionally, if copies of the legitimate message were given to more than one instances, it attempts to synthesize a consistent view of the appropriate response through the formation of a response consensus.

3.1 Security Model

Although DIGIT does not assume anything about the security of the cloud in which it operates, there should be security guarantees about its own components. The DIGIT proxy and its associated components should be protected against remote attacks from an adversary. This is analogous to the protection offered by a trusted platform module (TPM) [30] in single-system computing. As long as the TPM itself remains secure it can be effective in its role as a crypto-system.

3.2 Target Integration

Considering DIGIT as a gateway component in a cloud setup is only our initial approach. Effectiveness and scalability factors drive the question whether DIGIT could be realized closer to the actual system it protects. It would be interesting to investigate whether hardware, hypervisor or even application-driven approaches could introduce deceptive computation.

4 Decoy Generation

The key challenge in generating decoy traffic is that it should appear realistic and indistinguishable from actual user-generated traffic. We aim to satisfy this requirement based on the assumption that an attacker has a limited view of the cloud infrastructure and controls and monitors the behavior of a subset of the application server instances. Our goal is for decoy requests to carry the same properties as the actual user input and make the server to behave in the same way. We assume that actual and decoy computation on an application replica is the same as long as, given a real and a corresponding decoy request, similar or identical code execution paths are followed. Currently, we do not place any context-related constraints (e.g., a series of valid protocol messages or application requests that a user would be unlikely to perform in a specific order) as we assume that an attacker would not attempt to distinguish decoys in such manner. However, our approach can be extended to include more decoy evaluation heuristics.

Fig. 2 Decoy traffic generation based on an (optionally feedback-assisted) generation-evaluation approach. As more evaluation heuristics become available, the quality of generated decoys can adapt to actual user traffic. Decoy messages that achieve high fidelity are stored in a database for future use

Figure 2 presents the process of generating realistic computational decoys. Decoy generation begins with a set of templates for protocol messages generated by popular client applications (e.g., web browsers). Templates are used to generate random permutations in the acceptable value space for the parameters or content of a given message type. For instance, if the message is an HTTP GET request carrying the "PIN" parameter with a space of four numeric characters ($[0–9]\{4\}$) the system would generate all permutations. Alternatively, for a "search_word" parameter with a space defined by a dictionary of the English language we would generate an appropriate number of decoys or enough realistic decoys to satisfy a given quota.

The system then evaluates all generated decoys against the actual user input from a training set using the heuristics mentioned above. Decoy messages that exhibit similar or identical application server behavior are kept, while the rest are discarded. As dynamic binary instrumentation is computationally expensive, we make a time-space trade-off and store the produced decoys for future use rather than carry out real-time generation and evaluation.

4.1 Early Prototype

To assess our decoy generation approach we have implemented as an early prototype the common scenario of web applications in a cloud environment. The focus of our prototype is the automated generation of HTTP message decoys, an effort which is expected to act as a guideline on practical requirements in system components and procedures so that we may adjust our design if necessary.

Our HTTP server is Lighttpd, which uses a single-threaded queue-based workflow for processing user requests. We chose this server due to its simpler control flow compared to multi-threaded event-based server implementations, which enables us to create more easily compare the control flow graphs of real and decoy executions. In a production environment, an attacker might have to deal with the complexity introduced by multi-threaded event-based servers when trying to identify abnormal execution behavior.

We implemented a tool for the Pin dynamic binary instrumentation framework [19] to output the control flow graph of Lighttpd, initially at the function level, and later at the basic block level. The tool runs twice for the same legitimate user input, in our case an HTTP GET request, to identify the invariant parts of the control flow graph. We then run the tool for each generated decoy and compare the output graph to the invariant graph of the legitimate input to decide which variations of the original input qualify as realistic decoys.

Our example scenario consists of a simple service that handles single-keyword dictionary queries. The application returns an HTTP 404 "Not Found" status code and no content for queries with a keyword not contained in a pre-defined dictionary, and an HTTP 200 status and the relevant content for matching keywords. Our goal was to generate and evaluate decoys based only on the knowledge that the application expected HTTP GET requests that carried a parameter named "query," and that the parameter accepted input of arbitrary length in the character space a–z. Overall, assuming zero knowledge about the internals of the web application, we were able to produce decoy inputs that returned valid HTTP status codes and content given user inputs with the same behavior.

5 Related Work

The concept of deception in the context of computer systems and networks, with the aim to mislead intruders and reveal their presence and actions, has been applied in many variations and at multiple levels [24, 34].

The use of diversionary mechanisms for inducing intruders to spend precious time on non-essential part of a system, and eventually reveal their presence has been considered since the days of mainframe computers. Early proposals included the insertion of pseudo-flaws in existing system components and the installation of entrapment modules [17].

Fully-blown computer traps purposely set up and heavily monitored by security administrators to lure prospective intruders are widely known as honeypots [21, 22, 26, 28]. Honeypots do not have any legitimate users and do not provide any regular production service. Therefore, under normal conditions they should remain idle, neither receiving nor generating any traffic, or generating any other activity. Shadow honeypots [4] combine honeypots with network-level anomaly detection mechanisms to enable their integration with production systems.

Besides decoy systems or system components, the use of decoy information can also confuse intruders and unveil their actions. Decoys may consist of bogus medical records, credit card numbers, credentials, and other bait data relevant to each case, also known as honeytokens [27] or honeyfiles [33]. When a bait file is stolen and later accessed, it can transparently send an alert that reveals the location of the action. Bowen et al. have proposed techniques for generating believable decoys indistinguishable from actual data at the network and host level [8, 9]. They do so by capturing real-user actions in a production environment, such as opening documents and browsing the web, and then replaying within virtual machines to simulate the presence of a human operator, thus making them more believable to an infiltrating adversary. Bojinov et al. [7] propose a methodology for generating password decoys that closely resemble the ones of a particular user. To do so they analyze the grammatical properties of each password, output corresponding templates and use them to generate similar, thus realistic, passwords.

Currently, our system uses protocol message templates to generate realistically looking application traffic and activity. However, several techniques for automatically extracting protocol specifications from their corresponding implementations [5, 18, 32], or protocol messages [12, 14, 15] can also be employed. Wang et al. [31] have employed differential black-box protocol analysis to uncover the syntax and semantics of application-level single-sign-on protocols. They are thus able to automatically identify message attributes that are unique to the session, user or device as well as integrity-verification fields, parameter propagation chains and authentication-enabling secrets.

6 Conclusion

In this paper we have presented our work on DIGIT, a system which employs computational decoys to introduce uncertainty and deceive an adversary who has infiltrated a cloud setup for stealing user information. Our design can be overlaid on top of an existing infrastructure which remains agnostic to the use of decoys. We generate realistic application-specific decoys by requiring that they carry the same properties and result in the same behavior by the server instance located at the back-end of the cloud.

References

1. Hacker Posts 6.4 Million LinkedIn Passwords. http://www.technewsdaily.com/7839-linked-passwords-hack.html. December 2012.
2. Sony Hacked Again, 1 Million Passwords Exposed. http://www.informationweek.com/security/attacks/sony-hacked-again-1-million-passwords-ex/229900111.
3. Twitter detects and shuts down password data hack in progress. http://arstechnica.com/security/2013/02/twitter-detects-and-shuts-down-password-data-hack-in-progress/. February 2013.

4. Kostas G. Anagnostakis, Stelios Sidiroglou, Periklis Akritidis, Kostas Xinidis, Evangelos P. Markatos, and Angelos D. Keromytis. Detecting Targeted Attacks Using Shadow Honeypots. In *Proceedings of the 14th USENIX Security Symposium*, pages 129–144, August 2005.
5. Guangdong Bai, Jike Lei, Guozhu Meng, Sai Sathyanarayan Venkatraman, Prateek Saxena, Jun Sun, Yang Liu, and Jin Song Dong. AUTHSCAN: Automatic extraction of web authentication protocols from implementations. In *Proceedings of the 20th Network and Distributed Systems Security Symposium (NDSS)*, 2013.
6. H. Berghel. Identity theft and financial fraud: Some strangeness in the proportions. *Computer*, 45(1):86–89, Jan. 2012.
7. Hristo Bojinov, Elie Bursztein, Xavier Boyen, and Dan Boneh. Kamouflage: Loss-resistant password management. In *Proc. of ESORICS'10*, 2010.
8. Brian M. Bowen, Vasileios P. Kemerlis, Pratap V. Prabhu, Angelos D. Keromytis, and Salvatore J. Stolfo. A system for generating and injecting indistinguishable network decoys. *Journal of Computer Security*, 20(2–3):199–221, 2012.
9. Brian M. Bowen, Pratap Prabhu, Vasileios P. Kemerlis, Stelios Sidiroglou, Angelos D. Keromytis, and Salvatore J. Stolfo. Botswindler: tamper resistant injection of believable decoys in vm-based hosts for crimeware detection. In *Proceedings of the 13th international conference on Recent advances in intrusion detection*, RAID'10, pages 118–137, Berlin, Heidelberg, 2010. Springer-Verlag.
10. Kevin D. Bowers, Ari Juels, and Alina Oprea. HAIL: a High-Availability and Integrity Layer for Cloud Storage. In *Proc. of CCS*, pages 187–198, 2009.
11. Andrew Brown and Jeff Chase. Trusted Platform-as-a-Service: A Foundation for Trustworthy Cloud-Hosted Applications. In *Proc. of CCSW*, 2011.
12. Paolo Milani Comparetti, Gilbert Wondracek, Christopher Kruegel, and Engin Kirda. Prospex: Protocol specification extraction. In *Proceedings of the 30th IEEE Symposium on Security and Privacy*, pages 110–125, 2009.
13. Computerworld. Microsoft BPOS cloud service hit with data breach, Dec 2010. http://www.computerworld.com/s/article/9202078/Microsoft_BPOS_cloud_service_hit_with_data_breach.
14. Weidong Cui, Vern Paxson, Nicholas C. Weaver, and Y H. Katz. Protocol-independent adaptive replay of application dialog. In *Proceedings of the 13th Network and Distributed System Security Symposium (NDSS)*, 2006.
15. Holger Dreger, Anja Feldmann, Michael Mai, Vern Paxson, and Robin Sommer. Dynamic application-layer protocol analysis for network intrusion detection. In *Proceedings of the 15th USENIX Security Symposium*, 2006.
16. Chris Erway, Alptekin Küpçü, Charalampos Papamanthou, and Roberto Tamassia. Dynamic provable data possession. In *Proceedings of the 16th ACM conference on Computer and Communications Security (CCS)*, pages 213–222, 2009.
17. Dennis Hollingsworth. Enhancing computer system security. Technical Report P-5064, RAND Corporation, Aug 1973.
18. Zhiqiang Lin, Xuxian Jiang, Dongyan Xu, and Xiangyu Zhang. Automatic protocol format reverse engineering through context-aware monitored execution. In *Proceedings of the 15th Network and Distributed System Security Symposium (NDSS)*, 2008.
19. Chi-Keung Luk, Robert Cohn, Robert Muth, Harish Patil, Artur Klauser, Geoff Lowney, Steven Wallace, Vijay Janapa Reddi, and Kim Hazelwood. Pin: building customized program analysis tools with dynamic instrumentation. In *Proceedings of the 2005 ACM SIGPLAN conference on Programming language design and implementation*, PLDI '05, pages 190–200, New York, NY, USA, 2005. ACM.
20. Yogesh Mundada, Anirudh Ramachandran, and Nick Feamster. SilverLine: Data and Network Isolation for Cloud Services. In *Proc. of HotCloud*, 2011.
21. Niels Provos. A virtual honeypot framework. In *Proceedings of the 13th USENIX Security Symposium*, pages 1–14, August 2004.
22. Niels Provos and Thorsten Holz. *Virtual honeypots: from botnet tracking to intrusion detection*. Addison-Wesley Professional, 2007.

23. Thomas Ristenpart, Eran Tromer, Hovav Shacham, and Stefan Savage. Hey, you, get off of my cloud: exploring information leakage in third-party compute clouds. In *Proc. of CCS*, pages 199–212, 2009.
24. Neil C. Rowe and Hy S. Rothstein. Two taxonomies of deception for attacks on information systems. *Journal of Information Warfare*, 3(2):27–39, 2004.
25. Sophos. Groupon subsidiary leaks 300k logins, fixes fail, fails again, 2011 Jun. http://nakedsecurity.sophos.com/2011/06/30/groupon-subsidiary-leaks-300k-logins-fixes-fail-fails-again/.
26. Lance Spitzner. *Honeypots: Tracking Hackers*. Addison-Wesley Longman Publishing Co., Inc., 2002.
27. Lance Spitzner. Honeytokens: The other honeypot, Jul 2003. http://www.symantec.com/connect/articles/honeytokens-other-honeypot.
28. Clifford Stoll. Stalking the wily hacker. *Communications of the ACM*, 31(5):484–497, 1988.
29. The Wall Street Journal. Google Discloses Privacy Glitch, 2009 Mar. http://blogs.wsj.com/digits/2009/03/08/1214/.
30. Trusted Computing Group. TPM Main Specification. http://www.trustedcomputinggroup.org/resources/tpm_main_specification.
31. Rui Wang, Shuo Chen, and XiaoFeng Wang. Signing me onto your accounts through facebook and google: A traffic-guided security study of commercially deployed single-sign-on web services. In *Proceedings of the 2012 IEEE Symposium on Security and Privacy*, SP '12, pages 365–379, Washington, DC, USA, 2012. IEEE Computer Society.
32. Gilbert Wondracek, Paolo Milani Comparetti, Christopher Kruegel, and Engin Kirda. Automatic network protocol analysis. In *Proceedings of the 15th Network and Distributed System Security Symposium (NDSS)*, 2008.
33. J. Yuill, M. Zappe, D. Denning, and F. Feer. Honeyfiles: Deceptive files for intrusion detection. In *Proceedings of the 5th IEEE Workshop on Information Assurance*, pages 116–122, Jun 2004.
34. Jim Yuill, Dorothy Denning, and Fred Feer. Using deception to hide things from hackers: Processes, principles, and techniques. *Journal of Information Warfare*, 5(3):26–40, 2006.

Towards a Data-Centric Approach to Attribution in the Cloud

Wenchao Zhou

Abstract With an increasing number of applications being mirgrated to cloud, it becomes evident that faults in these applications or the underlying cloud platform can be costly. In cases where a system fault occurs, administrators often find themselves needing to answer *attribution* questions, to perform a variety of managerial tasks including system debugging, accountability enforcement, and attack analysis. In this chapter, we propose *Secure Time-Aware Provenance* (STAP), a data-centric approach that provides the fundamental functionality required to answer such attribution questions—the capability to "explain" the existence (or change) of a certain distributed system state at a given time in a potentially adversarial environment.

The proposed STAP model allows consistent and complete explanations of system state (and changes) in dynamic environments, and can be efficiently maintained and queried even in potentially adversarial environments. STAP incorporates tamper-evident properties, and guarantees eventual detection of compromised nodes that lie or falsely implicate correct nodes.

1 Introduction

The past few years have witnessed the success of cloud computing. An increasing number of applications and services being migrated and outsourced to cloud, and it becomes evident that faults in these applications or the underlying cloud platform can be costly. In cases where a system fault occurs, administrators of cloud applications may find themselves needing to answer *attribution* questions,

W. Zhou (✉)
Georgetown University, 37th & O St., Washington, DC, USA
e-mail: wzhou@cs.georgetown.edu

S. Jajodia et al. (eds.), *Secure Cloud Computing*, DOI 10.1007/978-1-4614-9278-8_13,   271

to understand why and how a system execution reaches a certain state, and who should be responsible for unexpected system faults. Such examples include, but are not limited to, the following scenarios:

- **System debugging.** A detected system fault in a system execution may indicate a subtle yet critical bug in the design or the implementation. The system designer would greatly benefit from knowing the execution trace that led to this unexpected state, and the ability to reconstruct it for debugging purposes.
- **Accountability.** In a deployment that crosses multiple administrative domains, each of the participating parties may act to maximize its own benefit regardless the (potentially negative) impact on the global system. Attribution questions that are answered in a collective and secure fashion are useful to enforce accountability—the ability to hold the parties to be accountable to their operations and outputs to the global system.
- **Attack analysis—root cause analysis.** In cases where a cloud application is under an ongoing attack, the operators must decide the root causes (e.g., intrusion by a malicious user) from the symptom (e.g., unavailability of the service provided by the cloud application), before they can take appropriate actions.
- **Attack analysis—damage assessment.** On the other hand, if an attack has been discovered, the operators must then determine its effects (i.e., its damage to the whole system), such as corrupted state on other nodes, so that the system can be repaired and brought back to a correct state.

Composing answers to attribution questions is not an easy task; in fact, the answers are often coupled with a particular *combination* of behaviors, both within the network and at different applications, which can be hard to find. The key challenge is to inspect the data flows, dependencies, and updates to distributed (networked) nodes' state—often in ways that are not predictable in advance. Existing domain-specific solutions [16, 42, 79] often work by recording log data at each node, e.g., a list of past routing changes, which are then used to answer the administrator's questions on demand. However, tailoring the schema and the introspection mechanisms to each new application is cumbersome and inflexible. It would be preferable to have a *generic* solution that can be applied to arbitrary distributed systems.

1.1 The Provenance Approach

The approach that we propose in this chapter is to adopt a data-centric approach, by constructing a distributed data structure called the *provenance* that, at a high level, tracks how data flows through the system. Data provenance itself is not a new concept—it has been extensively explored by the databases and the systems community, and has proven to be a useful and practical concept. It has been successfully applied to a variety of areas, including probabilistic databases [7, 68, 82], collaborative databases [27], file systems [34, 60, 61], scientific workflow computation [8, 11, 17, 63, 78], and cloud computing [36]. It is primarily used to answer questions concerning how query or computation results are derived and which data sources they come from. The capability of learning such information is essential to answer the cause-and-effect questions, and, therefore, enables provenance to be a promising approach for attribution in the cloud.

Backed by the provenance system, we can support a large variety of queries to answer attribution questions. For instance, system administrators may use state queries (*"Why does a certain state τ exist?"*), which explains the derivations of system state at query time, for fault detection, history queries (*"Why did τ exist at a previous time t?"*) for system debugging and accountability, dynamic queries (*"Why and how did τ (dis)appear?"*) for root cause analysis, and causal queries (*"What state on other nodes was derived from τ?"*), which explains which parts of the system have been affected, for attack analysis and system recovery.

1.2 Research Challenges

To support the full range of functionality required for enabling attribution in the cloud, there are a number of challenges arisen in (distributed) cloud systems: the attribution query may ask for a state change that no longer exists; a state change during query processing could result in inconsistency in the returned query results; furthermore, if a system fault is induced by an attacker, the attacker can fabricate plausible yet incorrect results. To support attribution queries in the cloud,

- We must be able to capture **historical** information about past states and interactions within the systems, not just about the current state. Only maintaining relationships among current state is not enough; historical provenance would require recording relationships among entries in event logs.
- We must guarantee **correct and complete** provenance results even in **transient state**. In reality, the state of a distributed system can be highly dynamic; there can even exist instabilities or oscillations, for instance, a typical Internet router can incur hundreds of updates per minute.
- We must have the ability to **distribute the storage** of the provenance to keep communication costs down: for performance reasons, centrally archiving the system's entire provenance is impractical. This means that we also need the ability to **detect when nodes tamper with the provenance**; otherwise, a compromised node could cover its traces and avoid detection.

Several prior work has proposed solutions that attack these research challenges *individually*. For instance, PASS [60] and several scientific workflow systems [8, 63, 78] present solutions for historical provenance; Orchestra [27], PA-S3fs [61] and RAMP [36] discuss distributed provenance maintenance and querying for specific applications; and Sprov [34] enforces the integrity of chain-structured provenance. (Section 5 summarizes and discusses the related work in greater details.) This chapter describes a comprehensive solution that addresses *all* the above research challenges. We demonstrate that *it is practical to develop a general-purpose provenance system for the cloud, that provides attribution of system behavior even in an untrusted and dynamic environment.*

This chapter proposes and develops the foundations of *Secure Time-aware Provenance* (STAP). STAP captures time, distribution, and dependencies of updates; it enables the administrator of a distributed system to pose "ad hoc" queries over the system's prior states, communications patterns, event orderings, and more.

2 Provenance Model

As a basis for the introduction of the provenance model, we first introduce, in Sect. 2.1 a distributed system model (based on distributed Datalog) and some basic concepts that will be useful for our formal definitions. We then use this system model to describe system execution traces in Sect. 2.2, and formalize the STAP model in Sect. 2.3.

2.1 System Model

For ease of exposition, we adopt a simple, declarative system model. We consider a distributed system that consists of a set of *nodes* $N = \{N_1, N_2, \ldots, N_n\}$ that are connected by a network and can communicate by sending messages. The state of a node at a given point in time can be expressed as a set of *tuples* (typically with fixed schemas). We model user input as tuples that are inserted or deleted directly by users, and computations performed by the system as *derivations* of new tuples from existing tuples. We say that a tuple is a *base tuple* if it was inserted directly by a user; otherwise we say that it is a *derived tuple*. Derived tuples can be sent from one node to another as messages.

We use *Network Datalog* (NDlog) [52–55], a distributed variant of Datalog, to describe the possible derivations and dependencies among tuples that can exist in the system. Such declarative language is expressive enough to specify a wide range of application domains including cloud computing [1], sensor networks [9], overlay network compositions [56], anonymity systems [75], mobile ad-hoc networks [49], and wireless channel selection [48]. (However, it should be possible to apply network provenance to distributed systems written in other languages, including legacy systems, as long as the dependencies between incoming and outgoing tuples can be modeled in a similar way; see, for example, [85, 87]).

Example: Network Routing

For concreteness, we consider a simple MinCost protocol for network routing as an example, in which the nodes compute the lowest-cost path between each pair of nodes using the following NDlog *rules*:

```
mc1 cost(@S,D,C)  :- link(@S,D,C).
mc2 cost(@S,D,C)  :- link(@Z,S,C1), mincost(@Z,D,C2), C=C1+C2.
mc3 mincost(@S,D,MIN<C>) :- cost(@S,D,C).
```

Fig. 1 An example network, where the best path between node c and a changed at time t_2, due a change of the network topology

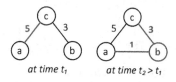

at time t_1 at time $t_2 > t_1$

As in traditional Datalog, each NDlog rule has the form `p :- q1, q2, ..., qn.`, which can be read informally as "p should be derived whenever `q1, q2, ...`, and `qn` all exist at the same time". NDlog supports a *location specifier* in each predicate, which is written as an @ symbol followed by the node on which the tuple resides. For example, any `cost` tuples that are derived via rule `mc1` should reside on the same node as the corresponding `link` tuples, as both carry the same location specifier `@S`.

In this program, the base tuple `link(@S,D,C)` exists if node S has a direct link to node D with cost C. The tuple `cost(@S,D,C)` is derived when S has a (possibly indirect) path to D with total cost C, which can either be a direct link (`mc1`) or a path through another node Z (`mc2`). Rule `mc3` aggregates all paths with the same sources and destinations to compute the minimal path cost. In NDlog, the protocol runs continuously, and tuples can be derived or underived in response to changes to base tuples. For instance, `mincost` tuples may be updated if the cost of a link changes, since this can change the lowest-cost route.

2.2 Execution Traces

The execution of an NDlog program can be characterized by the sequence of events that take place; we refer to this sequence as an *execution trace*. An execution trace can be used to explain a derivation that occurred during the execution; we can simply replay it and check which event triggered the derivation and which conditions held at that time. A full trace can recursively explain all derivations; if we are only interested in some specific derivations (e.g., the ones queried by the network operator), a subtrace is generally sufficient.

Figure 1 shows an example scenario during the execution of the MinCost program. At some past time t_2, the network protocol changed its min-cost path between node c and a in response to updated link information that claimed there existed a shorter path between the two nodes. Figure 2 shows a part of the corresponding execution during which +mincost(c,a,4) is derived. The explanation for this event consists of the following trace (event tuples are denoted in **bold**):

- At time $t_2 @ b$, node b discovered a new link to node a and thus inserted the base tuple **+link(@b,a,1)**.

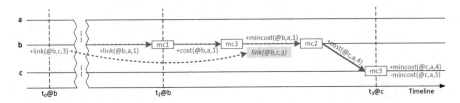

Fig. 2 An execution subtrace of the MinCost program that corresponds to scenario in Fig. 1 and provides an explanation of +mincost(@c,4). *Rectangles* indicate that a rule is fired, *dashed arrows* indicate local event triggering, *solid arrows* indicate cross-node messages, and *shaded boxes* indicate the conditions for events

- Rule mc1 was triggered by +link(@b,a,1), resulting in **+cost(@b,a,1)**.
- Rule mc3 was used to derive **+mincost(@b,a,1)** from +cost(@b,a,1).
- Rule mc2 (specifically its delta rule d3) was triggered by +mincost(@b,c,1). The condition was satisfied by the existing tuple link(@b,c,3) that had been derived at time t_0; the resulting update **+cost(@c,a,4)** was then shipped to c.
- At time $t_3 @ c$, node c received +cost(@c,a,4) from node b and derived **+mincost(@c,a,4)** using rule mc3, which then replaced the higher-cost mincost(@c,a,5).

Note that the ordering of edges (arrows) in Fig. 2 reflects dependencies, in the form of a *happens-before* relationship. For example, +link(@b,c,1) happens before +cost(@b,a,1) as a result of executing rule mc1.

2.3 Provenance Model

In this section, we present a (slightly) simplified version of STAP that assumes a trusted environment. We defer the discussion of STAP's security enhancement for untrusted environments to Sect. 4.

STAP encodes the provenance for a trace $\mathscr{E}$ in a graph $G(\mathscr{E}) = (V, E)$ in which each vertex $v \in V$ represents an event in $\mathscr{E}$, and each edge $(v_1, v_2) \in E$ represents a direct dependency between two such events. STAP's provenance graph can contain the following six types of vertices:

- INSERT(t, n, τ) and DELETE(t, n, τ): Tuple τ was inserted (deleted) on node n at time t.

- DERIVE(t, n, R, τ) and UNDERIVE(t, n, R, τ): Tuple τ was derived (underived) via rule R on node n at time t.
- SEND$(t, n, \triangle\tau, n')$ and RECEIVE$(t, n', \triangle\tau, n)$: An update $\triangle\tau$ was sent (received) on node n at time t to (from) node n'.

The last two vertices are needed because a derivation on one node can involve tuples on another; the corresponding messages are represented explicitly in G. The vertices are generated and connected according to the following rules:

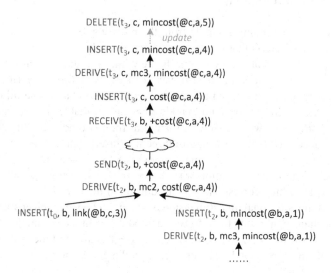

Fig. 3 The STAP provenance graph for explaining the deletion of `mincost(@c,a,5)`

- When a base tuple is inserted, an INSERT vertex is added.
- If a node N_i derives a tuple τ via rule r, a DERIVE vertex is added, which has incoming edges from all of r's preconditions, as well as from the triggering event, i.e., the INSERT that caused r to fire. The DERIVE vertex is then connected to a new INSERT vertex (if τ is local to N_i) or a new SEND vertex (if τ is sent to another node).
- When a message is received from another node, a RECEIVE vertex is added, with an incoming edge from the corresponding SEND vertex. This vertex is then connected to a new INSERT vertex.
- Whenever an INSERT vertex is added for a tuple τ that already has at least one derivation, an incoming edge is added to τ's most recent INSERT vertex (recall that tuples can have more than one derivation).
- When a tuple τ_1 replaces another tuple τ_2 due to a primary-key or aggregation constraint, an *update edge* is added from τ_1's INSERT vertex to τ_2's DELETE vertex.

The guidelines for deletions and underivations are analogous. Note that the graph is acyclic because edges are always added between an existing vertex and a new vertex, but never between two existing vertices. It is also monotonic because, as the execution continues, new vertices and edges are added but never removed.

Given the instantiated provenance graph $G(\mathcal{E})$, the provenance $G(\triangle\tau,\mathcal{E})$ of an update event $\triangle\tau$ on node N_i at time t is simply the subtree of $G(\mathcal{E})$ that is rooted at the corresponding INSERT(t,N_i,τ) (or DELETE(t,N_i,τ)) vertex. Reference [88] presents a formal correctness proof of the STAP model.

Example: MinCost Routing

We now revisit our running example from the previous sections. Figure 3 shows a piece of the STAP graph that explains the deletion of the tuple mincost(@c,a,5) on node c at time t_3 that resulted from the new link a-c that was inserted at time t_0. Specifically, the edge at the DELETE vertex of mincost(@c,a,5) (indicated by a dotted line) corresponds to an aggregation constraint—that is, the minimal cost changed because a lower-cost path to node a became available. The updated lowest cost (cost(@c,a,4)) was derived on node b at time t_2 (and subsequently sent to node c) because (a) a link b-c with cost three was inserted at time t_0 (and remained to exist at time t_2), and (b) the tuple mincost(@b,a,1) was newly derived at t_2 via rule mc3. The latter derivation was caused by the insertion of the base tuple link(@b,a,1), which corresponds to the addition of the new link.

Note that the additional time dimension on the provenance graph enables another use of provenance: querying the *effects* of an update event. For example, if we want to determine how the insertion of the new link a-b has affected the system, we can simply locate the corresponding INSERT vertex in the graph and traverse the edges in the reverse direction.

3   Provenance Maintenance and Querying

In this section, we explore the generic data management challenges posed by the distribution, querying, and maintenance of provenance in large-scale cloud deployment. Such scale has presented a unique challenge to provenance data management: applications in the cloud sometimes involve hundreds of nodes; moreover, provenance computations are required to share resources with existing cloud applications. Bandwidth efficiency and minimal impact on computation overhead are of significant importance.

3.1   Storage Model

This section defines the storage model used by STAP to store and maintain provenance in distributed systems. STAP's graph-based data model is amenable to storage using a distributed relational database, and is sufficiently general to be used as a basis for generating other provenance representations.

STAP stores the graph representation of provenance in a relational table in a format similar to that used in existing work [23, 25]. STAP makes use of four provenance tables—called `prov`, `ruleExec`, `send`, and `recv`—that are incrementally updated as the derivation rules that model the protocols are executed. These tables store STAP's provenance graph in a distributed fashion.

Tuple instances: The `prov` table maintains information about each tuple (including both current tuples and tuples that existed in the past) as well as the specific rule that triggered its derivation. Entry `prov(@N,VID,Time,RLoc,RID)` indicates that the tuple on node `N` with unique identifier `VID` was derived at time `Time` by a rule execution on node `RLoc` that is uniquely identified by `RID`. If `N` and `RLoc` are different, the tuple was sent from `RLoc` to `N`, and this communication is recorded in additional `recv` and `send` entries (see below). `VID` is generated based on a cryptographic hash of the contents of the tuple and the time of its derivation; similarly, `RID` is a hash of the rule identifier, node location, and `VID` of the derived tuple. For base tuples, `RID` is set to `null`, since they are not derived by any rule.

In order to correctly generate the above entries, NDlog programs undergo an automatic rewrite process to include the `RID` and `RLoc` information with each tuple derivation. This process ensures that the appropriate `prov` entry will be generated on the node to which the derivation is sent.

Rule execution instances: The `ruleExec` table maintains information about each execution of a rule (not just about each rule). Entry `ruleExec(@RLoc, RID, Rule, ExecTime,Event,CList)` indicates the execution of a `Rule` on `RLoc` at `ExecTime`, triggered by an event `Event` (i.e., a tuple that changed, appeared, or disappeared) while the preconditions in `CList` were holding.

Message transmissions: The `send` and `recv` tables maintain information about message exchanges. `send(@Sender,VID,STime,RID)` and `recv(@Receiver,VID, RTime,Sender,STime)` refer to the rule execution identified by `RID` that affected the tuple identified by `VID`; the corresponding message was sent by `Sender` at time `STime` and received at time `RTime`. Whenever a rule execution causes a message to be sent, `send` and `recv` entries are generated at the sender and receiver, respectively, and are timestamped using nodes' local clocks. To handle clock skew, the receiver stores the sender's timestamp at message transmission; this timestamp is included in each message along with the (un)derived tuple. This information is used during query processing to correctly match up `send` and `recv` entries.

Given the distributed nature of provenance storage, these tables are naturally partitioned based on their first attributes, and distributed among the nodes.

Example Tables

Tables 1–3 show the entries for the tables above, based on the example provenance tree shown in Fig. 3. The vertices defined by our provenance model (Sect. 2.3) are encoded in the provenance tables as follows: INSERT and DELETE vertices

Table 1 An example `prov` relation based on Fig. 3. The table is horizontally partitioned across all nodes, based on the location specifier `Loc`. The last column is not stored in the table; it is included here to show the derivation that corresponds to each entry. The first column indicates an insertion (+) or a deletion (−)

+/−	Loc	VID	Time	RLoc	RID	Derivation
+	b	VID1	t0	null	null	+link(@b,c,3)
+	b	VID2	t2	null	null	+link(@b,a,1)
+	b	VID3	t2	b	RID1	+mincost(@b,a,1)
+	c	VID4	t3	b	RID2	+cost(@c,a,4)
+	c	VID5	t3	c	RID3	+mincost(@c,a,4)
−	c	VID6	t3	c	RID3	-mincost(@c,a,5)

Table 2 An example `ruleExec` relation that corresponds to the DERIVE vertices. The last column shows the derivation rule that was executed in each instance

+/−	RLoc	RID	Rule	ExecTime	Event	CList	Derivation
+	b	RID1	mc3	t2	VID2	null	+mincost(@b,a,1)
+	b	RID2	mc2	t2	VID2	(VID1)	+cost(@c,a,4)
+	c	RID3	mc3	t3	VID4	null	+mincost(@c,a,4)

Table 3 Example `send` and `recv` relations that correspond to the SEND and RECEIVE vertices

Sender	VID	STime	RID	Derivation	
b	VID4	t2	RID2	+cost(@c,a,4)	
Receiver	VID	RTime	Sender	STime	Derivation
c	VID4	t3	b	t2	+cost(@c,a,4)

are respectively represented as tuple insertions (+prov) and deletions (-prov). Likewise, DERIVE and UNDERIVE are stored as +ruleExec and -ruleExec. Edges between INSERT/DERIVE and DELETE/UNDERIVE pairs are represented by the RID and VID pairings in each prov entry. recv and send entries correspond to the RECV and SEND vertices. For each tuple uniquely identified by its primary key, each EXIST vertex consists of all updates (i.e., +prov and -prov) ordered by their timestamps.

3.2 Provenance Maintenance

The STAP graph can be captured via the evaluation of delta rules of the form action :- event, conditions. In a delta rule of the form $\triangle p$:- $p_1,...,\triangle p_i,...,p_n$, the *event* (in this case, $\triangle p_i$) is represented as an INSERT or DELETE vertex, the *conditions* (the other p_k) are represented as a sequence of INSERT (or DELETE) vertices that support the existence of p_k (EXIST vertex), and the *action* ($\triangle p$) is represented as a DERIVE or UNDERIVE vertex. When a delta rule $\triangle p$:- $p_1,...,\triangle p_i,...,p_n$ is fired at time t, STAP performs the following steps:

- Generate a +ruleExec or -ruleExec tuple with timestamp t to represent the rule execution, and maintain pointers to the triggering event $\triangle p_i$ and preconditions $p_1, \ldots, p_n$ (excluding p_i).
- Generate a +prov or -prov tuple with timestamp t to represent the insertion or deletion event $\triangle p$, and to maintain a pointer to the generated +/-ruleExec tuple.
- If the generated event $\triangle p$ needs to be sent to another node, generate a pair of send and recv tuples at the sender and the receiver, respectively, with timestamps that correspond to nodes' local clocks.
- Finally, if the generated event $\triangle p$ results in a violation of a primary-key or aggregation constraint (e.g., the newly-generated tuple displaces another), generate an additional +prov or -prov tuple to represent the deletion caused by $\triangle p$. This corresponds to the update edge from Sect. 3.1.

To perform the provenance maintenance described above, we leverage the distributed querying processing capability of the declarative networking engine. Given *any* NDlog program, additional NDlog provenance maintenance rules are automatically generated. The detailed description with a pseudocode of the automated rewrite can be found in Ref. [89].

3.3 Proactive and Reactive Maintenance

To answer provenance queries about past tuples or updates, the STAP model contains a temporal dimension. Note that keeping full copies of the provenance is unnecessary because STAP provenance is *monotonic*: the provenance of historic updates and tuples (which eventually make up a major portion of a provenance graph) is immutable. STAP therefore maintains provenance incrementally, i.e., it considers only the "deltas" between adjacent versions, which are sufficient to reconstruct the full provenance graph. STAP stores these deltas in the following two different ways:

- **Explicit deltas (proactive).** In this approach, all of the +prov, -prov, +ruleExec and -ruleExec entries are stored explicitly in a temporally ordered log that is indexed by time. Compared to keeping each version of the provenance, the storage cost is considerably lower; however, the full provenance information must be reconstructed from the deltas before a query can be answered.

  The idea of keeping deltas between adjacent versions and reconstructing a specific version by merging deltas is known as a classic approach to perform efficient versioning. It has been extensively studied and adopted in many application domains, include transaction logs in database systems [24, 58], revision control systems [35, 80], and log-structure file systems [71, 73]. Several variants, such as forward deltas and reverse deltas [80], have been proposed to tailor the system performance for different system settings or requirements. We expect that similar treatment is applicable to the proactive provenance maintenance as well.

- **Per-node input logs (reactive).** In this approach, STAP maintains only the non-deterministic inputs (`recv` entries for incoming messages, as well as tuple insertions and deletions) at each node. If the underlying application is deterministic, STAP can replay these inputs at query time to reproduce the original execution of that node, and reconstruct the provenance on the fly. As an optimization, each derived tuple sent across nodes needs only to include the sender's timestamp.

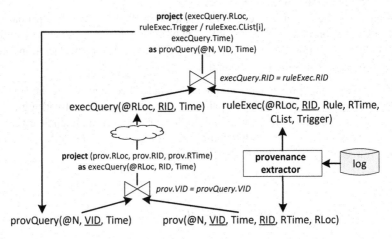

Fig. 4 Logical query plan for recursive provenance queries. *Underlined* attributes are primary keys

3.4 Provenance Querying

To query the provenance of an update, STAP executes a distributed recursive query that reconstructs the relevant subtree of the provenance graph from the four tables we have described in Sect. 3.1. Figure 4 shows the logical query plan for evaluating this distributed recursive query; the query starts at the root of the subtree and iteratively adds vertices and edges until a fixpoint is reached (at the base tuples). The results are then returned in the form of tuples from the `prov`, `ruleExec`, `send`, and `recv` tables that encode the relevant subtree.

In Fig. 4, the initial provenance query is represented as an input tuple `provQuery(@N,VID,Time)` to the logical plan. Based on this tuple, STAP carries out the following steps:

- **Step 1: Retrieve rule execution instances.** Since the VID uniquely identifies $\triangle\tau$, STAP uses it as a lookup into the `prov` table (via a database join) and then retrieves the corresponding RID used to derive the tuple, as well as the location RLoc at which the rule was fired. This corresponds to the generation of the DERIVE or UNDERIVE vertex. If RLoc is different from Loc (i.e., the tuple was derived from a remote rule execution), additional RECV and SEND vertices are generated by joining the VIDs of derived tuples with the recv and send tables[1]; for readability, these extra operations have been omitted from Fig. 4. Next, STAP generates execQuery tuples to trigger queries on the ruleExec table.

- **Step 2: Expand dependent derivations.** STAP ships the resulting execQuery(@RLoc,RID,Time) tuple to RLoc and there joins it with the local ruleExec table to recursively expand the child derivations that have resulted in $\triangle\tau$. Here, multiple additional provQuery tuples are generated: one for the trigger event for the delta rule RID, and another for each condition predicate value that occurred during the execution of RID. Each expansion generates an INSERT or DELETE vertex, depending on whether the trigger event was an insertion or a deletion, and each expanded condition generates an EXIST vertex, which includes additional INSERT and DELETE vertices to explain why the condition held at the relevant Time.

- **Repeat until fixpoint.** Steps 1 and 2 are performed recursively until all child nodes are expanded. As the query progresses, the provQuery events are recursively propagated from the root of the provenance tree (where the queried update resides) towards the child nodes in order to construct the entire subtree. Each level of the tree can be expanded in parallel at different nodes. Upon reaching the leaf nodes (which correspond to base tuples), the query results are returned back to the root along the reverse path. At each level, the parent node returns only its portion of the query result (subtree) after all the child nodes have completed their respective subqueries.

4 Secure Provenance

In the previous sections, we have assumed a trusted environment, in which nodes are cooperative and correctly follow the provenance maintenance and querying protocols. However, distributed systems may be deployed across multiple administrative domains, where nodes may refuse to cooperate or even intentionally misbehave for various reasons, such as tensions between competing parties or malicious attacks.

In this section, we consider attribution in an *adversarial* setting, that is, we assume that a faulty node does not necessarily crash but can also change its behavior and continue operating. Getting correct answers to attribution queries in an adversarial setting is difficult because the misbehaving nodes can lie to the querier. For example, the adversary can attempt to conceal his actions by causing his nodes to fabricate plausible (but incorrect) responses to attribution queries, or

---

[1]After retrieving the recv entry based on VID and RTime, we use the STime (sender's timestamp) attribute in recv to fetch the appropriate send entry on the sender's side. This avoids explicit time synchronization.

he can attempt to frame correct nodes by returning responses that blame his own misbehavior on them. Thus, the adversary can gain valuable time by misdirecting the operators and/or causing them to suspect a problem with the attribution system itself.

Existing solutions for attribution in an adversarial environment usually requires some trusted components, e.g., a trusted virtual-machine monitor [5, 42], a trusted host-level monitor [57], a trusted OS [60], or trusted hardware [10]. However, most components that are available today are not fully trustworthy; OSes and virtual machine monitors have bugs, which a powerful adversary could exploit, and even trusted hardware is sometimes compromised [40]. We argue that it is useful to have alternative techniques available that do not require this type of trust.

Towards this challenge, we introduce *Secure Time-aware Provenance* (STAP), a provenance system that can operate in a *completely untrusted* environment. We assume that the adversary may have compromised an arbitrary subset of the nodes, and that he may have complete control over these nodes. Despite the conservative threat model, a STAP system provides strong, provable guarantees: it ensures that an observable symptom of a fault or an attack can always be traced to a specific event—passive evasion or active misbehavior—on at least one faulty node, even when an adversary attempts to prevent this.

4.1   Threat Model and Assumptions

Since we would like to enable system administrators to investigate a wide range of problems, ranging from simple misconfigurations to hardware faults and even clandestine attacks, we conservatively assume Byzantine faults [46], i.e., that an adversary may have compromised an unknown subset of the nodes, and that he has complete control over them. Thus, the non-malicious problems are covered as a special case. We assume that the adversary can change both the primary system and the provenance system on these nodes, and he can read, forge, tamper with, or destroy any information they are holding. We also assume that no nodes or components of the system are inherently safe, i.e., system administrators do not a priori trust any node other than their own local machines. Reference [85] presents the detailed assumptions considered in STAP.

Compromises

Ideally, we would like to correctly answer provenance queries even when the system is under attack. However, given our conservative threat model, this is not always possible. Hence, we make the following two compromises: first, we only demand that the system answer provenance queries about behavior that is *observable by at least one correct node* [32]; in other words, if some of the adversary's actions never affect the state of any correct node, the system is allowed to omit them.

Second, we accept that the system may sometimes return an answer that is incorrect or incomplete, as long as the system administrator can (a) tell which parts of the answer are affected, and she can (b) learn the identity of at least one faulty node. In an attribution setting, this seems like a useful compromise: any unexpected behavior that can be noticed is observable by definition, and even a partial answer can help the system administrator determine whether a fault or misbehavior has occurred and which parts of the system have been affected.

4.2 Approach Overview

The provenance definition in previous sections assumes that, at least conceptually, the entire system execution $\mathscr{E}$ is known. However, in a distributed system without trusted components, no single node can have this information, especially when nodes are faulty and can tell lies. In this section, we present STAP, which constructs an approximation G_v of the "true" provenance graph G that is based on information available to correct nodes.

Approximate Provenance Using Evidence

Although each node can observe only its own local events, nodes can use messages from other nodes as *evidence* to reason about events on these nodes. We can require that messages be authenticated and acknowledged, such that each received message m is evidence of its own transmission. Once we discover inconsistencies from the input/output messages, the evidences can be used to tie faults to a particular node who is responsible for the inconsistency.

In addition, we can demand that nodes attach some additional information $\varphi(m)$, such as an explanation for the transmission of m. The validity of $\varphi(m)$ is checked against the expected execution logic and the evidence. For the purposes of this section, we will assume that $\varphi(m)$ describes the sender's entire execution prefix, i.e., all of its local events up to and including the transmission of m. Of course, this would be completely impractical; our implementation in sections "Secure Logging for Provenance Maintenance" and "Secure Provenance Querying" achieves a similar effect in a more efficient way.

When a provenance query is issued on a correct node, that node can collect some evidence $\bar{\mathscr{E}}$, such as messages it has locally received, and/or messages collected from other nodes. It can then use this evidence to construct an approximation $G_v(\bar{\mathscr{E}})$ of $G(\mathscr{E})$, from which the query can be answered.

We use the similar mechanisms presented in Sect. 3 to construct provenance from the evidence. In the construction of $G_v(\bar{\mathscr{E}})$, the legitimacy of the vertices depends on the evidence collected from the other nodes. We introduce a *color* for each vertex v in $G_v(\bar{\mathscr{E}})$, which is used to indicate whether v is legitimate: correct vertices are black, and faulty vertices are red. For example, if a faulty node N_i has no tuple τ

derived during the execution, but nevertheless sends a message $+\tau$ to another node. $+\tau$ has no legitimate provenance, so we use the red color to represent transmission of $+\tau$. Finally, we introduce a third color, yellow, for vertices whose true color is not yet known.

Definition: STAP

Based on the intuition presented in section "Approximate Provenance Using Evidence", we give the definition of STAP, which is formulated based on the following properties.

Definition 1 (Monotonicity). An approximation $G_v(\bar{\mathscr{E}})$ of $G(\mathscr{E})$ is *monotonic* if $G_v(\bar{\mathscr{E}})$ is a subgraph of $G_v(\bar{\mathscr{E}} + \bar{\mathscr{E}}')$ for additional evidence $\bar{\mathscr{E}}'$.

Definition 2 (Accuracy). $G_v(\bar{\mathscr{E}})$ is *accurate* if it faithfully reproduces all the vertices on correct nodes; in other words, if a vertex v on a correct node appears in $G_v(\bar{\mathscr{E}})$ then v must also exist in $G(\mathscr{E})$, be colored black, and have the same predecessors and successors.

Definition 3 (Completeness). $G_v(\bar{\mathscr{E}})$ is *complete* if, given sufficient evidence $\bar{\mathscr{E}}$ from the correct nodes, (a) each vertex in $G(\mathscr{E})$ on a correct node also appears in $G_v(\bar{\mathscr{E}})$, and (b) for each detectably faulty node, $G_v(\bar{\mathscr{E}})$ contains at least one red or yellow vertex.

Monotonicity is an important property because it prevents G_v from changing fundamentally once additional evidence becomes available, which could invalidate responses to earlier queries. Accuracy and completeness properties give guarantees that a correct node will never be falsely accused and that a detectably faulty node will be eventually detected. Based on these properties, we define STAP as follows:

Definition 4. Given an execution trace $\mathscr{E}$, we define STAP to be a monotonic approximation $G_v(\bar{\mathscr{E}})$ of the provenance graph $G(\mathscr{E})$ that is both complete and accurate in an untrusted setting.

4.3 Secure Maintenance and Querying

We next present the security enhancement to the provenance maintenance and querying for implementation a STAP system.

Secure Logging for Provenance Maintenance

Recall from Sect. 2.3 that provenance graph $G = (V, E)$ is designed so that each vertex $v \in V$ can be attributed to a specific node HOST(v). Thus, we can partition the graph so that each $v \in V$ is stored on HOST(v). To ensure accuracy, we must additionally keep evidence for each cross-node edge, i.e., $(v_1, v_2) \in E$ with HOST$(v_1) \neq$ HOST(v_2). Specifically, HOST(v_1) must be able to prove that HOST(v_2) has committed to v_2, and vice versa, so that each node can prove that its own vertex is legitimate, even if the other node is compromised. Finally, each node's subgraph of G is completely determined by its inputs and outputs; hence, it is sufficient to store messages and changes to base tuples. When necessary, the microquery module can reconstruct G from this information.

Logs and Authenticator Sets

STAP's log is a simplified version of the log from PeerReview [33]. The log λ_i of a node i consists of entries of the form $e_k := (t_k, y_k, c_k)$, where t_k is a timestamp, y_k is an entry type, and c_k is some type-specific content. There are five types of entries: SND and RCV record messages, ACK records acknowledgments, and INS and DEL record base tuple insertions and deletions. Note that log entries are different from vertex types. Each entry is associated with a hash value $h_k = H(h_{k-1} \| t_k \| y_k \| c_k)$ with $h_0 := 0$, where $H(\cdot)$ is a cryptographic hash function. Together, the h_k form a hash chain. A node i can issue an *authenticator* $a_k := (t_k, h_k, \sigma_i(t_k \| h_k))$; $\sigma_i(\cdot)$ denotes a signature with i's key. An authenticator is a signed commitment that e_k (and, through the hash chain, $e_1, \ldots, e_{k-1}$) must exist in i's log. Each node i stores the authenticators it receives from other nodes in its *authenticator set* A_i.

Commitment

When a node i needs to send a message $\pm\tau$ to another node j, it first appends a new entry $e_x := (t_x, \text{SND}, (\pm\tau, j))$ to its local log. Then it sends $(\pm\tau, h_{x-1}, t_x, \sigma_i(t_x \| h_x))$ to j. When a node j receives a message $(\pm\tau, a, b, c)$, j calculates $h'_x := H(a \| b \| \text{SND} \| (\pm\tau, j))$ and then checks whether the authenticator is properly signed, i.e., $\pi_i(c) = (b \| h'_x)$, and whether t_x is within $\Delta_{clock} + T_{prop}$ of its local time. If not, j discards the message. Otherwise, j adds (t_x, h'_x, c) to its authenticator set $A_{j,i}$, appends an entry $e_y := (k, \text{RCV}, (\pm\tau, i, a, b, c))$ to its own log, and sends $(\text{ACK}, t_x, h_{y-1}, t_y, \sigma_j(t_y \| h_y))$ back to i.

Once i receives (ACK, a, b, c, d) from j, it first checks its log to see whether there is an entry $e_x = (a, \text{SND}, (\pm\tau, j))$ in its log that has not been acknowledged yet. If not, it discards the message. i then calculates $h'_y := H(b \| c \| \text{RCV} \| (\pm\tau, i, h_{x-1}, t_x, \sigma_i(t_x \| h_x)))$, and checks whether $\pi_j(d) = (c \| h'_y)$ and t_y is within $\Delta_{clock} + T_{prop}$ of its local time. If not, i discards the message. Otherwise, i adds (c, h'_y, d) to its authenticator set $A_{i,j}$ and appends an entry $e_z := (t, \text{ACK}, a, b, c, d)$ to its log. If i does not receive a valid acknowledgment within $2 \cdot T_{prop}$, it immediately notifies the administrator of this.

Retrieval

The provenance maintenance module implements a primitive RETRIEVE(v, a_k^i) which, when invoked on $i := \text{HOST}(v)$ with a vertex v and an authenticator a_k^i of i, returns the prefix of the log in which v was generated. Typically, this is the prefix authenticated by a_k^i, but if v is an EXIST vertex that exists at e_k, the prefix is extended to either (a) the point where v ceases to exist, or (b) the current time. If the prefix extends beyond e_k, i must also return a new authenticator that covers the entire prefix. A correct node can always comply with such a request.

Secure Provenance Querying

STAP adopts a similar distributed recursive querying framework as STAP. To construct provenance in a secure manner, it uses a special primitive called MICROQUERY to navigate a STAP graph.[2] MICROQUERY has two arguments: a vertex v, and evidence $\bar{\mathscr{E}}$ such that $v \in G_v(\bar{\mathscr{E}})$. MICROQUERY returns one or two *color notifications* of the form BLACK(v), YELLOW(v), or RED(v). If two notifications are returned, the first one must be YELLOW(v). MICROQUERY can also return two sets P_v and S_v that contain the predecessors and successors of v in $G_v(\bar{\mathscr{E}})$, respectively. Each set consists of elements (v_i, e_i), where $\bar{\mathscr{E}}_i$ is additional evidence such that v_i and the edge between v_i and v appear in $G_v(\bar{\mathscr{E}} + e_i)$; this makes it possible to explore all of G_v by invoking MICROQUERY recursively.

The microquery module implements MICROQUERY(v, e), and uses the information in this log to implement MICROQUERY; it uses authenticators as a specific form of evidence. At a high level, this works by (1) using e to retrieve a log prefix from HOST(v), (2) replaying the log to regenerate HOST(v)'s partition of the provenance graph G, and (3) checking whether v exists in it. If v exists and was derived correctly, its predecessors and successors are returned, and v is colored black; otherwise v is colored red. A formal description of the querying process is presented in Ref. [85].

4.4 Evaluation

We evaluate STAP using three applications, including Quagga [66] routing deployment, Chord [77] distributed hash table, and Hadoop [30] MapReduce. Since we have already proven the correctness of the STAP algorithm in [86], we focus mostly on usability and performance. Specifically, our goal is to answer the following high-level questions: (i) can STAP answer useful attribution queries? (ii) how much overhead does STAP incur at runtime? and (iii) how expensive is it to ask a query?

---

[2]MICROQUERY returns a single vertex; provenance queries must invoke it repeatedly to explore G_v. Hence the name.

Due to space constraints, we present only the usability result (for the Hadoop experiment) here. The complete results are presented in Ref. [85].

Usability

In the Hadoop experiment, we ran the experiments on 20 c1.Medium instances on Amazon EC2 (in the us-east-1c region). The program we used (WordCount) counts the number of occurrences of each word in a 10.3 GB dataset consisting of the Wikipedia and 12/2010 Newspapers crawl from WebBase [81]. The provenance query **Hadoop-Squirrel** asks for the provenance of a given key-value pair in the output; for example, if the WordCount application produces the (unlikely) output (squirrel, 10000) to indicate that the word "squirrel" appeared 10,000 times in the input, this could be due to a faulty or compromised mapper. Such queries are useful to investigate computation results on outsourced Cloud databases [65].

Figure 5 shows the output of the Hadoop-Squirrel query, where one of the Mappers (i.e. Map-3) is configured to misbehave—in addition to emitting a (word, offset) tuple for each word in the text, it injects 9,991 additional (squirrel, offset) tuples. An analyst who is suspicious about the enormous prevalence of squirrels in this dataset can use STAP to query the provenance of the (squirrel, 10,000) output tuple. STAP responds by selectively reconstructing the provenance subgraph of the corresponding reduce task. Seeing that one mapper output 9,993

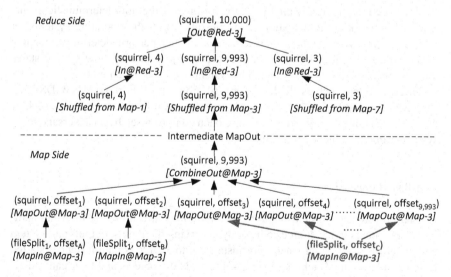

Fig. 5 Example result (with simplified notations) of the Hadoop-Squirrel query

squirrels while the others only reported 3 or 4, she can "zoom in" further by requesting the provenance of the (squirrel, 9,993) tuple, at which point STAP reconstructs the provenance subgraph of the corresponding map task. This reveals two legitimate occurrences and lots of additional bogus tuples, which are colored red.

5 Related Literature

The STAP system presented in this chapter expands upon previous results in the databases, networking and systems communities. In this section, we describe the related research in these areas.

5.1 Attribution in Distributed Systems

Attribution in distributed systems has received a lot of traction in the system research community. There has been a substantial amount of work in this area. We summarize the work in the related topics.

Replay-Based Debugging

Replay-based debugging is enabled by recording all the non-deterministic events (such as network communications and interrupts from the operating systems) at runtime. Once a system fault is detected, users can then perform deterministic replay to reproduce the fault. Diagnosis is performed by inspecting how system states progress towards the fault, facilitated by watchpoints and breakpoints.

These systems, such as P2 debugger [76], liblog [22], Friday [21], WiDS [51], MaceMC [41], and QI [64] are designed to diagnose non-malicious faults, such as bugs or race conditions. When nodes have been compromised by an adversary, these systems can return incorrect results.

Log-Based Forensics

Log-based forensics systems capture execution logs at runtime by inserting additional statements in the source code, or by observing the inputs, outputs and system calls of each system component. For instance, Pip [70] logs path instances started from outside inputs; Backtracker [42, 43] records the objects and their causalities; logs of Magpie [4] are in the form of path instances consisting of the used system components; and D3S [50] modifies the underlying operating systems to allow automatic injection of state exposers and predicate checkers. Based on the logs and snapshots taken at runtime, users are enabled to reason about the causalities between system states, with the support from visualization tools and query engines.

The STAP system presented in this chapter provides a general-purpose abstraction of dependencies, and enables richer functionalities. Among others, the main difference between STAP and these existing forensic systems is that STAP does not require trust in any components on the compromised nodes. For example, Backtracker [42, 43] and PASS [60] require a trusted kernel, cooperative ReVirt [5] a trusted VMM, and A2M [10] trusted hardware. ForNet [74] and NFA [83] assume a trusted infrastructure and collaboration across domains.

Accountability

Systems such as PeerReview [33] and NetReview [31] can automatically detect when a node deviates from the algorithm it is expected to run. Tamper-evident logs are introduced to prevent modifications on history from unauthorized peers. In addition, equivocation, i.e. making conflicting statements to different nodes, are prevented by allowing peers to exchange logs to examine consistency. Attestation-based trusted hardware, such as A2M [10] and TrInc [47], can be used to further reduce the auditing overhead.

These systems cannot detect problems that arise from interactions between multiple nodes, such as BadGadget [28] in interdomain routing, or problems that are related to inputs or unspecified aspects of the algorithm. Also, accountability systems merely report that a node is faulty, whereas provenance systems also offer support for diagnosing faults and for assessing their effects on other nodes.

Proofs of Misbehavior

Many systems that are designed to handle non-crash faults internally use proofs of misbehavior, such as the signed confessions in Ngan et al. [62], a set of conflicting tickets in SHARP [20], or the POM message in Zyzzyva [44]. In STAP, any evidence that creates a red vertex in G_v essentially constitutes a proof of misbehavior, but STAP's evidence is more general because it proves misbehavior with respect to the (arbitrary) primary system, rather than with respect to STAP itself. Systems such as PeerReview [33] can generate protocol-independent evidence as well, but, unlike STAP's evidence, PeerReview's evidence is not diagnostic: it only shows that a node is faulty, but not what went wrong.

5.2 Provenance

Since its importance was realized by the research community, provenance has been extensively studied, and successfully applied to a large range of application areas. Various provenance models have been proposed, and implemented in their corresponding systems. Our work presented in this chapter was inspired by the rich previous work in this domain.

Provenance Model

A classic approach to model provenance is to capture provenance as *graphs*. Provenance graphs reflect the relations between derived tuples and the base tuples that contribute to them. Each vertex represents a data object or an operation that transforms data objects (for instance, a database relational operator such as union, join, selection and projection), and each edge denotes a data flow among the vertices. This approach is also adopted by many of the scientific computation systems [8,11,63,78] and file systems [60], in which a directed-acyclic-graph (DAG) representation is used to describe dependencies.

Alternatively, data provenance may be more compactly represented using *algebraic representation* [7,26]. Algebraic representations encode provenance using the binary operations $+$ and $*$ (representing, for example, union and join). For instance, let α, β, and γ represent base tuples, a tuple τ with provenance of $\alpha + \beta * \gamma$ means that τ is derivable if α exists or both β and γ are existent.

There have been several efforts to generalize provenance models and allow provenance interoperability. Green et al. [26] proposed provenance semiring, a provenance model that is useful for a variety of applications and generalizes previous models of provenance (such as lineage [12], why-provenance [7]) and query answering on annotated relations. The Open Provenance Model (OPM) [59] is a standardization effort that proposes an amalgamation of concepts from existing provenance systems, and aims to improve the provenance interoperability.

Maintenance and Querying

Provenance data are usually stored as additional tuple fields or separate tables in relational databases (such as Orchestra [27] and PermDB [23]), XML files (such as Kepler [78], ES3 [19]) and RDF files (such as Taverna [63]). In our STAP system, provenance information is maintained in an internal distributed relational database. While potential inconsistencies due to transient state could be resolved by maintaining provenance in bi-temporal databases [38,45], STAP *inherently* captures and maintains temporal information along with the provenance data.

To facilitate access to the provenance data, provenance systems allow users to specify queries written in SQL [63,78], XQuery [17], or query languages specifically designed for provenance (such as ProQL [39]). ProQL supports a wide variety of applications with derived data, and can be used to assess trust and derivability, detect side effects, as well as compute data annotations in particular provenance semirings. To improve query performance, recent work [2, 3] studies provenance labeling for efficiently evaluating reachability queries over large provenance graphs in a variety of workflow settings.

Visualization, an alternative approach to retrieve information from provenance, has been previously studied in VisTrails [8], in which workflow specifications can be compared side by side, and workflow specifications can be adjusted by example-based refinement [72].

Applications

Provenance has been implemented and integrated in many practical systems. Probabilistic databases, such as Trio [82], Mystiq [68, 69], and Panda [37], have applied provenance for efficient management of temporal and/or uncertainties. Trio, in particular, supports an uncertainty data model by associating each tuple with a confidential level, and updating the confidential levels of derived tuples based on their provenance. Collaborative data sharing systems (CDSS), such as Orchestra [27], uses provenance for trust management and reconciling conflicts among data from multiple sources. PASS [60] and Sprov [34] track file modification histories and causalities in file systems. PA-S3fs [61] and RAMP [36] focus on file systems and MapReduce workloads on the emerging cloud platform. Workflow systems, such as VisTrails [8], myGrid/Taverna [63], Kepler [78], Chimera [17], and ZOOM [11], use provenance support in scientific computations, to facilitate verification, reproducibility, and collaboration. VisTrails, for instance, captures the evolution of workflow specifications—the history of refining a workflow specification (e.g., the addition or deletion of a module, and the modification of a parameter). Several surveys [6, 13, 18] provides further details about workflow provenance systems.

Provenance Security

McDaniel et al. [57] outlines requirements for secure network provenance, emphasizing the need for provenance to be tamper-proof and non-repudiable. Hasan et al. proposes Sprov [34] that implements secure chain-structured provenance for individual documents; however, it lacks important features that are required in a distributed system, e.g., a consistency check to ensure that nodes are processing messages in a way that is consistent with their current state. Pedigree [67] captures provenance at the network layer in the form of per-packet *tags* that store a history of all nodes and processes that manipulated the packet. It assumes a trusted environment, and its set-based provenance is less expressive compared to STAP's graph-based dependency structure.

Provenance Privacy

More recently, researchers have studies, more specifically, the tradeoffs between privacy and utility for workflow provenance. For example, [14, 15] proposed the *module privacy* that ensures that the probability of guessing the correct outputs of a module, given the revealed inputs in the provenance, is below a given threshold. This is achieved by hiding a subset of the inputs (or outputs) of the modules in the provenance graph exposed to the users.

6 Conclusion

This chapter describes a data-centric approach to attribution in the cloud. We present Secure Time-Aware Provenance (STAP), an approach that provides the fundamental functionality required for performing attribution queries—the capability to "explain" the existence (or change) of system state in a potentially adversarial environment. STAP reveals the dependencies between system states, and permits system operators to transitively tie observed faults to their potential causes, and to assess the damage that these faults may have caused to the rest of the system. We have identified several practical challenges in deploying STAP, and have presented the solutions that addressed each of the following main challenges:

- **Distribution.** A key challenge of supporting provenance in distributed system is to develop an abstract system model in which provenance data can be maintained efficiently. We demonstrated that it is achievable by modeling the system state as a set of distributed databases, and by extracting logical dependencies from system specifications and runtime. Enabled by the distributed query processing capabilities, provenance information is then incrementally maintained as views of system state during the execution. We analytically and empirically showed that the overhead incurred by provenance maintenance is linear in the cost of the base system, and, therefore, does not affect its scalability.
- **Time-awareness.** Another challenge is to track state changes over time in a relaxed system model, in which clocks are not synchronized and messages can be delayed, reordered or lost. To address this challenge, we examined the fundamental correlation between provenance and (observable) event ordering in distributed systems. We then presented an enhanced provenance model that provides a sound and complete representation that correctly captures the system dependencies.
- **Security.** A final challenge is to provide security guarantees in completely untrusted environments, in which the adversary may have compromised an arbitrary subset of the nodes, and that he may have complete control over these nodes. We showed that, despite the conservative threat model, our security enhancement in STAP still provides strong, provable guarantees: it ensures that an observable symptom of a fault or an attack can always be traced to a specific event|passive evasion or active misbehavior|on at least one faulty node, even when the adversary attempts to prevent this.

To demonstrate STAP's practicality and generality, we have applied it to a variety of different systems, including the Internet's interdomain routing system, the Chord distributed hash table, and the Hadoop MapReduce system. The evaluation has demonstrated that STAP is able to detect a number of different problems that had been previously described in the literature, and that STAP is practical, both in terms of its run-time overhead and in terms of the effort required to deploy it.

6.1   Future Research Directions

We conclude the chapter with a list of several promising research directions suggested by the presented research work.

Usability and Adoption

STAP automates fault diagnosis and debugging by systematically maintaining and querying state dependencies as the system execution progresses. Its usability, however, can be further improved to encourage its adoption in academia and industrial development settings.

One important aspect for future research is to enhance the "readability" of the returned provenance results. Provenance information could be overwhelmingly large in systems with complex dependency logic. To address this challenge, we intend to explore the following two complementary approaches: the first approach focuses on developing an expressive yet easy-to-use interface (e.g., a SQL-like declarative query language tailored for the STAP model), for users to annotate and prune provenance data based on a customizable pattern; alternatively, the size and complexity of provenance information can be controlled by introducing layering into the provenance system, in which case provenance data can be captured at a variety of granularities, and be interactively expanded.

Privacy and Confidentiality

STAP mainly explores the authenticity and integrity aspects of security in provenance systems. We plan to extend the exploration to their counterparts, privacy and confidentiality. It is intriguing to study the tension between privacy and verifiability, two seemingly contradictory properties. As a first step, the private and verifiable routing (PVR) [29, 84] provides initial evidence that strong privacy guarantees can be achieved in interdomain routing, where the functionality of each node is well-restricted to route selection and advertisement based on a customized ranking function. We intend to further understand the performance implications or limits when extending the guarantees to more general systems.

Fault Diagnosis and Recovery

STAP can be used to systematically diagnose faults, where "explanations" of a suspicious symptom are compiled as a set of state dependencies that recursively trace back to the root causes. As the basis for inferring state dependencies, the high-level dependency logic (captured as derivation rules in STAP) is of critical importance. To generalize and further automate the extraction of such dependency logic from a target application, one potential avenue that we intend to explore is to employ programming language techniques that perform static (or dynamic) analysis on the information flow of target systems.

In addition to debugging, one intriguing direction is the use of STAP for provenance-based recovery. STAP maintains sufficient information to reproduce the system execution trace individually for each node. This brings opportunities to undo the damages caused by an exposed system fault, by applying the inverse operations in the reverse order. For example, a mistakenly deleted system state can be restored by the corresponding insertion. In addition, provenance keeps the dependency information and thus allows minimal recovery, i.e., the recovery only impacts the nodes that are actually affected by the fault.

Provenance-Driven Invariant Generation

Formal verification is an alternative approach to enforce the safety and security of cloud applications. One important challenge in formal verification is for system designers to discover the safety properties (or invariants). The quality of these safety properties directly affects the quality of the verification results, however, there lacks a systematic approach to extract the safety properties, and the process largely relies on manual efforts today. To address this problem, we are interested in feeding the design bugs or security vulnerabilities exposed in fault diagnosis (as hints for the safety properties) to refine the invariants in the design and development phase.

Acknowledgements The research work presented in this chapter are performed in collaboration with Boon Thau Loo, Andreas Haeberlen and Zachary Ives from University of Pennsylvania, and Micah Sherr from Georgetown University.

References

1. Peter Alvaro, Tyson Condie, Neil Conway, Khaled Elmeleegy, Joseph M. Hellerstein, and Russell Sears. Boom Analytics: Exploring Data-Centric, Declarative Programming for the Cloud. In *Proceedings of the ACM SIGOPS/EuroSys European Conference on Computer Systems (EuroSys)*, 2010.
2. Zhuowei Bao, Susan B. Davidson, Sanjeev Khanna, and Sudeepa Roy. An optimal labeling scheme for workflow provenance using skeleton labels. In *Proceedings of ACM SIGMOD International Conference on Management of Data (SIGMOD)*, 2010.
3. Zhuowei Bao, Susan B. Davidson, and Tova Milo. Labeling recursive workflow executions on-the-fly. In *Proceedings of ACM SIGMOD International Conference on Management of Data (SIGMOD)*, 2011.
4. Paul Barham, Austin Donnelly, Rebecca Isaacs, and Richard Mortier. Using Magpie for request extraction and workload modelling. In *Proceedings of the USENIX Symposium on Operating Systems Design and Implementation (OSDI)*, 2004.
5. Murtaza Basrai and Peter M. Chen. Cooperative ReVirt: adapting message logging for intrusion analysis. Technical Report University of Michigan CSE-TR-504-04, 2004.

6. Rajendra Bose and James Frew. Lineage retrieval for scientific data processing: a survey. *ACM Computing Survey*, 37(1):1–28, 2005.

7. Peter Buneman, Sanjeev Khanna, and Wang Chiew Tan. Why and where: A characterization of data provenance. In *Proceedings of the International Conference on Database Theory (ICDT)*, 2001.

8. Steven Callahan, Juliana Freire, Emanuele Santos, Carlos Scheidegger, Claudio Silva, and Huy Vo. VisTrails: Visualization meets data management. In *Proceedings of ACM SIGMOD International Conference on Management of Data (SIGMOD)*, 2006.

9. David Chiyuan Chu, Lucian Popa, Arsalan Tavakoli, Joseph M. Hellerstein, Philip Levis, Scott Shenker, and Ion Stoica. The Design and Implementation of a Declarative Sensor Network System. In *Proceedings of ACM Conference on Embedded networked Sensor Systems (SenSys)*, 2007.

10. Byung-Gon Chun, Petros Maniatis, Scott Shenker, and John Kubiatowicz. Attested append-only memory: Making adversaries stick to their word. In *Proceedings of the ACM Symposium on Operating Systems Principles (SOSP)*, 2007.

11. Sarah Cohen-Boulakia, Olivier Biton, Shirley Cohen, and Susan Davidson. Addressing the provenance challenge using zoom. *Concurrency and Computation: Practice and Experience*, 20:497–506, 2008.

12. Yingwei Cui, Jennifer Widom, and Janet L.Wiener. Tracing the lineage of view data in a warehousing environment. *ACM Transaction on Database Systems (TODS)*, 25, 2000.

13. Susan B. Davidson, Sarah Cohen Boulakia, Anat Eyal, Bertram Ludäscher, Timothy M. McPhillips, Shawn Bowers, Manish Kumar Anand, and Juliana Freire. Provenance in scientific workflow systems. *IEEE Data Engineering Bulletin*, 30(4):44–50, 2007.

14. Susan B. Davidson, Sanjeev Khanna, Tova Milo, Debmalya Panigrahi, and Sudeepa Roy. Provenance views for module privacy. In *Proceedings of the ACM Symposium on Principles of Database Systems (PODS)*, 2011.

15. Susan B. Davidson, Sanjeev Khanna, Sudeepa Roy, Julia Stoyanovich, Val Tannen, Yi Chen, and Tova Milo. Enabling privacy in provenance-aware workflow systems. In *Proceedings of Biennial Conference on Innovative Data System Research (CIDR)*, 2011.

16. Anja Feldmann, Olaf Maennel, Z. Morley Mao, Arthur Berger, and Bruce Maggs. Locating internet routing instabilities. In *Proceedings of the Conference on Applications, Technologies, Architectures, and Protocols for Computer Communications (SIGCOMMM)*, 2004.

17. Ian T. Foster, Jens-S. Vöckler, Michael Wilde, and Yong Zhao. Chimera: A virtual data system for representing, querying, and automating data derivation. In *Proceedings of Scientific and Statistical Database Management Conference (SSDBM)*, 2002.

18. Juliana Freire, David Koop, Emanuele Santos, and Claudio T. Silva. Provenance for computational tasks: A survey. *Computing in Science and Engineering*, 10, 2008.

19. James Frew and Peter Slaughter. Provenance and annotation of data and processes. Chapter ES3: A Demonstration of Transparent Provenance for Scientific Computation, pages 200–207. Springer-Verlag, Berlin, Heidelberg, 2008.

20. Yun Fu, Jeffrey Chase, Brent Chun, Stephen Schwab, and Amin Vahdat. SHARP: An architecture for secure resource peering. In *Proceedings of ACM Symposium on Operating Systems Principles (SOSP)*, 2003.

21. Dennis Geels, Gautam Altekar, Petros Maniatis, Timothy Roscoe, and Ion Stoica. Friday: Global Comprehension for Distributed Replay. In *Proceedings of the USENIX Symposium on Networked Systems Design and Implementation (NSDI)*, 2007.

22. Dennis Geels, Gautam Altekar, Scott Shenker, and Ion Stoica. Replay Debugging for Distributed Applications. In *Proceedings of the USENIX Annual Technical Conference (USENIX ATC)*, 2006.

23. Boris Glavic and Gustavo Alonso. Perm: Processing provenance and data on the same data model through query rewriting. In *Proceedings of the IEEE International Conference on Data Engineering (ICDE)*, 2009.

24. Jim Gray, Paul McJones, Mike Blasgen, Bruce Lindsay, Raymond Lorie, Tom Price, Franco Putzolu, and Irving Traiger. The recovery manager of the system r database manager. *ACM Computing Survey*, 13(2):223–242, 1981.

25. Todd J. Green, Grigoris Karvounarakis, Zachary G. Ives, and Val Tannen. Update exchange with mappings and provenance. In *Proceedings of the International Conference on Very Large Databases (VLDB)*, 2007.

26. Todd J. Green, Grigoris Karvounarakis, and Val Tannen. Provenance semirings. In *Proceedings of the ACM Symposium on Principles of Database Systems (PODS)*, 2007.

27. Todd J. Green, Grigoris Karvounarakis, Nicholas E. Taylor, Olivier Biton, Zachary G. Ives, and Val Tannen. ORCHESTRA: Facilitating collaborative data sharing. In *Proceedings of ACM SIGMOD International Conference on Management of Data (SIGMOD)*, 2007.

28. Timothy G. Griffin, F. Bruce Shepherd, and Gordon Wilfong. The stable paths problem and interdomain routing. *IEEE/ACM Transactions on Networking*, 10(2):232–243, April 2002.

29. Alexander J. T. Gurney, Andreas Haeberlen, Wenchao Zhou, Micah Sherr, and Boon Thau Loo. Having your cake and eating it too: Routing security with privacy protections. In *Proceedings of the ACM Workshop on Hot Topics in Networks (HotNets-X)*, 2011.

30. Hadoop. http://hadoop.apache.org/.

31. Andreas Haeberlen, Ioannis Avramopoulos, Jennifer Rexford, and Peter Druschel. NetReview: Detecting when interdomain routing goes wrong. In *Proceedings of the USENIX Symposium on Networked Systems Design and Implementation (NSDI)*, 2009.

32. Andreas Haeberlen and Petr Kuznetsov. The Fault Detection Problem. In *Proceedings of the International Conference on Principles of Distributed Systems (OPODIS)*, 2009.

33. Andreas Haeberlen, Petr Kuznetsov, and Peter Druschel. PeerReview: Practical accountability for distributed systems. In *Proceedings of the ACM Symposium on Operating Systems Principles (SOSP)*, 2007.

34. Ragib Hasan, Radu Sion, and Marianne Winslett. Preventing history forgery with secure provenance. *ACM Transactions on Storage (TOS)*, 5(4):1–43, 2009.

35. James J. Hunt, Kiem-Phong Vo, and Walter F. Tichy. Delta algorithms: an empirical analysis. *ACM Transactions on Software Engineering and Methodology (TOSEM)*, 7(2):192–214, 1998.

36. Robert Ikeda, Hyunjung Park, and Jennifer Widom. Provenance for generalized map and reduce workflows. In *Proceedings of Biennial Conference on Innovative Data System Research (CIDR)*, 2011.

37. Robert Ikeda and Jennifer Widom. Panda: A system for provenance and data. *IEEE Data Engineering Bulletin, Special Issue on Data Provenance*, 33:42–49, 2010.

38. C. S. Jensen, J. Clifford, S. K. Gadia, A. Segev, and Richard Thomas Snodgrass. A glossary of temporal database concepts. *SIGMOD Record*, 21:35–43, 1992.

39. Grigoris Karvounarakis, Zachary G. Ives, and Val Tannen. Querying data provenance. In *Proceedings of ACM SIGMOD International Conference on Management of Data (SIGMOD)*, 2010.

40. Bernhard Kauer. OSLO: Improving the security of Trusted Computing. In *Proceedings of the USENIX Security Symposium (USENIX Security)*, 2007.

41. Charles Killian, James W. Anderson, Ranjit Jhala, and Amin Vahdat. Life, Death, and the Critical Transition: Finding Liveness Bugs in Systems Code. In *Proceedings of the USENIX Symposium on Networked Systems Design and Implementation (NSDI)*, 2007.

42. Samuel T. King and Peter M. Chen. Backtracking intrusions. *ACM Transactions on Computer Systems*, 23(1):51–76, 2005.

43. Samuel T. King, Z. Morley Mao, Dominic Lucchetti, and Peter Chen. Enriching intrusion alerts through multi-host causality. In *Proceedings of Network and Distributed System Security Symposium (NDSS)*, 2005.

44. Ramakrishna Kotla, Lorenzo Alvisi, Mike Dahlin, Allen Clement, and Edmund Wong. Zyzzyva: Speculative Byzantine fault tolerance. In *Proceedings of ACM Symposium on Operating Systems Principles (SOSP)*, 2007.

45. Anil Kumar, Vassilis J. Tsotras, and Christos Faloutsos. Designing access methods for bitemporal databases. *IEEE Transaction on Knowledge and Data Engineering (TKDE)*, 10:1–20, 1998.
46. Leslie Lamport, Robert Shostak, and Marshall Pease. The Byzantine generals problem. *ACM Transactions on Programming Languages and Systems (TOPLAS)*, 4(3):382–401, 1982.
47. Dave Levin, John R. Douceur, Jacob R. Lorch, and Thomas Moscibroda. TrInc: Small Trusted Hardware for Large Distributed Systems. In *Proceedings of the USENIX Symposium on Networked Systems Design and Implementation (NSDI)*, 2009.
48. Changbin Liu, Ricardo Correa, Harjot Gill, Tanveer Gill, Xiaozhou Li, Shivkumar Muthukumar, Taher Saeed, Boon Thau Loo, and Prithwish Basu. PUMA: Policy-based Unified Multiradio Architecture for Agile Mesh Networking. In *Proceedings of International Conference on Communication Systems and Networks (COMSNETS)*, 2012.
49. Changbin Liu, Richardo Correa, Xiaozhou Li, Prithwish Basu, Boon Thau Loo, and Yun Mao. Declarative policy-based adaptive mobile ad hoc networking. *IEEE/ACM Transactions on Networking (TON)*, 2011.
50. Xuezheng Liu, Zhenyu Guo, Xi Wang, Feibo Chen, Xiaochen Lian, Jian Tang, Ming Wu, M. Frans Kaashoek, and Zheng Zhang. D3S: debugging deployed distributed systems. In *Proceedings of the USENIX Symposium on Networked Systems Design and Implementation (NSDI)*, 2008.
51. Xuezheng Liu, Wei Lin, Aimin Pan, and Zheng Zhang. WiDS Checker: Combating Bugs in Distributed Systems. In *Proceedings of the USENIX Symposium on Networked Systems Design and Implementation (NSDI)*, 2007.
52. Boon Thau Loo, Tyson Condie, Minos Garofalakis, David E. Gay, Joseph M. Hellerstein, Petros Maniatis, Raghu Ramakrishnan, Timothy Roscoe, and Ion Stoica. Declarative Networking: Language, Execution and Optimization. In *Proceedings of ACM SIGMOD International Conference on Management of Data (SIGMOD)*, 2006.
53. Boon Thau Loo, Tyson Condie, Minos Garofalakis, David E. Gay, Joseph M. Hellerstein, Petros Maniatis, Raghu Ramakrishnan, Timothy Roscoe, and Ion Stoica. Declarative Networking. *Communication of ACM*, 2009.
54. Boon Thau Loo, Tyson Condie, Joseph M. Hellerstein, Petros Maniatis, Timothy Roscoe, and Ion Stoica. Implementing Declarative Overlays. In *Proceedings of the ACM Symposium on Operating Systems Principles (SOSP)*, 2005.
55. Boon Thau Loo, Joseph M. Hellerstein, Ion Stoica, and Raghu Ramakrishnan. Declarative routing: extensible routing with declarative queries. In *Proceedings of the Conference on Applications, Technologies, Architectures, and Protocols for Computer Communications (SIGCOMMM)*, 2005.
56. Yun Mao, Boon Thau Loo, Zachary Ives, and Jonathan M. Smith. MOSAIC: Unified Platform for Dynamic Overlay Selection and Composition. In *Proceedings of ACM International Conference on emerging Networking EXperiments and Technologies (CoNEXT)*, 2008.
57. Patrick McDaniel, Kevin Butler, Stephen McLaughlin, Radu Sion, Erez Zadok, and Marianne Winslett. Towards a Secure and Efficient System for End-to-End Provenance. In *Proceedings of the Workshop on the Theory and Practice of Provenance (TaPP)*, 2010.
58. C. Mohan, Don Haderle, Bruce Lindsay, Hamid Pirahesh, and Peter Schwarz. Aries: a transaction recovery method supporting fine-granularity locking and partial rollbacks using write-ahead logging. *ACM Transactions on Database Systems (TODS)*, 17(1):94–162, 1992.
59. Luc Moreau, Beth Plale, Simon Miles, Carole Goble, Paolo Missier, Roger Barga, Yogesh Simmhan, Joe Futrelle, Robert E. McGrath, Jim Myers, Patrick Paulson, Shawn Bowers, Bertram Ludaescher, Natalia Kwasnikowska, Jan Van den Bussche, Tommy Ellkvist, Juliana Freire, and Paul Groth. The open provenance model (v1.01). http://eprints.ecs.soton.ac.uk/16148/1/opm-v1.01.pdf.
60. Kiran-Kumar Muniswamy-Reddy, David A. Holland, Uri Braun, and Margo Seltzer. Provenance-aware storage systems. In *Proceedings of the USENIX Annual Technical Conference (USENIX ATC)*, 2006.

61. Kiran-Kumar Muniswamy-Reddy, Peter Macko, and Margo Seltzer. Provenance for the cloud. In *Proceedings of the USENIX Conference on File and Storage Technologies (FAST)*, 2010.
62. Tsuen-Wan Ngan, Dan Wallach, and Peter Druschel. Enforcing fair sharing of peer-to-peer resources. In *Proceedings of International Workshop on Peer-to-Peer Systems (IPTPS)*, 2003.
63. Tom Oinn, Matthew Addis, Justin Ferris, Darren Marvin, Tim Carver, Matthew R. Pocock, and Anil Wipat. Taverna: A tool for the composition and enactment of bioinformatics workflows. *Bioinformatics*, 20:3045–3054, 2004.
64. Adam J. Oliner and Alex Aiken. A query language for understanding component interactions in production systems. In *Proceedings of the ACM International Conference on Supercomputing (ICS)*, 2010.
65. Hweehwa Pang and Kian-Lee Tan. Verifying Completeness of Relational Query Answers from Online Servers. *ACM Transactions on Information and System Security (TISSEC)*, 11(2):1–50, 2008.
66. Quagga Routing Suite. http://www.quagga.net/.
67. Anirudh Ramachandran, Kaushik Bhandankar, Mukarram Bin Tariq, and Nick Feamster. Packets with provenance. Technical Report GT-CS-08-02, Georgia Tech, 2008.
68. Christopher Ré, Nilesh Dalvi, and Dan Suciu. Efficient top-k query evaluation on probabilistic data. In *Proceedings of the IEEE International Conference on Data Engineering (ICDE)*, 2007.
69. Christopher Ré and Dan Suciu. Approximate lineage for probabilistic databases. In *Proceedings of the International Conference on Very Large Databases (VLDB)*, 2008.
70. Patrick Reynolds, Charles Edwin Killian, Janet L. Wiener, Jeffrey C. Mogul, Mehul A. Shah, and Amin Vahdat. Pip: Detecting the Unexpected in Distributed Systems. In *Proceedings of the USENIX Symposium on Networked Systems Design and Implementation (NSDI)*, 2006.
71. Mendel Rosenblum and John K. Ousterhout. The design and implementation of a log-structured file system. *ACM Transactions on Computer Systems (TOCS)*, 10(1):26–52, 1992.
72. Carlos Eduardo Scheidegger, Huy T. Vo, David Koop, Juliana Freire, and Cláudio T. Silva. Querying and creating visualizations by analogy. *IEEE Transactions on Visualization and Computing Graphics (TOVCG)*, 13(6):1560–1567, 2007.
73. Margo Seltzer, Keith Bostic, Marshall Kirk Mckusick, and Carl Staelin. An implementation of a log-structured file system for unix. In *Proceedings of the USENIX Winter Conference (USENIX Winter)*, 1993.
74. Kulesh Shanmugasundaram, Nasir Memon, Anubhav Savant, and Herve Bronnimann. ForNet: A distributed forensics network. In *Proceedings of International Workshop on Mathematical Methods, Models and Architectures for Computer Networks Security (MMM-ACNS)*, 2003.
75. Micah Sherr, Andrew Mao, William R. Marczak, Wenchao Zhou, Boon Thau Loo, and Matt Blaze. A3: An Extensible Platform for Application-Aware Anonymity. In *Proceedings of Network and Distributed System Security (NDSS)*, 2010.
76. Atul Singh, Petros Maniatis, Timothy Roscoe, and Peter Druschel. Using queries for distributed monitoring and forensics. In *Proceedings of the ACM SIGOPS/EuroSys European Conference on Computer Systems (EuroSys)*, 2006.
77. Ion Stoica, Robert Morris, David Karger, M. Frans Kaashoek, and Hari Balakrishnan. Chord: A scalable peer-to-peer lookup service for internet applications. In *Proceedings of the Conference on Applications, Technologies, Architectures, and Protocols for Computer Communications (SIGCOMMM)*, 2001.
78. Workflow System, Ilkay Altintas, Oscar Barney, and Efrat Jaeger-frank. Provenance collection support in the kepler scientific workflow system. In *Proceedings of the International Provenance and Annotation Workshop (IPAW)*, 2006.
79. Renata Teixeira and Jennifer Rexford. A measurement framework for pin-pointing routing changes. In *Proceedings of the ACM SIGCOMM Network Troubleshooting Workshop*, 2004.
80. Walter F. Tichy. Design, implementation, and evaluation of a revision control system. In *Proceedings of the International Conference on Software Engineering (ICSE)*, 1982.
81. The Stanford WebBase Project. http://diglib.stanford.edu/~testbed/doc2/WebBase/.
82. Jennifer Widom. Trio: A system for integrated management of data, accuracy, and lineage. In *Proceedings of Biennial Conference on Innovative Data System Research (CIDR)*, 2005.

83. Yinglian Xie, Vyas Sekar, Mike Reiter, and Hui Zhang. Forensic analysis for epidemic attacks in federated networks. In *Proceedings of the IEEE International Conference on Network Protocols (ICNP)*, 2006.
84. Mingchen Zhao, Wenchao Zhou, Alexander J. T. Gurney, Andreas Haeberlen, Micah Sherr, and Boon Thau Loo. Private and verifiable interdomain routing decisions. In *Proceedings of the Conference on Applications, Technologies, Architectures, and Protocols for Computer Communications (SIGCOMMM)*, 2012.
85. Wenchao Zhou, Qiong Fei, Arjun Narayan, Andreas Haeberlen, Boon Thau Loo, and Micah Sherr. Secure network provenance. In *Proceedings of ACM Symposium on Operating Systems Principles (SOSP)*, 2011.
86. Wenchao Zhou, Qiong Fei, Arjun Narayan, Andreas Haeberlen, Boon Thau Loo, and Micah Sherr. Secure network provenance. Technical Report MS-CIS-11-14, University of Pennsylvania, 2011.
87. Wenchao Zhou, Qiong Fei, Shengzhi Sun, Tao Tao, Andreas Haeberlen, Zachary Ives, Boon Thau Loo, and Micah Sherr. NetTrails: A declarative platform for provenance maintenance and querying in distributed systems. In *Proceedings of ACM SIGMOD International Conference on Management of Data (SIGMOD) – demonstration*, 2011.
88. Wenchao Zhou, Suyog Mapara, Yiqing Ren, Yang Li, Andreas Haeberlen, Zachary Ives, Boon Thau Loo, and Micah Sherr. Distributed time-aware provenance. In *Proceedings of the International Conference on Very Large Data Bases (VLDB)*, 2013.
89. Wenchao Zhou, Micah Sherr, Tao Tao, Xiaozhou Li, Boon Thau Loo, and Yun Mao. Efficient querying and maintenance of network provenance at Internet-scale. In *Proceedings of ACM SIGMOD International Conference on Management of Data (SIGMOD)*, 2010.

Software Cruising: A New Technology for Building Concurrent Software Monitor

Dinghao Wu, Peng Liu, Qiang Zeng, and Donghai Tian

Abstract We introduce a novel concurrent software monitoring technology, called *software cruising*. It leverages multicore architectures and utilizes *lock-free* data structures and algorithms to achieve efficient and scalable security monitoring. Applications include, but are not limited to, heap buffer integrity checking, kernel memory cruising, data structure and object invariant checking, rootkit detection, and information provenance and flow checking. In the software cruising framework, one or more dedicated threads, called cruising threads, are running concurrently with the monitored user or kernel code, to constantly check, or cruise, for security violations. We believe the software cruising technology would result in a game-changing capability in security monitoring for the cloud-based and traditional computing and network systems.

We have developed two prototypical cruising systems: *Cruiser*, a lock-free concurrent heap buffer overflow monitor in user space, and *Kruiser*, a semi-synchronized non-blocking OS kernel cruiser. Our experimental results showed that software cruising can be deployed in practice with modest overhead. In user space, heap buffer overflow cruising incurs only 5 % performance overhead on average for the SPEC CPU2006 benchmark, and the Apache throughput slowdown is only 3 % maximum and negligible on average. In kernel space, it is negligible for SPEC, and 3.8 % for Apache. Both technologies can be deployed in large scale for cloud data centers and server farms in an automated manner.

D. Wu (✉) • P. Liu • Q. Zeng
Pennsylvania State University, University Park, PA 16802, USA
e-mail: dwu@ist.psu.edu; pliu@ist.psu.edu; quz105@psu.edu

D. Tian
Beijing Institute of Technology, Beijing, China
e-mail: dhai@bit.edu.cn

S. Jajodia et al. (eds.), *Secure Cloud Computing*, DOI 10.1007/978-1-4614-9278-8__14,   303
© Springer Science+Business Media New York 2014

1   Introduction

Existing security-related software monitoring techniques could be roughly broken down into two categories: control-receiving monitoring and non-control-receiving monitoring. Control-receiving monitoring is well captured by the classic concept of reference monitors. A reference monitor defines a set of requirements that governs the reference validation mechanism. As stated by Schneider [50], "A reference monitor is guaranteed to receive control whenever any operation in some specified set is invoked." This category can be further classified into several classes. For examples,

- Operating system kernels as a reference monitor for operations on system objects (e.g., files and processed).
- Memory mapping hardware as a reference monitor (for accesses to memory pages).
- Processors as a reference monitor. Using tagging memory support, enforcement of information flow security policies could be pushed into the processor itself [81].
- Inlined reference monitors such as Software-based Fault Isolation (SFI) [75] and Jif [35]. Through static instrumentation, SFI can monitor a distrusted module writing or jumping to an address outside its fault domain. Enforced at both compile time and run time, Jif can impose information flow control and access control.
- Dynamic taint analysis (DTA) as a reference monitor [37]. Through static or dynamic instrumentation, or a combination of static and dynamic instrumentation, DTA can monitor data flows among instructions at byte-level granularity.

Non-control-receiving monitoring is not always bounded with control receiving. Due to various reasons (e.g., performance overhead), quite a few classes of monitoring do not expect to receive any control. Their primary goal is to obtain some specified awareness of the system being protected. Control-receiving monitoring is active monitoring; in contrast, non-control-receiving monitoring is passive monitoring. For examples,

- OS level monitors can collect system call traces for intrusion detection [23] and backtracking purposes [28].
- Calling context monitors can obtain the calling context information of an application for performance analysis and debugging purposes.
- Memory performance (e.g., memory leak) monitors can obtain awareness about certain memory leak problems.
- Architecture level monitors (e.g., shadow gates [67]) could be added to track information flows.

Fine-grained software monitoring or security enforcement, such as inlined reference monitor, is often inlined, which delays the execution of the protected programs. In addition, inlined monitor code runs in the same address space as the program being monitored. This could cause safety and security issues. The inlined code may introduce security holes or cause robustness problems. If the monitor code fails, the original program will fail as well. If the monitor code is blocked, the original program is often blocked as well. Furthermore, it is difficult to monitor or enforce concurrency properties with inlined code since the monitor code is scattered and often needs additional synchronization.

It is quite challenging to parallelize control-receiving monitoring. An example is dynamic taint analysis, for which parallel monitoring is still not very practical primarily due to the pervasive data and control dependence among the monitor and normal program execution. This has been a main cause of high performance overhead, a major obstacle to adopt concurrent software monitoring in practice.

The performance overhead of concurrent monitors comes from two sources: logging/monitoring and synchronization between the monitored code (logging) and monitor threads (monitoring). The latter has implicit blocking cost if the synchronization primitives used are lock-based. When the monitor threads are blocked due to external events, such as IO and OS preemptive scheduling, the threads being monitored will also be blocked in a lock-based synchronization style even if the monitor threads are not monitoring.

Our key insight is that we can explore multicore architectures for concurrent security monitoring using novel lock-free (non-blocking) data structures and algorithms[1] to eliminate blocking cost and thus make the concurrent monitoring extremely attractive in terms of performance and scalability. Since the synchronization between the original program and the monitor is non-blocking, this also makes the monitoring system monitor kill-safe; that is, the original program won't fail even if the monitor is blocked or crashed.

2 Software Cruising

Software Cruising is a novel concurrent software monitoring technology that migrates security enforcement from the monitored code, either in user or kernel space, to a concurrent monitor thread. The technology leverages multicore and multiprocessor architectures and uses *lock-free* data structures and algorithms to achieve *non-blocking* and efficient synchronization between the monitor and monitored code.

---

[1]Technically speaking, lock-free and non-blocking are related, but different concepts. Here, we do not distinguish the difference and rather use them interchangeably to mean that it is not traditional lock-based and not blocking.

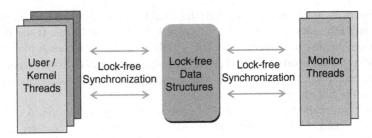

Fig. 1 The software cruising architecture

2.1 Architecture

In the software cruising framework, one or more dedicated threads, called *cruising threads*, are running concurrently with the monitored user- or kernel- code to constantly check, or *cruise*, for security violations. Figure 1 shows the architecture. It leverages the increasingly popular multicore architectures and lock-free (non-blocking) synchronizations.

The lock-free data structure is used to log information necessary for security monitoring. The monitored code in either user or kernel space and the monitor threads do not communicate directly, but rather through the lock-free data structures using non-blocking synchronization primitives. The key is to use lock-free data structures and algorithms to achieve the non-blocking property between the monitor and the code being monitored. The monitor thread(s) are always checking (cruising), possibly in spare cores on multicore processors, for security violations, but the user/kernel threads' executions are not blocked.

2.2 Features

The proposed software cruising technology has a number of distinct features that make it very attractive.

Leveraging Multicore Architectures for Concurrent Security Monitoring

The software cruising technology leverages multicore architectures with *lock-free* and *non-blocking* synchronization for security monitoring and enforcement. As the monitor threads running on separate cores, the execution of the original program is not largely affected, with loose coupled lock-free synchronization. With the increasingly popular multicore and multiprocessor architectures, this can minimize the performance overhead on the program being monitored. This also makes deployment in the cloud environment easier and more flexible since the monitor code can be run in separate virtual machines.

Protecting Monitor Threads from Malware

Malware, e.g., compromised user/kernel threads or untrusted kernel extensions hosting rootkits, could poison a monitor thread. To protect monitor threads, we could apply a new technology we developed recently [78]. Via HAP (hardware-assisted paging), this technology forces different subjects (e.g., user/kernel threads, monitor threads, untrusted kernel extensions, trusted kernel extensions, kernel core) to use different sets of page tables. The set of pages used by the monitor threads and the lock-free data structures can be flagged as unreadable, unwritable, or unexecutable as needed so that it can be protected from other threads running in the protected mode. Moreover, to prevent the monitor from being tampered and provide guaranteed performance isolation, we can utilize the virtualization technology and apply the SIM framework [58] to run the monitor process out of the monitored VM, while collecting heap memory allocation information inside the monitored VM in a secure and efficient way.

Non-blocking and Lock-Free

Our design is completely non-blocking between the monitor and the monitored program. Even if the monitor is blocked due to external IO events or OS preemptive scheduling, the program execution can still make progress without waiting. One of our designs for user-space heap buffer overflow monitoring adopts lock-free data structures. Our design of kernel cruising is semi-synchronized, but ensures correctness and non-blocking. Advantages of the lock-free and semi-synchronized designs include efficiency, scalability, deadlock-free, and kill-safe (see next paragraph on kill-safe).

Monitor Kill-Safe

Since our design is non-blocking and lock-free, it is safe to kill the monitor and any other cruising threads. We call this feature monitor kill-safe. In large-scale distributed systems such as cloud computing, hardware and software could fail frequently. The monitor kill-safe feature is particularly attractive in such scenarios.

Efficiency

The program being monitored incur very low performance overhead because (1) the monitoring code is in separate threads (possibly) running on separate cores, and (2) all communications are non-blocking so that even if the monitor is blocked due to external IO events or OS preemptive scheduling the program execution can still make progress without waiting.

Scalability

As software becomes more and more concurrent with more cores from hardware, the synchronization cost is more likely to become a bottleneck. The software cruising framework scales much better in this scenario since cruisers and user programs are running concurrently in a lock-free non-blocking manner.

One-to-One and One-to-Many Virtual Machine (VM) Monitoring

Software cruising can be deployed in large-scale (cloud) data centers and server farms. The software cruising framework has very flexible deployment options such as one-to-one and one-to-many monitoring. The one-to-one scheme is that one monitor corresponds to one virtual machine cruising, while the one-to-many is that one monitor cruises for multiple virtual machines. The one-to-many scheme is especially attractive for monitoring large-scale clouds.

2.3 Applications

With these distinct features, we sketch out a number of applications of software cruising. Software cruising can be applied to both user-space and kernel-space software monitoring. We have conducted two cases studies, one in user space and the other in kernel space. The security property we choose to monitor is heap buffer overflow. In user space, we developed *Cruiser*, a lock-free concurrent heap buffer overflow monitor (See Sect. 3 for more details). In kernel space, we developed *Kruiser*, a semi-synchronized non-blocking OS kernel cruiser (See Sect. 4 for more details).

Software cruising has flexible deployment options. It can be applied to application and system software running in a single computer, as well as large-scale distributed and networked systems such as data centers in the cloud computing environment. In such scenario, the monitor can be run in separate virtual machines with different protection level and makes the cruising system more scalable and more secure.

Other applications of software cruising include, but are not limited to, data structure and object invariant checking, rootkit detection, and information provenance and flow checking. For some good engineering reasons, low-level system code often contains features, e.g. custom linked list, that are hard to abstract and verify statically [11, 13, 31]. Instead, we can apply software cruising to dynamically check invariants; that is, we cruise to check that the data structure in memory is a well-formed.

3 Cruiser: Lock-Free Concurrent Heap Buffer Overflow Monitoring

In this section, we introduce the design of *Cruiser*, a lock-free concurrent heap buffer overflow monitor in user space. Interested readers are referred to Zeng, Wu, and Liu [82] for more technical details.

3.1 Introduction

Buffer overflow attacks are often the first step taken by multistage exploits. For example, the multistage attack example shown in MulVAL [40] starts with either CVE-2002-0392 [71] or CVE-2003-0252 [72], both are buffer overflow related vulnerabilities. Despite many counter measures developed, buffer overflow based attacks are still a great threat.

As a case study, we have applied software cruising to the heap buffer overflow problem and developed a novel dynamic heap buffer overflow detector, called *Cruiser*. The key ideas are (1) to create a dedicated monitor thread, which runs concurrently with user threads to cruise over, or keep checking constantly, dynamically allocated buffers against overflows; and (2) to utilize lock-free data structures and non-blocking algorithms, through which user threads communicate with the monitor thread with minimum overhead and without being blocked. The first idea leverages increasingly popular multicore architectures for security monitoring, and the second minimizes the communication and synchronization cost by removing the blocking overhead.

3.2 Design

Our method is canary-based [15]. Each dynamically allocated buffer is surrounded by two canary words; as long as a canary is found corrupted, an overflow is detected. Buffer addresses are collected in a lock-free data structure efficiently without blocking user threads. By traversing the data structure, buffers on heap are under constant surveillance of the concurrent monitor thread.

Cruiser Architecture

To efficiently maintain dynamic memory allocation information, we design the cruiser architecture such that the communication between the original program and the monitor is loosely coupled and non-blocking. As shown in Fig. 2, malloc calls are intercepted to allocate additional space for canary and place the allocated buffer information onto a list of ring data structures. There is one ring per user thread so

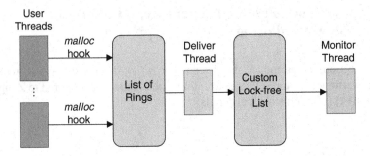

Fig. 2 The cruiser architecture

that there is no race conditions between two malloc calls. The malloc calls then return promptly, and one or several deliver threads move the metadata from rings to a custom lock-free linked list. The monitor thread cruises over the segmented list to check buffer overflows.

Ring

The ring data structure is based on the single-producer single-consumer FIFO wait-free ring buffer proposed by Lamport [32]. This algorithm allows a producer and a consumer to operate concurrently, with very low synchronization overhead as the producer and the consumer are synchronized via simple read/write instructions on the two control variables, the ring head and tail.

Segmented Lock-Free Linked List

Our custom lock-free linked list is segmented. The list consists of segments, each of which is a linked list itself. We construct one segment for each user thread to minimize the race conditions on list operations. Each segment has a dummy node head which is never removed. Also, the first non-dummy node will not be deleted until a new node is inserted before it. Thus the lock-free node insertion after the dummy node can be simply implemented using an atomic compare-and-swap (CAS) instruction. The buffer release and node deletion in the lock-free linked list is more complicated and we refer readers to our Cruiser paper [82] on the technical details. This custom lock-free linked list is very efficient and has the following distinct features: (1) Wait-free access and zero-contention; (2) No ABA problem [25]; and (3) No need to use special memory reclamation such as reference counters or hazard pointers [33].

3.3 Results

We evaluated Cruiser on its effectiveness, execution overhead, and scalability with varying number of threads.

Effectiveness

We tested the effectiveness of Cruiser on the SAMATE Reference Dataset (SRD) [38], as well as a set of well-known real-world exploits (wu-ftpd [51], Sudo [52], CVS [53], libHX [55], Lynx [56], and Firefox [54]). The experiments show that Cruiser can detect all the overflows, duplicate and invalid buffer frees.

Performance Overhead

We evaluated the performance overhead of Cruiser with the SPEC CPU2006 Integer benchmark suite. The results show that Cruiser incurs very low execution overhead: 5 % on average for the eager buffer release option and 12.5 % for the lazy option.

Scalability

We also evaluated Cruiser on the multithreaded setting. We configured the Apache web server with different number of concurrent requests (from 1 to 110) and tested Cruiser's scalability. The experimental results show that Cruiser scales well. The maximum slowdown of the Apache throughput is about 3 % and the average slowdown is negligible.

4 Kruiser: Semi-synchronized Non-blocking OS Kernel Cruising

In this section, we introduce the design of *Kruiser*, a semi-synchronized non-blocking OS kernel cruiser. Interested readers are referred to Tian et al. [66] for more technical details.

4.1 Introduction

It is desirable to adopt software cruising to monitor OS kernel memory integrity and other safety and liveness properties. The lock-free and non-blocking properties of software cruising are especially attractive in kernel space since there are many tasks, events, and execution threads working simultaneously in kernel. If we use lock-based synchronizations for monitoring, it is likely that it will affect the kernel performance and execution characteristics.

Cruiser, as presented in the previous section, cannot be directly applied to monitor kernel buffer overflows due to the following reasons: (1) user- and kernel-space heap management schemes are quite different; (2) the runtime execution characteristics of kernel is quite different from user programs; and (3) OS kernel usually is not just one standalone program like typical user-space programs.

We have developed a prototype—called *Kruiser*, which stands for *kernel cruising*—that can monitor integrity of OS kernel memory. In kernel space, objects (or buffers) with the same size (from kernel or user-space programs) are usually allocated in the same page(s). Kruiser leverages this kernel memory management characteristic information and cruises over pages at first level, and individual buffers at the second level. Kruiser poses minimal changes to the existing OS kernel and can be deployed in large-scale cloud data centers to monitor many virtual machines scalably with the one-to-many virtual machine monitoring scheme.

4.2 Design

Kernel space presents new and more difficult challenges in designing software cruising systems.

Challenges

Synchronization

Synchronization is vital to ensure the monitor process locate and check live buffers efficiently and reliably without incurring false positives. To achieve highly efficient concurrent monitoring, we explore page-level information and design a semi-synchronized algorithm which introduces zero contention into kernel operations and performs non-blocking heap monitoring without incurring false positives or suspending the system.

Self-Protection

As a countermeasure against buffer overflow attacks, our component can become an attack target itself. We rely on a monitor process that keeps checking constantly—that is, cruising—the kernel heap integrity. This busy process can be an explicit attack target. By killing the monitor process, attackers completely disable the detection. Attackers can also tamper the data structure needed by our component to mislead or evade the detection. Thus we need to protect the safety of the monitor process and ensure the integrity of related data structures. To address this challenge, we apply the virtualization technology to deploy the monitor process

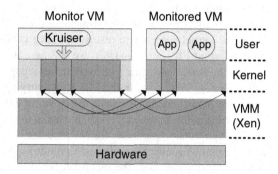

Fig. 3 The Kruiser architecture (using virtualization and direct memory mapping)

into a trusted environment. To ensure the same efficiency as in-the-box monitoring, we leverage the Direct Memory Mapping (DMM) technique, which allows the monitor process to access the monitored OS memory. To protect our data structure from being overflowed or underflowed, we apply two write-protected pages surrounding the data structure.

Architecture

Kruiser attaches one canary word at the end of each heap buffer and runs a separate monitor process, which keeps scanning, or cruises, the canaries to detect buffer overflows and runs concurrently with the monitored system. As shown in Fig. 3, Kruiser, or the monitor process, is run in a separate VM than the monitored OS to strengthen self-protection. The heap buffer metadata is kept in the monitored VM to achieve efficient updating. The monitor cruises over the heap metadata via an efficient technique called direct memory mapping. Once a kernel heap buffer canary is found corrupted, an overflow is reported.

The design of Kruiser is based on Linux and the Xen hypervisor. The Kruiser system can be divided into three parts: VMM, Dom0 VM, and DomU VM (the monitored VM). Dom0 VM contains the monitor process and the custom driver, which reside in user space and kernel space, respectively. The custom driver is used to help the monitor process release memory *but with its page tables retained*. A tiny component, namely Memory Mapper, inside the VMM is used to map the kernel memory of the monitored VM to the page table entries retained by the custom driver. A static array, called Page Identity Array (PIA), stores all the metadata at page level, and the interposition code reside in the kernel space of DomU VM.

Kernel Cruising

Kruiser keeps the metadata at page level and stores them in a static array called Page Identity Array (PIA). This array, however, can incur a variety of race conditions and atomicity issues. Introducing additional complex synchronization on PIA will inevitably affect the kernel performance. Instead, we design a novel algorithm that leverages kernel behavior to resolve the race conditions. To avoid race conditions on concurrent PIA entry updates, we leverage the critical section that are already exist in the kernel code that adds or removes a page from the page table to get a free ride with negligible cost for the PIA array entry update. Concurrent PIA entry read and write may cause inconsistent values being used. Instead of avoiding this read-write race condition, we let it occur, but avoid using inconsistent values by detecting inconsistent version numbers. Each PIA entry contains a version number which is incremented whenever the page corresponding to the PIA entry is added or removed from the heap page pool. The inconsistent values can be detected by comparing the version numbers before and after the read.

This non-blocking algorithm is constructed using simple reads, writes, and memory barriers without complicated and expensive synchronization mechanisms. The monitor process is lightly synchronized by reading version numbers twice, while other processes manipulating heap pages make progress without being synchronized or blocked by the monitor. In other words, the synchronization is one-way. That is why we call it *semi-synchronized non-blocking kernel cruising*. It is semi-synchronized in another sense. On the PIA entries, write-write is synchronized with a free-ride from the existing kernel functions, while read-write is not synchronized. It resolves the concern of a variety of subtle race conditions without the need to freeze the entire system for recheck, but still *does not incur any false positives*.

4.3   Results

To evaluate Kruiser, we developed a prototype based on 32-bit Linux and the Xen hypervisor.

Effectiveness

We conducted effectiveness tests on three vulnerabilities [47, 62] deliberately introduced in the Linux kernel and two real-world heap buffer overflow vulnerabilities [69, 70] in Linux. Our experimental results indicate that Kruiser is effective in defending against kernel heap buffer overflow attacks.

Performance Overhead

We evaluated the performance overhead of Kruiser on the SPEC CPU2006 benchmark. Our results showed that the average execution performance overhead is negligible. When the slab allocation is frequent, the performance overhead is a little bit higher, such as in gcc, but the maximal performance overhead is still less than 3 %.

Scalability

We also evaluated the scalability of Kruiser on the Apache server in a multithreaded setting. The setup is similar to that of Cruiser (see Sect. 3.3). Our experimental results showed that the average slowdown of the Apache throughput is 3.8 and 7.9 % for a more secure Kruiser option.

5 Discussion

In this section, we discuss several advanced options and potential future application of software cruising.

5.1 Detection Latency

Since our software cruising is non-blocking, our monitoring does not suspend the system being monitored for detection. Thus, the detection latency becomes a critical indicator of the detection effectiveness. The time it takes a software cruising system to complete whole system monitoring once is called cruising cycle. It is important to keep the cruising cycle short so that we can detect an exploit quick enough. For the two applications we developed, the cruising cycles are both tunable; that is, we can configure the software cruising systems make small cruising cycle. Cruiser can achieve this with more than one monitor thread and keep the cruising list short enough. Each monitor thread only cruises part of the linked list. This can be achieved easily since the lock-free linked list is segmented. Kruiser can achieve this in a similar way. We can logically divide the metadata data structure into several segments and deploy equal number of monitor threads, so that each monitor thread only needs to be responsible for one segment.

5.2 Guaranteed Detection

Our cruising systems race with attackers: As long as an exploit cannot succeed within a cruise cycle after a canary is corrupted, it is bound to be *prevented*. In addition, even an attacker has compromised the system by exploiting a (kernel) heap buffer overflow vulnerability and enabled a remote shell with root privileges, the canary corrupt should be detected before the attacker keys in the first command, since a cruise cycle is normally less than a few milliseconds. In this sense, we "raised a bar" for attackers. However, automatic attack vectors such as worms can be fast and advanced attacks may directly manipulate our data structures or try to recover the corrupted canaries using the keys. Moving the data structures and keys to a separate VM gains security but can lead to high performance overhead. Instead, we combine Secure-In-VM (SIM) [58] and *secure canary generation* to prevent attackers from recovering the corrupted canary, even after the system has been compromised and entirely controlled by attackers.

With the In-VM protection and secure canary generation, attackers can not hide their attacks in that: (1) The In-VM protection prevent attackers from manipulating metadata; and (2) The canary generation based on the stream cipher guarantees the difficulty for attackers to recover the corrupted canaries within one cruising cycle. Therefore, the attacks are bound to be detected within one cruising cycle after compromising the system, unless the attackers know the exact canary value to be corrupted beforehand, which usually implies the overread and overrun vulnerabilities overlap for exactly the same buffer area and which is very rare.

Here we assume that the attacker does not reboot the system after a successful exploit to evade detection. We can add an additional cruiser check, to see whether the system has been compromised or not, in the system shutdown (reboot) routine to relax this assumption. Combined with the checkpoints technique, this guarantee enables a system to recover the nearest clean state.

5.3   Cloud Cruising

The software cruising approach leverages increasingly popular multicore architectures; its efficiency and scalability show that it can be applied to data centers and server farms in practice. Cruiser can be applied to shrink-wrapped software in an automated manner with negligible cost. The scheme in our prototype Kruiser is one-to-one monitoring on VMs. An advanced option in this design space is the one-to-many scheme; that is, one VM (monitor) cruises over multiple VMs, especially for the VMs that reside in the same physical machine. This is vital to the scalable online monitoring for cloud data centers and server farms.

Large data centers using shipping-containers packed with thousands of servers each are common nowadays. Therefore, scalable deployment is a critical requirement for intrusion detection measures in data centers. Unlike traditional interposition-based monitors, which may intervene normal functionalities frequently, Kruiser imposes minimal interference and performs monitoring in parallel with the monitored VM. Moreover, with the one-to-many option, one Kruiser instance is able to monitor multiple VMs given an acceptable detection latency much longer than the cruising cycle, without affecting the guaranteed detection property. In addition, the performance isolation provided by the underlying VMM ensures the monitor process and the monitored VM do not abuse computing resources to interfere with each other, which is a desirable property for users.

With the popularity of multicore architectures, servers built with many cores are more and more common. The hardware evolution trend embraces the concurrent monitoring fashion, as the cost for a unit core running a monitor instance decreases sharply, and the extra energy consumption by one core is relatively low for machines with hundreds of cores. Therefore, the scalability and low cost properties imply that Cruiser and Kruiser can be practically applied to large data centers and server farms, as one of the intrusion detection instruments in practice.

6 Related Work

In this section, we present related work on buffer overflow detection, system integrity, information flow integrity, and self-healing software.

6.1 Buffer Overflow Detection

Over the past few decades, there has been extensive research in this area, including buffer bounds checking [2–4, 7, 18, 26, 36, 48, 68, 74], canary checking [15, 24, 46], return address shadow stack or stack split [12, 21, 44, 64, 79], non-executable memory [61, 65], non-accessible memory [20, 22, 73], randomization and obfuscation [6, 9, 14, 65], and execution monitoring [1, 10, 16, 29, 49].

Despite so many countermeasures, only a few of them, such as StackGuard [15], ASLR (Address Space Layout Randomization) [9, 65], NX memory [61, 65], and DieHard [8] and DieHarder [39], are widely deployed in production systems. In Table 1, we compare Cruiser with those widely deployed tools and techniques.

Table 1 Comparison of some widely deployed tools and technologies with Cruiser

	Stack-Guard	ASLR	NX	DieHard & DieHarder	Cruiser
Low performance overhead	•	•	•	○	•
Easy to deploy and apply	•	•	•	○	•
No false alarms	•	•	•	•	•
Mainstream platform compatible	•	•	•	•	•
Program semantics loyalty	•	•	•	•	•
Legacy code compatible	•		•		•
Binary code compatible			•		•
No need for recompilation			•		•
Able to locate corrupted buffers				•	•
Leveraging multicore architectures					•
Guaranteed detection or prevention		○	•	○	•
Deployed to the field	•	•	•	•	⋆

Legend: • means positive; ○ means partially or almost; ⋆ means just open-sourced

Software cruising shares many features with these techniques, including low performance overhead, easiness to deploy and apply, no false alarms, compatibility with mainstream platforms, and program semantics loyalty.

Cruiser bears many similar features with StackGuard [15]. Kruiser exhibits excellent performance on system kernel integrity checking, with novel features such as *secure monitor protection* and *guaranteed detection* (even after an initial successful exploit). In addition, Software cruising systems also have the following features: non-blocking and lock-free monitoring, monitor kill-safe, compatibility with legacy code, no need for recompilation, i.e. working with binary executables, ability to leverage multicore architectures, guaranteed detection of attacks (not bypassable), secure monitor protection, and ability to precisely locate corrupted buffers, which is critical for testing, debugging, and security monitoring.

6.2   System Integrity

Existing OS integrity protection techniques can be broken down into three categories: (1) code integrity [45, 57], (2) data integrity [5, 63], (3) control flow integrity and control data integrity [1, 42, 76, 77]. Software cruising for data structure and object invariants in general falls into the third category. HookSafe [76] protects kernel hooks by relocating them to a dedicated page-aligned memory space. In contrast, software cruising does not do any hook relocating. The technique proposed by Petroni and Hicks [42] detects kernel control flow attacks by identifying persistent yet unexpected modifications of the kernel's CFG. It does not use any canaries. In contrast, software cruising can be applied to detect control flow attacks by comparing linkages between canaries with the linkages between the corresponding kernel data structures. Soft-Timer [77] uses soft timer interrupts while software cruising does not use any interrupt.

6.3   Information Flow Integrity

Security models for information flow controls were studied many years ago [17]. Recently, Decentralized Information Flow Control (DIFC) [19, 30, 34, 80] has attracted much interest. Compared to classic information flow control researches, which are model-oriented, DIFC is targeting pragmatic, system-oriented information flow control. DIFC projects have developed more practical and more usable declassification measures and information flow tracking (also called "taint tracking") mechanisms. Although taint tracking has been implemented in design-from-scratch DIFC systems such as HiStar [80], so far fine-grained information flow tracking still cannot be made practical in commodity software systems. This problem is a main motivation behind our plan to apply software cruising to information provenance and flow integrity checking.

6.4 Self-Healing Software

Self-healing (or self-fixing, self-repairing) software such as the Network Worm Vaccine Architecture [27, 43, 60], ClearView [41], and SHADOWS [59], aims to fix itself when something monitored goes wrong. However, runtime protection or monitoring mechanisms are often too expensive in practice to be applied in large scale. None of these solutions utilize non-blocking lock-free data structures and algorithms to reduce monitoring overhead. The software cruising technology can be combined with the self-healing software technology to make it more affordable since to be self-healing it has to be self-monitoring first!

7 Conclusion

We have presented a novel concurrent software monitoring technology, called *software cruising*. It leverages multicore architectures and utilizes *lock-free* data structures and algorithms to achieve efficient and scalable security monitoring. Applications include, but are not limited to, heap buffer integrity checking, kernel memory cruising, data structure and object invariant checking, rootkit detection, and information provenance and flow checking. In the software cruising framework, one or more dedicated threads, called cruising threads, are running concurrently with the monitored user or kernel code, to constantly check, or cruise, for security violations. We believe the software cruising technology would result in a game-changing capability in security monitoring for the cloud-based and traditional computing and network systems.

We have developed two prototypical systems: *Cruiser*, a lock-free concurrent heap buffer overflow monitor in user space, and *Kruiser*, a semi-synchronized non-blocking OS kernel cruiser. Cruiser is legacy code compatible and can be automatically applied to protect shrink-wrapped software and systems (source code or binary executables) transparently, and thus can gain extra security with virtually no cost for heap buffer overflow checking as StackGuard for stack buffers. Kruiser has a novel algorithm on concurrent, but *semi-synchronized non-blocking*, kernel heap integrity cruising. It is not fully synchronized, to reduce the performance overhead, but still ensures correctness regarding race conditions, deadlocks, and other typical concurrency issues.

Our preliminary results showed that software cruising can be deployed in practice with modest overhead. In user space, heap buffer overflow cruising incurs only 5 % performance overhead on average for the SPEC CPU2006 benchmark, and the Apache throughput slowdown is only 3 % maximum and negligible on average. In kernel space, it is negligible for SPEC, and 3.8 % for Apache. Both technologies can be deployed in large scale for (cloud) data centers and server farms in an automated manner.

Acknowledgements This research was supported in part by the National Science Foundation (NSF) under the grants CNS-1223710 and CNS-0905131, the Army Research Office (ARO) under the grant W911NF-09-1-0525 (MURI), and the Air Force Office of Scientific Research (AFOSR) under the grant W911NF1210055.

References

1. Abadi, M., Budiu, M., Erlingsson, U., Ligatti, J.: Control-flow integrity. In: Proceedings of the 12th ACM Conference on Computer and Communications Security (CCS '05), pp. 340–353 (2005)
2. Akritidis, P., Costa, M., Castro, M., Hand, S.: Baggy bounds checking: an efficient and backwards-compatible defense against out-of-bounds errors. In: USENIX Security '09, pp. 51–66 (2009)
3. Austin, T.M., Breach, S.E., Sohi, G.S.: Efficient detection of all pointer and array access errors. In: Proceedings of the ACM SIGPLAN conference on Programming language design and implementation, PLDI '04, pp. 290–301 (2004)
4. Avijit, K., Gupta, P.: Tied, libsafeplus, tools for runtime buffer overflow protection. In: USENIX Security '04, pp. 4–4 (2004)
5. Baliga, A., Ganapathy, V., Iftode, L.: Automatic inference and enforcement of kernel data structure invariants. In: ACSAC '08: Proceedings of the 2008 Annual Computer Security Applications Conference, pp. 77–86. IEEE Computer Society, Washington, DC, USA (2008). DOI http://dx.doi.org/10.1109/ACSAC.2008.29
6. Barrantes, E.G., Ackley, D.H., Palmer, T.S., Stefanovic, D., Zovi, D.D.: Randomized instruction set emulation to disrupt binary code injection attacks. In: Proceedings of the ACM conference on Computer and communications security, CCS '03, pp. 281–289 (2003)
7. Berger, E.D.: HeapShield: Library-based heap overflow protection for free. Tech. Report UMCS TR-2006-28, Univ. of Mass. Amherst (2006)
8. Berger, E.D., Zorn, B.G.: DieHard: probabilistic memory safety for unsafe languages. In: Proceedings of the 2006 ACM SIGPLAN conference on Programming language design and implementation, PLDI '06, pp. 158–168. ACM, New York, NY, USA (2006). DOI http://doi.acm.org/10.1145/1133981.1134000. URL http://doi.acm.org/10.1145/1133981. 1134000
9. Bhatkar, E., Duvarney, D.C., Sekar, R.: Address obfuscation: an efficient approach to combat a broad range of memory error exploits. In: USENIX Security '03, pp. 105–120 (2003)
10. Castro, M., Costa, M., Harris, T.: Securing software by enforcing data-flow integrity. In: Proceedings of the 7th symposium on Operating systems design and implementation, OSDI '06, pp. 147–160. USENIX Association, Berkeley, CA, USA (2006). URL http://dl.acm.org/citation.cfm?id=1298455.1298470
11. Chatterjee, S., Lahiri, S., Qadeer, S., Rakamaric, Z.: A reachability predicate for analyzing low-level software. In: O. Grumberg, M. Huth (eds.) Proceedings of the 13th international conference on Tools and Algorithms for the Construction and Analysis of Systems (TACAS'07), *Lecture Notes in Computer Science*, vol. 4424, pp. 19–33. Springer Berlin Heidelberg (2007). DOI 10.1007/978-3-540-71209-1_4. URL http://dx.doi.org/10.1007/978-3-540-71209-1_4
12. Chiueh, T.C., Hsu, F.H.: RAD: A compile-time solution to buffer overflow attacks. In: Proceedings of the The 21st International Conference on Distributed Computing Systems (ICDCS '01), pp. 409–417 (2001)
13. Condit, J., Hackett, B., Lahiri, S.K., Qadeer, S.: Unifying type checking and property checking for low-level code. In: Proceedings of the 36th annual ACM SIGPLAN-SIGACT symposium on Principles of programming languages, POPL '09, pp. 302–314. ACM, New York, NY, USA (2009). DOI http://doi.acm.org/10.1145/1480881.1480921. URL http://doi.acm.org/10.1145/ 1480881.1480921

14. Cowan, C., Beattie, S.: PointGuard: protecting pointers from buffer overflow vulnerabilities. In: USENIX Security '03, pp. 91–104 (2003)
15. Cowan, C., Pu, C.: StackGuard: automatic adaptive detection and prevention of buffer-overflow attacks. In: USENIX Security '98, pp. 63–78 (1998)
16. Cox, B., Evans, D., Filipi, A., Rowanhill, J., Hu, W., Davidson, J., Knight, J., Nguyen-Tuong, A., Hiser, J.: N-variant systems: a secretless framework for security through diversity. In: USENIX Security '06, pp. 105–120 (2006)
17. Denning, D.: A lattice model of secure information flow. Communications of the ACM 19(5), 236–243 (1976)
18. Dor, N., Rodeh, M., Sagiv, M.: CSSV: towards a realistic tool for statically detecting all buffer overflows in C. In: Proceedings of the ACM SIGPLAN conference on Programming language design and implementation, PLDI '03, pp. 155–167 (2003)
19. Efstathopoulos, P., Krohn, M., VanDeBogart, S., Frey, C., Ziegler, D., Kohler, E., Mazieres, D., Kaashoek, F., Morris, R.: Labels and event processes in the Asbestos operating system. In: Proceedings of the Nineteenth ACM SIGOPS symposium on Operating systems principles, SOSP '05 (2005)
20. Electric Fence: Malloc debugger. Http://directory.fsf.org/project/ElectricFence/
21. Frantzen, M., Shuey, M.: StackGhost: Hardware facilitated stack protection. In: USENIX Security '01, pp. 55–66 (2001)
22. Hastings, R., Joyce, B.: Purify: Fast detection of memory leaks and access errors. In: the Winter 1992 Usenix Conference, pp. 125–136 (1992)
23. Hofmeyr, S.A., Forrest, S., Somayaji, A.: Intrusion detection using sequences of system calls. Journal of Computer Security 6(3), 151–180 (1998). URL http://dl.acm.org/citation.cfm?id=1298081.1298084
24. IBM: ProPolice detector. Http://www.trl.ibm.com/projects/security/ssp/
25. IBM System/370 Extended Architecture, Principles of Operations: IBM Publication No. SA22-7085 (1983)
26. Jim, T., Morrisett, J.G., Grossman, D., Hicks, M.W., Cheney, J., Wang, Y.: Cyclone: A safe dialect of C. In: USENIX Annual Technical Conference (ATC '02), pp. 275–288 (2002)
27. Keromytis, A.D.: The case for self-healing software. In: Aspects of Network and Information Security: Proceedings NATO Advanced Studies Institute (ASI) on Network Security and Intrusion Detection (2005)
28. King, S.T., Chen, P.M.: Backtracking intrusions. In: Proceedings of the nineteenth ACM symposium on Operating systems principles, SOSP '03, pp. 223–236. ACM, New York, NY, USA (2003). DOI 10.1145/945445.945467. URL http://doi.acm.org/10.1145/945445.945467
29. Kiriansky, V., Bruening, D., Amarasinghe, S.P.: Secure execution via program shepherding. In: USENIX Security '02, pp. 191–206 (2002)
30. Krohn, M., Yip, A., Brodsky, M., Cliffer, N., Kaashoek, M.F., Kohler, E., Morris, R.: Information flow control for standard OS abstractions. In: Proceedings of the twenty-first ACM SIGOPS symposium on Operating systems principles, SOSP (2007)
31. Lahiri, S.K., Qadeer, S.: Verifying properties of well-founded linked lists. In: Conference record of the 33rd ACM SIGPLAN-SIGACT symposium on Principles of programming languages, POPL '06, pp. 115–126. ACM, New York, NY, USA (2006). DOI http://doi.acm.org/10.1145/1111037.1111048. URL http://doi.acm.org/10.1145/1111037.1111048
32. Lamport, L.: Proving the correctness of multiprocess programs. IEEE Trans. Softw. Eng. 3(2), 125–143 (1977)
33. Michael, M.M.: Hazard pointers: Safe memory reclamation for lock-free objects. IEEE Trans. Parallel Distrib. Syst. 15(6), 491–504 (2004)
34. Myers, A., Liskov, B.: Protecting privacy using the decentralized label model. ACM Transactions on Computer Systems (2000)

35. Myers, A.C., Liskov, B.: A decentralized model for information flow control. In: Proceedings of the sixteenth ACM symposium on Operating systems principles, SOSP '97, pp. 129–142. ACM, New York, NY, USA (1997). DOI 10.1145/268998.266669. URL http://doi.acm.org/10.1145/268998.266669

36. Necula, G.C., Condit, J., Harren, M., McPeak, S., Weimer, W.: CCured: type-safe retrofitting of legacy software. ACM Trans. Program. Lang. Syst. **27**(3), 477–526 (2005)

37. Newsome, J., Song, D.: Dynamic taint analysis for automatic detection, analysis, and signature-generation of exploits on commodity software. In: Proceedings of the Network and Distributed System Security Symposium (NDSS '05) (2005)

38. NIST. SAMATE Reference Dataset: Http://samate.nist.gov/SRD

39. Novark, G., Berger, E.D.: DieHarder: securing the heap. In: Proceedings of the 17th ACM conference on Computer and communications security, CCS '10, pp. 573–584. ACM, New York, NY, USA (2010). DOI http://doi.acm.org/10.1145/1866307.1866371. URL http://doi.acm.org/10.1145/1866307.1866371

40. Ou, X., Govindavajhala, S., Appel, A.W.: MulVAL: a logic-based network security analyzer. In: Proceedings of the 14th conference on USENIX Security Symposium - Volume 14, pp. 113–128. USENIX Association, Berkeley, CA, USA (2005). URL http://dl.acm.org/citation.cfm?id=1251398.1251406

41. Perkins, J.H., Kim, S., Larsen, S., Amarasinghe, S., Bachrach, J., Carbin, M., Pacheco, C., Sherwood, F., Sidiroglou, S., Sullivan, G., Wong, W.F., Zibin, Y., Ernst, M.D., Rinard, M.: Automatically patching errors in deployed software. In: Proceedings of the ACM SIGOPS 22nd symposium on Operating systems principles, SOSP '09, pp. 87–102. ACM, New York, NY, USA (2009). DOI http://doi.acm.org/10.1145/1629575.1629585. URL http://doi.acm.org/10.1145/1629575.1629585

42. Petroni Jr., N.L., Hicks, M.: Automated detection of persistent kernel control-flow attacks. In: Proceedings of the 14th ACM conference on Computer and communications security, CCS '07, pp. 103–115 (2007)

43. Portokalidis, G., Keromytis, A.D.: REASSURE: A self-contained mechanism for healing software using rescue points. In: Advances in Information and Computer Security—6th International Workshop, IWSEC 2011, Tokyo, Japan, November 8–10, 2011. Proceedings, *Lecture Notes in Computer Science*, vol. 7038, pp. 16–32. Springer (2011)

44. Prasad, M., Chiueh, T.C.: A binary rewriting defense against stack based buffer overflow attacks. In: Usenix Annual Technical Conference (Usenix ATC '03), pp. 211–224 (2003)

45. Riley, R., Jiang, X., Xu, D.: Guest-transparent prevention of kernel rootkits with VMM-based memory shadowing. In: Proceedings of the 11th international conference on Recent advances in intrusion detection, RAID '08 (2008)

46. Robertson, W., Kruegel, C., Mutz, D., Valeur, F.: Run-time detection of heap-based overflows. In: Proceedings of the 17th Usenix Conference on System Administration (LISA '03), pp. 51–60. Usenix Association, Berkeley, CA, USA (2003)

47. Roethlisberge, D.: Omnikey Cardman 4040 Linux driver buffer overflow (2007). http://www.securiteam.com/unixfocus/5CP0D0AKUA.html

48. Ruwase, O., Lam, M.S.: A practical dynamic buffer overflow detector. In: Proceedings of the 11th Annual Network and Distributed System Security Symposium (NDSS '04), pp. 159–169 (2004)

49. Salamat, B., Jackson, T., Gal, A., Franz, M.: Orchestra: intrusion detection using parallel execution and monitoring of program variants in user-space. In: Proceedings of the 4th ACM European conference on Computer systems (EuroSys '09), pp. 33–46 (2009)

50. Schneider, F.: Blueprint for a science of cybersecurity. The Next Wave **19**(2), 47–57 (2012)

51. SecurityFocus: Wu-ftpd file globbing heap corruption (2001). http://www.securityfocus.com/bid/3581

52. SecurityFocus: Sudo password prompt heap overflow (2002). http://www.securityfocus.com/bid/4593

53. SecurityFocus: CVS directory request double free heap corruption (2003). http://www.securityfocus.com/bid/6650

54. SecurityFocus: Mozilla Firefox and Seamonkey regular expression parsing heap buffer overflow (2009). http://www.securityfocus.com/bid/35891
55. SecurityFocus: libHX 'HX_split()' remote heap-based buffer overflow (2010). http://www.securityfocus.com/bid/42592
56. SecurityFocus: Lynx browser 'convert_to_idna()' function remote heap based buffer overflow (2010). http://www.securityfocus.com/bid/42316
57. Seshadri, A., Luk, M., Qu, N., Perrig, A.: SecVisor: a tiny hypervisor to provide lifetime kernel code integrity for commodity OSes. In: Proceedings of the twenty-first ACM SIGOPS symposium on Operating systems principles, SOSP '07, pp. 335–350 (2007)
58. Sharif, M.I., Lee, W., Cui, W., Lanzi, A.: Secure in-VM monitoring using hardware virtualization. In: Proceedings of the 16th ACM conference on Computer and communications security, CCS '09, pp. 477–487 (2009)
59. Shehory, O.: SHADOWS: Self-healing complex software systems. In: Automated Software Engineering, pp. 71–76 (2008). DOI 10.1109/ASEW.2008.4686296
60. Sidiroglou, S., Laadan, O., Perez, C., Viennot, N., Nieh, J., Keromytis, A.D.: ASSURE: automatic software self-healing using rescue points. In: M.L. Soffa, M.J. Irwin (eds.) ASPLOS, pp. 37–48. ACM (2009)
61. Solar Designer: Non-executable user stack (1997). Http://www.openwall.com/linux/
62. sqrkkyu, twzi: Attacking the core: Kernel exploiting notes (2007). Http://phrack.org/issues.html
63. Srivastava, A., Erete, I., Giffin, J.: Kernel data integrity protection via memory access control. Tech. Rep. GT-CS-09-04, Georgia Institute of Technology (2009)
64. StackShield: (2000). Http://www.angelfire.com/sk/stackshield/
65. The PaX project: Http://pax.grsecurity.net/
66. Tian, D., Zeng, Q., Wu, D., Liu, P., Hu, C.: Kruiser: Semi-synchronized non-blocking concurrent kernel heap buffer overflow monitoring. In: Proceedings of the 19th Network and Distributed System Security Symposium, NDSS '12 (2012)
67. Tiwari, M., Wassel, H.M., Mazloom, B., Mysore, S., Chong, F.T., Sherwood, T.: Complete information flow tracking from the gates up. In: Proceedings of the 14th international conference on Architectural support for programming languages and operating systems, ASPLOS XIV, pp. 109–120. ACM, New York, NY, USA (2009). DOI 10.1145/1508244.1508258. URL http://doi.acm.org/10.1145/1508244.1508258
68. Tsai, T.K., Singh, N.: Libsafe: Transparent system-wide protection against buffer overflow attacks. In: Proceedings of the 2002 International Conference on Dependable Systems and Networks (DSN '02), pp. 541–541 (2002)
69. US-CERT/NIST: CVE-2008-1673. Http://web.nvd.nist.gov/view/vuln/detail?vulnId=CVE-2008-1673
70. US-CERT/NIST: CVE-2009-2407. Http://web.nvd.nist.gov/view/vuln/detail?vulnId=CVE-2009-2407
71. US-CERT/NIST: National vulnerability database, CVE-2002-0392. http://web.nvd.nist.gov/view/vuln/detail?vulnId=CVE-2002-0392
72. US-CERT/NIST: National vulnerability database, CVE-2003-0252. http://web.nvd.nist.gov/view/vuln/detail?vulnId=CVE-2003-0252
73. Valgrind: Http://valgrind.org/
74. Wagner, D., Foster, J.S., Brewer, E.A., Aiken, A.: A first step towards automated detection of buffer overrun vulnerabilities. In: Proceedings of the 7th Network and Distributed System Security Symposium, NDSS '00, pp. 3–17 (2000)
75. Wahbe, R., Lucco, S., Anderson, T.E., Graham, S.L.: Efficient software-based fault isolation. In: Proceedings of the fourteenth ACM symposium on Operating systems principles, SOSP '93, pp. 203–216. ACM, New York, NY, USA (1993). DOI 10.1145/168619.168635. URL http://doi.acm.org/10.1145/168619.168635
76. Wang, Z., Jiang, X., Cui, W., Ning, P.: Countering kernel rootkits with lightweight hook protection. In: CCS '09: Proceedings of the 16th ACM Conference on Computer and Communications Security (2009)

77. Wei, J., Payne, B.D., Giffin, J., Pu, C.: Soft-timer driven transient kernel control flow attacks and defense. In: ACSAC '08: Proceedings of the 2008 Annual Computer Security Applications Conference, pp. 97–107. IEEE Computer Society, Washington, DC, USA (2008). DOI http://dx.doi.org/10.1109/ACSAC.2008.40

78. Xiong, X., Tian, D., Liu, P.: Practical protection of kernel integrity for commodity OS from untrusted extensions. In: Proceedings of the Network and Distributed System Security Symposium, NDSS '11. The Internet Society (2011)

79. Xu, J., Kalbarczyk, Z., Patel, S., Iyer, R.: Architecture support for defending against buffer overflow attacks. In: Workshop Evaluating & Architecting Sys. Depend. (2002)

80. Zeldovich, N., Boyd-Wickizer, S., Kohler, E., Mazieres, D.: Making information flow explicit in HiStar. Communications of the ACM (2011)

81. Zeldovich, N., Kannan, H., Dalton, M., Kozyrakis, C.: Hardware enforcement of application security policies using tagged memory. In: Proceedings of the 8th USENIX conference on Operating systems design and implementation, OSDI'08, pp. 225–240. USENIX Association, Berkeley, CA, USA (2008). URL http://dl.acm.org/citation.cfm?id=1855741.1855757

82. Zeng, Q., Wu, D., Liu, P.: Cruiser: Concurrent heap buffer overflow monitoring using lock-free data structures. In: Proceedings of the 32nd ACM SIGPLAN conference on Programming language design and implementation, PLDI '11, pp. 367–377. ACM, New York, NY, USA (2011). DOI http://doi.acm.org/10.1145/1993498.1993541. URL http://doi.acm.org/10.1145/1993498.1993541

Controllability and Observability of Risk and Resilience in Cyber-Physical Cloud Systems

Hasan Cam

Abstract Effective management of risk and resilience in a dynamic cyber-physical system is essential for ensuring successful completion of missions by minimizing the adverse impact of attacks and physical failures. With the accurate risk assessment and efficient resilience control of security events and operations, a cyber-physical system can keep performing satisfactorily by adapting to the dynamic changes occurring due to various cybersecurity events and operations, such as exploiting vulnerabilities, detecting intrusions, and recovering compromised nodes. To the best of our knowledge, this book chapter is the first one to present a model with system state equations of linear and non-linear, based on cybersecurity parameters such as cyber assets' vulnerabilities, criticalities, dependencies, influences, attack types, intrusions, recovery rate, patching rate, normal and compromised nodes. Using this model, this book chapter describes how to apply the controllability and observability aspects of linear/non-linear systems to manage cybersecurity risk and resilience of cyber-physical systems. The purpose of employing controllability is to steer a system from an abnormal security state to a normal security state. That is, by implementing recovery and resilience operations on compromised nodes and assets of a system, it is steered from an abnormal state with compromised nodes towards a state with a fewer or no compromised nodes. Observability is used to determine the system security state by having appropriate cyber output measurements. The challenges for implementing controllability and observability are discussed. An example is provided to illustrate how controllability could be used to achieve resilience within a network.

H. Cam (✉)
Network Science Division, U.S. Army Research Laboratory, Adelphi, MD 20783, USA
e-mail: hasan.cam.civ@mail.mil

S. Jajodia et al. (eds.), *Secure Cloud Computing*, DOI 10.1007/978-1-4614-9278-8_15,   325
© Springer Science+Business Media New York 2014

1 Introduction

As the emerging technologies such as cloud services and mobile computing are increasingly integrated with the current distributed control systems, their control and security become more challenging because they involve the uncertainties and disturbances of not only physical world but also cyber space. Control systems and critical infrastructures may include all those physical systems that make vital contributions to national security, economic stability, public health, or safety. Given that cloud service providers support millions of customers, cloud systems and infrastructure can be considered as a critical infrastructure to the extent that the failure of an important cloud computing system may have great national impact. Therefore, the cloud computing systems should be designed and managed together with the cyber systems so that their security and resilience can be taken into account at every layer of design and management [1]. To this end, this book chapter addresses how cybersecurity events and operations of cyber-physical systems can be modeled, and then applies the controllability and observability concepts of control theory to manage cybersecurity risk and resilience of cyber-physical systems.

Cloud computing is becoming one of the most explosively expanding technologies in the computing industry. It is obvious that cloud computing fundamentally changes the way that computing and information technology services are delivered to customers and organizations. It enables users to migrate their data and computation to a remote location with minimal impact on their system performance. Cloud computing benefits include flexibility, reduced cost, improved automation, and sustainability. But, when failures occur in cloud computing systems due to various reasons such as cyber attacks or physical disturbances, they could result in grave damages to economy, security, or social life. Therefore, this book chapter addresses how impact of such failures and damages can be minimized by applying controllability and observability techniques of control theory to the management of cybersecurity risk and resilience in cyber-physical systems.

As the complexity of existing physical systems and the sophistication of threats increase, the current hardware/software cyber and computing systems continue to suffer from zero-day threats and vulnerabilities. Because having full defense against the penetration of these advanced persistent threats is not realistic, we must ensure how physical and cyber systems can keep functioning effectively despite the presence of cyber attacks. Adaptive and cost-effective techniques should be developed to enable the continuity of mission-critical operations in the presence of advanced attacks. This requires risk and resilience management to accomplish mission assurance [2, 3]. In general, risk refers to the probability that an adverse event or action occurs and results in a negative impact or consequence. In the context of cyber security, risk is defined as being the expected likelihood and consequences of threats or attacks on cyber assets. Risk assessment involves identifying threats and vulnerabilities, computing the occurrence likelihood of threats, and then determining the impact and consequences of exploiting vulnerabilities by threats. Risk management is basically the process of first assessing risk and then taking necessary actions to avoid, transfer, mitigate, or control it to an acceptable level by considering the costs and benefits of the actions. We define the resiliency of a system as being the ability of (i) resisting against any failures or cyber attacks, (ii) keep functioning, possibly with a degraded performance, to complete mission in the presence of some failures and attacks, and (iii) identifying and recovering the failed entities of the system.

In control theory, a dynamic system is defined as being *controllable* if a set of inputs can drive it from an initial state to any desired final state within a finite time, and *observable* if its complete internal state can be constructed from its outputs [4–8]. Controllability and observability are considered in the design of autonomic computing systems for web services [9], and self-adaptive systems [10]. Currently, there is no real-time modeling and management of cybersecurity events and operations in linear/non-linear time-invariant systems, with the purpose of applying the controllability and observability of control-theory to manage risk and resilience. To the best of our knowledge, this book chapter is the first one to present a cybersecurity model for controllability and observability of linear/non-linear systems for cybersecurity events and operations. The model is constructed by developing differential equations to capture cyber assets vulnerabilities, recovery, attacks, etc., so that controllability and observability of control theory can be applied to the development of risk and resilience in cyber-physical systems. A preliminary version of this model is presented in [11]. We also describe how the differential equations of a model for nonlinear systems can be linearized. Risk and resilience management of a cyber-physical system is discussed using the cybersecurity parameters such as cyber assets' vulnerabilities, criticalities, dependencies, influences, attack types, intrusion, recovery rate, patching rate, and compromised nodes. The controllability and observability aspects of linear/non-linear systems are discussed to significantly enhance real-time risk and resilience management of cyber-physical systems.

The rest of this book chapter is organized as follows. Section 2 presents the problem statement, along with controllability and observability concepts of control theory. Section 3 lays out the proposed cybersecurity model for linear and non-linear cyber-physical systems. Section 4 presents an approach and an example to deploying controllable input signals at critical network nodes. Section 5 concludes the chapter with final remarks.

2   Controllability, Observability, and Problem Statement

Control theory offers a powerful mechanism to deal with disturbances, unpredictable changes, and uncertainties in modeling, analyzing, and designing resource control and feedback systems. Controller aims to maintain the difference between the reference input (e.g., performance targets as desired values) and the measured output (e.g., measured performance metrics), in spite of disturbance, noise, or attack that are not under control (Fig. 1).

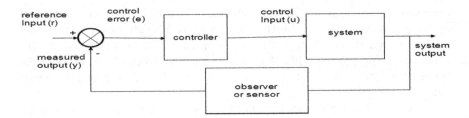

Fig. 1 Block diagram of a control system

Most real systems are non-linear, and their controllability is similar to that of linear systems in many aspects [7]. A cyber-physical dynamical system can be modeled as a linear time-invariant dynamic system using a combination of N system state equations and K output equations as follows.

$$\dot{x}(t) = Ax(t) + Bu(t)$$

$$y(t) = Cx(t) + Du(t)$$

where

- The vector $x(t) = (x_1(t), \ldots, x_N(t))^T$ corresponds to the N system state variables that capture the state of a network with N nodes at time t,
- The $N \times N$ matrix A describes the network's connectivity and interaction strength between nodes,
- The $N \times M$ input matrix B identifies the nodes that are controlled by an outside controller, where $(M <= N)$,
- The system is controlled by a time-dependent input vector $u(t) = (u_1(t), \ldots, u_M(t))^T$ that is imposed by the controller,
- The vector $y(t) = (y_1(t), \ldots, y_K(t))^T$ denotes the K system outputs corresponding to K system state variables of interest, where $(K <= N)$,
- The $K \times N$ matrix C describes the coefficients that weight the state variables, and
- The $K \times M$ matrix D describes the coefficients that weight the system inputs.

When an attacker's input u_a, process noise w_p, and measurement noise w_m are added to a linear time-invariant dynamic system, the system can be described as

$$dx(t)/dt = Ax(t) + Bu(t) + u_a(t) + w_p(t)$$

$$y(t) = Cx(t) + Du(t) + w_m(t)$$

Controllability is related to the ability of forcing the system into a particular state by using an appropriate control signal. If the $N \times NM$ controllability matrix $[B, AB, A^2B, \ldots, A^{N-1}B]$ has full rank N, then the system is controllable, according to Kallman's controllability rank condition. A system is called *controllable* if it can be driven from any initial state to any desired final state in finite time using a suitable choice of input. This is like capturing an ability to guide a system's behavior towards a desired state via proper manipulation of input variables.

Observability is related to the possibility of observing states of a system via output measurements. The state equation is observable if for any input state x_0 and for any input signal u, finite the output y sequence determines uniquely x_0. The pair (A,C) or the system is observable if the observability matrix has full rank N: $[C, CA, \ldots, CA^{N-1}]^T$. A system is called *observable* if its complete internal state can be reconstructed from its outputs.

Problem Statement A cyber-physical system such as a cloud computing system features a tight coupling and coordination of computing, communication, sensing, and physical elements that interact with physical inputs and outputs. Managing risk and resilience in real-time is essential to achieve mission assurance. However, it is a very challenging issue, due to the lack of modeling, incomplete information on vulnerabilities and threats, and dynamic network environment with uncertainties and unexplained activities in traffic.

Given incomplete information on vulnerabilities, threats, attacks, fully/partially compromised nodes, topology, and uncertainties over a cyber-physical system, the objective is to assess and manage dynamically the risk and resilience of the system, and then steer a system with compromised nodes towards a system without compromised nodes by implementing recovery and resilience operations on compromised nodes and assets, and strengthening resilience of the system. To achieve this, this chapter discusses first how to model the assets and cybersecurity operations of a cyber-physical system as a linear/non-linear time-invariant dynamic system, and then use controllability and observability techniques of control theory in order to determine: (*i*) a set of independent input signals and nodes that are needed to drive the system from an abnormal state with compromised elements towards a normal state with a fewer or no compromised elements, and (*ii*) a set of output measurements and sensors that are needed to observe and characterize the system state.

In this regard, *controllability*-related main problems are: (*i*) how to characterize and predict driver nodes, and (*ii*) how to identify the minimum number of driver nodes to achieve controllability. Similarly, *observability*-related main problems are: (*i*) how to identify minimum set of sensors whose measurements can allow us to determine all state variables, and (*ii*) how to determine the impact of noise and measurement uncertainties on determining the minimum number of sensors.

3   Cybersecurity Modeling of a Cyber-Physical System

A cyber-physical control system comprises various types of assets such as sensors, intrusion detection systems, scanners, controllers, and actuators. The minimal requirement for the risk assessment of any system is to characterize threats, vulnerabilities, effectiveness and operational status of the system's defenses for particular threats. In addition, determining the capabilities of an attacker or adversary helps determine the occurrence likelihood of an attack, leading to a better risk assessment and management. But, due to the lack of information on determining adversarial behaviors, probability of attack occurrence, and potential negative impact, risk assessment and management should be based on a model where all uncertainties, constraints, and assumptions are expressed clearly. This model should also represent accurately defense characteristics, threats, the overall system, and their timing relationships, based on the known characteristics and/or accurate measurements of threats, control defense characteristics, and systems.

A more realistic model contributes to performing a more accurate risk management, leading to more meaningful security metrics. The model provides insight into quantifying and improving security status of systems for various threats with different defense systems. In addition, incorporating timing relationships into a model of risk and resilience management is highly desirable, as systems increasingly become more dynamic.

To model a cyber-physical system using the linear/non-linear time-invariant systems, we consider a network or system of N nodes, where

- $N(t) = G(t) + V(t) + E(t) + C(t) + E(t) + F(t)$, and $N(t)$ is the total number of nodes in the system at time t,
- $G(t)$ denote the number of those nodes that do not have any known vulnerability at time t,
- $V(t)$ denote the number of those nodes that have some known vulnerabilities at time t, but are not exploited yet,
- $C(t)$ denote the number of those nodes that are compromised partially/fully through the exploitation of their vulnerabilities,
- $E(t)$ denote the number of those nodes that are evicted due to that they cannot be recovered,
- $F(t)$ denote the number of those nodes that have failed and do not operate due to physical failures.

3.1 Modeling a Linear Cybersecurity System

The cybersecurity environment of a cyber-physical system can be modeled as a linear system. Our cybersecurity model with linear system equations for such a system is illustrated in Fig. 2.

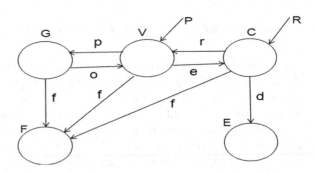

Fig. 2 The cybersecurity model of a linear system

Let:

$R(t)$: recovery support services rate,
$P(t)$: patching support services rate,
$o(t_0)$: vulnerability occurrence rate,
$p(t_0)$: vulnerability patching rate,
$e(t_0)$: vulnerability exploitability rate,
$r(t_0)$: compromised systems recovery rate,
$d(t_0)$: cyber compromised-node eviction rate, and
$f(t_0)$: physical failure rate.

Let $P(t)$ and $R(t)$ denote the inputs, based on recovery and patching support operations, respectively. Also, let $C(t)$ and $V(t)$ denote the outputs that can be measured. Then, the system can be described as follows:

$$\dot{x}(t) = (\dot{G}(t), \dot{V}(t), \dot{C}(t), \dot{E}(t), \dot{F}(t))$$
$$u(t) = (P(t),\ R(t))$$
$$y(t) = (C(t),\ V(t))$$

Differential equations of the model shown in Fig. 2 can be written as

$$\dot{G}(t) = pV(t) - oG(t) - fG(t)$$
$$\dot{V}(t) = oG(t) + rC(t) - pV(t) - eV(t) - fV(t) + P(t)$$
$$\dot{C}(t) = eV(t) - rC(t) - dE(t) - fC(t) + R(t)$$
$$\dot{E}(t) = dC(t)$$
$$\dot{F}(t) = fG(t) + fV(t) + fC(t)$$

Assuming that system state variables $G(t)$, $V(t)$, $C(t)$, $E(t)$, and $F(t)$ are linear, the system state can be expressed using the first-order linear differential equations as follows.

$$\dot{x}(t) = Ax(t) + Bu(t)$$

$$\begin{bmatrix} \dot{G}(t) \\ \dot{V}(t) \\ \dot{C}(t) \\ \dot{E}(t) \\ \dot{F}(t) \end{bmatrix} = \begin{bmatrix} -f-o & p & 0 & 0 & 0 \\ o & -e-f-p & r & 0 & 0 \\ 0 & e & -r-f & -d & 0 \\ 0 & 0 & d & 0 & 0 \\ f & f & f & 0 & 0 \end{bmatrix} \begin{bmatrix} G(t) \\ V(t) \\ C(t) \\ E(t) \\ F(t) \end{bmatrix} + \begin{bmatrix} 0 & 0 \\ 1 & 0 \\ 0 & 1 \\ 0 & 0 \\ 0 & 0 \end{bmatrix} \begin{bmatrix} P(t) \\ R(t) \end{bmatrix}$$

$$\begin{bmatrix} C(t) \\ V(t) \end{bmatrix} = \begin{bmatrix} 0 & 0 & 1 & 0 & 0 \\ 0 & 1 & 0 & 0 & 0 \end{bmatrix} \begin{bmatrix} G(t) \\ V(t) \\ C(t) \\ E(t) \\ F(t) \end{bmatrix}$$

3.2   Modeling a Nonlinear Cybersecurity System

The cybersecurity environment of a cyber-physical system can also be modeled as
a nonlinear system. Our cybersecurity model with nonlinear system equations for
such a system is illustrated in Fig. 3. Obviously, the dynamics of the system can be
described in various ways.

Fig. 3 The cybersecurity
model of a non-linear system

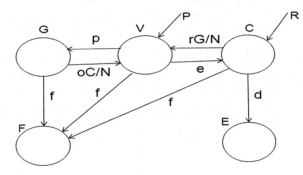

Differential equations of the model shown in Fig. 3 can be written as

$$\dot{G}(t) = pV(t) - oG(t)C(t)/N(t) - fG(t) \tag{1}$$

$$\dot{V}(t) = oG(t) + rC(t)G(t)/N(t) - pV(t) - eV(t) - fV(t) + P(t) \tag{2}$$

$$\dot{C}(t) = eV(t) - rC(t)G(t)/N(t) - dE(t) - fC(t) + R(t) \tag{3}$$

$$\dot{E}(t) = d\ C(t) \tag{4}$$

$$\dot{F}(t) = f\ G(t) + f\ V(t) + f\ C(t) \tag{5}$$

The Eqs. 1, 2, and 3 are nonlinear (due to the presence of the product term
$G(t)C(t)$). In order to approximate a nonlinear system by a linear one around an
equilibrium point of time t_0, we employ Jacobian linearization as follows. Note
that nonlinear perturbations around the equilibrium point of time t_0 are ignored,
compared to the (lower order) linear terms.

$$f(G(t), V(t), C(t), E(t), F(t)) \approx f(G(t_0), V(t_0), C(t_0), E(t_0), F(t_0)) +$$

$$\begin{bmatrix} f_{G(t)}(t_0) & f_{V(t)}(t_0) & f_{C(t)}(t_0) & f_{E(t)}(t_0) & f_{F(t)}(t_0) \end{bmatrix} \begin{bmatrix} G(t) - G(t_0) \\ V(t) - V(t_0) \\ C(t) - C(t_0) \\ E(t) - E(t_0) \\ F(t) - F(t_0) \end{bmatrix}$$

where, for $x(t) \in \{G(t), V(t), C(t), E(t), F(t)\}$,

$$f_{x(t)}(t_0) = \frac{\partial f(G(t), V(t), C(t), E(t), F(t))}{\partial x(t)} \text{ at } t = t_0.$$

Now, let's linearize the non-linear equation 1 using the above Jacobian technique.

$$
\begin{aligned}
\dot{G}(t) &= pV(t) - oG(t)C(t)/N(t) - fG(t) \\
&= pV(t_0) - oG(t_0)C(t_0)/N(t_0) - fG(t_0) +
\end{aligned}
$$

$$
\begin{bmatrix} -f - oC(t_0)/N(t_0) & p & oG(t_0)/N(t_0) & 0 & 0 \end{bmatrix}
\begin{bmatrix}
G(t) - G(t_0) \\
V(t) - V(t_0) \\
C(t) - C(t_0) \\
E(t) - E(t_0) \\
F(t) - F(t_0)
\end{bmatrix}
$$

$$
\begin{aligned}
&= (-f - oC(t_0)/N(t_0))G(t) + pV(t) + (oG(t_0)/N(t_0)) \\
&\quad C(t) - oG(t_0)C(t_0)/N(t_0)
\end{aligned}
$$

Let $a_{11} = -f - oC(t_0)/N(t_0)$, $a_{12} = p$, $a_{13} = o\ G(t_0)/N(t_0)$, $a_{14} = 0$, $a_{15} = 0$, and $u_1 = -o\ G(t_0)C(t_0)/N(t_0)$.

Similarly the non-linear equation 2 can be linearized as follows.

$$
\begin{aligned}
\dot{V}(t) &= oG(t) + rC(t)G(t)/N(t) - pV(t) - eV(t) - fV(t) + P(t) \\
&= oG(t_0) + rC(t_0)G(t_0)/N(t_0) - pV(t_0) - eV(t_0) - fV(t_0) + P(t_0) +
\end{aligned}
$$

$$
\begin{bmatrix} o + rC(t_0)/N(t_0) - p - e - frG(t_0)/N(t_0) & 0 & 0 \end{bmatrix}
\begin{bmatrix}
G(t) - G(t_0) \\
V(t) - V(t_0) \\
C(t) - C(t_0) \\
E(t) - E(t_0) \\
F(t) - F(t_0)
\end{bmatrix}
$$

$$
\begin{aligned}
&= (o + rC(t_0)/N(t_0))G(t) + (-p - e - f)V(t) + (rG(t_0)/N(t_0)) \\
&\quad C(t) + P(t_0) - rG(t_0)C(t_0)/N(t_0)
\end{aligned}
$$

Let $a_{21} = o + rC(t_0)/N(t_0)$, $a_{22} = -p - e - f$, $a_{23} = r\ G(t_0)/N(t_0)$, $a_{24} = 0$, $a_{25} = 0$, and $u_2 = P(t_0) - rG(t_0)C(t_0)/N(t_0)$.

The non-linear equation 3 can be linearized as follows.

$$\dot{C}(t) = eV(t) - rC(t)G(t)/N(t) - dE(t) - fC(t) + R(t)$$

$$= eV(t_0) - rC(t_0)G(t_0)/N(t_0) - dE(t_0) - fC(t_0) + R(t_0) +$$

$$\left[-rC(t_0)/N(t_0) \quad e \quad -f - rG(t_0)/N(t_0) \quad -d \quad 0 \right] \begin{bmatrix} G(t) - G(t_0) \\ V(t) - V(t_0) \\ C(t) - C(t_0) \\ E(t) - E(t_0) \\ F(t) - F(t_0) \end{bmatrix}$$

$$= (-rC(t_0)/N(t_0))G(t) + eV(t) + \left(-f - rG(t_0)\right)/N(t_0)\Big)$$

$$C(t) - dE(t) + rG(t_0)C(t_0)/N(t_0) + R(t_0)$$

Let $a_{31} = -rC(t_0)/N(t_0)$, $a_{32} = e$, $a_{33} = -f - rG(t_0)/N(t_0)$, $a_{34} = -d$, $a_{35} = 0$, and $u_3 = rG(t_0)C(t_0)/N(t_0) + R(t_0)$.

Finally, all the linearized system state equations of the nonlinear system can be expressed as

$$\begin{bmatrix} \dot{G}(t) \\ \dot{V}(t) \\ \dot{C}(t) \\ \dot{E}(t) \\ \dot{F}(t) \end{bmatrix} = \begin{bmatrix} a_{11} & a_{12} & a_{13} & 0 & 0 \\ a_{21} & a_{22} & a_{23} & 0 & 0 \\ a_{31} & a_{32} & a_{33} & a_{34} & 0 \\ 0 & 0 & d & 0 & 0 \\ 0 & 0 & 0 & 0 & 0 \end{bmatrix} \begin{bmatrix} G(t) \\ V(t) \\ C(t) \\ E(t) \\ F(t) \end{bmatrix} + \begin{bmatrix} 1 & 0 & 0 \\ 0 & 1 & 0 \\ 0 & 0 & 1 \\ 0 & 0 & 0 \\ 0 & 0 & 0 \end{bmatrix} \begin{bmatrix} u_1 \\ u_2 \\ u_3 \end{bmatrix}$$

$$\begin{bmatrix} C(t) \\ V(t) \end{bmatrix} = \begin{bmatrix} 0 & 0 & 1 & 0 & 0 \\ 0 & 1 & 0 & 0 & 0 \end{bmatrix} \begin{bmatrix} G(t) \\ V(t) \\ C(t) \\ E(t) \\ F(t) \end{bmatrix}$$

where

$a_{11} = -f - oC(t_0)/N(t_0)$, $a_{12} = p$, $a_{13} = o\ G(t_0)/N(t_0)$, $u_1 = -o\ G(t_0)C(t_0)/N(t_0)$;
$a_{21} = o + rC(t_0)/N(t_0)$, $a_{22} = -p - e - f$, $a_{23} = r\ G(t_0)/N(t_0)$, $a_{24} = 0$, $a_{25} = 0$,
    $u_2 = P(t_0) - rG(t_0)C(t_0)/N(t_0)$;
$a_{31} = -rC(t_0)/N$, $a_{32} = e$, $a_{33} = -f - rG(t_0)/N$, $a_{34} = -d$, $a_{35} = 0$, and).
    $u_3 = rG(t_0)C(t_0)/N + R(t_0$

3.3 Shaping Functions of Inputs and System State Variables in Model for Controllability and Observability

Once system state and output equations of model are derived, the controllability and observability of the system can be determined by checking whether the controllability matrix $[B, AB, A^2B, \ldots, A^{N-1}B]$ and the observability matrix $[C, CA, \ldots, CA^{N-1}]^T$ have full rank N.

If any one of the controllability and observability matrices does not have the rank N, then their entries may be modified properly by re-shaping the functions of inputs and system state variables, along with selecting a different set of assets for measuring outputs or applying inputs, in accordance with meeting a given objective of the system. For instance, in order to provide risk and/or resilience, the functions of system state variables $G(t)$, $V(t)$, $C(t)$, $E(t)$, and $F(t)$ are shaped based on available risk and resilience mechanisms and services of the system. More control defense systems and resilience mechanisms could be added to a set of selected (critical) nodes that are controlled by independent input signals.

4 Deployment of Controllable Input Signals at Critical Network Nodes

This section describes a protocol, called Protocol for security Control, Resilience, and Controllability Collaboration (CRCC), and discusses its steps in depth. The main objective of this protocol is to identify critical nodes from the perspective of risk and resilience, and then feed the selected critical nodes with independent input signals to assist controllability of risk and resilience management of the system. Because critical nodes are identified in terms of risk and resilience, the protocol first computes the risk and resilience of nodes individually and collectively, and then ranks the nodes based on their attributes such as risk, resilience, and influence.

Protocol CRCC

Input: Conditional probability tables of cyber assets for Bayesian network, inventory of security control and resilience mechanisms at each asset or node, topology information and control effectiveness of network.

Output: Identifying critical assets, and feeding them with independent input signals for assisting controllability.

1. Compute *risk*, *control effectiveness* and *resilience* of cyber assets using a Bayesian network.
2. Identify and prioritize the *critical nodes* of network with respect to network connectivity and the attributes of resilience, control, and influence by introducing an enhanced Hierarchically Well-Separated Tree.
3. Feed selected critical nodes with *independent input signals* for assisting system *controllability*.

4.1 Risk, Control, and Resilience Scores of Nodes Using Bayesian Network

Risk assessment involves identifying threats and vulnerabilities, computing the occurrence likelihood of threats, and then determining the impact and consequences of exploiting vulnerabilities by threats. Risk management is the process of first assessing risk and then taking necessary actions to avoid, transfer, mitigate, or control it to an acceptable level by considering the costs and benefits of the actions. The minimal requirement for the risk assessment of any system is to characterize threats, vulnerabilities, effectiveness and operational status of the system's defenses for particular threats. In addition, determining the capabilities of an adversary helps determine the likelihood of an attack, leading to a better risk assessment.

Risk assessment needs the scoring of vulnerabilities. In this regard, the Security Content Automation Program (SCAP), developed by the National Institute of Standards and Technology (NIST), supports the National Vulnerability Database (NVD) providing a repository for known vulnerabilities and software that contains these vulnerabilities. As part of SCAP, the Common Vulnerability Scoring System (CVSS) provides a score for each new software vulnerability discovered that prioritizes the importance of the vulnerability. Once vulnerabilities and exploits are scored, Bayesian network is one commonly used technique to perform risk assessment. Bayesian networks (or Belief networks) are graphical models representing the probabilistic relationships among a set of variables under uncertainty. In the Bayesian network, the graph nodes represent random variables, and edges show dependencies among nodes.

Bayesian networks are usually used for risk assessment by representing threats, vulnerabilities, and their dependencies. However, this section extends Bayesian network to integrate risk assessment with determining the effectiveness of control defense systems and resilience mechanisms of an individual host machine. That is, additional random variables are added to the Bayesian network of risk assessment to represent control effectiveness, resilience, and recovery.

This leads to the integration of risk assessment with the measurements of effectiveness of control, resilience, and recovery attributes of cyber assets, as illustrated in Fig. 4.

$P(A)$, $P(B)$: probability that node receives various threats.
$P(C)$, $P(D)$: probability that node has vulnerabilities that can be exploited by threats.
$P(E)$: probability that node receives aggregated threat.
$P(F)$: probability that node has aggregated vulnerabilities that can be exploited by threats.
$P(G)$: probability that vulnerability can be exploited at node.
$P(H)$: probability that node is infected despite the presence of control mechanisms.
$P(I)$: probability that node has proper internal/external recovery mechanisms for mitigating node's infection.
$P(J)$: probability that node infection is mitigated.

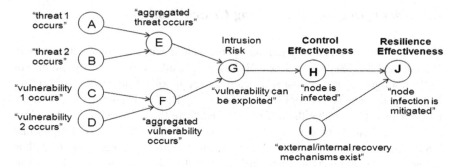

Fig. 4 An example of a Bayesian network for the analysis of risk, control, and resilience of an individual node (e.g., host) in a network The random variables are $A, B, C, D, E, F, G, H, I$, and J. The expressions of events corresponding to these random variables are enclosed within quotation marks

In Bayesian network, vertices represent the (binary) variables of system and the dependence relations among these variables are expressed in terms of conditional probabilities in conditional probability tables (CPTs). Bayesian reasoning uses Bayes' theorem of $P(X|Y) = P(Y|X)P(X)/P(Y)$, where $P(X|Y)$ and $P(Y|X)$ are conditional probabilities of random variables X and Y that represents two events. Note that $P(X,Y) = P(X|Y)P(Y)$, and $P(X,Y) = P(Y|X)P(X)$, where $P(X,Y)$ be the probability that both events corresponding to variables X and Y have occurred. When this product rule is generalized by extending it to n variables, it is called the *chain rule*:

$$P(X_1, X_2, \ldots, X_n) = P(X_1) P\left(X_2 \middle| X_1\right) P\left(X_3 \middle| X_1, X_2\right) \ldots P\left(X_n \middle| X_1, X_2, \ldots, X_{n-1}\right)$$
$$= P(X_1) \prod_{i=2}^{n} P\left(X_i \middle| X_1, \ldots, X_{i-1}\right)$$

The (posterior) joint probability distribution as well as the intrusion risk, control effectiveness, and resilience effectiveness are computed as follows.

$$P(A,B,C,D,E,F,G,H,I,J) = P(A)P(B)P(C)P(D)P\left(E \middle| A,B\right) P\left(F \middle| C,D\right)$$
$$P\left(G \middle| E,F\right) P\left(H \middle| G\right) P(I)P\left(J \middle| H,I\right)$$

Intrusion Risk : $P(G = True) = \sum_{A,B,C,D,E,F \in \{T,F\}} P(G = True, A, B, C, D, E, F)$.

Control Effectiveness : $P(H = False)$

$$= \sum_{A,B,C,D,E,F,G \in \{T,F\}} P(H = False, A, B, C, D, E, F, G).$$

Resilience Effectiveness : $P(J = True)$

$$= \sum_{A,B,C,D,E,F,G,H,I \in \{T,F\}} P(J = True, A, B, C, D, E, F, G, H, I).$$

4.2   Identifying and Prioritizing Critical Nodes

To achieve resource matching and management along with information distribution, Hierarchical Well-Separated Trees (HSTs) are considered to be a very useful tool [12], although they are originally developed to approximate arbitrary metrics using trees [13]. For a given network G, a corresponding HST is constructed as an overlay network over G such that the nodes of the HST are the nodes of G, but the edges of HST are virtual and can map to some paths of different lengths in G, so that HST approximates G by a logarithmic distortion factor. Specifically, an α-HST is defined as a rooted weighted tree such that (*i*) the edge weights from the root to leaf decrease by a factor of α, (*ii*) all root-to-leaf paths have the same hop distance, and (*iii*) the weights from each node to its children are the same. To identify critical nodes of a network based on the values of their attributes such as resilience, control, and influence, this section employs our Hierarchically well-Separated Tree with Attributes (HSTA) [3] that is an extended version of HST.

HST assumes a random permutation of ranks for nodes, which probably does not matter for the problems like finding an empty slot in a garage for an incoming car. However, in cybersecurity domain, not only that the values of every node's attributes could vary, but also the criticality of attributes may change in space and time. Therefore, HSTA of this section considers one or more attributes during nomination process. These multiple attributes of nodes are ordered like primary, secondary, and tertiary attribute. During the ancestor nomination process, the primary attribute values of nodes are considered first for comparison and nomination. If the primary attribute values of two nodes happen to be very close to each other according to its threshold, then the next high-ranking attribute (i.e., secondary attribute) values of these two nodes are compared to break the tie. This tie-breaking process is applied until the tie is broken.

For each attribute k, we introduce a "closeness" threshold T_k in the sense that, if the difference between two adjacent values of an attribute is equal of smaller than the attribute's threshold, then these two values are assumed to be the same. During the ancestor nomination process of nodes, if such two values of an attribute happen to the numbers to be compared, then they are considered the same. To break the tie in such a case, the values of the next attribute in ranking are considered for ancestor nomination. But, if the tie cannot be broken by the lowest rank attribute either, then one of these two nodes is chosen randomly. Let T_r, T_c, and T_i denote the closeness thresholds of the resilience, control, and influence attributes, respectively. In this section, the attributes of resilience, control, and influence are ordered from highest to lowest, so that the primary attribute is the resilience attribute.

Next, this section proposes Algorithm Critical Nodes (CN) and an example to show how α-HSTA can be implemented for $\alpha = 2$ and a few attributes. Algorithm CN constructs a 2-HSTA from its leaves level towards the root level, by assuming that all the nodes of a given network initially form the leaves level of the tree. If we denote the leaves level by level 1, then the 2-HSTA starts determining the level 1 ancestors, and keeps building the tree towards the root node.

Algorithm CN

Input: A network of N nodes, each having three attribute values, namely, resilience, control, and influence ranked from highest to lowest. Let $\alpha=2$, $\beta=1$, and $p=0$, ..., $\lceil \log_2 N \rceil$. . Let T_r, T_c, and T_i denote the closeness thresholds of the resilience, control, and influence attributes, respectively.

Output: The most critical nodes of the network are identified with respect to three attributes and network hop distances.

```
Begin
    /* Comment: Initially, no node has any ancestor. */
    Let p be either ⌈log₂N⌉ or a desirable number
smaller than ⌈log₂N⌉ that is good enough to nominate
desirable number of high-level ancestor nodes;
    Let the given network of N nodes be represented by a
graph with the same connectivity of network links;
    for i = 0 to p
        1. Each candidate node floods up to 2ᵖβ hops
           distance to determine all its potential ancestor
           nodes;
        2. Each candidate node compares its primary
           attribute (i.e., resilience) values with the
           primary attribute
           values of all those potential ancestor nodes that
           are located at 2ᵖβ hops distance;
            a. If the difference of the primary
               attribute values of any two nodes is greater
               than Tᵣ, then consider these attribute
               values in Step 3 and go to Step 3; otherwise,
               compare the secondary attribute values of
               these two nodes to break the tie. If the
               difference of their secondary attribute
               values is greater than Tᵤ, then consider
               these attribute values in Step 3 and go to
               Step 3; otherwise, compare the tertiary
               attribute values of these two nodes to break
               the tie; if the tie is not broken, choose
               one of these nodes. If the difference of
               their tertiary attribute values is greater
               than Tᵢ, then consider these attribute
               values in Step 3 and go to Step 3.
            b. Each candidate node nominates the node that
               has the highest attribute value as its
```

p^{th}-round ancestor node among its all
potential ancestor nodes and itself;
(Note: a node may nominate itself as an
ancestor node);

3. At the end of the round, only nominated
   ancestor nodes are considered in the next round;

end for

end

Example 1 Algorithm CN constructs a 2-HSTA for the given 20-node network by assuming that all the nodes of the network initially form the leaves level of the 2-HSTA. Let $T_r = 0.05$, $T_c = 0.1$ and $T_i = 0.08$. Only the resilience attribute values that range from 0.1 to 1.0 are shown with subscript R in Fig. 5, where 1.0 is the highest desirable attribute value. In the first iteration (i.e., p = 0) of the *for* loop in Algorithm CN, each candidate node floods 1 hop, compares resilience values, and then choose the highest resilience value as its level 1 ancestors (node labels in blue) if the difference of their resilience values is greater than $T_r = 0.05$; otherwise, consider their control values. For instance, note that the difference of the resilience values of N_{10} is N_{11} is less than $T_r = 0.05$, as illustrated in Fig. 5. Therefore, their control attribute values (i.e., 0.60 and 0.45) need to be compared, which causes N_{11} to nominate itself rather than N_{10}. At the end of iteration 1, the nominated ancestor nodes of level 1 are N_2, N_5, N_6, N_9, N_{11}, N_{15}, N_{16}, N_{17}, and N_{20}. In the second iteration (i.e., p = 1) and third iteration (i.e., p = 2) of the for loop in Algorithm CN, each candidate node floods up to 2 hops and 4 hops, respectively, as shown in Fig. 6. At the end of the second iteration, the nominated ancestor nodes of level 2 are N_6, N_9, and N_{16}, while only N_6 is nominated as an ancestor node at level 3.

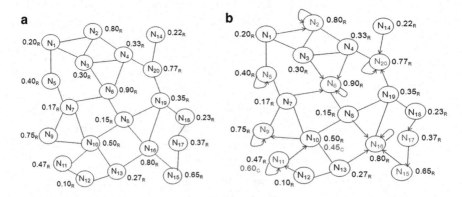

Fig. 5 (**a**) The 20-node network, where only the resiliency attribute values range from 0.1 to 1.0 are shown, where 1.0 is the highest desirable attribute value. (**b**) Flooding 1-hop and nominating the level 1 ancestors at the first round of 2-HSTA. The nominated ancestor nodes of level 1 are N_2, N_5, N_6, N_9, N_{11}, N_{15}, N_{16}, N_{17}, and N_{20} that are pointed to by *arrowheads* in *blue*

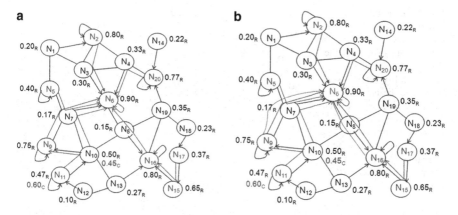

Fig. 6 (**a**) Flooding 2-hops and nominating the level 2 ancestors at the second round of 2-HSTA. The nominated ancestor nodes of level 2 are N_6, N_9, and N_{16} that are pointed to by *arrowheads* in *red*. (**b**) Flooding 4-hops and nominating the level 3 ancestors at the third round of 2-HSTA. The nominated ancestor node at level 3 is N_6 that is pointed to by *arrowheads* in *green*, indicating that N_6 is identified as the most critical node. Hence, HSTA integrates the network connectivity information with the information of attributes in identifying critical nodes of a network at every round

4.3 Feeding Critical Nodes with Independent Input Signals for Assisting Controllability

Once the critical resilience nodes are chosen using the 2-HSTA in the previous section, we examine their resilience mechanisms and services, in addition to their system capabilities and resources such as computing power, storage space, recovery and monitoring mechanism, mobile agents, etc. Their capability of supporting the resilience operations can be strengthened by adding more resilience and control effectiveness mechanisms. Finally, those nodes whose capability of supporting resilience operations can be represented by external independent signals are selected and fed by independent inputs. These selected nodes can be considered as driver nodes [7], and controllability is posed as identifying the minimum number of driver nodes such that rank(C) = N. Recall that, if the rank of the $N \times NM$ controllability matrix $C = (B, AB, A^2B, \ldots, A^{N-1}B)$ equals N, then the network/system is said to be controllable, according to Kallman's controllability rank condition.

Example 2 Let's assume that the resiliency critical nodes of level 2 (i.e., N_6, N_9, N_{16}) in the example of 2-HSTA have external inputs controlled by an outside controller. These critical nodes N_6, N_9, N_{16} are also called the driver nodes from the network controllability perspective. In our interpretation, this implies that these driver nodes become responsible for restoring network nodes to normal operation whenever they are compromised partially and fully. The external inputs $u_6(t)$, $u_9(t)$, and $u_{16}(t)$ of these nodes are non-zero, and all the other external inputs of nodes are zero. This implies that the entries b_6, b_9, and b_{16} of the 20×3 matrix B

Fig. 7 The nominated ancestor nodes of level 2 in the 2-HSTA, namely, N_6, N_9, and N_{16}, are selected as the driver nodes for network controllability in resilience operations, based on their resilience asset values. That is, these nodes become responsible for restoring network nodes to their normal operation whenever they get compromised. Matrix B^T is the transpose of matrix B

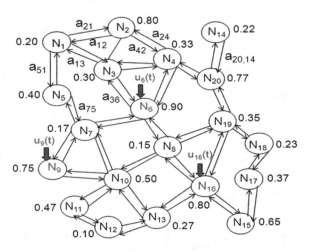

are non-zero. As for the entries a_{ij} of the 20×20 matrix A, they depend on the network connectivity links. Figure 7 shows the weights of resiliency dependencies or influences a_{ij} and a_{ji} between neighboring nodes i and j, for all nodes, where a_{ij} is the weight associated with the directed edge from j to i in the graph. The same type of weights could be computed for other types of attributes such as control, and vulnerability. Note that the $N \times NM$ controllability matrix: $C = (B, AB, A^2B, \ldots, A^{N-1}B)$, and the system is controllable if $\text{rank}(C) = N$, where $N = 20$ and $M = 3$.

$$
A = \begin{bmatrix} a_{11} & \cdots & a_{1,20} \\ \vdots & \ddots & \vdots \\ a_{20,1} & \cdots & a_{20,20} \end{bmatrix}, \quad B^T = \begin{bmatrix} 0\,0\,0\,0\,0\,b_6\,0\,0\,0\,0\,0\,0\,0\,0\,0\,0\,0\,0\,0\,0 \\ 0\,0\,0\,0\,0\,0\,0\,0\,b_9\,0\,0\,0\,0\,0\,0\,0\,0\,0\,0\,0 \\ 0\,0\,0\,0\,0\,0\,0\,0\,0\,0\,0\,0\,0\,0\,0\,b_{16}\,0\,0\,0\,0 \end{bmatrix}^T
$$

5 Conclusions

This book chapter presents a model with differential equations representing the relationships among various events, operations, and security modes of assets, vulnerabilities, impact of attacks, and control inputs. Using this model, this book chapter has described how to apply the controllability and observability concepts of linear/non-linear systems to enhance real-time risk and resilience management of cyber-physical systems. The model has considered cybersecurity parameters such as cyber assets' vulnerabilities, criticalities, dependencies, influences, attack types, intrusions, recovery rate, patching rate, normal and compromised nodes. The purpose of employing controllability is to steer a system with some compromised nodes towards a system without any compromised node by implementing recovery and resilience operations on compromised nodes and assets, and strengthening resilience of the system. Observability is used to determine the state of the system by employing appropriate cyber output measurements. An approach to determining critical nodes and feeding them with independent input signals for assisting controllability is provided.

References

1. D. Catteddu et al., "Security and Resilience in Government Clouds," ENISA, http://www.enisa. europa.eu/act/rm/files/deliverables/cloud-computing-risk-assessment, Jan. 2011
2. N. Poolsappasit, R. Dewri, and I. Ray, "Dynamic Security Risk Management Using Bayesian Attack Graphs," IEEE Trans. on Dependable and Secure Computing, vol. 9, no. 1, Jan./Feb. 2012.
3. H. Cam, "PeerShield: Determining Control and Resilience Criticality of Collaborative Cyber Assets in Networks," *Cyber Sensing 2012, SPIE Defense, Security, and Sensing*, 23–27 April 2012, Baltimore, MD, USA.
4. R.E. Kalman, "Mathematical description of linear dynamical systems,". J. Soc. Indus. Appl. Math. Ser. A 1, 152–192 (1963).
5. D.G. Luenberger, Introduction to Dynamic Systems: Theory, Models, & Applications (Wiley, 1979).
6. J.-J. Slotine and W. Li. Applied Nonlinear Control (Prentice-Hall, 1991).
7. Y-Y. Liu, J-J. Slotine, A-L. Barabasi, "Controllability of Complex Systems," Nature, vol. 473, 12 May 2011.
8. Y-Y. Liu, J-J. Slotine, A-L. Barabasi, "Observability of Complex Systems," *Proc. of the National Academy of Sciences of the USA*, Feb 12, 2013.
9. L. Checiu, B. Solomon, D. Ionescu, M. Litoiu, G. Iszlai, "Observability and controllability of autonomic computing systems for composed web services," Proc. of the 6th IEEE International Symposium on Applied Computational Intelligence and Informatics, pp. 269–274, 2011.
10. Y. Brun, R. Desmarais, K. Geihs, M. Litoiu, A. Lopes, M. Smit, "A design space for self-adaptive systems," R. Lemos et al. (Eds.), Self-Adaptive Systems, Lecture notes in computer science (LNCS), Vol. 7475, Springer, Berlin Heidelberg (2013), pp. 33–50.
11. H. Cam, " Risk and Resilience Controllability-Observability in Cloud Computing Security", *ARO (Army Research Office) Cloud Security Workshop*, March 11–12, 2013, George Mason University.
12. J. Gao, L.J. Guibas, N. Milosavljevic, and D. Zhou, "Distributed Resource Management and Matching in Sensor Networks," *Proc. of the 8th International Symposium on Information Processing in Sensor Networks (IPSN'09)*, 97–108, April, 2009.
13. Subrata Chakraborty and Chung-Hsing Yeh, "A simulation based comparitive study of normalization procedures in multiattribute decision making," in *6th WSEAS Intl. Conference on Artificial Intelligence, Knowledge Engineering and Databases*, Corfu Island, Greece, 2007.

Printed in the United States
By Bookmasters